THE MAKING OF A PERIPHERY

Columbia Studies in International and Global History

COLUMBIA STUDIES IN INTERNATIONAL AND GLOBAL HISTORY

Cemil Aydin, Timothy Nunan, and Dominic Sachsenmaier, Series Editors

This series presents some of the finest and most innovative work coming out of the current landscapes of international and global historical scholarship. Grounded in empirical research, these titles transcend the usual area boundaries and address how history can help us understand contemporary problems, including poverty, inequality, power, political violence, and accountability beyond the nation-state. The series covers processes of flows, exchanges, and entanglements—and moments of blockage, friction, and fracture—not only between "the West" and "the Rest" but also among parts of what has variously been dubbed the "Third World" or the "Global South." Scholarship in international and global history remains indispensable for a better sense of current complex regional and global economic transformations. Such approaches are vital in understanding the making of our present world.

For a complete list of books in the series, see page 305.

The Making of
a Periphery

How Island Southeast Asia Became
a Mass Exporter of Labor

Ulbe Bosma

Columbia University Press   *New York*

Columbia University Press
Publishers Since 1893
New York   Chichester, West Sussex
cup.columbia.edu

Library of Congress Cataloging-in-Publication Data
Names: Bosma, Ulbe, 1962– author.
Title: The making of a periphery : how island Southeast Asia became a mass exporter
    of labor / Ulbe Bosma.
Description: New York : Columbia University Press, [2019] | Series: Columbia studies
    in international and global history | Includes bibliographical references and index.
Identifiers: LCCN 2018054001 (print) | LCCN 2018057960 (ebook) |
    ISBN 9780231188524 (cloth : alk. paper) | ISBN 9780231547901 (e-book)
Subjects: LCSH: Foreign workers, Southeast Asian—History. | Labor market—Southeast
    Asia—History. | Southeast Asia—Population—History. | Southeast Asia—Dependency
    on foreign countries—History. | Southeast Asia—Economic conditions—19th century. |
    Southeast Asia—Economic conditions—20th century.
Classification: LCC HD8690.8 (ebook) | LCC HD8690.8 .B67 2019 (print) |
    DDC 331.6/259—dc23
LC record available at https://lccn.loc.gov/2018054001

∞

Columbia University Press books are printed on permanent and durable acid-free paper.
Printed in the United States of America

Cover design: Milenda Nan Ok Lee

Cover art: © British Library Board / Robana / Art Resources NY

Contents

Tables, Maps, and Figures

FIGURES

Acknowledgments

The writing of this book has been an exiting and complicated exercise in comparative global history. I was extremely fortunate to be in environments where I found all the facilities and encouragement I needed to engage with the range of topics I cover here, such as epidemic disease, piracy, slavery, indentured labor, plantation regimes, and intense spatial mobility, all within the context of an expanding global economy. The choice of Island Southeast Asia as a unit of analysis may seem a complicated one because it encompasses the possessions of three different colonial empires, but, considering that this region is marked by deep historical connections, the choice is also logical. The region is a showcase for the wide-ranging effects of economic globalization.

While working on my book, I could test my ideas at the seminars I gave during my month-long stints as guest professor at the École des Haute Études en Sciences Sociales over three consecutive years. I am deeply grateful to Alessandro Stanziani for inviting me and to Nancy Green, Rémy Madinier, and Laurent Berger for having me in their classes and lecture series. With Alessandro I had many conversations about slavery and bonded labor in this part of the world. Moreover, I had the good fortune that Matthias van Rossum became my colleague at the International Institute of Social History (IISH). His approach to slavery under the Dutch East India Company and mine, which focuses on the subsequent nineteenth century, share many commonalities. We are both fascinated by the question how local forms of slavery became connected to regimes of production for global markets. Xanthe van der Horst and Linda van der Pol went through the files of the Ministry of the Colonies at the National Archive in The Hague to find many nineteenth-century documents pertaining to slavery in the Indonesian archipelago.

I also found inspiration and encouragement among my colleagues at the helm of the Commodity of Empire project: first, Jean Stubbs and Jonathan Curry-Machado, later joined by William Clarence-Smith. They have also been part of the effort to build a large network for the study of commodity frontiers, launched in 2014 and led by Sven Beckert, Mindi Schneider, Eric Vanhaute, and me. This book shares many of the concerns of this network, which studies the incorporation of the "global country-side" in the global capitalist economy and its long-term effects.

This book is also about global labor history, a field developed at my institute, the IISH. Actually, it applies comparative methods of studying labor relations across space and time, methods that have been developed at the IISH in the "Global Collaboratory for the History of Labor Relations."

I would like to thank Marcel van der Linden and Corey Ross for helping me shape the introduction of this book. I am grateful to the anonymous reviewers for their carefully written and very helpful comments. Richard Bowles and Anne Lee corrected and polished the manuscript. Last but not least, I would like to thank the series editors for taking this book on board and Caelyn Cobb, my editor at Columbia University Press, for guiding me through the review and production process.

THE MAKING OF A PERIPHERY

Introduction

Located off a corner of Eurasia, Island Southeast Asia was once a thriving region, an exporter of precious tropical products that found willing consumers around the world, from China to Europe.[1] Today, the Philippines and Indonesia are forced to specialize in exporting their surplus of cheap labor. What explains this reversal of fortune? This book focuses on two prominent causes: high demographic growth and a long history of bonded labor embedded in patron-client relationships. These conditions enabled colonial powers to transform this region, consisting of today's Indonesia, the Philippines, and Malaysia, into a major exporter of products such as sugar, coffee, tobacco, rubber, and palm oil. Underlying the general trend were major subregional differences regarding colonial regimes and the concrete constellations of production, labor recruitment, and migration. The trajectories of the Malay Peninsula, Sumatra, and Borneo have been markedly different from those of Java or Luzon, for example. By elaborating such contrasts, I will argue that today's massive labor exports are rooted in demography and have been structured by colonial and even precolonial patterns of labor recruitment.

Smallpox vaccination, in conjunction with the suppression of wars and piracy during the early nineteenth century in the northern Philippines and Java, resulted in a form of demographic growth unique in Asia. This was contemporaneous with Britain's rapid population growth but

MAP 0.1 Island Southeast Asia.

ushered in trajectories markedly different from those of the Industrial Revolution. Mass migrations did emerge, but the movement of people was to commodity frontiers financed by corporate plantations and mining rather than to cities and factories. Over the past decades, the industrial and service sectors of Indonesia and the Philippines have failed to absorb the rural landless masses, many of whom are now trying to improve their lives as migrant workers. In 2010, an estimated 5.3 million Filipinos and 3.9 million Indonesians were working abroad, but these are conservative figures that do not include the many undocumented migrants. Moreover, the numbers would be considerably higher if we were to add the naturalized migrants from Island Southeast Asia living around the globe.[2] Rapid demographic growth has been an undeniable factor in a region with a proportion of the world population that has increased from just 1.7 percent in 1800 to 5 percent by the year 2000.[3] However, demography and unemployment alone cannot explain this explosion of mobility, which widely exceeded the emigration flows of countries with comparable degrees of overpopulation and poverty. Moreover, these factors cannot explain why 1.8 million citizens from Malaysia, a relatively wealthy immigrant country, are working abroad.[4] Other factors are at play here, such as the way in which colonial British Malaya was forged as an immigrant society with strong transnational linkages, on the one hand, and internal communal tensions, on the other. Migrations have their apparent social, cultural, and systemic contexts and, with that, their historical roots, too.[5]

These migration systems, as well as the many worrisome trafficking practices surrounding them, are, I will argue, rooted in the way the region became incorporated in the global economy as a producer of bulk commodities. The resulting almost exclusive reliance on the export of tropical crops produced with cheap labor, in return for manufactured articles from industrialized countries, is usually—and particularly in world-systems research—termed a "peripheral" condition. This notion has its provenance in Latin America, where economists such as Rául Prebisch authored the "dependency theory," claiming that the exchange of this continent's commodities for U.S. and European manufactured goods has led to underdevelopment. Over the past decades, this notion, despite its problematic character, has also been applied to Island Southeast Asia.

World-systems research divides the world into macroregions: a core, a periphery, and a semiperiphery. It connects the emergence of the periphery to the ascendency of global capitalism: a small group of early capitalist and industrializing countries in Western Europe and North America reduced most of the other countries of the world to commodity exporters. Following this line of reasoning, the impoverishment of the Global South was the corollary of the economic supremacy of the North. One of the most obvious flaws in this argument is that depressed wages and impoverishment are not the inevitable outcomes of economic reliance on the export of primary products. Australia, Norway, Canada, and, last but not least, Malaysia are clear examples of the opposite. Countries can specialize in the export of commodities rather than in manufactured goods for perfectly sound economic reasons and thrive. We should therefore not apply "peripheral" to all commodity-exporting countries but only to those that over time experienced economic stagnation or even impoverishment. Most of these countries are former colonies. Colonial domination obviously played a key role in coercing local economies into commodity production. Colonialism was, however, often a limited and negotiated phenomenon with spatially highly differentiated effects even within single colonies. Both world-systems and macroeconomic explanations tend to ignore the spatially diverse effects of colonialism and the enormous variety of production and labor regimes involved. This obscures our understanding of peripheralization as a process.

If we understand peripheralization as a subservient and in many ways coerced incorporation of societies to produce commodities for capitalist core countries, it certainly applies to *parts* of Island Southeast Asia, as well as *parts* of Latin America, but not to entire regions or continents.[6] The question we could ask, then, is: What enabled these peripheral incorporations and concomitant intense migrations to emerge in the case of Island Southeast Asia? I would propose that it was a combination of sudden demographic growth with modes of labor control already in place in precolonial times. This allowed colonial powers to mobilize rural populations for commodity production on a massive scale. This initially happened only in northern Java and the Philippines, through three colonial interventions, first, by recasting existing modes of taxation and patrimonial relations to increase commodity exports; second, by creating conditions for rapid demographic growth through reducing violence, famine, and, especially, the threat of smallpox through vaccination programs; and, third, by facilitating corporate plantation and extraction enterprises through providing cheap land and through tolerating—and even sanctioning—oppressive labor regimes. This book aims to revisit the theme of the peripheralization of parts of Island Southeast Asia by following the histories of demography and modes of labor control. It is an exercise in global labor history, a field of study developed at the International Institute of Social History in Amsterdam.

THE REVERSAL OF FORTUNE AND ITS MECHANISMS

Why Nations Fail is the title of a bestseller that brought to the attention of a large audience the role of colonialism in today's global inequality.[7] The book was the culmination of a long discussion that has a direct bearing on the subject of peripheralization and that was launched in the year

2000 by the economic historians Kenneth Sokoloff and Stanley Engerman. They observed that societies that were relatively advanced before 1800 had become poor by the turn of the twenty-first century.[8] Their idea was further developed by Daron Acemoglu, Simon Johnson, and James Robinson in their famous cliometric articles on the "reversal of fortune" and the "colonial origins of comparative development" and then in *Why Nations Fail*, Acemoglu and Robinson's widely read and translated book. The authors were intrigued by the phenomenon that "exploitation colonies" experienced lower economic growth after decolonization than "settler colonies," even though the former category emerged in the richer and more densely populated parts of the world and the latter in poorer, less inhabited areas. This reversal of fortune has been explained as the upshot of colonial powers recasting existing extractive systems or institutions in exploitation colonies for their own purposes, which inflicted lasting damage on the institutional arrangements. By comparison, in the usually temperate settler colonies, Europeans were able to introduce their own agricultural systems and build their own institutions, with secure property rights modeled on their country of origin.[9]

While Acemoglu, Johnson, and Robinson can be commended for launching a strong, simple, and elegant explanation for today's global economic divergences and for restoring the historical dimension to the economic debate, they also—and deservedly—attracted criticism for holding up the European model to the rest of the world.[10] It is, after all, one thing to explain the successes of Europe and its settler colonies by their inclusive institutions but another to explain the "failures" of the Global South by the want of such institutions. Apart from being Eurocentric, the empirical basis for a binary division between secure property rights in settler colonies and extractive institutions in exploitation colonies is weak, if not absent, first, because indigenous property rights were not that insecure and, second, because colonial governments in Island Southeast Asia—as elsewhere in the world, for that matter—*did* emulate the European model by enforcing individual property rights. However, this did little to protect local populations from exploitation by plantations or other agencies.[11] On the contrary, by declaring all waste land to be the domain of the colonial state, for example, they set in motion a process of enclosures that favored plantation enterprise. The protection of property rights by the colonial states did not at all impede what

Acemoglu, Johnson, and Robinson label as "extractive institutions." The way these authors define them, namely, as institutions that "concentrate power in the hands of a small elite and create a high risk of expropriation for the majority of the population," perfectly applies to how colonial legislation protected the operations of plantation and mining conglomerates.[12]

To date, social historians have left this debate on the historical origins of postcolonial social inequalities and high unemployment in Island Southeast Asia to economic historians. They should not stay silent, however, because two crucial dimensions are glaringly absent from this institutionalist debate, namely, labor relations and demography. This is despite the fact that their importance can easily be deduced from the timing of the reversal of fortune. Acemoglu, Johnson, and Robinson seem to suggest—although they are not entirely consistent on this point—that the reversal was set in motion at the time of the Industrial Revolution.[13] In Asia at that time, colonial powers first entered the countryside in the most densely populated parts of the region. In Island Southeast Asia, this inaugurated strongly divergent trajectories of demographic growth and the mobilization of labor for colonial cash-crop production. The northern Philippines and Java were subsumed under systems of colonial commodity production, whereas the rest of the region was more attuned to China for most of the nineteenth century.

The northern Philippines and Java were prosperous wet rice-growing regions that became severely impoverished in the twentieth century. In general, it has been observed that it was precisely the most densely populated and prosperous wet rice deltas of Southeast Asia that belong to the poorest parts of Asia today.[14] A reversal of fortune basically means, after all, that what once amounted to the sources of prosperity became the roots of misery over time. In this case, it was a combination of soil fertility, agricultural skills—such as in wet rice cultivation—and political stability. As Wilbur Zelinsky phrased it decades ago: "density of settlement in the deltas is the function of the antiquity of a stable rice culture."[15] These stable rice-producing regions, not all of which were deltaic, stood in the economic vanguard of the Sino-Malay space around the South China Sea, and this included Luzon, Java, and adjacent Bali. The empire of Majapahit (1293–1500), located in East Java, with its fertile volcanic soils and wet rice cultivation, emerged as the dominant economic and political power in the Malay world.[16]

Yet for the argument advanced in this book, it matters a great deal that this prosperity was based on successful modes of labor control rather than on specific ecological conditions. After all, wet rice cultivation was not confined to monsoon Asia or to fertile deltas, for that matter. It was, for example, also practiced by the Minangkabau in the tropical interior of Sumatra, in the Ifugao Mountains in the Philippines, and on the rice terraces of Bali. In other words, far more locations in Island Southeast Asia were suited to wet rice cultivation than would become famous for it. Ecology was a limiting factor, but it is equally true that landscapes can be the result of labor systems. The secret of the power of empires such as the Majapahit is that they were capable of attracting, and sometimes abducting, peasants to their wet rice complexes and keeping them there.[17] Without denying that ecological constraints did matter, I would argue that markets and effective mechanisms of labor recruitment were decisive in creating agricultural surpluses and high population densities.[18] As Michael Dove has pointed out for Majapahit, state formation was all about enhancing revenue collection by turning peripatetic swidden cultivators into a sedentary peasantry, a policy further pursued by the European colonizers.[19]

It is also important to note that we are not dealing here with hydraulic empires, in which central courts organized agriculture. In the rich wet rice–growing parts of Java and Luzon (most notably Ilocos), it was not the rulers but the local communities that were engaged in land clearance and water control. Even in Java, which had the most centralized polities, rulers at best facilitated land reclamation through taxation measures.[20] In his study for the Ford Foundation, published in 1956, Clifford Geertz was among the first to point out the role of the local communities and their elites in exerting control over labor. He describes how, in precolonial history, the elites of such communities—and he refers both to Java and the Philippines—were entitled to the labor of their dependents. Geertz could have used the concept of the patron-client relationship, but this term was not yet en vogue in the 1950s.[21] Nonetheless, patron-client mechanisms play a key role in his argument about agricultural involution. When labor scarcity turned into labor abundance in the nineteenth century, the same mechanism stayed in place to regulate entitlements to increasingly scarce land.[22]

The word "patron," derived from the Latin word *pater*, suggests a parental relationship between a powerful person and his dependent, a relationship that proved to be remarkably resilient over time. Patron-client relations facilitated the opening up of new land in fourteenth-century Java and gave twentieth-century sugar factories access to land and labor. In most cases, it was shored up by debt bondage, which resisted the numerous laws against it enacted by European and American colonizers in Island Southeast Asia. As has been remarked so often—for the Philippines, for example—the continuation of patron-client relationships made wage labor just a nominal issue.[23] In many ways, patron-client relationships have been crucial in rural economies in which food scarcity was ubiquitous in the months preceding the harvest and in which food security, as well as social security in general, was not arranged in a mutualistic way but through hierarchies: the strong helped the poor but at the price of the former turning the latter into their dependents. Eventually, massive rural unemployment would change the balance in such a way that in rural societies the patron relationship between landlord and peasant—or between rich peasant and dependent—lost its protective character. Patrons were no longer interested in securing a loyal labor force once there was such a surplus of labor available.[24] However, while the role of patron-client mechanisms may have diminished in agrarian societies, it definitely resurfaced in migration networks that function through the same hierarchical bonds of mutual obligations. Today, many international labor migrants rely on their parents' funding or on sponsorship by wealthier villagers, which keeps them tied to their village of origin by debts.[25] In the absence of banking institutions and social security, the age-old mechanisms of patronage are far from outdated in Island Southeast Asia and in many other regions in the world today.

EMERGING PLANTATIONS ERODING STATE REVENUE

The reversal of fortune stemmed from early-nineteenth-century demographic acceleration in communities that had already successfully mobilized labor for wet rice growing in patron-client relationships. Obviously, these societies were easier to tax than peripatetic communities engaged in swidden agriculture, and this enabled the existence of political super-structures. In this respect, the situation in Central Java was different from that across most of the Malay Peninsula, for example.[26] The reversal of fortune was not simply the result of the overtaxation of easily controlla-ble, rapidly growing populations; colonialism also played a distinctive role. The emergence of this part of the world as a bulk-commodity pro-ducer went along with a shift from revenue extraction for the state toward extraction of labor for plantation interests. While the strong rulers—and colonial state bureaucracies definitely fall into that category—had become increasingly effective in raising revenue and conscripting labor and military services from rural households, the emergence of plantation economies in the nineteenth century turned the clock back and eroded the state's revenue basis, which had been strengthened over time in Java and the northern Philippines. This point merits further explanation.

State formation entails bringing subjects under the direct control of the ruler and court, to increase revenue and enhance military strength. Strong polities in Southeast Asia such as Siam and Burma—as well as the Indonesian sultanates of Mataram, Banten, and Bone—enslaved pop-ulations of conquered territories and settled them in their heartlands, usually as sharecroppers.[27] In their statecraft, slavery just played a tran-sient role, if only because it was a relatively costly mode of labor control requiring permanent supervision and because slaves were rarely con-scripted into armies.[28] The need for a sustained revenue basis and a male population that could be conscripted into the defense of the ruling elites against foreign invaders propelled the transfer of enslaved people into a class of enserfed commoners. Rural populations were usually heav-ily taxed. In precolonial Java, taxation ranged from 30 to 40 percent on agricultural output, on top of which came the burden of the many toll-houses, which took revenue from all kinds of trade. Despite the fact that taxation was widely evaded, the overall level of extraction was still con-siderably higher than in late-colonial Java.[29]

Colonial powers continued these policies of creating sedentary and heavily taxed rural societies by curtailing the spatial mobility of peas-ants.[30] The Spanish did this by forcing all Christian Filipinos to live within earshot of a church bell, in practice resettling them in villages around churches. Nobody was allowed to leave this community, the *pueblo*, without permission from the priest. Recalcitrant peasants were put on the galleons connecting Manila with Acapulco (Mexico). In the nineteenth century, the colonial authorities of the Netherlands Indies punished peasants who migrated without permission with a rattan beating. To a certain extent, colonial states used the extractive powers of the precolonial rulers to finance the colonial state—as well as to send considerable funds back to the metropolis—either through taxation or by directing tributary labor to the infrastructure or to cash-crop production.

Victor Clark, an American who made an extensive study of labor conditions in the Philippines and Java at the turn of the twentieth century, painted with a few imaginative strokes the colonial state as the inheritor of the extractive powers of the precolonial rulers: "These national savings went to enrich the hoards of oriental despots and to support the luxury of a sensual court. Under modern colonial government they are devoted to the construction of works of general utility. Public buildings, roads, bridges, irrigation works, wharves and railways represent the crystallized savings of the Javanese."[31]

Nevertheless, a lot more could have been spent on infrastructure, education, and health had the colonial state not eroded the extractive powers it had inherited from the precolonial rulers. Particularly in Java, it relinquished its own claims on forced labor in the nineteenth century to give room to private enterprise and alleviate the plight of the rural populations. In general, colonial states favored plantation estates, expecting that these would dramatically widen the revenue basis, as I argue in chapter 3.[32] However, corporate plantation enterprises strongly resisted taxation, including duties on their exports. *In the end, colonialism restricted rather than strengthened the extractive powers of the state.*

During the dismemberment of the patrimonial state and the elimination of many of its revenue-extracting mechanisms, the patron-client relationships at the local level remained unimpaired. These became pivotal for the plantations, which had neither the coercive powers of the state to recruit their workforce nor the supplies of proletarianized labor, despite the fact that rapid population growth was leading to increasing pressure on land. Labor was abundantly available for export agriculture, but only if planters could tie their labor in patron-client relationships, which is exactly what happened in Java, Luzon, and the Visayas. More than any of the other larger islands of the Indonesian archipelago, Java became a plantation island. In 1930, 85 percent of the added value of its export crops came from plantations, compared with a mere 36 percent in all the other Indonesian islands, which I will henceforth describe by the colonial administrative term "Outer Islands." In Java, plantations dominated export agriculture, whereas for Borneo and most of Sumatra, smallholders did. It was not specific crops that can explain why Java became a plantation island while the Outer Islands were dominated by smallholder production. In Java, rubber was a plantation crop, enabled by enclosures, whereas in the Outer Islands and Malaysia rubber was widely grown as a smallholder crop. It is the differences in population density, population growth, and the concentration of plantations that drove a perfect reversal of fortune: the originally less populated and probably poorer Outer Islands—where plantations had not found the servile labor that was available in Java—benefited more from the commodity boom in the decades around 1900 than Java's peasantry.[33] Java turned from the most prosperous and powerful island of Southeast Asia into one of the poorest.

THE PERIPHERY AND THE COMMODITY FRONTIERS

The reversal of fortune befell stable rice-producing societies in Island Southeast Asia because their effective modes of labor recruitment were enmeshed in patron-client relationships. The stability and resilience of these modes of labor control proved to be of great value to the colonial administrations of the Philippines and Java when they embarked on the promotion of commodity exports. Together with strong demographic growth and a vigorous global demand for commodities, this was the basis for the emergence of plantation-style commodity production that peripheralized the societies in which the plantations were embedded.

The claim that the one-sided orientation of colonial economies on export commodities was the result of deliberate policies of the metropolitan state government is an old one. It started with Indian nationalist economic writing and was given academic credibility by the thesis of underdevelopment of the periphery through the core, as was elaborated by pioneering development economists such as Albert O. Hirschman and Raúl Prebisch. Others have argued, however, that this "underdevelopment" was the result of imperial policies only to a limited extent and was predominantly the upshot of economic specialization, in which colonial regimes were not necessarily instrumental. The increasing availability of cheap industrial cotton cloth and the growing demand for tropical commodities in industrial countries made it attractive to farmers in the tropics to abandon weaving and instead to grow cash crops. Nevertheless, Bassino and Williamson might overstate their case when they note that "Southeast Asia underwent the biggest terms of trade boom, the biggest Dutch disease, and the biggest de-industrialisation in the global periphery."[34] The extent to which this part of the world was industrialized was modest. Much of the manufacturing was actually cottage production, which was carried out in slack hours. Java, for example, was always 80 percent an agricultural economy until the Second World War, and its most important manufacturing was of textiles. According to recent research findings, cottage textile production continued to exist during the commodity boom and the decades around 1900.[35]

There can be no doubt, however, that the world's periphery was driven toward commodity exports and away from industrialization. By the late nineteenth century, there was a general trend of declining prices for industrially manufactured goods in comparison with tropical agricultural products.[36] Meanwhile, continuously shrinking freight costs facilitated the incorporation of Island Southeast Asia into the global economy as a mass producer. After all, initially, only high-value items such as spices, ceramics, camphor, birds' nests, pearls, diamonds, textiles, tin, and sugar were transported over the oceans. In the early nineteenth century, Asian rice seldom reached European markets unless carried as ballast. This all changed with the arrival of the steel steamships, which were faster, could carry more, and were—in contrast to rigged vessels— allowed to pass through the Suez Canal, something particularly relevant to Asia. The emerging global market for mass commodities came about at the time when population pressures began to become evident in the most densely populated parts of Java and the Philippines, and it enabled an overflow of labor to commodity frontiers.[37]

Certainly, national economies relying on commodity production are at a disadvantage compared with industrial nations for a number of reasons, one of which is the higher volatility of commodity prices than those for manufactured articles. However, specialization in tropical commodities did make sense for Island Southeast Asia and, contrary to widely held beliefs, was not necessarily detrimental to economic development. Parts of Island Southeast Asia did well. Malaysia is the key example here, as it achieved impressive economic growth figures with its specialization in tin, rubber, and palm oil. Rather than focusing on a dichotomy between industry and agriculture, this book foregrounds the role of labor control and the mechanisms that siphoned off local wealth. Here, the distinction between plantations and smallholders emerges as a crucial variable. Plantations also figure prominently in the article by Sokoloff and Engerman that set the agenda for research on the reversal of fortune. They observe that sugar plantations were highly efficient in their time but also generated extreme inequality, which, the authors suggest, was eventually responsible for the Caribbean region's falling behind the initially poorer North American territories.[38] For more contemporary times and on a more micro level, it has also been observed that plantations compare badly with smallholder cash-crop production in terms of benefits to the actual workers and local economies.[39] It is an observation of direct relevance for contemporary discussions concerning sustainable commodity production. The United Nations Conference on Trade and Development (UNCTAD), for example, placed the smallholder commodity producer high on the agenda in its 2015 report.[40]

Plantations not only yield fewer benefits for local rural societies but also subject the economy to more price volatility, first of all because of their high degree of specialization. While early-nineteenth-century European estates in Central Java, for example, still spread their risks over a variety of crops—such as coffee, tobacco, indigo, and sugar—plantations became larger over time and, particularly in the case of sugar, more capital intensive and intertwined with international banking interests. These conglomerates had an edge over individual plantations when overcoming bad harvests or sudden drops in market prices, which leads to the second reason economies dominated by European plantations suffered more from the cyclical nature of commodity prices than smallholders: plantations developed into formidable interest groups that entrenched themselves solidly in the decision-making processes of the colonial administrations and metropolitan governments. These politically and socially entrenched entities were capable of resisting higher taxation during boom times and of wresting tax cuts from the government and squeezing payments to the workers in times of bust. These conditions are termed "extractive institutions" by Acemoglu, Johnson, and Robinson. The economically oppressive alliance among local elites, the state, and corporate enterprise that played such a prominent role in the diagnosis of rural poverty by the Dependency School is indeed undeniably present within the colonial and postcolonial histories of the Philippines and Indonesia.[41]

The notion of the "plantation conglomerate" excellently fits the definition of Acemoglu, Johnson, and Robinson of an extractive institution as "a high concentration of political power in the hands of a few who extracted resources from the rest of the population."[42] The plantation is a powerful tool for controlling labor and robbing cultivators of their negotiating power to divert to other crops; it is also a pivot in the global commodity chain. This is succinctly formulated from a world-systems perspective by Dale Tomich in his article "Rethinking the Plantation": "World market and division of labor and social relations of production are integrated with one another through the institutional matrix of the plantation."[43] However, rather than the sugar plantation in the early-modern New World, which was an insular phenomenon, we need to understand the plantation in Asia in a broader sense, namely, as a conglomerate of estates firmly entrenched in the colonial state and capable of controlling a countryside and a labor force, even without being the proprietor of either of them. Control was, after all, exerted via patron-client relationships, which in the twentieth century were coupled with advanced methods of control over plantation workers by issuing passes with fingerprints. Although the "plantation" was a business model engrained in the imperial mind, backed up by a powerful colonial state and therefore initially discarded by the postcolonial states, it did make a remarkable comeback over later decades.

Plantations need the constant support of the state, because smallholders are almost invariably capable of producing at lower cost: they do not need supervision, use slack hours for raising cash crops, and are better motivated because they keep the rewards of their work, as I argue in chapter 3. Ordinary workers barely shared in the profits made by plantations. This was particularly the case when planters had to pay high recruitment fees to obtain labor and squeezed the maximum profit out of their laborers by resorting to physical coercion, taking justice into their own hands, or enlisting the collaboration of state officials in their oppression. Colonial governments enacted labor contracts with a penal sanction on desertion in an attempt to remedy the evils of human trafficking and the abuse of plantation workers, though this sacrificed the bargaining power of the laborers. The penal sanction imposed labor discipline and suppressed any collective action against payments far below market levels. The plantation belt in East Sumatra was notorious in this respect.

Individual labor contracts with a penal sanction proved to be inferior to patron-client relationships in terms of ensuring a stable workforce, as I explain in chapter 4. For that reason, the penal sanction disappeared after a brief existence in Java in the 1870s and was never introduced in the Philippines. In Malaysia, it was abolished when the booming rubber sector in the 1910s led to serious labor shortages and to a massive desertion of labor gangs toward smallholder cash-crop production. *Kongsis* (Chinese labor gangs) of tin miners escaped to more lucrative mining outside the concessions granted to corporate enterprise. The labor gangs had beaten the indentured-labor system, and wages rose, particularly in the rubber plantations.[44] Throughout Island Southeast Asia, patron-client relationships in a diversity of settings—ranging from labor gangs in Javanese cane fields to Chinese tin *kongsis*—greased the wheels of colonial extraction. The only locations where the penal sanction continued to exist until the end of colonial rule were plantations and mines in Indonesia's Outer Islands, where wages were the lowest in the region and, not coincidentally, where Javanese workers were not recruited in labor gangs but through professional agencies. Patron-client systems coupled with land scarcity allowed plantations to thrive, a fact that applied most notably to Java, where commodity production was dominated by plantations.

DIVERGENT LABOR REGIMES, DIVERGENT ECONOMIC TRAJECTORIES

Within Island Southeast Asia, the plantation economy was most dominant in Java, which not coincidentally was also clearly lagging behind the rest of the region in terms of economic performance (see table 0.1). This certainly does not mean that the relationship between plantation dominance and the reversal of fortune is a monocausal one. First of all, the example of British Malaya shows that plantations and mines cannot ignore the laws of labor demand and supply. The Lewisian elasticity of labor supplies is, according to Arthur W. Lewis, not necessarily permanent. While the capitalist plantation and mining sectors expanded, they drew labor from the countryside, which resulted in higher returns on capital and, eventually, further demand for labor. At a certain stage of economic development—which is termed the Lewisian turning point—emerging shortages of labor will lead to rising wages. Even within the peripheral economy of Java, laborers benefited from the cyclical commodity booms of the 1860s to 1870s and of the early twentieth century.[45] The final decade before the First World War allowed a 2.5 percent annual growth of per capita income in Indonesia, which trickled down to poorer segments of the rural population.[46] However, this was a temporary phenomenon, particularly in Java, where living conditions deteriorated in the course of the 1920s, leading to, among other things, undernourished workers streaming toward the East Sumatra plantations.[47] Java's per capita income stagnated after 1913, despite the fact that the island had a buoyant and well-managed plantation economy dominated by one of the most efficient and best capitalized sugar industries in the world.

Two other factors need to be considered in order to explain Java's economic stagnation. First, land scarcity: the availability of land was a key determinant in the living standards of the still overwhelmingly rural populations in this part of the world.[48] The crux of the matter is that in the context of Island Southeast Asia, the plantations and population density are highly correlated and also connected by modes of labor recruitment. The second factor, which again is intertwined with the plantation interests and population density, is the rate of colonial-metropolitan remittances. The Dutch economist Jacob van Gelderen observed in the late 1920s that over the two previous decades, the colony's positive trade balance had widely exceeded that of the Philippines. While the latter was still receiving substantial investment in the plantation sector, as well as in irrigation and industry in the 1910s, the Netherlands Indies massively remitted corporate profits and expatriate pensions abroad.[49] Because of the entangled character of peripheralization, it is important to compare different production systems and their relationship with local and metropolitan economies. Island Southeast Asia offers a rich field for such comparisons: In early-twentieth-century Java, metropolitan plantation agriculture dominated. In the northern Philippines, it was indigenous plantocracies, and in Indonesia's Outer Islands and Malaysia, smallholder cash-crop production abounded.

The comparative analysis is important in order to explain not only short-term economic performance but also further prospects for growth, which are, in addition, determined by the potential for economic diversification. Tropical commodity producers *can* achieve a meaningful diversification of their economies, as Findlay and Lundahl have shown, but the question is, of course, under what conditions.[50] This is an issue central to this book and directly related to the question of how this part of the world was able to become a mass exporter of labor. In Java, for example, some forward and backward linkages developed during the boom years, but they were apparently too weak to create a robust sector with a relatively high productivity to bring about a sustained rise of real wages for a rapidly growing population. However, was this because of plantations or because of commodity production in general? Under certain conditions commodity exporters can compete very well with industrializing countries in terms of economic performance. In the early years of the twentieth century, Japan had not yet presented the convincing argument that labor-intensive industrialization could catapult a country well beyond being a producer of primary products in terms of per capita income (see table 0.1).

The paths of economic growth are volatile, and fortunes could turn dramatically in the course of a few decades, as table 0.1 shows. The Philippines were doing much better than Java in the first half of the twentieth century, with a more varied economy, less population pressure, better education, and less dominant plantation interests. With the highest per capita income among the Southeast Asian countries in the 1950s, the Philippines were expected to follow Japan in a surge of industrial growth. Instead, the Philippines would become the poorest country in Island Southeast Asia thirty years later. While there is no unanimity about the causes of this deeply disappointing development, the detrimental effects of demographic growth rates (of over 3 percent per year in the 1960s) are too obvious to be ignored. In line with this observation, it should be noted that much of the predicament of the Philippines under Ferdinand Marcos had already been in the making in the late-colonial era,

TABLE 0.1
GDP per capita, 1880–2000 (in 1990 USD)

Country/Year	1880	1910	1930	1939	1970	2000
The Philippines	624	874	1,382	1,508	1,764	2,349
Malaysia	663 (1870)	801 (1911)	1,636	1,609	2,079	7,788
Indonesia (Java)*	475	715	983	934		3,135
Indonesia (Outer* Islands)	1,042	1,003	1,184	1,236		3,449
Singapore	682	1,839	2,269	2,803	4,439	21,263
Japan	863	1,304	1,850	2,816	9,714	20,481

* The 1880 figures show more divergence between Java and the Outer Islands than is realistic. This is because of an extrapolation that has been applied to compensate for the paucity of data for the nineteenth century.

Source: CLIO-INFRA. For Java and the Outer Islands, see Bosma, "GDP per Capita Netherlands Indies," in Bosma, "Data on Demography, Migration, Slavery, and Employment for the Netherlands Indies, the Philippines, and British Malaya 1800–1950," http://hdl .handle.net/10622/NCJVLW.

when plantation agriculture became increasingly dominant, exploiting the growing population pressure.

British Malaya, and later on Malaysia, tells a story of paths of sustained growth based on commodity exports. This experience also suggests that investment in agriculture and irrigation might have been a more effective scenario than entering into competition with, for example, manufacturing in Hong Kong and Japan. This is what some observers had actually suggested in the early twentieth century as a way out for the stagnating economy of Java.[51] Plantations were, however, often capable of offering better wages than such industries. Accordingly, specialization in commodities made sense, and it apparently went well in Malaysia after the Second World War. Nevertheless, Malaysia did not reach the economic growth achieved by the industrializing countries of East and Southeast

Asia. Today, it has an economy that offers abundant employment for unskilled and low-skilled labor but not enough for the higher educated, who have been migrating in large numbers over the past decades.

For Island Southeast Asia as a whole, at least three different strata of migration emerged in colonial times: first, the labor or "coolie" migration toward the plantations; second, the educated urban toward Singapore and Manila; and, third, the peasant settlers' migration. In the Philippines, where education stood at a relatively high level in colonial times, the trek to the city was already substantial under the American administration.[52] In Java, massive by-employment of marginal and landless peasants in plantations and in the infrastructure brought about intensive circular labor migrations. The peasant settler migration would eventually cover the entire area of Island Southeast Asia. In the cases of the Philippines and Indonesia, it brought only temporary relief from the pressures of high demographic growth. In the Philippines, it became massive in the 1970s and replaced the ailing sugar industry as a source of foreign currency in the subsequent decade. Java had better prospects of releasing its "surplus population" to the Outer Islands, but here the limits of colonization were also reached in the decade to follow. Moreover, the new postcolonial plantations in the thinly populated islands of Southeast Asia were different from their colonial equivalents because they needed far less labor per hectare under cultivation. We can think of the huge sugar plantations in New Guinea, where the cane is harvested by combines. Since the capacity of the frontiers to absorb settlers or plantation laborers was limited, international migration became the way out. Indonesian and Philippine migration patterns transcended their national boundaries toward a widening circle of richer East Asian countries and Gulf States.

THE BOOK'S OUTLINE

The investigation into the "making of the periphery" examines the precolonial and colonial roots of postcolonial global inequalities. This is an ambition shared both by world-systems scholars and by the practitioners of the new institutional economic history. In this regard, it is salient that the concept of "extractive institutions," which is part of the "reversal of fortune" thesis, overlaps strongly with Dale Tomich's description of the plantation as a pivot in the global economy. Precisely this pivotal role of plantations in peripheralization should make us critical about macroanalytical explanations of global economic inequalities. Not all of Island Southeast Asia was covered by plantations, and the main argument in this book is that rural societies became integrated in the global market in various ways, covering the full gamut from slavery, sharecropping, indentured coolie labor, and wage labor to independent smallholdings. These trajectories have their own historical specificities.[53]

A reversal of fortune occurred in Island Southeast Asia not in the seventeenth century, as Anthony Reid argues in his brilliant and evocative *Southeast Asia in the Age of Commerce*, but almost two centuries later. Chapter 1 describes how smallpox vaccination in the early nineteenth century in the northern Philippines and Java resulted in demographic growth figures that were unique for Asia: twice as high as the already remarkable annual demographic growth of 0.7 percent attained by China at that time. Only the British possessions on the Malay Peninsula kept abreast with this growth, not through reduced mortality but thanks to growing numbers of Chinese and Tamil immigrants. Demographic stagnation continued for most of the remaining 60 to 70 percent of the territory of archipelagic Southeast Asia, where with a colonial presence hardly tangible for most of the nineteenth century, vaccinations were as infrequent as slavery was rife. Chapter 2 focuses on the so-called Outer Islands of Indonesia in the mid–nineteenth century, where, similar to the situation in West Africa, some slaveholding polities were beyond colonial control and hence capable of resisting colonial expansion by trading spices and forest and sea products for arms and other commodities.

Meanwhile, smallpox vaccinations in the northern Philippines and Java led to population growth and abundant supplies of labor for the emerging plantation economies, as I detail in chapter 3. By the mid–nineteenth century, both territories saw extensive migrations from overpopulated regions toward commodity-producing frontiers. In the interwar years, declining commodity prices coupled with increasing population pressures in these densely populated parts of Island Southeast Asia led to rural poverty and even malnutrition. The chapter concludes with an analysis of the deeper causes of this reversal of fortune, pointing to the mutually reinforcing mechanisms of plantation dominance and population pressure. In chapter 4, the focus shifts to British Malaya and Indonesia's Outer Islands at the time of the rubber boom in the wake of the Second Industrial Revolution. The trajectories of commodity production in the Malay Peninsula, Sumatra, and Borneo in the early twentieth century offer important counterpoints to those of Java, Luzon, and the western Visayas. Wherever population densities were low, smallholders reaped substantial benefits from commodity booms, wages went up, and plantations had great difficulty in attracting workers. Chapter 4 explains how the worlds of high and low population densities came together through intensive and unscrupulous recruiters who supplied the Javanese as indentured workers for the plantations in Sumatra in the early twentieth century. This demonstrates how much the demographic imbalances within Island Southeast Asia were intrinsically part of the dynamics of peripheralization. These imbalances shaped the migration systems and practices of human trafficking that still abound in the region today.

Economic peripheralization can be measured, as is explained in chapter 5, by assessing the imprint of colonial commodity production on the societies of Island Southeast Asia in the early twentieth century. How many people were reliant on these colonial plantation and mining conglomerates and their related infrastructures in the final decades of colonial rule? What was the structure of employment in late-colonial societies, how precarious was it, and what migration circuits developed? Chapter 5 also presents the argument that the deindustrializing effects of the region's specialization on exporting cash crops have been exaggerated, whereas the detrimental effects of cheap rice imports on the rural economy of Java have largely gone unnoticed. In this regard, Java was very different from the Philippines, where the American administration imposed tariffs on rice imports. Moreover, the northern Philippines— less underdeveloped by the Spanish colonizers than their American colonizers have suggested—had a relatively highly educated and increasingly urban population. In densely populated colonial Java, where education was poor, the massive by-employment of marginal and landless peasants in plantations and in the infrastructure brought about intensive circular labor migrations. British Malaya saw both coolie migration toward mines and plantations and the permanent settlement of skilled workers in its trading hubs. The increasingly urban and educated migrant flows of the Philippines and Malaysia and the contrasting rural and low-skilled mobility in Indonesia would set patterns still clearly discernible today in the international emigration flows both within and from this part of the world.

Chapter 6 completes the book's exploration of the historical roots of today's mass emigration within and from the region. First, plantation agriculture did not disappear with colonialism. On the contrary, over recent decades there has been massive land grabbing for palm oil, pineapple, and other plantations, crops that require less employment than the old colonial estates. Second, the circular migrations of the low skilled and the urbanization of the educated have been continuously expanding since the early twentieth century. Today's migrations are structured on recruitment mechanisms that were born in the early nineteenth century, in times of rapid demographic growth and emerging colonial plantation economies. In late-colonial society, these migrations became not only more urbanized but also increasingly feminized. Migration systems ranged from mutual-support networks built on increasing migrant social capital, to subcontracting, and to outright trafficking, which existed alongside as well as in competition with one another. Both from the past and the present, myriad stories can be told of individual migrants who preferred illicit migration channels, mediated through patron-client relationships, to the licensed but exploitative arrangements of the colonial and postcolonial states.

The six chapters together aim to show that the dependence on commodity exports is far too easy an answer to the question of how a reversal of fortune or peripheralization could happen. We at least have to add to our analysis the high level of demographic growth and specific modes of labor control in this part of the world. Demographic change coincided with the transition of the European presence from trading companies to territorial states, which were capable of encapsulating rural populations in systems of global commodity production via patron-client systems. Strong demographic growth did not lead to Malthusian situations, but it did make rural populations dependent on plantation employment. Plantation owners cashed the profits from the booms and shifted the losses incurred during busts to the rural workers. Conversely, thinly populated areas allowed smallholders to engage in the cultivation of export crops without being subjected to such exploitation. The roots of this divergence within Island Southeast Asia lie in the early nineteenth century.

CHAPTER ONE

Smallpox Vaccination and Demographic Divergences in the Nineteenth Century

The way in which Acemoglu, Johnson, and Robinson formulate the "reversal of fortune" thesis not only overstates the importance of property rights—or, to put it more precisely, the importance of their codification—but also takes for granted the claim made by the dependency school that colonization in early modern history led to the destruction of local commerce and manufacturing.[1] This point also remained almost uncontested in the case of Island Southeast Asia. Reid wrote extensively in his classic *The Age of Commerce* about how European intrusions played a major role in destroying the once flourishing maritime world, initiating the peripheralization of the Malay world.[2] In fact, as Lieberman has emphasized, the economic centers of gravity were not the trading emporia but the consolidated territorial polities, and thus the impact of the European chartered companies could not have been as dramatic as Reid suggests.[3] Moreover, from recent historical research it appears that precolonial port cities were not as magnificent as Reid portrayed them.

This is not to deny the plunder, violence, and demographic contraction that attended the early European encounters with Island Southeast Asia and also took place in Latin America and Africa. The northern Philippines were sliced up into *encomiendas* and divided among the conquistadores, while the spice islands of the Moluccas were ruthlessly incorporated by the VOC (the Dutch East India Company). Yet despite all the death and destruction wreaked in these early stages of colonialism, Wallerstein's observation that in the case of Southeast Asia a meaningful colonial territorialization and incorporation of local labor and land in global capitalism only occurred by the late eighteenth century is still valid. Until that time, Island Southeast Asia was still part of the *external arena* of the modern world-system.[4] After all, the Philippines produced little for Spain except losses, and the VOC's exports from its extensive territories accounted for a marginal 2 percent of local net domestic product. The main commodities this trading company was interested in—namely, pepper, cloves, and sugar—represented just 11 percent of Southeast Asia's exports.[5] The presence of the European trading companies was local and confined to particular sectors of commerce and manufacturing.

Nonetheless, the marginality of the VOC's trade within the economy of Southeast Asia does not exclude its potentially ruinous effects on urban life, maritime trade, and artisanship. The violent monopolization of clove cultivation and the enforced concentration of sugar production around Batavia, for example, were indubitably detrimental to Indonesia's economy. The decline in Java's exports was temporary, however, and was followed by a recovery after 1740. There is, further, no reason to assume, as some historians have done, that the VOC brought about an atrophy of once flourishing port cities or, for that matter, of the textile sector of Southeast Asia.[6] The perception that cities with over one hundred thousand inhabitants crumbled under the weight of seventeenth-century European colonialism has been disavowed by more recent scholarship for being colored by early-modern European discoverers, who did not mind exaggerating the size of the Asian cities they visited in order to secure their place in the explorer's hall of fame.[7] The emporia were neither as large as suggested by contemporary travelogues, nor were they manifold. Usually, only one or two acted as the hubs for the most valuable items, such as pepper and sandalwood, luxury cloth, gold, and camphor—the latter used as a disinfectant during a plague epidemic. Maritime leadership was ephemeral because competitors were quick to take over the leading positions: between 1511 and 1683, Malacca, Brunei, Makassar, Banten, and Batavia succeeded one another as trading hubs for Indian textiles, Chinese ceramics, and Southeast Asian sea and forest products. There is nothing specifically Asian about this, because centers of maritime commerce are by nature unstable, as we have also seen on the other side of the globe, in the Low Countries. There, within a period of 120 years, Bruges, Ghent, Antwerp, and Amsterdam succeeded one another as the dominant commercial centers of their time.[8] One port's loss was another's gain.

Precolonial cities were particularly vulnerable if they relied on maritime food imports. The trading hubs of Palembang and Makassar still had their own bases of rice production, but Malacca, Banten, and Aceh were heavily dependent on rice imports, and Brunei notoriously so.[9] It is true that in Island Southeast Asia an important rice trade existed, carried by tall ships built with the craftsmanship for which this part of the world was known.[10] However, to feed cities with tens of thousands of inhabitants through overseas rice imports was logistically a daunting task, one exposed to naval threats and the superior firepower of European ships in particular. This is what the proud sultanate of Banten, at the center of the pepper trade, experienced during repeated Dutch blockades in the seventeenth century.[11] Compact cities of over fifty thousand inhabitants, resembling those in Europe, were the exceptions or even nonexistent in Island Southeast Asia. Instead, all over Southeast Asia—and South Asia, for that matter—settlements showed a mix of rural and urban, which scholars have termed "rurban" and which could be economically advanced and monetized.[12]

The corollary of this is that the colonial capital Batavia, founded by the VOC in 1619, yielded in nothing to any of the emporia it had blockaded, destroyed, or brought under its control. With fifty thousand inhabitants, it was probably the largest city of Island Southeast Asia around 1700, but while on its way to becoming one of the world's largest colonial towns, its health conditions deteriorated, probably because of the rapidly expanding number of fishponds near its outskirts. These offered an ideal breeding ground for mosquitoes, turning Batavia into a malaria-infested place, where in bad years 80 percent of the newly arrived Europeans lost their lives. The rich citizens and their slave retinues moved out of the city to their mansions in the so-called Ommelanden (surrounding districts), which were dotted with sugar mills and where another hundred thousand people lived.[13] This unique situation of 150,000 people largely dependent on outside food supplies owed its existence to adequate rice supplies arranged by the powerful VOC. It is inconceivable that any of the grand emporia that preceded Batavia—with the possible exception of Makassar—could ever have procured such stable supplies for so many people.

Batavia's example might raise the question why Manila did not live up to its promise of becoming the central entrepôt of Island Southeast Asia after the Spanish had subdued its main competitor, Brunei.[14] Initially, the town followed the Asian model of attracting merchants and their retinues, and it was an example for the founders of Batavia. In the course of the sixteenth century, Manila emerged as the trading hub of Chinese traders. Some forty or fifty ships per year called at its port at that time, and an extensive Chinese quarter was inhabited by 16,000 people: a community annihilated by the massacre of 1603.[15] The murder of its Chinese population was the immediate cause of the town's demise, but it was not the only factor. Manila's aspirations were also thwarted by competition from Malacca, Makassar, and the VOC. Last but not least, Spanish trade policies that had established the so-called Galleon Trade between Manila and Acapulco across the Pacific only seemingly gave the city its global stature, while they actually severely limited its trade and condemned the city to a languishing existence. With its commerce more or less confined to the transshipment of goods from Asia destined for Mexico, the town's population size stayed below ten thousand until it mushroomed into a primate city in the nineteenth century.

DEMOGRAPHIC STAGNATION

Although the European intrusions did not destroy urban life, artisanship, and commerce, Southeast Asia certainly went through a phase of demographic decline and economic contraction between 1600 and 1750. Climate change, smallpox epidemics, and frequent military conflict were responsible for this. For obvious reasons, the relative weight of these factors remains obscure, and the extent of the demographic decline can only be sketched in rough figures. Data are particularly scarce for the years before 1800, with the notable exception of the northern Philippines, where tributary registers and parish records kept track of the number of inhabitants and of their marriages, births, movements, and occupations. Based on this data, Newson concludes in her thorough study that the population of Luzon and the Visayas, which still numbered 1.4 million in the 1560s, had been almost halved by 1700. Smallpox was a major cause, because of intensifying trade contacts with China by the late sixteenth century, but the ravages of the Spanish conquest and piracy were, at the least, important additional causes.[16] The disasters that befell the Filipinos were immense and wiped out the positive effects of enhanced agricultural production through the introduction of the plow by the Spanish authorities in the final decade of the sixteenth century.[17]

Maritime raiding as such was rooted in ancient habits. Long before the Spanish conquest, slave raiding was endemic all over the Philippines, but it reached unprecedented heights during the so-called Spanish–Moro Conflict that began in 1569 with the first sea battle between Spanish and Brunei vessels. Pirates from Mindanao, North Borneo, and the Sulu sultanate relentlessly attacked Luzon and the Visayas. The attacks were not only aimed at the churches, with their gold and silver treasures, but also—or even more so—at their surrounding populations. Other key targets were the Spanish shipyards in the Philippine islands: the Moros were always keen to abduct competent carpenters. In the late sixteenth and early seventeenth centuries, the Spanish were beleaguered by the nearby Moros polities of Sulu and Mindanao, from the west by huge Chinese pirate fleets, from the south by the Dutch in the Moluccas, and in one case even by a joint attack by the Moluccan sultans of Ternate and Tidore and the VOC. Piracy abated after the Spanish had strengthened their control over Mindanao and thawed their relations with the sultan of Sulu. But this was just an interlude lasting from the 1720s until the deposition of this ruler in 1748.[18] From then on, the raids resumed with renewed ferocity, which could have completely devastated the Visayas and the western provinces of Luzon had many people not resettled in larger and better-defendable villages or vacated the coastal areas.[19]

One can only guess at how many people were abducted from the Philippines between the 1560s and 1800. In relatively quiet times, it might have been just a thousand per year, but the number of abducted could easily peak at over four thousand, as happened in the three decades after 1750. Still to be added are the numerous victims of the collateral violence: on average, for every two abducted people, a third might have been killed during the raid.[20] Such an average annual loss of four to five thousand people amounted to 0.5 percent of the total Filipino population. Existing birth and marriage practices—including abortion, infanticide, and bridewealth paid in the form of slaves—as well as the institution of slavery must have depressed natural demographic growth in the Philippines for most of the eighteenth century.[21] Although the tributary population in Luzon and the Visayas saw an annual increase of 1.4 percent in the early eighteenth century, this seems to have been predominantly the result of improved counting methods and, to some extent, of abating piracy. Moreover, it is almost certain that increased levels of piracy and the spread of smallpox led to a new demographic stagnation by the mid–eighteenth century.[22] The basis for sustained demographic growth was only established in the final decades of the eighteenth century, when the Spanish authorities constructed a string of fortresses on the western coast of Luzon and around the Visayas. At that time, Manila began to fulfill its initial promise of becoming a trading hub; textile-manufacturing centers emerged in the western Visayas, while Pampanga and some Tagalog provinces in Central Luzon embarked on sugar production. Last but not least, the government of the Philippines boosted its revenues by introducing forced cultivation, with tobacco as the most important crop.

In contrast to the Philippines, detailed demographic data for the Indonesian archipelago is scarce. However, from the snippets of information available, we can reconstruct some important shifts in the demographic history of Java in a long-term perspective. In the fourteenth century, the empire of Majapahit stood at its zenith, and its agricultural output had just been considerably augmented by the innovation of the double cropping of rice in the Brantas delta. Increasing monetization also testifies to an expanding and diversifying economy. These factors taken together would justify an estimation of Java's population of approximately five million in the early fifteenth century.[23] After that, it probably increased by 0.2 percent annually up to the mid–sixteenth century but stagnated at 6.5 million afterward under the effects of intensifying violence and extensive slave exports. From the 1660s onward, the general trend in the Indonesian archipelago was one of demographic decline.[24]

Java went through horrible times in the late seventeenth century. The people suffered from famines caused by droughts and by epidemics of rinderpest. Meanwhile, the rulers of Mataram were engaged in almost incessant warfare, and if this was still not enough, smallpox surged. Already present when the Portuguese arrived on this island, new waves were carried into Batavia by slaves arriving from South Asia.[25] From here, the disease spread into the interior, where it wreaked havoc in the densely populated heartland of Mataram. Smallpox, droughts, and wars caused a population decline of 20 percent between the late seventeenth and the mid–eighteenth century. By then, the size of Java's population was likely back to where it had stood by the late fifteenth century: just under six million.

In the Outer Islands, meanwhile, smallpox visited many of the Moluccan islands every twenty years from the seventeenth century onward,[26] and with a case fatality of between 20 and 30 percent, it raised overall mortality by an additional 0.7 to 1 percent. Mortality further rose through the VOC's violent imposition of its clove and nutmeg monopolies and in the political and economic chaos after the destruction of Makassar in 1669.[27] Some recovery of demographic growth did happen—for example in Ambon, resulting from a combination of higher birth rates, resettlements, and slave imports—but this growth soon leveled off.[28]

By the end of the eighteenth century, Java and the northern Philippines were the first to show signs of economic and demographic recovery. At that time, the VOC had achieved dominance over Java and was well on its way to turning this island into a producer of commodities such as timber, coffee, rice, and sugar. This drove up real wages and through that probably birth rates as well. Carey depicts a cheerful return of prosperity in the heartlands of the former empire of Mataram in the second half of the eighteenth century. Despite a regular recurrence of smallpox, natural annual demographic growth could have reached approximately 0.7 percent in Java. This resulted in a total population for Java and Madura of 7.5 million by the early years of the nineteenth century.[29]

While economic recovery in Java and the Philippines can be attributed to the *pax imperialis* and the economic policies of the VOC and the Philippine government, elsewhere in Island Southeast Asia a new wave of Chinese maritime dynamism reverberated in the coasts around the Java Sea and the South China Sea. The demand for tin, gambier, pepper, sandalwood, trepang (sea cucumber), pearls, and bird's nests rose. Makassar emerged as a transit harbor for the trade between the eastern part of the archipelago and China, in the process of which Amoy (Xiamen) replaced Batavia as its most important trading partner. China bone was traded all over Island Southeast Asia, from the north of the Philippines to the southern islands of the Moluccas, as well as to the interior of Borneo. The growing demand for forest and sea products from China lured thousands of Bajau (sea nomads) to the east coast of Sulawesi to catch trepang.[30] Others were less fortunate and were enslaved by pirates to collect bird's nests, wax, trepan, and pearls in the Sulu archipelago and its dependencies.[31]

That extensive slave raiding and trafficking had serious demographic repercussions will be discussed in more detail in the next chapter.[32] Here, it suffices to point out that slavery strengthened some polities while weakening others. Sulu and Aceh saw their exports grow and increased their working populations by raiding or buying slaves. Sulu controlled a population of about four hundred thousand people in its densely populated archipelago and through its sizeable Bornean dependencies; it therefore constituted a major power in the region.[33] Almost equal in population was Aceh, which emerged as the world's most important pepper producer in the course of the eighteenth century.[34] Like Sulu, this sultanate was a major importer of slaves, who were employed in all sections of society and, similar to Sulu, were easily integrated: many Acehnese of lower rank were descendants of slaves.[35] The major rice-producing principalities in the Indonesian archipelago, such as Bali, Lombok, and the Bone kingdom, with its fertile central plains and dependencies sprawling over southeast Sulawesi,[36] were prolific importers and exporters of slaves and probably experienced stagnant population numbers. The same stagnation marked the extensive territories of the northern Moluccan sultanates of Tidore and Ternate, which suffered from piracy, revolts against their rulers, and internal strife.[37]

While slavery was the most important form of labor migration in these still autonomous sultanates and other principalities of Southeast Asia, in Borneo and the Malay Peninsula, Chinese *kongsis* (self-organized groups of immigrant laborers) were the dominant immigrant category. In the eighteenth century, West Kalimantan (Kalimantan is the name for Indonesian Borneo) was swarmed by Chinese gold miners, who had come at the invitation of the local rulers.[38] In Montrado and Mandor, located at Kalimantan's most western tip, Chinese gold and diamond diggers arrived from the 1780s onward and rapidly grew into a population of over forty thousand.[39] In addition to the Chinese, Malay settlements dotted

TABLE 1.1

Chinese immigrant labor in mines and plantations in Indonesia and Malaysia, c. 1800

West Kalimantan	40,000–50,000	Southeast Kalimantan	5,000
Bangka	10,000–25,000	Pahang/Kelantan	10,000–20,000
Riau	10,000	Terengganu	10,000–12,000
Perak/Selangor	1,000	Java	30,000
Penang/Wellesley Bengkulu	10,000	Brunei	30,000
Total			156,000–193,000

Source: Bosma, "Methodological Paper," 9, table 1.5.1.

West Kalimantan, populated by Bugis, fugitives from Java, and pirates and their descendants.[40] Gold, diamonds, and forest products made the Chinese settlements of West Kalimantan partners for the emerging city of Singapore, a connection maintained by Chinese vessels.[41] Later on, large coconut plantations emerged, owned by Arab, Bugis, and Malay entrepreneurs, which were likewise connected to the global market by Chinese traders.

Gold and diamond miners also came to southeastern Kalimantan and went from Banjarmasin upriver in the Barito. Little is on record about the number of miners involved, but snippets of evidence suggest that five to ten thousand Chinese and Malay were sieving the diamonds from the sediment at the riverbeds and river shores.[42] Thousands of Chinese labor migrants delved for tin in Bangka or grew gambier in the gardens of Riau. The sultanates of Kelantan and Terengganu, located on the east coast of the Malay Peninsula, had become the residence of ten to twenty thousand Chinese miners and other Chinese immigrants, who were lured by the commerce and opportunities in these thriving centers for textile manufacturing, pepper, and gold production.[43] Thousands of Chinese operated the sugar mills along the north coast of Java and had settled as sugar planters in Kedah (on the west coast of the Malay Peninsula) and Penang. Thousands, again, had become pepper planters in Brunei. Indeed,

Chinese miners and planters had fanned out over the whole of Island Southeast Asia, with the exception of the Philippines, where Chinese immigrants had been massively expelled after having sided with the British occupiers in the early 1760s. Only a few dozen Chinese miners were allowed to stay.[44] All in all, the total number of Chinese labor immigrants in the mines and plantations of Island Southeast Asia must have ranged between 150,000 and 200,000 around 1800; particularly in Java, this was just a fraction of the entire ethnic Chinese population.[45] Over the course of the nineteenth century, their numbers in Island Southeast Asia steadfastly increased, along with the further growth of Chinese mining and plantation enterprises. In the Malay Peninsula in particular, a sizeable Chinese migrant population was already present before the arrival of Western private enterprise.

DEMOGRAPHIC DIVERGENCES IN THE NINETEENTH CENTURY

After three centuries of demographic stagnation and decline, population growth returned to Java and the northern Philippines. This occurred at a pace that approximated Great Britain's during the Industrial Revolution. In the Philippines, a natural growth rate of 1.5 to 1.8 percent per annum was recorded for most of the nineteenth century. Figures from the early years of that century already suggest rapid population growth, although this might simply represent better counting. Consistently high demographic growth was, however, reported after the mid–nineteenth century.[46] In Java, population growth climbed to an average 1.25 percent in the first half of the nineteenth century and subsequently to 1.6 percent.[47] The Straits Settlements experienced the same growth rates, thanks to massive immigration. This was unique for Asia, where even the remarkable doubling of China's population between 1750 and 1850 only required a modest average 0.7 percent growth per annum. In most of Southeast Asia, meanwhile, natural growth stayed well below even this figure for the entire nineteenth century.[48] The eastern part of the Indonesian archipelago in particular went through demographic stagnation or even outright decline, as this area was heavily affected by smallpox and piracy.[49] While at the turn of the twentieth century the average demographic growth of Indonesia's Outer Islands may have approximated to 0.8 percent, in the eastern sectors of the Indonesian archipelago it was still stagnating, if not declining.

Wherever the *pax imperialis* ruled in Island Southeast Asia, populations started to grow, and as a result, demographic centers of gravity shifted. While the population of Indonesia's Outer Islands still equaled that of Java in the early nineteenth century, a hundred years later the balance had shifted to thirty million for Java and eleven million for the Outer Islands. In the same century, the proportion of the Muslim population of Sulu and Mindanao within the population of the Philippine archipelago fell from 10 percent to 5 percent.[50] An even more pronounced shift took place in the Malay Peninsula, where the population of the Straits quintupled between 1830 and 1900, whereas elsewhere in the peninsula growth barely exceeded 0.2 per annum because of wars, piratical depredations, and smallpox.[51] The exception was the western coast of the Malay Peninsula, where plantations and tin mines were located.[52] The demographic balance would have shifted even more to the southwestern parts of the peninsula if the vaccination regime had not been so weak in the Straits Settlements, as I will argue.

Figure 1.1 shows clear upward demographic growth shifts for Java, the Philippines, and the Straits in the early nineteenth century. Indonesia's Outer Islands and the Malay States went through this transition much later. This divergence can be explained by strong natural demographic growth in the case of Java and the Philippines through smallpox vaccinations, as I will argue, and by immigration for the Straits. A secondary but far from negligible role in this divergence was played by slavery and slave raiding, which had rampaged up and down the coasts of the Philippines for centuries but began to move to the Indonesian archipelago by about 1780. I will return in the next chapter to the role of slavery in the demographic divergence in Island Southeast Asia.

WAS IT SMALLPOX VACCINATION?

There can be no doubt that the northern Philippines and Java experienced precocious demographic growth in the nineteenth century. For Java, Boomgaard has pointed to smallpox vaccination as a crucial factor in this. Smallpox was a major killer all over the world, and successful vaccination programs reduced mortality by up to a full 1 percent per

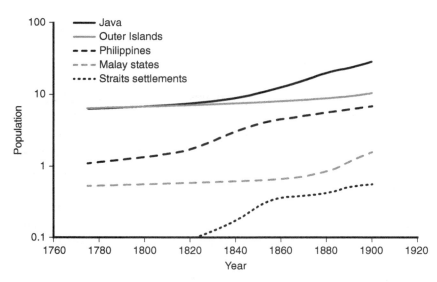

FIGURE 1.1 Population growth in Island Southeast Asia, 1760–1900. *Source*: Bosma, "Methodological Paper," 9, table 1.6. Population is based on log scale.

year—all other factors staying equal—and were hence a major factor in nineteenth-century demographic growth.[53] Improving food availability was a necessary additional step in preventing a fall into the Malthusian trap. That smallpox vaccination must have been behind the diverging demographic growth of Island Southeast Asia can also be deduced by a simple process of elimination. The region was under the same regime of natural and human-inflicted disasters, after all. Malaria was abundant, with the exception of higher altitudes. Cholera was a major killer that frequently visited almost every location in Southeast Asia. But as a cholera vaccine only became available after 1900, this disease played no role in the demographic divergences within Island Southeast Asia in the nineteenth century.[54]

Health conditions did not vary much across Island Southeast Asia; neither did exposure to calamities such as natural disasters or violence. Volcanic eruptions, earthquakes, tsunamis, cyclones, typhoons, and hurricanes occurred all over the region, and some of these resulted in scores of casualties. The eruption of the Tambora volcano on the island of Sumbawa in 1815, the largest volcanic eruption in modern history, alone caused the death of 120,000 people.[55] In general, these were local phenomena, however, and in that respect they were of less consequence than the epidemics that regularly scourged the entire region. Neither can the many colonial wars explain demographic divergences within Island Southeast Asia. The two major colonial wars in Sumatra, the Padri War and the Aceh War, probably had two to three hundred thousand victims, but the Java War was equally devastating.[56] Moreover, the Philippine Revolution and War of Independence around 1900 assumed apocalyptic dimensions, with hundreds of thousands of direct and indirect casualties.[57]

In sum, natural disasters and military conflicts do little to explain the sharp demographic divergences across regions in Island Southeast Asia. Improving living standards and availability of food are much more important, if only because bad nutritional conditions as a rule exacerbated susceptibility to disease and reduced marital fertility. There are strong indications of rising real wages in Java—as well as in the northern Philippines, for that matter—by the end of the eighteenth century because of the policies of economic encouragement.[58] Moreover, sweet potato (a Columbian crop) became popular in Java in the early nineteenth century, followed by cassava half a century later. Both crops were already quite common in Java before they spread across the Outer Islands. Thanks to an increase in the quantity and quality of food in Java, coupled with an improved infrastructure, this island became less famine prone over the course of the nineteenth century, despite its rapidly growing population.[59] In the Philippines, the increased safety of the western coasts enabled the emergence of rice frontiers in Antique (the western part of the island of Panay) and Pangasinan (Northern Luzon). For the Visayas, it has been suggested that the transition from millet to maize enabled crucial gains in the food situation.[60]

Not only were the improving nutritional levels a source of demographic growth, but they also explain the lasting success of smallpox vaccinations. There is worldwide evidence that under favorable economic conditions, vaccination (with bovine material) or variolation (with human material) had a strong positive effect on demographic growth. Variolation appears to have been a decisive factor in the rapid population growth in England at the eve of the Industrial Revolution, for example.[61] Jennerian vaccination played a pivotal role in the early-nineteenth-century demographic transition in Europe, in Costa Rica, and also a little later in Guangdong (Southeast China).[62] In the Madras and Bombay Presidencies, systematic smallpox vaccination, which started in the 1860s, contributed to substantial demographic growth as well, although this was partly undone by the El Niño–related famines of the late nineteenth century.[63]

In the northern Philippines and Java, smallpox vaccination took place under relatively favorable nutritional conditions, compared with most of the rest of Island Southeast Asia. This was also expressed in relatively high birth rates. Whereas in the Philippines and Java these moved up toward forty-five per thousand (and after 1830 in Java even between forty-eight and fifty-seven per thousand),[64] elsewhere in Island Southeast Asia the figure stayed in the low thirties. Few families could be found that had more than two or three children; women would consider more than that number impossible to rear and used a variety of means of birth control, ranging from late weaning to abortion and even infanticide.[65] For the island of Nias, for example, the harsh labor conditions for women have been cited as a cause of low birth rates.[66] This was also the case among the Dayaks of North Borneo, about whom the ethnographer Henry Ling Roth wrote that couples could only have a few children because of arduous female working conditions:

A Dyak woman generally spends the whole day in the field, and carries home every night a heavy load of vegetables and firewood, often for several miles, over tough and hilly paths, and not infrequently has to climb up a rocky mountain by ladders and over slippery stepping-stones, to an elevation of a thousand feet. Besides this, she has an hour's work every evening to pound the rice with a heavy wooden stamper, which violently strains every part of the body.[67]

In some islands, populations stayed below Malthusian boundaries, in others these might have been hit cyclically, but most islands in the Indonesian archipelago were not the resource-limited isolated biotopes that one would associate with Malthusian conditions.[68] Maize had been introduced by the Spaniards and Portuguese, and rice was a foodstuff that was generally traded all over the archipelago and thus available to whoever could afford it. These crops readily found their way to where they were in demand, and after 1860, telegraph connections facilitated speedy information about possible food shortages. All kinds of consumer items, from China bone to industrially manufactured utensils, found their way to every corner of Island Southeast Asia, from the hamlets at creeks deep inside Borneo to the Aru Islands near New Guinea, famous for their pearls and birds of paradise.[69] It is not unlikely that the reverberations of China's new economic dynamism and improved communications elevated birth rates, although this did not necessarily translate into demographic growth as long as the Outer Islands of Indonesia were still scourged by smallpox and pirates.

SMALLPOX VACCINATION IN AN ASIAN PERSPECTIVE

Shortly after 1800, the smallpox vaccine reached Southeast Asia from different directions. From the West it came from Bombay and Mauritius and from the East via Latin America. The rulers of Siam, Burma, and Vietnam invited European doctors to introduce this new preventive measure against the deadly disease.[70] The vaccine was distributed from Macao, Manila, and Batavia throughout the region and reached even to Japan, but during the first half of the nineteenth century, vaccination only made palpable progress in Java, the northern Philippines, and Guangdong. Although the courts of Siam, Vietnam, and Burma were in favor of the practice, and though missionaries regularly imported the vaccine, viable vaccination programs did not emerge for want of infrastructure and popular support. Variolation had sometimes become popular, which made it hard for authorities—including colonial civil servants—to convince people of the superiority of vaccination.[71] However, in most of Southeast Asia, variolation was not popular either. In Burma, vaccinations started in the 1880s, but only in 1909 were serious measures taken against the permanent influx of smallpox in Rangoon carried by immigrant workers from India. In Thailand, vaccination began in 1906 and became compulsory in 1914. In Tonkin, where smallpox was ubiquitous if not endemic, serious vaccination did not commence until the French had established their Institute Pasteur at Hanoi in 1924.[72]

Even where colonial rule was more than nominal, vaccination practices were often wanting, as was the case in the Straits Settlements, which initially struggled with low-quality inoculants from India.[73] Since the government had failed to quarantine sailors on board infected ships, the disease flared up time and again. This happened, for example, during the First Anglo-China War, or Opium War (from 1839 to 1842), when troop ships called at Singapore on their way from India to China.[74] Having learned their lesson, the Straits' authorities turned to Batavia for Java fresh vaccine, but as long as their efforts to contain the disease were neither systematic nor compulsory, smallpox would prevail among the native population of these colonial settlements. Europeans, meanwhile, obtained vaccinations from private practitioners, but quite often the vaccine was not available or of dubious quality. Such was the mortality in Singapore that it halted the growth of this booming city in the late 1840s despite the constant influx of immigrants.[75]

Things improved for the Malay and Chinese quarters of the Straits' harbor cities once the Straits Settlements became a crown colony in 1867, which invested the authorities of Singapore with wider administrative authority. Following similar legislation in metropolitan Britain, a quarantine ordinance was enacted in 1868. One year later, vaccination was declared compulsory, with the consent of the leaders of the city's Hindu, Muslim, and Chinese communities.[76] Despite these measures, smallpox was still occurring in the Straits by the late 1880s and proved hard to eradicate because of the open connections with the rest of Asia. Penang, for example, suffered repeatedly from epidemics caused by Indian immigrants transferred via Rangoon.[77] Meanwhile, British vaccination programs in the newly annexed Malay sultanates met with considerable resistance, and a comprehensive vaccination program only took root in the 1920s.[78]

Although smallpox vaccine arrived in various administrative centers throughout Southeast Asia in 1804 through 1806, only in Java, the northern Philippines, and Guangdong (China) did a reasonably effective smallpox vaccination program emerge at this early stage. While there is no single explanation for this, it is certain that the role of intermediary structures and agents such as ecclesiastical or other spiritual authorities was crucial; they were equally if not more vital than the state to the success of vaccination campaigns. This factor becomes even more marked when we note that the Catholic priests of the Philippines and the Muslim *penghulus* of Java not only performed religious but also administrative tasks. Local communities and local initiatives played a crucial role, as we know from variolation in late-eighteenth-century England, and they explain the success of vaccination in early-nineteenth-century Guangdong and its capital Guangzhou (Canton).[79] In the same vein, the histories of smallpox vaccination in Mexico, parts of the Philippines, and Java testify to the importance of collaboration between government and "civil society."[80]

Mexico and the Philippines were both included in a grand Spanish scheme to combat smallpox. The Spanish Empire was an early adopter of smallpox vaccination after King Carlos IV decided to dispatch a mission to bring the vaccine to all his subjects. The vaccine was preserved during the voyages over the oceans by using orphans as a chain of human vaccine carriers. It was Francisco Xavier Balmis, one of the three physicians sent out by the king, who defied the opposition of the viceroy of New Spain and brought the vaccine across the Pacific on a regular Manila-bound galleon, where the poor treatment of the boys almost ruined his mission.[81] Once the expedition had arrived in Manila, the vaccinators immediately treated thousands of children in this central port town. Intentionally or not, by doing so they created a firewall against incoming germs.

After Balmis's team had traveled across the Philippines, Governor-General Rafael Aguilar established and personally chaired a Bureau of Vaccination (*Junta Central de la Vacuna*) in line with the example of Spanish America and issued regulations for public vaccinations as well as ordering the establishment of regional branches of this junta.[82] He was ardently supported by the Philippine archbishop Zuliabar, who circulated a letter to all his priests impressing on them the need to advance this cause wherever they could. Church attendants were summoned to cooperate with the vaccination campaign, and it has been reported that force was applied, if necessary, to bring reluctant Filipinos to the vaccinator.[83] According to a nineteenth-century public health officer of the Philippines, his administration in Manila was better capable of preserving the vaccine and implementing a vaccination program than many of the higher-developed European countries. On paper, it looked impressive enough, with a Central Junta, general vaccinators at the provincial levels, and one or two paid assistant-vaccinators in every village. Yet even a defender of the system such as J. P. Bantug mentions that outbreaks of smallpox still occurred.[84]

No doubt, this Spanish vaccination regime was incomplete. Even Emilio Aguinaldo, the scion of a rich Cavite family and first president of the Philippines, caught the disease as a toddler.[85] However, while De Bevoise claims that this Philippine regime compared badly to that of Java, his estimate of the annual percentage of casualties for the entire Philippines of 0.1 to 0.2 percent by the 1870s and 1880s still points to a situation far better than that in the Outer Islands of the Netherlands Indies. Actually, there are many similarities with Java: the regime was relatively tight in the coastal cities and other more intensely colonized parts, whereas the peripheries saw hardly any vaccinators. Accordingly, smallpox vaccination in provinces with a strong Spanish colonial presence and relatively high levels of literacy, such as metropolitan Manila and Ilocos, might have been fairly effective.[86] Elsewhere, vaccination efforts easily dissipated because of underpayments to vaccinators and a lack of supervision by the civil service and medical doctors. Authorities both in the Philippines and the Netherlands Indies could hardly have been expected to oversee vaccinations on the myriad islands in their districts, where training of local vaccinators was just a matter of some basic instruction.[87] The poor quality of the vaccine and slow responses to outbreaks of smallpox—because the vaccine was only stored in the colonial capitals Batavia and Manila—were not helpful either.[88]

Java is generally considered a success story with regard to smallpox vaccination. It began in 1804 in the midst of the Napoleonic wars, after a ship had carried nine Javanese and six slave children to Ile de France (Mauritius) to bring the vaccine back to Batavia.[89] Vaccination efforts were intensified by Governor-General Thomas Stamford Raffles (1811–1815), who placed them on a solid footing in Java, particularly in the port cities of Surabaya, Semarang, and Batavia.[90] His work was carried on by his successor, Godert van der Capellen (1816–1826), who successfully mobilized the *penghulus* (village priests or experts in Islamic law) and other village notables regarding vaccination in most of Java.[91] The number of vaccinated might well have reached one million in the early 1820s and after the disruptive Java War (1825–1830) gradually rose to almost half of the population by the 1860s. In this decade, Java suffered the last serious outbreak of smallpox, probably because migrations brought into contact with the outside world relatively isolated districts that hitherto had been neglected by vaccinators. The disease would disappear entirely in the 1930s.[92]

The vaccination efforts in Java were strikingly well conceived from an epidemiological point of view. First, as Boomgaard has observed, vaccination teams concentrated their efforts on children, being aware that most of the adults were immune after earlier epidemics. Second, as soon as cases of smallpox were discovered, teams were sent out to isolate the nidus of the disease by vaccinating the surrounding area.[93] Third, the fact that Europeans out of self-interest started to vaccinate Indonesians with whom they came in direct contact also played out in a fortunate way.[94] In the early nineteenth century, Java and the Philippines were relatively isolated from the outside world, particularly in comparison with the Straits. In the Philippines, only a few ports were visited by ships from abroad, Manila being the most important one in the early nineteenth century and the only one formally open to international shipping.

Meanwhile, vaccinations first took place where the European populations were concentrated, namely in the larger port cities, which were coincidentally also the locations where the virus went ashore. In the Netherlands Indies, this not only pertained to the key port cities of Java but also of Sumatra, namely Padang, Bengkulu, and Palembang, where vaccination discipline had been maintained since the early nineteenth century and may have prevented the disease from spreading into the hinterland. Since most of the long-distance travel went via these cities, the number of casualties from smallpox in this part of the archipelago must have been low.[95] With increasing maritime commerce, quarantine became pivotal to compensate for lacunae in vaccination regimes. The Philippines wisely introduced these measures in the same year, 1855, in which they opened up new harbors for international shipping. This made them the first in Island Southeast Asia.[96] The Straits followed in 1869, constructing huge quarantine camps at its ports and not allowing migrant workers into the cities.[97] The Netherlands Indies enacted quarantine measures in 1871, requiring all ships with epidemic diseases on board to raise a yellow flag upon their arrival in Dutch waters.[98]

While quarantine enhanced the effects of a still far from perfect vaccination regime, it did not keep abreast with expanding commercial contacts and increasing mobility. Java experienced an outbreak of the already mentioned smallpox epidemic in the late 1860s, at the time of the rapid expansion of plantation agriculture and concomitant intensifying migration. For the same reason, quite a few provinces of the Philippines suffered from smallpox epidemics in the 1870s and 1880s. The revolution and war of the 1890s, in which American soldiers transferred new variants of the smallpox germ, raised the mortality from smallpox to eighteenth-century levels.[99]

Most severely affected by increased commerce were the health conditions in the Outer Islands of the Netherlands Indies. In the nineteenth century, an increasing number of ships reached the South Moluccan islands, New Guinea, and Central Sulawesi. Islands south of the coast of New Guinea, for example, were annually visited by Chinese vessels or brigs sailing via Makassar to buy the harvest of sea cucumbers (trepang), pearls, and other items available in the eastern part of the Indonesian archipelago.[100] Similar to what would happen later on with the influenza epidemic of 1918–1919, steam liners and railways spread diseases rapidly. Since the KPM (Royal Packet Navigation Company) maintained regular connections between over two hundred ports of the archipelago at the turn of the twentieth century, the spread of diseases to the most remote corners was just a matter of days.[101] Where medical care was practically absent, people were left to their own devices and often reacted by abandoning the sick and fleeing into the forests, where their chances of survival were slim.[102]

The relative absence of medical care was compounded by religious and cultural norms that stood in the way of vaccination campaigns in more peripheral parts of the Netherlands Indies and the Philippines, which, again, was very different from the situation in Java or the Northern Ilocos, for example.[103] Local notions of medicine throughout the Philippines led to frequent dodging of vaccination.[104] Likewise, one can draw up a long list of cases of resistance in the Outer Islands. Bali ranked as the most notorious: on this Hindu island, smallpox was seen as a gift from the gods, and serious vaccination only began during the First World War. Incidentally, most—if not all—resistance in the Outer Islands occurred in non-Muslim areas.[105] Although the expansion of direct rule over the Netherlands Indies was often accompanied by vaccination programs, many blank spots remained, where smallpox was still endemic in the early twentieth century.[106] In fact, Sarawak, Brunei, the Sulu Islands, and parts of the Malay Peninsula were no better.[107]

To conclude, the authorities of the northern Philippines and Java were the first in Asia to preserve the vaccine in their colonial capitals and systematically combat smallpox with compulsory vaccination, and while far from perfect, it was a precocious approach, even measured by European standards.[108] Not coincidentally, the most thoroughly colonized and densely populated parts of Island Southeast Asia became the earliest adopters of vaccination, giving them a demographic lead in Island Southeast Asia. Economic incentives also definitely played their role in the high demographic growth in Java, Luzon, and the Visayas, but jumping from the 0.2 percent population growth common in Asia to 1.5 to 1.8 percent required a unique combination of increased living standards, improved health conditions, and—particularly important in the case of the Philippines—a decline of the number of piratical depredations. Slave raiding would shift toward the Outer Islands of Indonesia, as we will see in the next chapter.

CHAPTER TWO

The External Arena

Local Slavery and International Trade

Across the globe, the ban on the slave trade that was initiated by the British parliament in 1807 was undermined by a growing demand for slave labor for commodity production. The example of the extensive palm-oil plantations in northern Nigeria is well recorded, where hundreds of thousands of slaves were put to work as late as the turn of the twentieth century.[1] The cultivators of spices in Zanzibar and pearl diving in the Gulf were also well-known slave-labor-driven industries.[2] Similar to Africa, in Island Southeast Asia the involvement of slaves in production for the market would only increase after the prohibition of the slave trade gained global traction. In the still independent sultanates of Sulu and Aceh—as well as the principalities of Bone, Bali, and Lombok—slave-based production received a boost from a growing overseas demand for rice and sea and forest products. The result of growing economic opportunities through expanding global markets exerted a strong demand for slave labor, as Warren and Mann have pointed out for maritime Asia.[3] Further, the extensive slave raiding in Laos by the rulers of Siam in the early nineteenth century served the purpose of capturing slaves to collect forest products for the Chinese market.[4] These scholars' perspective sharply diverges, actually, from the older historiography, which influenced Reid's *Southeast Asia in the Age of Commerce* and attributes the upsurge of piracy to declining indigenous maritime commerce caused by European colonialism.[5]

A proliferation of firearms and opium, as well as the liquor trade, which reached even the remotest corners of Island Southeast Asia, augmented existing practices of abductions into a full-blown slave trade. Arms were traded freely from Singapore until the Dutch convinced the British in 1863 that a ban of this traffic was imperative to combat piracy successfully.[6] The combination of increased trade in commodities, luxuries, and arms encouraged the widespread practice of coastal populations and nonmonotheistic populations in the hinterland to engage in interisland raiding.[7] Pirates, meanwhile, were not deterred by the fact that their victims were also Muslims and indiscriminately pillaged villages and captured ships. At best, they released Islamic priests and had some respect for hajis.[8] Although piracy was the most visible link between global markets and local production in Island Southeast Asia, debt slavery was no less intertwined with the increasing commodification of this part of the world. While Muslim or Christian polities as a rule did not enslave coreligionists, let alone members of their own societies, debt pawnship was allowed in most Malay societies, and once trapped in this condition, permanent and hereditary slavery was almost unavoidable. Moreover, thousands were enslaved by organized gambling sessions specifically designed to lure men into debt in order to enslave them.

In their struggle to suppress the enslavement of people, colonial powers were restrained by their tenuous hold on their territories. In the early nineteenth century, even the protection of the colonial core areas such as Java, the Straits, and the northern Philippines was an almost impossible mission. However, once these territories were relatively safe and yielded sufficient revenue, the battle against slave raiding and trading could be gradually expanded, culminating in the violent subjugation of the last bases of these activities at the turn of the twentieth century. The undoing of the independence of the restive sultanates and kingdoms of Island Southeast Asia also spelled the end of systems of commodity production for the global market—and for China in particular—that were not peripheral, not subservient to the industrial core, but still located in what Wallerstein has termed the external arena. The nineteenth-century history shows that Island Southeast Asia became engaged with distant markets via a plurality of trajectories. Some societies saw lucrative opportunities to produce for the market, whereas others were forced by colonial powers to do so.[9] While for enslaved or enserfed individuals it did not make much of a difference, the distinction is a crucial one in terms of the transfer of wealth to the world's core countries. This is, after all, what peripheralization is about.

THE SHIFT IN AND SURGE OF PIRACY IN THE NINETEENTH CENTURY

The epicenter of piracy that for centuries had scourged the coasts of the Philippines was the town of Jolo, located in the Sulu archipelago northeast of Borneo. The Sulu sultanate was located precisely at the crossroads of the trade between the eastern part of the Indonesian archipelago and southeastern China. It acted as a transit for slaves and goods and as a producer of commodities that were in growing demand in China by the late eighteenth century.[10] Slaves were employed to collect wax, turtle shells, bird's nests, and pearls, in return for which the Tausug traders of the Sulu archipelago obtained items for China.[11] They were also put on the land to grow food for their new masters.[12] Last but not least, enslaved men had to replace the growing numbers of casualties among these pirates, inflicted by European navy ships. Many sailors on the pirate ships were former captives, turning these crews into multiethnic communities with a provenance from all over Southeast Asia.[13] Piracy had risen to overwhelming proportions, according to contemporary sources. The most feared pirates were the ten thousand to 15,000 so-called Iranun, who were the clients of the Sulu sultanate. Another roughly nine thousand pirates had their bases at the eastern shores of Sumatra and the western coast of Kalimantan under the protection of the sultans of the Malay Peninsula. Thousands of local pirates also terrorized Moluccan waters. All in all, the total number of pirates might have ranged from twenty thousand to 25,000, enough to man between seven hundred and eight hundred vessels.[14]

Shortly after 1780, the Iranun shifted some of their raiding from the Philippines to the Indonesian archipelago.[15] They took advantage of the fourth Anglo-Dutch War (1780–1784), which dealt a serious blow to the maritime power of the VOC. This created a power vacuum that lured pirate fleets into the Straits of Malacca, further down the east coast of Sumatra, and into the eastern part of the Indonesian archipelago.

They were also driven in that direction once the Philippines began to repulse piratical depredations and even go on the offensive. During the reign of Governor-General José Basco y Vargas (1778–1787) coastal defenses were beefed up, most notably by the construction of a string of small fortifications throughout the archipelago. A few years later, Governor-General Rafael Aguilar (1793–1806) upgraded the naval forces to go after the pirates.[16] In 1818, the Spanish squadrons inflicted heavy damage to the fleets of these pirates, and six years later, it destroyed some pirate bases in the Sulu Sea.[17]

While moving further south in the Indonesian archipelago, the Iranun found junior partners in the pirates of Riau and West Kalimantan and in the Tobelorese (Alfurs from Halmahera) in the Moluccan waters. Meanwhile, practically all the coasts of Borneo became their safe havens. At Tempasuk, on the north coast of this island where once the Chinese had mined gold, the Iranun built a formidable base, from where they staged their operations into the Straits of Malacca toward Bangka and even as far as to the coasts of Java.[18] Taking advantage of the weakening Dutch maritime power, they obtained footholds in the western part of the Indonesian archipelago as well as along the west coast of the Malay Peninsula, on the opposite shores of Sumatra, and along the west coast of Kalimantan.[19]

In Moluccan waters, the upsurge of piracy coincided with the British intrusion into this part of the archipelago, which thwarted attempts by the VOC to suppress piracy and slave raiding in the area and to establish control over East Ceram, a center of slave trafficking as well as a smuggling center eroding their spice monopoly. British-Dutch competition in the Moluccas between the 1770s and 1815 marked forty years of political turmoil, in which the area twice changed hands between these two countries. Some strategically located islands in the north Moluccan Sea as well as East Ceram—located close to New Guinea—became refuges for sailors, exiles from the courts of the sultans of Tidore and Ternate, rebels from the failed large-scale Moluccan insurrection of Pattimura in 1817, and released or escaped slaves. All had flocked together to engage in piratical pursuits. Their fleets caused havoc in the densely populated islands and busy sea lanes of South Sulawesi, depopulating smaller islands and sometimes, when they joined forces, large ones as well.[20]

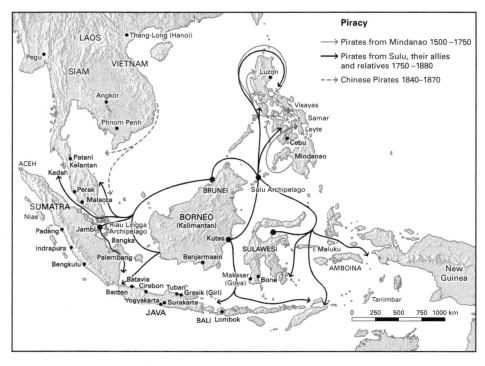

MAP 2.1 Slave-raiding routes, 1750–1880.

The Iranun and their local allies barely left any coast of the Indonesian archipelago—or the Malay Peninsula, for that matter—in peace.[21] From the 1780s, the annual pirate visits along the coast of Java assumed dimensions unthinkable in the days when the VOC was still the uncontested regional power.[22] In the early nineteenth century, pirates captured European schooners and brigs along the coast of Java, sometimes in sight of a main harbor town such as Surabaya. They even sacked post houses.[23] The Iranun also operated in sight of Singapore, apparently not bothered by the fact that the merchants of this city maintained warm relations with their patron, the Sulu sultanate. Vessels coming from Siam as well as from the Indonesian archipelago loaded with sandalwood, coffee, and spices avoided Singapore, knowing they could be attacked even within sight of the harbor.[24] In the early nineteenth century, the patrols of the cumbrous European rigged navy ships waged an uphill battle against these fast and easily maneuverable vessels, which evaded their patrols and found shelter in the countless creeks in the archipelago. Venting his frustration, Resident John Crawfurd of Singapore wrote in a local newspaper:

> A Glance at the Map of the Indian Islands will convince us that this region of the Globe must from its natural configuration and locality be peculiarly liable to become the seat of Piracy. These Islands form an immense cluster, lying as if it were in the highroad which connects the commercial nations of Europe and Asia with each other, and affords thus a hundred fastnesses from which to waylay the traveller.[25]

Crawfurd had set his hopes on the naval steamships, but even after their deployment in the 1830s, the task of suppressing piracy remained immense.[26] Meanwhile, collaboration between the Dutch and the British to combat piracy, to which they had agreed by treaty and for which they held regular consultations, including at the highest level between Calcutta and Batavia, was far from smooth.[27] Commercial rivalry between the British and Dutch and the fact that both still had local allies involved in slave raiding only compounded this struggle. The Dutch were intent on rolling back the considerable economic British presence in the Netherlands Indies by imposing discriminatory tariffs and restrictions on British shipping and by acting against the local partners of British interlopers in Indonesian waters. Since the late eighteenth century, British country traders had imported large quantities of opium and alcohol to Sukudana, Montrado, and Pontianak (all located on the west coast of Kalimantan) for the Chinese gold miners and also for further retail in Makassar and Bali, from where it was smuggled into Java.[28] To quell these smuggling lines, the Dutch landed three consecutive military expeditions on Bali in the late 1840s to force the rulers of this island into compliance and stop the slave and opium trade and their involvement in piracy. That the British extended their sphere of influence further to North Borneo—a pursuit that was greatly advanced when James Brooke assumed the position of raja of Sarawak in 1841—was not particularly conducive to good relations with the Dutch, either.

By the mid–nineteenth century, the Dutch and British had overcome their imperial jealousies, however, and intensified their collaboration. The

Spanish, on the other hand, were much more reluctant to work with the British and Dutch naval forces. Direct communication lines between the navy commanders of the fleets of the Netherlands and the Philippines were nonexistent: any exchange of information went via The Hague and Madrid. This allowed the Iranun to shift their operations and recover from the assaults by the Spanish navy.[29] Even after the Spanish raided the Iranun bases at the Balangingi Islands, followed by the Sulu capital Jolo in 1859, the sultanate was far from defeated, and its Iranun clients were still capable of capturing hundreds or perhaps even more than a thousand people per year.[30] Iranun actions in the waters of the Indonesian archipelago actually surged in the early 1860s, and an Iranun fleet was spotted by the Dutch colonial navy as late as 1869.

The Tausug of Sulu and their Iranun clients were able to resist the Spanish onslaught thanks to the sultanate's links with Chinese and Singapore commercial circles. This motley crowd of traders from different European countries supplied them with the necessary weapons.[31] To cut these links, the Spanish imposed a naval blockade around Jolo in 1871, and when they had to lift the blockade under British and German pressure in 1876, they only did this to take the even more drastic step of occupying Jolo in the same year with seven thousand soldiers. Yet even after this near mortal blow, the Tausug were still able to employ enslaved people from all over Island Southeast Asia to collect forest and sea products in and around northeastern Borneo.[32] Neither the British and Dutch naval patrols in this area nor the fact that the British had gained a foothold on the northeastern tip of Borneo (called Sabah) had much effect in this regard.[33] This "twilight zone" was only cleared in 1906, when oil production started at the Dutch island of Tarakan, just offshore. In Brunei too, it was only after the drill hit the immensely rich oil layers of this sultanate in 1929 that slavery disappeared, almost thirty years after it had become a British protectorate.[34]

ENSLAVING INDONESIANS: THE NUMBERS

Although pirate raids and kidnappings may have abated from the 1850s onward, the kidnapping of seven hundred people in one stroke was reported in 1855, and as late as 1862, Dutch newspapers in the Netherlands Indies reported about 428 people having been captured by pirates and 616 liberated by Dutch and British naval forces in Indonesian waters. We can be reasonably sure that not all the raids and kidnappings reached the newspaper columns.[35] The coasts of the eastern Indonesian archipelago continued to be hit by piratical raids long after British and Dutch navy ships had become more and more successful in the western part of the Indonesian archipelago. While Sarawak, Riau, Western Kalimantan, and Bangka became increasingly less hospitable for pirates from the 1840s, the dry and poor eastern sector of the Indonesian archipelago emerged as the central theater of slave raiding by various marauding groups, first of all because the Spanish had pushed the Iranun toward this area, where the latter had aligned themselves with the Tobelorese from Halmahera.[36] Pirates were also based south of Sulawesi and around the Savu Sea on the coasts of Flores and Sumbawa.[37] Capturing slaves was also an accepted practice among local rulers. The sultan of Tidore, the overlord of Papua New Guinea, sent regular expeditions to these coasts to conduct slave raids, and before the 1870s the Dutch colonial authorities were incapable of forcing the sultan to stop these practices.[38]

If this was not already bad enough, terrestrial raiding appeared to be near inextinguishable, and it lingered on until the early years of the twentieth century, fueled by the import of firearms into the islands in the Eastern Moluccas and Nusa Tenggara as well as to the interiors of Borneo, Sumatra, and Sulawesi.[39] In the eastern Moluccas, slave trafficking from New Guinea proved to be resilient even after the sultanates of Ternate and Tidore had given in to Dutch pressure to quit human trafficking in 1879.[40] Neither did intensified naval patrols quell slave transports between Sulawesi and Kalimantan, nor between Sumba and Bali and the east coast of Lombok. In fact, as late as 1888 the rulers of Lombok vehemently objected to Batavia's announcement that its navy would inspect the ports of this island for slave trading.[41] Extensive trade of debt slaves was going on between Sulawesi and western Borneo, conducted by Bugis traders who supplied the emerging coconut plantations with labor. Four ships equipped by ethnic Arabian merchants of Pontianak were spotted taking on board slaves in Sulawesi in 1870. A legal prosecution of this trafficking was aborted because of the prospect of serious unrest among the local elites of this city.[42] A vigorous demand was noted as late as the 1890s for East Kalimantan, where the dangerous jobs of rattan and bird's nests gathering were carried out by slaves, whose ranks needed permanent replenishing given the high mortality rates.[43] Because trafficking shifted to smaller vessels that could more easily escape the gaze of the tightening navy patrols, it lingered on until the early years of the twentieth century.[44]

Any assessment of the number of people captured and traded, as well as the number of the collateral casualties in the Indonesian waters, is surrounded by uncertainties, but this should not deter us from distilling estimates from observations made by contemporary sources as well as from the figures reconstructed by Warren. By the mid–nineteenth century, when piracy was already past its peak, the actual number of maritime kidnappings in Island Southeast Asia still must have ranged from six thousand to eight thousand annually, half of which I would argue took place in Indonesian waters.[45] To this figure of three to four thousand, we need to add the victims of the slave trade. Contemporary sources suggest that this may have involved some four to five thousand enslaved annually. For Nias, the number might have been 1,500 before the attempts by the Dutch to suppress enslaving practices by brute force in 1863. Many of these slaves ended up in Aceh, through Acehnese traders who were based in the island of Nias and who bought the slaves from warring heads who had kidnapped them.[46] From various ports of Sulawesi, hundreds of slaves were carried to the resource-rich environments of East and West Kalimantan.[47] Estimates of the number of slaves sold from Bali in the early nineteenth century range from five hundred to 1,200 annually, despite efforts by British and Dutch naval expeditions to stop this trafficking.[48] In the Savu Sea area—dominated by the islands of Sumba, Timor, and Flores—the trade involved five hundred to a thousand slaves annually for each of the major islands (and this is probably in addition to the slave raids).[49] To these figures we still have to add the slaves carried away from New Guinea, the Batak lands and Lampung in Sumatra, and the Riau Archipelago. The maritime slave trade was so widespread that in all likelihood it surpassed the kidnappings in numbers. By the mid–nineteenth century, seven thousand to nine thousand enslaved people each year might have been transported either on ships of pirates or traders over the waters of the Indonesian archipelago.

This dismal story is still not complete, however, because there is abundant evidence of the high number of killings during the raids, starvation on board the pirate ships, and casualties as the consequence of unsuccessful attempts to escape. Quite often, crews of vessels under attack from pirates fought back with all their means, knowing what their fate would be.[50] There are chilling witness accounts of mistreatment, malnourishment, and severe dehydration. For want of anything else, the captives drank seawater on the pirate vessels.[51] The conditions on the Iranun ships were harrowing, but those on board the ordinary slave traders were only marginally better, as is shown by a description of a transport of slaves from Nias:

> The circumstances that attend this traffic are no less revolting to humanity, than those which marked it on the coast of Africa. The unhappy victims, torn by violence from their friends and country, and delivered, pinioned hand and foot, to the dealers in human flesh, are kept bound during the whole course of the voyage . . . on a moderate calculation it may be estimated, that, of the total number purchased, one fourth never reach their destination, but fall victims to the various circumstances above mentioned.[52]

The available evidence suggests that for every two captives who arrived at a slave market, a third might have died during the violent raids or during transport.

The raids also caused death through the destruction of sources of livelihood. Fields of crops were destroyed, and the tiny fishing boats that were easy booty for the pirates were sunk or left drifting. In the longer term, the impoverishment and loss of nutritional variety as a result of declining fisheries impinged badly on the general health of communities.[53] Unavoidably, coastal villages were abandoned all over Island Southeast Asia, or people regrouped in larger settlements of 1,500 inhabitants or more, as often happened in the Philippines. Alternatively, people moved far into the hinterland, as was the case in Sumatra.[54] In the southeastern corner of Sulawesi and the islands off its shore, inhabitants responded by fleeing into the interior of the island or by building their villages on cliffs and surrounding them by palisades.[55]

The demographic consequences on the communities affected by raids were substantial but difficult to quantify, and they are therefore not included in table 2.1. It should be noted that the demographic consequences of slavery were geographically concentrated because most of

TABLE 2.1

Conjectural demographic consequences of slave trading and raiding in the Indonesian archipelago, 1820–1850 (annual average)

Activity	(1) Number deported	(2) Casualties during raids (50%)	(3) Casualties during transport (25%)	(4) Sold outside the archipelago	(5) Total demographic loss, columns 2, 3, and 4
Slave trade	4,000–5,000	—	1,000–1,250	1,000	2,000–2,250
Slave raids	3,000–4,000	1,500–2,000	750–1,000	1,000	3,250–4,000
Total	7,000–9,000	1,500–2,000	1,750–2,250	2,000	5,250–6,250

the raids occurred on nonmonotheistic islands or mountainous interiors, which apart from Nias were largely concentrated in the eastern part of the Indonesian archipelago, such as the Savu islands, New Guinea, Central Sulawesi (Toraja), and Bali. So many people were abducted from the eastern part of the Indonesian archipelago that societies must have been destroyed "beyond repair," as Van Welie observed.[56] As a consequence, in the eastern part of the Indonesian archipelago, where smallpox and slavery still abounded, demographic growth must have been close to zero, if not negative, and it certainly never exceeded 0.5 percent.[57] Slavery played a tangible role in the demographic divergence of nineteenth-century Island Southeast Asia, with the demographic positives for the Philippines and Java counterbalanced by the negatives for eastern Indonesia.

This story of enslavement was part of the wider history of slavery in the southern islands of the Philippines, British Malaya, and Indonesia's Outer Islands. It also pertains to the fact that enslavement was essential to maintain slave populations.[58] Unless settled family-wise on the land, slave populations declined precipitously, and therefore slave markets thrived and slave raids perpetual.[59] Yet we know little about how these slave voyages were related to slavery as an indigenous institution, on the one hand, and to maritime commerce, on the other. In the next few pages,

I will present some tentative figures about the proportion of captive slaves within the total slave population in Island Southeast Asia, which has always been assumed to be predominantly debt slavery. I will also submit that the lines between debt and captive slavery and between customary and commodified slavery were much more blurred than colonial civil servants—followed by scholarly literature—have suggested. The institution of slavery was both reshaped and strengthened through the incorporation of the region into the global economy.

SLAVERY IN ISLAND SOUTHEAST ASIA: THE NUMBERS

Slavery as an indigenous institution was a phenomenon conspicuously absent from colonial statistics for most of the nineteenth century. The total slave population in Island Southeast Asia and its economic importance have been grossly underestimated in colonial reporting. The official figures for the number of registered slaves in the Netherlands Indies, for example, only concerned those of owners who were due to pay taxes on their property and lived in a territory under direct Dutch rule, and they indicate a decline from twenty to ten thousand between 1820 and 1841.[60] This figure represents just the tip of the iceberg. Thanks to government records, reports about slave registrations, accounts of civil servants, travelogues, and sometimes detailed enumerations drafted by explorers, we can gain an impression of the numbers involved in nineteenth-century slavery in Island Southeast Asia. Although we cannot reconstruct the numbers as meticulously as has been done with regard to Atlantic slavery, the available material still allows us to produce a reasonable estimate.

In terms of absolute figures, the percentages indicated in map 2.2 would amount to 567,000 to 806,000 slaves in the Indonesian archipelago. To complete the picture for the whole of Island Southeast Asia, we could add the following conjectures: between thirty and sixty thousand slaves for the Malay Peninsula, another 67,000 for Sulu and its dependencies (which until the 1830s included not only North Borneo but also Brunei and Sarawak), and lastly 37,500 for Mindanao. All in all, the total number of slaves within Island Southeast Asia may well have ranged from 701,500 to 970,500 in the early nineteenth century.[61] Sulu, Aceh, Banda, the Moluccas, and Lombok were the most important importers of slaves,

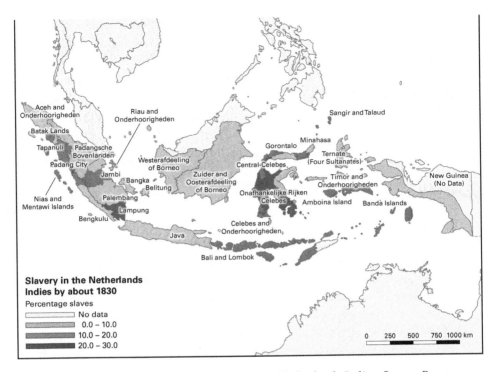

MAP 2.2 Slavery in early-nineteenth-century Netherlands Indies. *Source*: Bosma, "Methodological Paper," 34–37.

whereas Bali, Lombok, and the Bugis principalities were both importers and exporters. A second group of islands or regions with extensive slave-holding consisted of Sulawesi, Sangir and Talaud, Tapanuli, Minangka-bau, Bali, and Lombok, as well as Mindanao.

This total estimate allows us to gauge the importance of maritime raiding or trafficking in maintaining the institution of slavery in Island Southeast Asia. Table 2.2 presents a conjecture of the total number of people annually kidnapped or traded within the region. An important assumption made here is that even though slaves were captured in the Christian Philippine Islands and Malaya Peninsula, these territories did not commercially export slaves. Moreover, and as mentioned before, the annual maritime abductions for the whole of Island Southeast Asia might have ranged from six thousand to eight thousand, which again is a conservative estimate made for the mid–nineteenth century. Not all those

TABLE 2.2

Conjectural numbers for slave trading and raiding for Island Southeast Asia, 1820–1850 (annual average)

Activity	(1) number deported	(2) Casualties during transport (25%)	(3) Slave supplies (1 – 2)
Slave trade	4,000–5,000	1,000–1,250	3,000–3,750
Slave raids	6,000–8,000	1,500–2,000	4,500–6,000
Total	10,000–13,000	2,500–3,250	7,500–9,750

enslaved stayed within the region, of course, but this category constituted only a tiny minority.

Assuming that each person lived for another fifteen years after enslavement, the total population of the first generation enslaved would have ranged from 112,500 to 146,250, or about 15 to 18 percent of all the slaves in Island Southeast Asia. This is a conservative estimate and does not take into account the victims of terrestrial raiding who stayed on their islands. Nor does it include the children and grandchildren of these enslaved people. Little is known about the birthrates among enslaved populations or about the level of integration of their offspring into slave-holding societies. At any rate, the gender ratio of the captives was male biased, and the birthrate among the slave population was low. However, if we assume that the second- and third-generation offspring of these maritime captives numbered just forty or fifty thousand, it would still bring the total to about 20 to 25 percent of all slaves in Island Southeast Asia. This still might be a substantial underestimate because it does not include captives of local conflicts who were not shipped away. With regard to the Toraja in Central Sulawesi, for example, early-twentieth-century ethnographers concluded that the majority of the slaves were descendants of captives.[62] In fact, there are more indications that captives and their descendants might have made up a far larger segment of the total slave population in Southeast Asia. For Siam, Bowie has shown that over two-thirds of the slave population were captives or their descendants and only a quarter debt slaves and their offspring.[63]

It is safe to conclude that captive and commercially traded slaves made up a large minority of the total slave population in Island Southeast Asia. Slaves in Southeast Asia were property, traded and abused, and widely employed to produce for markets.[64] Slavery and enslavement were institutions regulated by Islamic judicial practices that also prescribed how debtors could become slaves and through that, commercial objects.[65] This has important ramifications regarding how we perceive the institution of slavery in this part of the world. Colonial administrators tended to underplay the institutional and commercial aspects of slavery in Southeast Asia and contrasted it with Atlantic colonial chattel slavery as being more benign to play down the urgency of abolition in this part of the world.[66] Even though the majority of the slaves in Island South Asia stayed within their own communities, and though most of them were debt slaves or had been slaves for many generations, enslavement was never an act of mercy. Many debt slaves were victims of usury, social oppression, or gambling.[67] British colonial civil servants in the Malay Peninsula reported instances of the gruesome treatment of debt slaves: the killing of runaways and the wide abuse of female debt slaves as prostitutes.[68]

Meanwhile, the role of debt slavery as a survival strategy, as a means to escape starvation, was relatively limited in this part of the world. Famines did occur in Island Southeast Asia, and these could also drive families to sell their children, usually their daughters.[69] People also sometimes sold themselves into slavery as a survival mechanism, but this mostly concerned survivors of disasters such as the eruption of the Tambora volcano in 1815, which produced a diaspora of people who arrived, starving, on the shores of other islands.[70] As a rule, however, families and clans were under social pressure to take over the debts of their individual members—and in some societies, they were even obligated to do so—to avoid enslavement of their kin.[71]

Debt slavery, I would argue, did go along with social stratification and commodification. In the least stratified itinerant societies, such as hunting or gathering communities, slavery was actually nonexistent, for the obvious reason that slaves were of no practical use and only meant additional mouths to feed. It was instead the rice-cultivating societies, or more generally the societies that usually produced agricultural surpluses, whose members ran the risk of being enslaved or sold as slaves.[72] In these societies, providing credit was a way for its richer and more powerful members to obtain labor, which was usually more valuable than the belongings of the debtor.[73] In smaller communities, mechanisms of credit and debt usually stayed within the bounds of a patron-client relationship, but when the debtor-creditor relationship became less personal and societies more market oriented, the frequency of labor bondage and enslavement increased. In addition to rice-exporting regions, sea- and forest-producing areas were typical sites where traders used the instrument of debt to obtain labor, which was the most valuable commodity in these societies. There are many examples of their practices. In the Aru Islands, famous for their trepang (sea cucumber), pearls, and birds of paradise, the local population was kept indebted by traders through the lavish distribution of Dutch gin.[74] Much of this was based on the custom that debts gave the creditor the right to someone's labor, a mechanism that still exists among rattan collectors in southern Sumatra today, for example.[75] The Dayaks of Borneo lived in permanent danger of becoming ensnared in peonage by Malay or Chinese traders or by Chinese mining *kongsis*.[76] Dayak women, and also children, were always in jeopardy of being sold to Chinese or Malay bachelors in order to settle debts.[77]

Meanwhile, the ruling elites abused their powers to inflict heavy punishments on commoners for petty crimes, as was, for example, recorded by a Dutch civil servant in Southeast Kalimantan, where many hands were needed for the gathering and transport of forest produce. Elsewhere, the number of convictions went up at the time that the annual arrival of the slave-trading *prahus* were expected.[78] Fines were reportedly still an important means of making debt slaves for local rulers by the end of the nineteenth century, for example in West Kalimantan and northern Sulawesi.[79] Customary law was on the side of the creditors, as outstanding debts were usually doubled every year, making slavery almost inescapable. Family members could also be drawn into slavery, either because the accumulated debts easily exceeded the price of a single slave or simply as an arbitrary act of power.[80] As a result, debt slavery often spread like an inkblot to children and other kin of the enslaved debtors.[81] Debt bondage was occasioned by deep social inequalities and wanting capital markets, with interest rates ranging from 30 to 100 percent per year. The absence of an independent judiciary left ample room for usury and extortion; indeed, debts were frequently conjured up.[82]

All these debt traps, and the fluid and changing character of slavery itself, signaled a progressive commodification of the economy. The combination of a craving for money at the expense of freedom and the demand for cheap labor resulted in widespread slavery, observed the governor of southwestern Sulawesi in 1861.[83] Many people became indebted as a result of deliberate acts to enslave them. Traders in Bali or Bugis traders at Toraja markets in Sulawesi organized gambling sessions and betting on cock fighting, providing loans to those who accumulated gambling debts in order to draft them into slavery.[84] The victims were put on the same ships as the captives of raiders in the interior of Sulawesi, sailing to sites of commodity production in Kalimantan.[85] Not only were slaves highly valued for their labor power; they were also bartered for precious items, such as Indian cloth, China bone, and European firearms. This slaves-for-arms trade would continue well into the nineteenth century and could include children, mostly orphans. In Timor, children were reportedly sold for elephant's teeth or cattle; from New Guinea, they were bartered for cloth and ironware.[86]

ENSLAVEMENT AS A TRANSIENT PHASE

Literature concerning slavery in Island Southeast Asia is replete with references to firearms, gambling, and luxury items involved in the slave trade. It underwrites the violent and commercial character of slavery in this part of the world. Thousands of slaves were employed in the production of spices in the Banda islands in the Moluccas before and under colonial rule. Slaves tended the pepper groves in Sumatra (Lampung, Palembang, Jambi, Aceh, and Padang) and in southeastern Kalimantan.[87] Slaves and bonded laborers were also, for example, employed for the production of cloth at Selayar, an island south of the coast of Sulawesi that was widely known for its cotton production.[88] Slaves were imported for rice production by the kingdoms of Lombok, Bone, and Bali; in the sultanate of Aceh and by the chieftains of Mindanao, slaves were even imported from India to cultivate rice.[89] Slaves could be encountered on fishing boats off the coasts of Banten, Aceh, and Malacca and around

Ambon.[90] Slaves from Siak were put to work on the tobacco, coconut, and nutmeg plantations of the sultan of Deli.[91] Toraja slaves gathered rattan and dammar gum with their masters.[92] Balinese slaves dug tin in the sultanate of Pahang on the Malay Peninsula. Pearl divers and textile workers were slaves of local rulers of Sulu, Mindanao, and in earlier times also in Manila and Cebu. Slaves in East Kalimantan gathered forest products and bird's nests, dived for pearls, or fished for trepang. Slaves were employed by the Igorot of the northern Philippines in their gold mines.[93] Slaves, to conclude a still far from exhaustive list, were the consorts in the maritime pursuits of the Bugis, Acehnese, and Tausug, who might entrust them with commercial responsibilities.

Still, one may wonder why in the age of imperialism (1870–1914) slavery in Island Southeast Asia was not as widespread as it was in West Africa, where slave-based copra and groundnut cultivation in particular catered to the margarine industry in industrial countries. In the Sokoto Caliphate or in Kano (present-day Nigeria), between 25 and 50 percent of the population lived in slavery at the turn of the twentieth century, which in absolute figures meant millions of people.[94] Although Island Southeast Asia was no less responsive than West Africa to the demand of overseas markets for commodities, the number of slaves involved was modest in comparison and probably smaller than that of the Chinese workers gathered in the *kongsis* at the commodity frontiers of the region at the time. A plausible explanation for this is that over the course of the nineteenth century, colonial navy vessels seriously degraded the supply lines of slaves toward the sites of commodity production. Extensive naval patrolling far from eliminated slavery, but it did prevent the slave-based economies of Sulu, Aceh, and Bone from taking full advantage of the commodity boom in the decades preceding the First World War.

The other explanation is that enslavement was usually a transient phase. The underlying logic is that since slavery required supervision, it was far more costly as a productive system than, for example, settling enslaved people as sharecroppers. In addition, because of the required supervision, keeping thousands of people as slaves might even have been impossible.[95] Most importantly, however, rulers of territories did not need to own people to extract labor from them. Siamese and Burmese kings and the sultans of Aceh, Mataram, and Banten did enslave and abduct populations during conquests, and while some were sold to private individuals, the majority were resettled in these rulers' heartlands. Likewise, in Timor, South Sulawesi, and Gorontalo—as well as among certain Dayak populations—slaves were quite often put to work on the fields to take care of their own living.[96] Alternatively, part of the slave population, usually those newly captured, were kept in households, whereas their offspring might be settled on a plot of land as sharecroppers. In Bali, for example, a distinction was made between slaves who were purchased or raided from other islands and indigenous slaves, who were kept in bondage for rice production and whose conditions were similar to those of serfs.[97] In precolonial Philippines, a sliding scale existed between the more recently enslaved, who were part of the household, and others who were allowed some private life as sharecroppers with their own house on a plot of land.[98]

While usufruct of the land and the possession of a house set serfs or *colonati* apart from slaves in Roman law,[99] such a legal distinction did not amount to much in Southeast Asia. There was certainly some legal basis for European administrators to contrast debt bondsmen or serfs, who had to perform certain tasks, to slaves purchased on the market or simply raided and who were quite usually of a distinct ethnic or religious background.[100] However, many slaves who were put on the land did not become serfs but remained personal property and a tradable commodity. In Sumba, for example, they might have had their own house and family yet still be traded like cattle; their value was literally equated to that of a horse. They would be sold as soon as their owners felt that their slave population had produced sufficient offspring.[101] That the rice-exporting polities in South Sulawesi, Bali, Lombok, and Nias were also slave exporters again underscores the commercial character of slavery: slave and rice exports substituted for each other. Market conditions determined whether slaves were treated as chattels or put on their own fields: strong demand for slaves drove up prices, making it potentially more lucrative to sell them than to put them on the land. Conversely, rising rice prices encouraged owners to put their slaves to work on the land rather than to sell them off. This is what the rajas of Lombok did when their rice exports became increasingly profitable over the course of the nineteenth century.[102]

At any rate, in strong polities throughout Southeast Asia, transformations from slavery into serfdom were irreversible, as Reid has pointed out.[103] In fact, the sliding scale from slavery to servitude is not exclusive to Island Southeast Asia but also occurred, for example, in medieval Europe.[104] It is, rather, the dichotomy between slave and citizen and the very notion of citizen itself that is exceptional, as it is more or less confined to European antiquity, the plantation societies of the New World, and, last but not least, the VOC port cities. Similar to Caribbean societies, manumitted slaves in these Asian cities did not become serfs but "free burghers," with the right to wear shoes and to serve in public functions and the duty to serve in the civil militia. In the Asian countryside, the situation was different. Here, the only available status apart from slavery was that of a commoner, who was subjected to corvée, which—as was the case in Central Java, for example—could entail the obligation to hand over more than half of the harvest to the court and to perform military service.

As long as legal citizenship did not exist and personal freedom was not adequately protected, any declaration by colonial administrations that the ownership of human beings was illegal remained a dead letter. For many of the enslaved, their formal emancipation changed little to nothing, as their bonded condition had escaped official gaze. Embedded in client-patron relationships, these conditions survived far into the twentieth century and still define hierarchies in the social and political domain today.[105] Slavery, peonage, corvée, and tributary labor represented different ways and sometimes subsequent stages in which the labor power of enslaved people was put to use. It was not the economic role of slavery that was different from the Atlantic world and the colonial enclaves in Asia but its pliability and the way it lingered on in servitude and patron-client relationships. This very malleability allowed for labor to be incorporated in colonial commodity production all over Island Southeast Asia.

THE SLOW DEATH OF SLAVERY
IN THE ERA OF IMPERIALISM

Servile relationships enabled colonial authorities to put rural populations to work for their cause. Initially this included slavery, which still existed in the rice fields of Pampanga as a mode of production in the seventeenth century and for a century longer in the cane fields of Batavia. However, both Spanish and Dutch colonial administrations began to develop other methods of labor control, partly in response to the fact that they were aware of slavery as a potential source of upheaval. Moreover, wherever labor was bonded to local aristocrats, the colonial state had no direct access to it.[106] Hence, both in Java and in the northern Philippines, the governments were intent on replacing personal bondage by tying people to their village or district in order to create a sedentary peasantry that would be chargeable with taxes and corvée. Both the VOC and the Spanish government endeavored to reduce debt bondage, which was a source of social unrest, particularly in the Philippines. In their struggle against peonage, the Spanish administrators set a maximum figure for loans that landholding elites could provide to tenants.[107]

By the early nineteenth century, most of the slaves held by Europeans were kept for domestic purposes, with the notable exception of the Banda islands, where they were employed in the nutmeg groves. In the Malay Peninsula, the British had control of Penang and introduced the institution of plantation slavery by bringing slaves from Africa. They were soon joined by convict laborers from India. Together with free Chinese immigrants, these slaves and coerced workers grew cloves, pepper, and sugar and worked at construction sites until slavery was formally abolished in the Straits Settlements in 1833.[108] In the Netherlands Indies, the abolition of slavery progressed more slowly. Although the purchase of newly enslaved people belonged to the past after the British had banned the maritime slave trade during their interregnum, further measures against slavery and peonage were confined to registration in 1822, and then only in the territories under direct rule.[109]

In Island Southeast Asia, comprehensive abolition would only occur when the Dutch, British, and Americans consolidated their hold on their internationally recognized colonial conquests. In the 1870s, the British extended their rule over the entire Malay Peninsula, the Spanish blockaded the Sulu archipelago, the French colonized Cochin China and Hanoi, while the Dutch ignited three decades of war against the Aceh sultanate. Colonial expansionism found its obvious legitimation in the eradication of piracy and the widespread existence of slavery. The Dutch and British consolidation of their rule over the Netherlands Indies and British Malaya was formalized by agreements with local rulers that included clauses about the gradual abolition of slavery. Usually, the first step in such a trajectory was registration. This was followed by transferring all registered slaves to the status of peons under the obligation to work for their master for another five years or so, a measure that had some resemblance to the intermediate status of apprentice that had preceded abolition in the British West Indies. Alternatively, the colonial government made funds available to compensate slaveholders for the immediate manumission of their slaves. Such an action was usually crowned by a festive emancipation day, in which the colonial officials summoned all the local grandees and praised them in public for accepting the enlightened principles of colonial rule. In general, however, European colonizers were wary of enforcing compliance because of the costs involved. Territorial expansion was financed on a shoestring, after all. Above all, colonial authorities were anxious to avoid the social upheaval or even outright rebellion of the elites that enforced abolition might trigger.

Concerns about social stability also explain the resistance of the American administration and the colonial government in the Philippines against the pressure of the U.S. Congress to root out slavery in this newly acquired colonial dominion. At that time in the southern Muslim territories, the proportion of the population that was enslaved might have amounted to 25 percent.[110] Under these circumstances, the American authorities were content with the liberation of the Christian slaves in Sulu and Mindanao.[111] Yet even this heedful course could not avoid a rebellion in Mindanao and Sulu. It was the beginning of ten years of dirty colonial war, ending with the massacre of the last remnants of the Moro's armed resistance against the American occupation at Jolo Island in 1913.[112] This was not the only story about slavery in the Philippines. Just after 1900, Americans discovered enslaved children serving in Christian households and observed widespread hereditary servitude in Christian Luzon. Objections by the Filipino members of the Philippine Assembly that these children were part of the family rather than slaves did not at all appeal to the American authorities. The Moro Province Anti-Slavery Law of 1903 was extended to the entire Philippines, symbolically in the same year that Jolo was reduced to rubble by the U.S. army.[113]

After the British had left the Netherlands Indies, the question of the abolition of slavery remained on the back burner until the late 1840s, when abolitionism began to resonate in Dutch politics. Eventually, the emancipation of the slaves and the prohibition of peonage or debt bondage were effectuated on December 31, 1859, but only for territories under direct Dutch rule, and even within these limits, it was not complete. In the decades to follow, the government continued its policy of achieving the subjugation of formally autonomous rulers. This began brutally with an expedition to Nias in 1863 to suppress slave trading, which killed seven hundred people,[114] and it ended brutally with the collapse of the principality of Bali in a blaze of fire and blood in 1908.

As a rule, however, Batavia avoided military action. Local rulers were pressed into signing a treaty with Batavia, in which enslaving people and slave trading were outlawed, and the registration of slaves was put in place to make sure that no new slaves would be made.[115] However, even this strategy often met with considerable resistance, and the colonial government in Batavia did not hesitate to put emancipation on hold if it anticipated a rebellion.[116] In West Kalimantan, brought under direct rule in 1855, registration of slaves was discontinued after it had incited serious discontent among the local elites.[117] Serious opposition was feared in southwestern Sulawesi (the Residency of "Sulawesi and Onderhoorigheden") that had been brought under direct Dutch rule as early as 1825, and registration started in 1863 with an apprenticeship of five years at most. By the mid-1870s, there were still over ten thousand registered slaves and many others who had not been registered. Plans were discussed to move abolition forward, but nothing happened, and Batavia decided eventually that rather than provoking a revolt it was better to wait for another twenty or thirty years to allow slavery to peter out in southwestern Sulawesi.[118]

The Residents of Timor and West Kalimantan received strict orders from Batavia in 1878 not to enforce abolitionist measures, as these were deemed both unfeasible to implement and politically dangerous.[119] The Dutch colonial government was anxious to avoid another military conflict at a time when the colonial army had suffered huge losses in the Aceh War (1873–1903).[120] Ironically, despite that the long colonial war against Aceh had started in a bid to end its piracy and slave trading, it did much to delay the abolition of slavery elsewhere in the Netherlands Indies. By the 1890s, in some districts or even residencies registration had not yet started. In the case of Aceh, the import of enslaved people was still going on at that time.[121] The colonial government expected that it would slowly disappear with the expansion of territories under direct colonial rule. These indeed began to function as safe havens for slaves fleeing areas still under the jurisdiction of local rulers who had not yet abolished slavery. In 1889 alone, 109 fugitive slaves in East Kalimantan reached such enclaves under direct Dutch rule.[122] Only after the Dutch had proclaimed their victory in Aceh were they prepared to move ahead with abolition throughout the Indonesian archipelago. Yet the formal abolition of slavery in Nias still had to wait until 1914, whereas in many other places in the Outer Islands it lingered on under the guise of patron-client relationships.[123]

The abolition of slavery that followed the extension of the Pax Britannica in British Malaya has much in common with the Dutch struggles with this issue. Beyond the Straits Settlements, feudal service and slavery coexisted, and both categories of labor could be put to work alongside each other, for example in commercial rice production in Muda, the irrigated rice belt along the coast of Kedah, where there were large appanage lands that could cover up to three hundred hectares.[124] By annexing the hitherto independent sultanates of Perak and Selangor as well as the ethnically Minangkabau polity of Negeri Sembilan in 1873, the British had assumed the task of eliminating these complexes of bonded labor.[125] Rulers considered slaves as key assets and were prepared to defend the institution even if it required the murder of a British civil servant. Resident J. W. W. Birch of Perak, who facilitated the escape of some of the sultan's harem slaves, paid for this act with his life in 1875.[126] The road to abolition in Pahang was surrounded by even more vicissitudes; years of resistance against abolition eventually culminated in open revolt in 1891.[127] Slavery in the Malay Peninsula lingered on the longest in the northeastern sultanate of Terengganu, where the existence of debt slavery was still seen in 1917.[128] For most of Sarawak and North Borneo, formal abolition had to wait until 1928. At that time, formal slavery in Brunei came to an end as well, as a concomitant of the development of the oil industry and rubber plantations.[129]

THE LEGACIES OF SLAVERY

Slavery, debt bondage, and peonage were fluid categories, and their malleability attests to the dynamics of an ongoing commodification of the economy of Island Southeast Asia. Local administrators were keenly aware of this, as is apparent from their reporting to Batavia, but it was far from exceptional that they were ordered not to intervene. The fact that Batavia often did not want to be confronted with too many inconvenient truths partly explains why the economic importance of slavery in the Outer Islands of Indonesia might have been downplayed. At any rate, the upsurge of slave raiding in the late eighteenth and early nineteenth centuries and the extensive slave trade toward the resource-rich environments of Borneo, which continued up until the very end of the nineteenth century, attest to the fact that the spread of international market relations imbued the entire institution of slavery.

In tandem with the spread of capitalism, enslavement through violent abduction and debt traps proliferated. This history of slavery in Island Southeast Asia and its connection to the global market has been obliterated from the narrative of the colonial winners. However, it is concrete proof that the engagement with the global market was marked by a diversity of trajectories, in which slavery, Chinese *kongsis*, and smallholders coexisted and competed with European hegemonic aspirations. Both the upsurge of slavery and the massive expansion of smallholder rubber and copra cultivation in Island Southeast Asia demonstrate the role of local initiative in the engagement of this part of the world with the global economy. These initiatives strengthened resistance against subservient incorporation and thus against peripheralization. The colonial subjugation of the slave-based economies in Island Southeast Asia was lengthy and often brutal: think, for example, of the violent Nias expedition, the Aceh War, and the expeditions against South Sulawesi and Bali.

In economic terms, slavery was not totally incommensurable with nineteenth-century plantation systems, as both the low-technology plantations in Nigeria and the high-technology sugar estates in Cuba in their own way exemplify. However, global capitalism not only engendered enslavement in Island Southeast Asia; it also solidified patron-client relationships, first, because the vertical or hierarchical solidarity ingrained in these relationships at least offered some protection during times of precarity and in societies where an independent judiciary did not exist, and second, because slave labor was expensive compared with the increasing supplies of servile labor in the colonial heartlands of the Philippines and the Netherlands Indies. When the global trade in bulk commodities reached serious dimensions, competitive prices were set by the global markets, and labor costs began to matter a lot more than earlier, when luxuries still dominated. These factors reinforced sharecropping as the most cost-effective way of producing agricultural export crops in bulk. It became the backbone of the rapidly growing commodity exports of the northern Philippines and Java, as will be discussed in the next chapter.

The end of slavery coincided with the most jingoistic phase of imperialism. The European press, both metropolitan and colonial, warmly supported imperial expansion and the violent subjugation of the slaveholding polities in particular. Newspapers exposed the outrageous character of slavery and the way in which the term "pawnship" was used to disguise its existence. Early in 1890, Dutch newspapers in Java reported that a six-year-old child had been given by its parents to an Arabian businessman to settle a debt of sixty-eight guilders; this episode came to the public eye after it was discovered that the poor girl had almost been starved to death.[130] Another newspaper article that appeared around the same time detailed the cruel treatment of slaves by an Arabian merchant in Ampenan (Lombok). This raised concerns in Batavia over the outrage such a story might create in the international press, which would taint the reputation of Dutch colonial rule.[131]

It was not just concern, of course, because exposing the cruelty of Hadramauti enslavers also served the colonials' self-image of being enlightened liberal Christians. The colonial press firmly upheld the ideas of European superiority and of free markets and enterprise and deemed coerced labor to be inferior to free labor. Yet the same colonial press was part of a colonial economy shaped by plantation capitalism, with its own modes of coercion to deal with labor scarcity. At that time, forced and bonded labor was also ubiquitous in Java and began to emerge rapidly in the notorious plantation belt of East Sumatra. In fact, coerced labor did not fade out in a linear fashion: it is a constantly resurfacing phenomenon that has moved on the rhythms of expanding capitalism, and it still exists to this very day. Some of the paths of the slave raiders in the

Indonesian waters are still the routes followed by contemporary human traffickers. Today, from the once slave-exporting island of Nias and of Nusa Tenggara, thousands of migrant workers are still smuggled into the plantation belts of Sumatra and Sabah to work under a regime of debt bondage.[132]

CHAPTER THREE

Saved from Smallpox but Starving in the Sugar Cane Fields

Java and the Northwestern Philippines

When the abolition of slavery brought Asia into the fold as an alternative supplier of indigo, coffee, and sugar for European markets, the plantation, in the format in which it had matured in the Caribbean, was still the business model of the day. Embedding it in Asian rural life was a process of trial and error with many failures and few successes. Imperial archives contain numerous reports of collapsed schemes for plantations all over the colonized territories of Asia—and Africa, for that matter. Indonesia's sparsely populated Outer Islands and the southern Philippines were entirely unfit for labor-intensive cultivation. In the Malay Peninsula, meanwhile, British attempts to encourage European planters to develop plantations came to little for most of the nineteenth century. Chinese entrepreneurs were more successful, thanks to their connections back home in China, from where they recruited their labor.[1] But even in densely populated Java and the Philippines, the colonial administrations struggled to develop plantation economies. As long as there was still enough land available, there was no cheap labor to be had for colonial cash-crop production. However, by the mid–nineteenth century the children saved by smallpox vaccination had grown up and began to flock toward the commodity frontiers in East and West Java, Luzon, and the Visayas. In the postslavery world, Java and the Philippines emerged as the second- and fourth-largest cane-sugar exporters in the early twentieth century, respectively, a development that was entwined with the darker story of the "reversal of fortune." The story of how Java and parts of the northern Philippines became plantation peripheries is the subject of this chapter.

By the late eighteenth century, economic prospects had improved for Luzon, the Visayas and Java. After almost a century of stagnation or even decline, Java experienced economic growth, and large swaths of land were cleared, particularly in Central Java, where growing rice for export and tobacco for local consumption mushroomed.[2] Coerced coffee production filled the coffers of the VOC, and Chinese millers made Java a sugar exporter of some consequence. By the late eighteenth century, Java had become the mainstay of the VOC, which obtained coffee, timber, rice, sugar, cotton yarn, and some indigo from this island. To pay for these commodities and other services, rapidly increasing quantities of copper money were shipped to the island. A similar budding dynamism marked the Philippines. The resurgence of this colony was orchestrated by the powerful governor-general José Basco y Vargas (1778–1787), who was convinced that the battle against piracy had to be stepped up, which urgently required an expansion of government revenue. As his most far-reaching measure, he introduced a tobacco monopoly in 1782, an institution that had already been in place in Cuba since 1717. Within a few years of its introduction in the Philippines, it was extended over most of Luzon.[3] The church admonished its flock to comply, and the elites were lured into collaboration with lucrative administrative positions to oversee the monopoly system. By the end of the eighteenth century, tobacco, betel nut, and wine monopolies—as well as tribute—accounted for more than 60 percent of the Philippine government's revenue.[4] As an important side effect, the tobacco monopoly encouraged the monetization of the economy, since the consumers were obliged to pay for their daily tobacco needs with coins.[5] The Philippines also saw the introduction of cotton production and the emergence of a textile sector, which was soon burgeoning in Ilocos (Luzon) and Iloilo (on the island of Panay in the Visayas) to serve markets in China.[6] In 1789, the harbor of Manila was opened up to foreign vessels, including American ships from Salem (Massachusetts), a town prominent in the Southeast Asian trade. Much of the Manila exports in these years were either indigo or sugar.[7]

FROM TRIBUTARY LABOR TO THE CULTIVATION SYSTEM, 1830–1870

Once the VOC had secured its sovereignty over most of Java's northern coast and its western regions, it started to develop the island as its economic mainstay. It began to order local rulers to deliver timber, although some room for negotiations about the price remained.[8] It introduced the coffee tree in 1707 and initially paid cultivators relatively well for their beans in order to encourage the dissemination of this crop. The authorities in Batavia backtracked on their generosity, however, when the results widely exceeded their expectations, and they came to realize that this rash monetization of the economy would create an ideal hunting ground for Chinese moneylenders. With their economic power accumulated as tax farmers for the sultan of Mataram, they were suspected of being capable of wresting the cultivation from the VOC's control.[9] Batavia decided to turn coffee growing into forced cultivation in return for minimal financial compensation for labor and land. It shored up its monopoly by pushing out smallholder coffee and barring Chinese traders from West Java.[10]

The expansion of forced cultivation and increasing reliance on tax revenue, still collected by the Chinese tax farmers, went along with measures by the colonial government to curb swidden agriculture and to recast a rural society dominated by personal bonds between peasants and local lords into a territorially anchored peasantry. Freedom of movement was curtailed within the territory under VOC jurisdiction, to prevent peasants from moving to new land elsewhere, a risk that was particularly high in the case of swidden cultivators. Accordingly, a person was only able to travel from one department Regency to another with government permission.[11] In the Priangan, where the measure was adopted first, its objective was to facilitate the conscription of the local population into forced coffee cultivation. Shortly after Java had been returned to the Dutch by the British, who had ruled the island from 1811 to 1816, the colonial government followed up on previous restrictive measures with a system of permits (*passenstelsel*) to ensure that landholders performed their conscript services and paid their land rent. The Javanese were not allowed to travel beyond their own Regency without permission from their village head and from the office of the assistant Resident, the highest Dutch official of each Regency. Anyone caught without a pass could expect a beating with a rattan or to be put to work on public construction sites.[12]

While the colonial authorities restricted the movement of the peasantry to widen the government's tax base and shore up systems of labor conscription, it was also keen to encourage a "free wage" labor market, so in 1819 it prescribed individual labor contracting and prohibited subcontracting via village heads. This liberal labor legislation suited the growing contingent of wage laborers in Java, a development strongly encouraged by the VOC in the late eighteenth century and attended by the distribution of large amounts of copper coins. The maritime sector, shipbuilding, the construction of fortifications, sugar plantations, dockworkers, riverine transport, and the colonial army together required a labor force of about 150,000 men by 1800.[13] Almost 15 percent of all men without their own farm performed wage labor, many in the form of labor gangs under *mandurs* (foremen), a clear sign of an emerging labor market.[14]

It was a labor market within bounds, however, incapable of meeting the objective of restoring Java's profitability as a colony. Fruitless attempts were made to accelerate the pace of rural capitalism and proletarianization. Inspired by the example set by Thomas Munro in the Presidency of Madras, Governor-General Thomas Stamford Raffles (1811–1816) had taken the bold step of taxing individual landholding peasants. This fixed land rent was based on the value of land and not on its actual yields, the rationale for which was that it left a larger share of the harvest to capable rather than to sloppy cultivators.[15] Ideally, this taxation system would have furthered individual landholding and the marketability of land. Raffles expected that richer farmers would buy out the smaller ones, who might then turn to plantations for work. In West Java, he had already handed out large tracts of land to his own entourage, who had, however, a hard time attracting labor. The British merchant houses in Batavia that had imported steam-driven cane crushers to their estates saw them rusting as the workers stayed away from the cane fields.[16]

The land rent did not create the large class of proletarians that Raffles had envisioned. In this cash-strapped economy, Javanese and Chinese moneylenders stepped in to provide advances on the crops in return for substantial interest rates.[17] These moneylenders did not disown their debtors, because ethnic Chinese were not entitled to own land, and Javanese lenders kept indebted peasants as sharecroppers rather than appropriating their plots. As long as labor was more valuable than land, the introduction of the land rent ushered in immiserization rather than proletarianization. While property relations were a serious impediment to the liberal idea of land rent as a way to enhance agricultural productivity, the idea was also technically unfeasible. The land rent could not be exacted from individual cultivators as long as the colonial government had no staff to conduct proper land registration, let alone cadastral surveys. Raffles resorted to entrusting the village heads with the responsibility for collecting the land rent, a measure that would undo much of the basic idea of taxes paid on an individual basis and on the value of land.[18]

In 1829, after twenty years of frustrating experiments with free labor and a land market to launch a plantation sector, Johannes van den Bosch, the most prominent advisor to the Dutch king on colonial matters, concluded that only by forcing the rural population to produce cash crops could the debt-making colony become profitable again. Under this so-called Cultivation System, work was imposed on about 35 to 40 percent of all households in Java in the 1840s, which amounted to over 60 percent of the rural households in the Residencies under its sway.[19] Peasants received a plant wage as compensation for the labor and land conscripted by the colonial civil service. From this compensation, they were supposed to pay their land rent. Javanese district officials belonged to the aristocracy, and village chiefs were assigned by the government in Batavia to implement the system, their initial resistance deflected by giving them a share in the profits of the Cultivation System. The conscripted peasantry, meanwhile, now had to work for the colonial government and still perform their customary service to the local nobility, who were unwilling relinquish their claims in this regard. With consorts of retainees often exceeding 250 people, the hereditary Javanese regional rulers (*bupati*)—who were formally integrated in a subordinate position in the colonial civil service—had considerable expenses and were not prepared to abandon their lifestyle and prerogatives. They did not need to, however, because their incorporation in the colonial bureaucracy had just shored up their position vis-à-vis the peasantry.

The role of the indigenous ruling class was eventually phased out from the Cultivation System, and the personal services the nobility could exact from the peasantry were curtailed. By contrast, village heads and village elites strengthened their positions as stakeholders in the cultivation of export crops by shifting the workload to their dependents, while keeping at least part of the compensation. They became interested in allowing newcomers a share in the communal *sawahs* (wet rice fields) in order to divide between as many people as possible the cultivation conscription and other assignments that came together with landowning. Usually, this concerned a relatively small plot, as these village societies were far from egalitarian.[20] They became dependents of wealthier farmers, who employed them as replacements to fulfill the obligations of the Cultivation System and perform tributary labor.[21] Despite the lack of egalitarian relations, as Boomgaard has observed, the fact that the Cultivation System put a premium on sharing wet rice *sawahs* initially enhanced food security for the rural population, and this in turn might have been a factor in rising natality.[22]

Patron-client relationships also facilitated the replacement of conscript labor by wage labor over the course of the Cultivation System. Village heads and other village elites became the suppliers of workers for the plantations that emerged from the 1850s onward, when the Cultivation System was being phased out. The role of labor intermediaries had previously been performed by village functionaries.[23] Likewise, the village elites ensured the sugar factories had access to land once the government no longer assigned plots of land to be planted with cane. The factories paid a handsome bonus for coercing impoverished peasants to lease out their share in the communal *sawah* landholdings. That this practice was outlawed by the colonial administration did not alter the facts on the ground.[24]

The growing army of wage laborers was recruited from marginal cultivators who could no longer subsist from their land, since by the mid–nineteenth century, Java's stunning population growth had ushered in land scarcity. Sugar factories and the surrounding villages attracted peasants who received a share in the *sawah* and in return performed their part in the cultivation conscription and other obligations.[25] By as early as the mid–nineteenth century, almost 56 percent of all agricultural workers who lived in the vicinity of a sugar factory were economically dependent on it for by-employment.[26] Precarious labor also found its way to sugar factories independently, as mid-nineteenth-century factory managers reported that they employed all kinds of people, including "vagabonds and itinerants." It is impossible to establish whether seasonal or permanent migration dominated, but there is ample evidence that the employers stabilized at least part of their workforce by providing housing and small gardens in the factory compounds. In the 1860s, such settlements housed between one thousand and two thousand people, and since there were about one hundred sugar factories in Java at that time, the total number involved would have ranged from one hundred to two hundred thousand people.[27]

It was not just demographic growth but also an array of other measures that smoothed the phasing out of conscript labor without jeopardizing the supply of cheap labor. This was accomplished by reducing the amount of statutory labor. The constitutional regulations of the colony (*Regeeringsreglement*) of 1854, which had announced the abolition of slavery, also contained a clause about the gradual abolition of pawnship and corvée labor, the so-called *pancen* or *heerendiensten*. Tributary service (for road construction or irrigation) was reduced from fifty-two to forty-two days per year in 1882, by converting part of the compulsory labor into a head tax. In 1914, all tributary labor for road construction and irrigation in Java—at that time still estimated at an annual three million working days—was converted into a head tax.[28]

The trend toward freeing up bonded labor for commodity production was general in Southeast Asia. The Siamese and Burmese governments, for example, eliminated servitude and corvée instead to impose land rent and head tax while they were on their way to become the world's most important rice exporters. Specific to the Netherlands Indies, however, was the fierce opposition to the government-imposed Cultivation System that was implanted in the patrimonial political economy of Java. The rhetoric of these opponents was one of creating the maximum space for private enterprise and of reducing the power of the colonial state, which at that time indubitably controlled much of economic life. Plantation owners and managers happily invoked a humanitarian agenda of liberating rural populations from depressing levels of forced labor imposed by the colonial government and the indigenous nobility. The famines in Java in the late 1840s gave them additional ammunition to condemn the

Cultivation System.[29] The liberal opposition raised the banner of "laissez faire" and accused Van den Bosch of having reversed, in their view, the healthy development toward rural capitalism.

However, the measures by liberal colonial statesmen to terminate labor conscription for government monopolies, and later on for infrastructural works, did little to establish a regime of free labor. The alleviation of the burdens imposed on rural society was, moreover, only temporary. The fact that less of the profits of the colonial economy ended up in the metropolitan exchequer contributed to improving living standards in rural Java, but only until the agricultural crisis of 1884. At that time, the downside of liberal colonial policies that had brought about a considerable net transfer of gains from the government to private planters became painfully clear. An increasingly wanting revenue base was heavily overstretched by the costly colonial war in Aceh. Meanwhile, the liberal assault on communal landholding to give room to a productive farmers' class was stalled by the village elites, who preferred to retain a growing population of marginal landowners and sharecroppers in subservience they could use to replace their own labor for corvée or to meet the requests of plantations for workers. The restoration of the 1819 regulation on individual labor contracting by the liberal colonial statesmen in the 1860s was just a paper tiger, since the village elites had in fact become traffickers in coolie labor for plantations.[30] The more Batavia dismantled the patrimonial structures after they had served their purpose of imposing the production of exports in Java's countryside, the more plantation estates and sugar factories dealt directly with the village elites, and, through that, the patron-client relationships within the villages were reinforced.

THE FRONTIERS OF THE EASTERN SALIENT AND THE PRIANGAN

The transformation from government-imposed commodity production embedded in the patrimonial state toward private estates was facilitated by patron-client relationships. Land scarcity was the second factor aiding the emerging plantation economies. Population pressures led to migration movements between the increasingly land-scarce Residencies of Central Java and new frontiers of commodity production located at

TABLE 3.1

Geographical division of Java's population, 1815–1930 (%)

Year	1815	1826	1845	1867	1930
West Java	24.0	22.0	26.2	25.0	27.3
Central Java	57.1	55.8	47.9	49.1	36.6
East Java	18.9	22.2	25.8	25.9	36.1

Source: For 1815, see Hugo, "Population Movements in Indonesia," 104. For 1826, see "Bevolking van Java en Madoera," 162–63. For 1845, see Bleeker, "Algemeene Staat der Inlandsche bevolking van Java," 204. For 1867, see Bleeker, "Nieuwe Bijdragen," 456. For 1930, see *Volkstelling 1930*, 8:60–70.

the extremes of the island (see table 3.1), a trend spurred by the Java War from 1825 to 1830. The proliferation of plantations in Central Java by the mid–nineteenth century halted this development, but it regained traction after newly constructed railroads connected these densely populated areas with the sugar, tobacco, and coffee frontiers of East Java.

After the 1830s, ever-increasing quantities of coffee, sugarcane, indigo, and other products of the Cultivation System had to be transported and at least partly processed before being shipped abroad. Java's wage economy rapidly expanded at factory compounds, in the transport sector, at warehouses, and in the ports. The measures described in the previous section to enhance the supplies of labor for the emerging plantation sector solved the problem of labor shortages that had crippled plantation estates in the early years of the nineteenth century. Available data for the 1860s suggests that in every single year, at least two hundred thousand Javanese moved to another district, many of them toward the sugar frontier in East Java, where labor shortages had emerged and wages were rising.[31] Meanwhile, the proportion of wage laborers among the gainfully employed men increased rapidly from almost zero under the Cultivation System to 6 percent in 1885.[32]

In other sectors of plantation production, the demand for labor also ushered in new migration flows. From the 1840s, the cultivation of tobacco and tea was given free for private enterprise, and a decade later the government allowed the rental of waste land—which it had declared state property—for plantation purposes. These decisions cleared the way for the first tobacco plantations in Rembang and Besuki and the tea estates in Priangan. The opportunities for private planters were hugely expanded by the introduction of the Agrarian Law of 1870, which facilitated the long-term leasing of large tracts of waste land by plantation enterprises. These areas were often more inhabited than "waste land" suggested; these lease holdings quite often enclosed existing villages. Such encroachments were only aggravated by the Land Reclamation Act of 1874, a measure by the colonial government to privilege sedentary agriculture and plantations over swidden agriculture. In practice, it just further reduced the availability of land for a growing sedentary peasantry. Enclosures exacerbated the already increasing land scarcity and drove Javanese landless peasants to nearby plantations for work or to migrate to the plantation belts in the Eastern Salient of the island and the Priangan.

In addition to mobility to nearby sugar factories and tobacco estates, longer-distance migrations extended to the large belts of cash-crop production, for example, tobacco in Jember (Besuki), coffee production on the slopes of the Tengger mountains in East Java, and last but not least the tea plantations of the mountainous Priangan in West Java. In the final three decades of the nineteenth century, over a million people (about 5 percent of the island's population) moved from one Residency to another in Java more or less permanently; the Residencies of Semarang, Banten, Yogyakarta, and Kedu each saw about one hundred thousand people leaving, and Madura even as many as three hundred thousand.[33] The majority of the migrants came from areas that suffered from population pressure, heavy tributary and corvée labor, poor soil, or combinations of these. The explanation for the push to migrate was not a shortage of arable land as such but low productivity per acre and a lack of opportunities for by-employment.[34] Since plantations were generally located in more fertile parts of Java and the sugar factories in irrigated fields, by-employment and high productivity per acre were usually linked. Cultural factors also played a role. The seafaring Madurese were accustomed to a roving maritime existence, whereas the Javanese were said to cherish the link to their village of origin, which limited their migration options.[35] Cultural dispositions can certainly not be ignored, but much of the migration toward the plantations was dominated by push and pull factors, as is apparent from the largest emigrant flows from Madura, Banten, and Yogyakarta.

The Madurese escaped from being packed together on a relatively barren island, which had soil unfit for plantation agriculture and only offered fisheries and saltpans for by-employment. For the maritime-oriented Madurese, it was easier to travel to East Java than across their own island, and the ties across the sea lane were strengthened by marriage bonds between the local rulers from Besuki and Madura.[36] From the late eighteenth century onward, they jointly encouraged the migration of Madurese to this part of Java to rehabilitate cultivated land that had fallen prey to the forests after decades of ravaging war. As early as the mid–nineteenth century, almost half of the ethnic Madurese population lived in East Java.[37]

Like Madura, large parts of Banten consist of nonfertile land, which is, moreover, not suitable for irrigation. It had been an emigration area for centuries, from where many left for Lampung (South Sumatra) to work in the pepper groves, either as seasonal laborers or as permanent migrants, or to escape more permanently from the oppression of the Bantenese rulers. This Residency had endured a chain of natural disasters by the late nineteenth century. First, 73 percent of all its buffaloes died from rinderpest in 1878, followed only a few years later by a severe cholera epidemic and in 1883 by the eruption of Krakatau, which took the lives of 22,000 Bantenese.[38]

The Madurese and Bantenese were joined by emigrants from Central Java, in particular, from the Principalities (Yogyakarta and Surakarta). In these semi-independent principalities, the descendants of the resettled captives of the Mataram empire suffered from heavy corvée and taxation. Together with rapid demographic growth, as well as adverse soil conditions in some parts of this area, the exploitation engendered famines, massive resistance, and extensive migration.[39] The small and densely populated Residency of Yogyakarta was particularly notorious for the exploitation of the peasantry by planters conniving with local rulers. There are manifold stories of peasants who gave up their land and houses once the burdens of compulsory labor became unbearable.[40]

Not all left their villages for good, however. Every year, trains carried hundreds of thousands of migrants who used this method of transport to stay in touch with the *desa* where they were born and raised. At sugar factories in East Java, daily wages were 5 to 10 cents higher than Java's average 20 to 25 cents, and in port cities, they could be as high as

80 cents or even an exceptional guilder per day.[41] The sugar-producing Residencies each attracted between sixty thousand and one hundred thousand immigrants, and Kediri saw an influx of over 140,000 immigrants in the final three decades of the nineteenth century. However, even before that, this Residency was one of the frontiers where peasants from Yogyakarta had found refuge. In some districts of Kediri where sugar production was rapidly expanding, the population tripled between 1845 and 1867.[42] The tea plantations of the Priangan topped the list of migration destinations and may have attracted as many as three hundred thousand migrants in the final decades of the nineteenth century.[43] While already impressive, these figures only represent migrations between residencies. Below the Residency level, mobility toward plantations was even more intense, as many Javanese sought by-employment at plantations and with wealthier farmers, preferably at some distance from their villages, because wage labor was seen as demeaning.[44]

Railways, meanwhile, allowed migrants to move over ever-larger distances. In the early twentieth century, Besuki had become the prime frontier Residency of East Java, where sugar and tobacco estates had spread from the north to the south over the preceding hundred years.

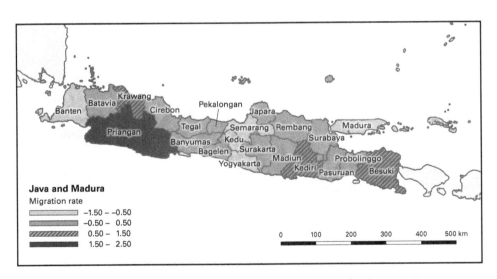

MAP 3.1 Reconstruction of annual average net migration of indigenous Javanese population between Residencies, 1867–1894.

The railway running across Besuki established a connection to the rest of the island and facilitated intense migration, much of it seasonal, but also an annual seven thousand immigrants settled permanently near its coffee and rubber estates.[45] In addition to employment in plantations, these migrants also found land thanks to the construction of large-scale irrigation works. In 1930, Besuki counted 320,000 first-generation migrants from Java and 150,000 from Madura, out of a total population of two million.[46] In South Sumatra, divided from West Java by a narrow sea lane, the construction of railways spurred new waves of migrations from Java and from the impoverished Residency of Banten in particular.

THE NORTHERN PHILIPPINES

The plantation was the colonial business model of the day in the early nineteenth century, but it turned out to be as ill-suited to the Philippines as it was to Java, simply because there was neither slave nor proletarian labor available. From the mid–eighteenth century onward, many experiments were undertaken to encourage the production of commercial crops, a pursuit that after much trial and error was crowned with success for only a limited number of them.[47] Ill-fated, for example, was the order issued in 1750 by the Spanish colonial government that each rural family ought to plant ten bushes of pepper or cacao or ten betel or coconut palm trees annually. With no provincial agencies available to implement it, this decree went nowhere.[48] Many such experiments failed, but the initially inauspicious hemp and indigo pursuits turned into major export crops together with sugar. Hemp, or abaca, catered to a booming demand for maritime rope and became the prime export commodity of the Philippines from 1887 to the 1920s.[49]

Commodity production therefore had to be operated via state coercion and patron-client relations, but this worked slightly differently in the Philippines than it did in the Netherlands Indies.[50] Dutch colonial agrarian policies from the early nineteenth century onward were based on the principle that land stayed within the property of Javanese village communities. The colonial state had imposed coerced cash-crop cultivation via Javanese aristocratic officials and village heads. Such patrimonial structures were absent in the precolonial Philippines, where polities were smaller in scale and had never become as socially stratified as in Java. Whatever statehood existed consisted of federations of *barangay* (communities comprising thirty to one hundred households) under their own *datu* (village head) and usually stratified into warriors, freemen, and slaves.[51]

In the Philippines, the patrimonial state was of a colonial making and operated through the Spanish *encomienda* system, which started as fiefs granted by the governor-general to loyal conquistadores and to the church. By 1591, there were thirty-six crown and 236 private *encomiendas* in the Philippines. To facilitate revenue or tribute collection as well as the recruitment of corvée labor, the precolonial *barangay* were concentrated into *pueblos*. The *datu* received the title *principale* (or *cacique*) and was assigned the task of collecting the tax and remitting it to the *encomienda*. Not least because of the greed of the *encomienda* holders, the whole system turned out to be highly exploitative.[52] In addition to a head tax, the Spanish had imposed a system of corvée labor, or *polo*, for defenses, shipbuilding, and rice supplies. In the course of the eighteenth century, a portion of these corvée-labor obligations was channeled into cash-crop monopolies, tobacco being the most important one. In a further step toward monetization, and similar to Java, corvée labor to be performed by all able-bodied men was reduced from forty to fifteen days per year in 1882, with the option of commuting it into a cash tax.[53]

In the seventeenth century, the private *encomiendas* one after another returned to government hands or came into the possession of monasteries. Large swathes of this land were leased out or sold to the *principales*, who had been on their way to becoming a powerful landed class since the beginning of Spanish rule.[54] The Spanish conquistadores of the sixteenth century had also encouraged individual landholding, which over time ended up in the hands of the *principales* as well through the device of the *pacto de retroventa* or *pacto de retrovendendo*. This was a mortgage not so much on the land, of which ownership was hardly registered, but one carried as a personal debt by the peasants, who were degraded to sharecropping serfs and could even be sold together with their land.[55] The *principales* lent their land to tenants on usurious terms, which further increased the class of bonded clients. Attempts by the colonial administration to protect the peasantry by setting limits on the amount of each lending transaction were to no avail as long as debts were such an effective instrument of labor control—and as long as land *with* servile sharecroppers was worth far more than a piece of empty land. This patron-client servitude was still widespread under American rule.[56]

The power of the landed *principales* had grown over time through their merger with their Christianized Mestizo-Chinese moneylenders, who via the *pacto de retroventa* acquired land on the default of their debtors.[57] Through intermarriage between these moneylenders and *principales* entrepreneurial acumen became coupled with entrenchment in the rural economy. In this respect, the Philippines became distinctly different from the Netherlands Indies. While European corporations had been able to obtain large tracts of land in lease after 1870, the emergence of a Mestizo gentry was something the Dutch authorities had always been anxious to prevent. Such a nonindigenous parasitic landed class would radically change the social order of rural Java, it was feared, and pose a real threat to Dutch rule. Therefore, the Dutch colonial rulers did not grant legal possession of land to anyone who had the legal status of "Foreign Orientals" (mainly Chinese) or Europeans, irrespective of whether they had been born in the Netherlands Indies. Also distinctly different was that in the Netherlands Indies, Chinese, Javanese, and European elites rarely intermingled. Indies Creole planters, although economically and politically powerful, did not become intertwined with the Javanese gentry.

In the Philippines, however, local family networks developed into a national landowning class. First, a sugar and rice plantocracy emerged in Pampanga, followed by Pangasinan. The Visayan island of Negros was turned into a sugar island, a tobacco plantocracy gained hold of Cagayan, and rice and coffee haciendas were established in Nueva Ecija and Batangas. As John A. Larkin put it: "Monopoly of credit, control of information and higher education, an intricate web of strategic marriages, and a strong network of ritual kin helped the rich retain power and wealth and deny these to others."[58] The sugar planters would become the dominant planters' party in late colonial society, and the way in which they shaped society has been aptly termed "sugarlandia."[59] By that time, the Philippine Mestizo *hacendero* class had unfolded into a nationwide oligarchy who over the course of the nineteenth century vacated their mansions in the countryside to become culturally fully oriented toward Manila and even to Spain.[60]

Similar to Java, the Philippines saw substantial permanent migrations from overpopulated lands from the early nineteenth century onward, in this case the northwestern Ilocos. At the turn of the twentieth century, over one-third of all people considering themselves Ilocanos were living outside their provinces of origin.[61] Like the Madurese, the Ilocanos were seafarers, but their land was initially not as dry and poor. On the eve of the Spanish colonization, it was still an economically prosperous wet rice area, maintaining commercial relations with China and Japan.[62] Fertile soil enabled large agricultural communities to live densely packed together, which had the additional advantage of being better defendable against the incursions of pirates.[63] Smallpox vaccinations, which were reportedly reasonably effective, may have played a role in sustaining demographic growth, aggravating population pressure. It did not take long before overpopulation set large caravans of Ilocano migrants in motion, first to establish new villages in the emerging rice and sugar belt of Pangasinan and over time farther down into Nueva Ecija in Central Luzon. Initially, an annual five hundred to one thousand Ilocanos moved from their overpopulated coastal homelands toward the Central Luzon plains, but by the 1840s, the annual exodus had grown to about ten thousand.[64] Over the course of the nineteenth century, Pangasinan, Cayagan Valley, Isabela, Tarlac, and most of the Visayas had become their immigration destinations.[65]

Similar to the situation in Java, these migrations must be linked to the availability of food. Bassino, Dovis, and Komlos have concluded that the decreasing availability of food because of rapid population growth was the most likely cause for the declining height of Filipinos born after 1870, precisely at the time that rice became scarcer and the Philippines had to start importing it.[66] Since the average height of military recruits from the frontier regions was above the national average, however, we may assume that here, as in Java, a push and pull mechanism was in play and that migrants improved their well-being by moving toward these frontiers.

The migrations that had commenced early in the nineteenth century would accelerate in the twentieth. The numbers involved rose to over ten thousand per year after 1910 for Nueva Ecija alone, when the American administration facilitated colonization by smallholder peasants through the Homestead Law of 1903. This law offered the

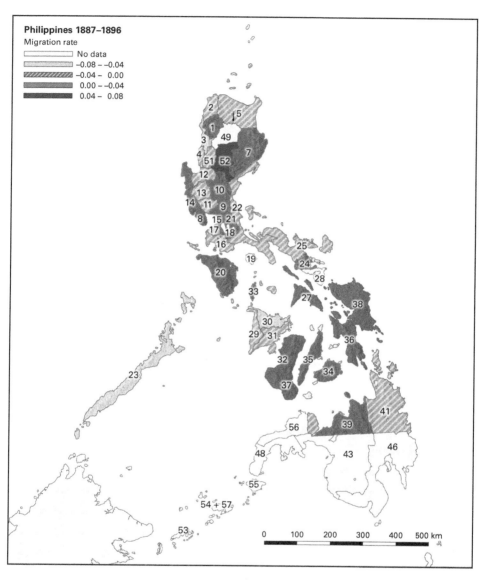

MAP 3.2 Reconstruction of migration between Provinces in the northern Philippines, 1887–1903.

Provinces: 1. Abra; 2. Ilocos Norte; 3. Ilocos Sur; 4. La Union; 5. Cagayan; 7. Isabela; 8. Bataan; 9. Bulacan; 10. Nueva Ecija; 11. Pampanga; 12. Pangasinan; 13. Tarlac; 14. Zambales; 15. Manila; 16. Batangas; 17. Cavite; 18. Laguna; 19. Marinduque; 20. Mindoro; 21. Rizal; 22. Tayabas; 23a. Paragua Sur; 23b. Paragua; 24. Albay; 25. Ambos Camarines; 27. Masbate; 28. Sorsogon; 29. Antique; 30. Capiz; 31. Iloilo; 32. Negros Occidental; 33. Romblon; 34. Bohol; 35. Cebu; 36. Leyte; 37. Negros Oriental; 38. Samar; 39. Misamis; 41. Surigao; 43. Cotabato; 46. Davao; 48. Zamboanga; 49 Lepanto-Bontoc; 51. Benguet; 52. Nueva Vizcaya; 53. Tawi-Tawi; 54. Siassi; 55. Basilan; 56. Dapitan; 57. Jolo opportunity for individuals to claim forty-acre lots of public waste land for a small sum of money. The homesteaders were to clear the land and cultivate most of it within five years or otherwise forfeit their land title. In addition, the American administration purchased friar lands to offer them for affordable prices.[67] While idle land was brought into cultivation by homesteading, corporate enterprise opened up new frontiers as well. In 1912, the massive Canlubang sugar central in Laguna was put into production and connected to the Philippine railway network five years later.[68] The expansion of the railway network and particularly the construction of roads—which had been nearly absent in the Philippines under Spanish rule—shortened the distance of these frontiers to Manila from weeks to days or even hours, which greatly facilitated seasonal migration. The census of 1939 shows huge gender discrepancies in the employable age for different provinces, which points to substantial single male immigrant flows in addition to family migrations: 48,346 in the sugar island of Negros, 32,000 in the plantation belt of Davao in Mindanao, 14,863 in the mining-intensive Mountain Province, and 13,062 in Manila. These men left their families behind in Cebu (31,133), Pangasinan (24,481), and the Ilocos provinces (36,039).[69]

JAVA AND PHILIPPINE SUGARLANDIAS

Sugar was king in Java from the late nineteenth century until the collapse of this industry in 1930, then it was king in the Philippines from the 1930s until 1985. In the Philippines, 12 percent of the population was economically dependent on the sugar sector in the 1930s.[70] This was not greatly different from Java on the eve of the Great Depression, when the sugar industry was by far the largest employer in Java, making up about 10 percent of the island's GDP and providing work for at least part of the year to 10 percent of the male and 3.6 percent of the female employable population.[71] Hundreds of thousands of migrants belonged to this workforce, many of whom had left their homes, propelled by a shortage of land. This applied to the Eastern Salient of Java and even more to Negros. The nutritional conditions in the sugar belts initially compared favorably with those in the overpopulated areas such as Central Java and Ilocos, but the picture was reversed in the 1920s for the Visayan island of Negros, where land scarcity made workers entirely dependent on plantation employment for their livelihood.

The story of the emergence of the Negros plantation belt, a frontier populated by immigrants and seasonal laborers from Iloilo and later on Ilocos, commenced in 1855 after the opening up of the port city of Iloilo (on the island of Panay) to foreign commerce. The British established a vice-consulate in this city, and the first to be entrusted with this office was Nicholas Loney, an agent for several Manchester textile firms. Intent on opening up the Philippines for British cloth, he may have judged the production of sugar of secondary importance, although Britain was a major purchaser of Philippine sugar.[72] In any case, Loney supplied equipment such as steam-driven cane crushers and, if necessary, credit.[73] At that time, an attempt had already been made to apply industrial equipment to sugar production in Negros by another foreigner, the Frenchman Leopold Germain Gaston. He was brought from Mauritius by an important Mestizo-Spanish planter in Batangas in 1837, which speaks to the global breadth of sugar production and the peripatetic character of expertise in cash-crop production. Gaston's example was followed by prominent ethnic Chinese from Iloilo, who were supplied with equipment by Loney.[74]

Negros's unfolding misery was partly the result of monocropping, made possible by the emigration of hundreds of thousands of labor migrants to the mushrooming sugar belt and by massive land grabs.[75] Much of the land was cleared by immigrants from Iloilo, who either came as clients of Mestizo entrepreneurs or on their own account.[76] Most pioneers needed crop loans from the sugar entrepreneurs, who provided these at an interest rate of 25 percent, which was not especially high but still difficult to repay. Many farmers lost their land within a year of entering into their contract loans.[77] To expel those who managed to hold on, the landlords would hire armed gangs. In this way, the *hacenderos* grabbed large swathes of land between the 1860s and 1880s and reduced the pioneers first to tenants and subsequently to sharecroppers.[78] For harvesting and haulage, the planters relied on *sacadas*, seasonal laborers, arriving in gangs of twenty or so men led by a *kapatas*, or patron.[79]

What generally separated sharecroppers from cane cutters in the Philippine sugar districts was that they still had their own working animals, although this was an advantage they lost when rinderpest in the early years of the twentieth century deprived them of their means of production.[80] Even then their bargaining position was still not bad, and it improved after their ranks had been thinned by the War of Independence. Moreover, the mechanization of the sugar factories had been sluggish.[81] Railway tracks did not yet connect field to factory, as was the case in Java, for example. However, the labor shortages that were still abundant by 1910 had vanished by the 1920s, when American investments had concentrated the processing of cane from 820 mills into seventeen centrifugal centrals and had fully mechanized haulage via a dense web of narrow-gauge railways. Meanwhile, the population had continued to increase rapidly.[82]

The word "sugarlandia," which was coined for the Philippines, Negros in particular, is equally applicable to Java, where over 8.6 percent of the most valuable land, namely *sawah* (wet rice) land, was committed to cane. The factories also deeply affected agricultural cycles, as they were a driving force behind the expansion of irrigated land but also the dominant co-users, putting their own interests above rice cultivation.[83] In the wake of the Brussels Convention of 1902, which reined in the dumping of European beet sugar on the global market, sugar brought some prosperity to rural Java. Sugar accounted for half of the plantation employment in Java, which doubled between 1900 and 1920 and brought a substantial increase of per capita income.[84] The Brussels Convention expired, however, during the First World War; sugar prices declined, and in the course of the 1920s, marginal peasants again fell on hard times. Many were forced to rent out their land to sugar factories for subeconomic prices and often under conditions detrimental to a timely start of the rice cycle. Resistance by poor peasants and cane cutters to their deteriorating conditions, leading to cane fires, was answered by the sugar factories establishing an extensive private police force to guard the fields during the sugar campaign.[85] While the role of the village heads and *mandurs* in controlling labor continued to be crucial, new instruments were added to the arsenal, such as the gathering of 160,000 fingerprints to detect known political propagandists among the labor force in the factories and among the field *mandurs*.[86] Meanwhile, the wages of the field laborers who did most of the work made up just 25 percent of the cost price of the Java sugar. While sugar workers in the Philippines did not receive a larger share, they earned more thanks to a protected U.S. sugar market. The incomes of Java's peasant families were further depressed by heavy taxation on land.[87]

Poverty and malnutrition proliferated in the plantation belts of the northern Philippines and Java, the consequences of which were aggravated by the widespread occurrence of malaria and hookworm. In Java, rice consumption declined from the late nineteenth century onward, although this was compensated for by the cultivation and consumption of cassava, sweet potatoes, and maize.[88] Yet even at the time that Java's per capita income and food supplies had increased substantially, the high casualty rate from the influenza epidemic in the Netherlands Indies sheds a less favorable light on the nutritional conditions and general health of Java's rural population. Casualty rates from influenza are highly correlated to nutritional as well as general health. There were relatively few casualties among well-fed people, who did not suffer from malaria or hookworm. Despite the fact that, for example, the barracks of the Dutch colonial army and the miners of Belitung were breeding places for the flu, only 0.3 percent of these soldiers and miners died. Among East Sumatra's malnourished coolies originating from Central Java, 3.5 percent succumbed, compared with 1 percent among the Chinese in the same plantations.[89] Within Asia, the Netherlands Indies and India were the worst affected by influenza, with a mortality rate of 5 to 6 percent of the population.[90] By contrast, the casualty rate from the pandemic hovered between 2 and 3 percent in British Malaya, the Philippines, and Burma.[91] That bad nutritional conditions in Java might have played a major role in this relatively high mortality rate seems even more likely considering that the casualty rate was also remarkably high in some densely populated rural provinces of Ilocos, Pangasinan, and, last but not least, the plantation belt of Negros.[92]

In the sugarlandias of both the Philippines and Java, the nutritional conditions further worsened during the early years of the Depression, although for different reasons. In Java, they were already precarious by the late 1920s, when protein intake declined to the alarming level of about 80 percent of the necessary minimum.[93] Things went from bad to worse in the wake of the collapse of the Java sugar industry during the Great Depression, which reduced the average intake to 1,500 to 1,600 kilocalories per day, well below the necessary minimum of 1,800 to 2,000. In the Philippines, food supplies still increased in the 1920s thanks to measures by the American administration to expand the acreage of land under rice, combined with import tariffs on this cereal to protect local production. This was good for rural income, but in practice, wage workers and share-croppers suffered, and their conditions further deteriorated when rice production stagnated in the 1930s.

Workers in the sugar and rice belts of Negros and Central Luzon were exposed to malnutrition. In Negros, they were employed for only half of the year, and then for just two or three days per week. While having enough time to grow food, they had little opportunity to do so because most arable land on that island was taken up by cane. Workers were completely in the thrall of their employers, who provided them with food from their canteens: sometimes "planters paid wages with nothing but the commodities bought from these canteens."[94] More than half of the families of cane workers were in debt. In the other Philippine sugar belt, Pampanga, proletarianization had progressed more slowly, but population pressure mounted here as well and was exacerbated by a steady stream of laborers from the densely populated Ilocos provinces toward Central Luzon. They must have found it increasingly difficult to find employment, since the sugar industry had embarked on the mechanization of plowing and haulage.[95]

Sugar workers and seasonal migrants were not the only groups suffering from deteriorating nutritional conditions in the 1930s. Landlords increasingly enjoyed the luxury of abundant supplies of labor and during the rice-scarce final months before the harvest felt no urge to provide rice to their sharecroppers to rescue them from starvation, which implies a serious erosion of the old patron-client relationship.[96] By the late 1930s, 70 percent of the population of Pampanga was landless, permanently in debt, and therefore—as a contemporary observer noted— actually living in a state of serfdom.[97] Meanwhile, relatively high rice prices, in which speculation played a role, led to a decline of the availability of this cereal by 35 percent in the 1930s for the entire Philippine population.[98] Sugar plantation workers were seriously undernourished in the 1930s; a figure even below 1,400 kilocalories for adults was mentioned in an investigation by the Institute of Pacific Relations. Such alarming figures were also to be found among coolies in Java plantations in 1939, for that matter.[99] Hunger and oppression by *hacenderos* provoked widespread resistance, manifesting itself in the torching of many a cane field.

Over time, this would turn increasingly violent and more organized in the shape of the well-known Huk movement.[100] To avoid an expansion of this peasant uprising in Central Luzon, the Philippine government imported and distributed relief rice. Generally, agricultural wages were far below, if not less than half, of the one-peso equivalent of half a U.S. dollar per day, which was considered to be a subsistence wage by the late 1930s.[101]

COLONIAL DOMINATION OR SPECIALIZATION?

The grim stories of the sugarlandias of Java and the Philippines seem to serve as classical cases of underdevelopment by colonial capitalism. What complicates the picture, however, is that most of the Philippine sugar barons were born in the Philippines, and more than half of the Java factories were owned by families with deep roots in Java. They belonged both to powerful Mestizo or Creole strata, classes that were definitely exploitative but did not rely on metropolitan capitalism.[102] There is another, and probably more important, reason why a straightforward connection between the extent of economic dependency of a colony on its core country and impoverishment is unlikely. Colonialism, and colonial plantation and mining sectors in particular, obviously had enormous transformative effects on societies under its subjugation, but this took many different forms and involved many different actors. This complexity seems to have escaped from theorizing on colonial exploitation and economic dependency as it has developed since the Second World War.

In 1945, Albert O. Hirschman, who would later on claim his "grandfathership of the dependency theory," postulated that colonial domination created peripheries that were to produce items suffering from unfavorable terms of trade: "An initial power supremacy enables the imperial power to shape the direction and composition of the colony's trade, and the trade relations which are thus established in turn strengthen markedly the original power position held by the imperial power."[103] As an indicator of dependency, Hirschman developed an index that still carries his name, in which figures above 40 signal an unhealthy concentration of the trade of a colony with its mother country. For the Netherlands Indies, the Philippines, Malaysia, and—for the sake of comparison—British India, his formula produced the data presented in table 3.2.

TABLE 3.2

Hirschman index, 1913 and 1938

Country	1913 exports	1913 imports	1938 exports	1938 imports
Netherlands Indies	38.1	42.1	32.4	34.1
Philippines	43.0	52.5	78.0	69.4
British Malaya	38.3	33.8	37.0	38.3
British India	31.4	65.2	37.8	38.5

Source: Hirschman, *National Power*, 104–5.

Table 3.2 shows that the colonies in question, with the notable exception of the Philippines, had a relatively diverse set of economic relations both with respect to their imports and their exports. In terms of dependency, the Philippines stood out as increasingly oriented toward its colonizer, which was the only market for its sugar, and sugar had become its most important export commodity by the 1930s. Moreover, the removal of import tariffs for U.S. goods opened up the Philippine market for a range of manufactured goods, including textiles.[104] Meanwhile, remarkably few trade ties were established between the Philippines and neighboring countries, making the "racial and cultural ties of the Malayan peoples throughout South-eastern Asia . . . an empty phrase," as a contemporary observer noted.[105] India, the Netherlands Indies, and Malaysia were economically less dependent on their colonial motherland, but this was not unequivocal good news. Indonesia's decreasing dependency index figure for exports, for example, was also the result of the collapse of its sugar industry during the Depression years.

The Hirschman index obviously does not allow for any categorical conclusions concerning the effects of the metropolitan dependency of Island Southeast Asia, but neither does it justify a denial of the substantial effects of colonialism on trade relations. In this regard, Patrick O'Brien might have been overstating his case when he claimed that it was not colonial power but the "underlying structural possibilities" that forced tropical dependencies to focus on a limited number of commodities.[106]

As a rule, metropolitan governments defended their own producers and refiners against competition from tropical producers. The protection of metropolitan beet sugar is the most notorious example, one that even hurt the Philippines despite their privileged access to the U.S. market. The U.S. sugar quota in 1934, imposed under pressure from the country's beet sugar industry, compelled the Philippines to destroy a third of its harvest in the year that followed, for which the planters were partly compensated by the government as a matter of fact.[107] Moreover, the United States issued a regulation that the maximum amount of public land a corporation could apply for in the Philippines was 1,024 hectares. This act was adopted by the American Congress as an anti-imperialist gesture but had its provenance in the American beet sugar interests that had lobbied for this law to prevent American capital from establishing strong and competitive sugar plantations in the Philippines.[108]

The United States also favored its own producers of natural fats by imposing an excise on processed coconut oil, which was returned to the Philippine exchequer—but only with the obnoxious clause that such funds would not be invested in the coconut sector.[109] This kept the Philippine coconut sector relatively inefficient. Despite all this, the Philippines were in an enviable position with regard to their coconut oil exports compared with the Netherlands Indies, as the Philippine oil factories had survived the glut of the market of the early 1920s, when those in the Netherlands Indies were mostly bankrupted and closed. The forty Philippine mills—which were overwhelmingly in U.S. and British hands—were recapitalized, however, and maintained themselves against competitors in the United States.[110] In contrast to the Philippines, coconut oil exports from the Netherlands Indies were of marginal importance, and most of the oil was consumed by the local market.[111] Philippine coconut oil even enjoyed preferential and duty-free access to the United States, which did not protect its own copra-processing industry, in contrast to the European countries.[112] This would change somewhat in 1934, when the United States imposed a tax on processed coconut oil. However, it still mattered a great deal to the coconut fat producers in Island Southeast Asia whether they had to deal with Europe or the United States.

Metropolitan interests indubitably inhibited the upgrading of tropical commodities toward export products with higher added value, but nonetheless it made sense for the colonial administrations in Island

Southeast Asia to develop and facilitate the export of primary products. In that respect, O'Brien is right. The long nineteenth century (1789–1914) was a time in which Asian, African, and Latin American economies experienced a period of favorable terms of trade for their primary products.[113] The specialization in a limited number of commodities, noted by O'Brien, was part of the game and not deliberately pursued by colonial governments, at least not initially. When the Spanish and Dutch colonial administrations promoted exports to increase their revenue in the late eighteenth century, they aimed to play a role in the global economy in a wide range of products, varying from luxuries, to textiles, to rice. Until the 1830s, dozens of ships left from Batavia, Manila, and harbor towns at the Gulf of Lingayen filled with rice for Canton, where it was imported to help feed famine-stricken southeastern China.[114] Java and the Philippines continued to export rice up to the 1860s.

Estates producing more than a single crop became less and less the rule over time. This was particularly the case in Java, where successful planters went all-in on sugar, the most profitable crop.[115] The increasingly capital-intensive outlays of the sugar factories provided a strong disincentive to shift to other commodities if these drew better prices on the world market. They kept extensive financial reserves for the bad years to protect their valuable property from being bankrupted. This conservative management style was markedly strong in Java's sugar industry. Although planters were well aware of the risk of monocropping, they were usually not capable of resisting the economic logic. The exception that proved the rule was the American investor who built the large Canlubang sugar factory in the Philippines in 1912. He had deep pockets, commanded plenty of land, and could therefore afford to combine sugar with copra in his enterprise.[116]

While monocropping was driven by an admittedly short-term economic rationale of favorable terms of trade, it definitely impinged negatively on manufacturing and particularly on food production. The precarious nutritional conditions of large segments of the population of Java were directly linked to these terms of trade. In Java, where cheap imports were still being allowed in, rice growing was less profitable than cane, which discouraged rice production. Java lost its role as a rice exporter, and the fact that it did not become a large importer was simply because cassava, maize, and sweet potatoes increasingly replaced rice on the daily menu. Only Sumatra's west coast, Bali, and Lombok were still selling part of their rice crop in the early twentieth century, and any attempts to expand rice cultivation outside Java failed because growing coffee, rubber, or copra paid much better.[117] The situation in British Malaya was even worse, as it had to import 65 percent of its rice in the early twentieth century, mostly from Burma.[118] Attempts by British authorities to encourage rice production failed as long as farmers could earn more from rubber or tobacco.[119] The downside of this economic specialization was that it inhibited the development of food production in British Malaya and distorted the rice market in Java, and this had serious consequences for the farmers who had to pay their land rent by selling part of their paddy harvest. With low prices for this crop, they might have preferred to produce less of it and work longer at the plantations. The Americans had made it a priority from the onset of their administration of the Philippines to wean the country off its rice imports from Siam and Saigon.[120] It was beneficial to the Philippine economy, although, as mentioned already, there was a downside in the shape of relatively high rice prices and in the 1930s the undernourishment of wage workers and sharecroppers.

With the exception of the Philippines, which were pulled into the U.S. economic orbit, the economic integration of Southeast and East Asia forged ahead in the early twentieth century. Japan emerged as a major industrial manufacturer for the region, exporting bicycles, sewing machines, and textiles to Southeast Asia and importing commodities such as sugar. The division of labor between cash-crop plantation belts and auxiliary rice frontiers emerged all over Asia, and its scale expanded.[121] In South Asia, the plantations of Ceylon drew their rice from the Kaveri delta (Madras Presidency), which also supplied British Malaya.[122] The drive toward specialization was relentless and practically unstoppable by colonial governments. An attempt by the administration of Burma to introduce coffee and cotton cultivation was thwarted by British and German traders, whose response was to offer better prices for rice. Nevertheless, the price of Burmese rice was low enough to flood even the Kaveri delta in the 1920s, to prevent food self-sufficiency in British Malaya, and to degrade the income-generating capacity of rice cultivators in Java.[123]

DIVERGING LIVING STANDARDS: ESTATES VERSUS SMALLHOLDERS

Since the Hirschman index does not explain the divergence of living standards in Island Southeast Asia as much as, for example, an examination of rice markets does, we can shift our focus to the types of crops and the types of labor relations as possible explanatory factors. The type of crop undeniably played a role in the unequal spread of the growth of specialization in cash crops. Sugar prices were declining under pressure from the major beet sugar–producing countries in continental Europe, which considered sugar a strategic alimentary commodity and not only protected their own markets but also provided their industries with the wherewithal to dump their surpluses on the world market. Crops such as coffee and tobacco—and up to 1940, rubber and cotton—were less vulnerable to protective measures or substitution by industrial countries.[124]

Even though the type of crop mattered in terms of effects on local purchasing power, of overriding importance seems to have been the difference between smallholders and plantation estates. The case of the Netherlands Indies definitely points in this direction. The histories of Java and the Outer Islands diverge widely with respect to their production systems of cash crops. In 1930, about 85 percent of all cash crops produced in Java came from plantation estates (mainly sugar, tea, coffee, rubber, and tobacco) compared with a mere 36 percent in the Outer Islands.[125] Coffee and rubber, for example, were predominantly plantation crops in Java, but they were smallholder crops or at least in the hands of local entrepreneurs in the Outer Islands.[126]

Copra is the exception to the rule that crops generally grown on estates in Java belonged predominantly to the domain of smallholders in the Outer Islands. By the late 1920s, only 5 percent of the coconut palms in the Netherlands Indies belonged to European-owned plantations, and the figure was even lower for Java than for the Outer Islands.[127] Copra emerged as a booming commodity in the early twentieth century, when coconut oil—previously only used in indigenous cuisine—became a major source for the production of soap and margarine. Island Southeast Asia soon became the dominant producer, with a share of 70 percent of the global output by the mid-1930s.[128] Both in the Outer Islands of the Netherlands Indies and in the Philippines, copra was initially a smallholder crop, with intermediaries—usually Chinese or Mestizo Chinese—taking care of the transport to, respectively, Singapore and Manila.[129] Copra cultivation brought considerable wealth to local populations, although smallholdings might end up in the hands of elites who then transformed the production sites into plantations; this happened less in Java than it did elsewhere.[130] A plantation belt emerged in Kalimantan near Pontianak, which was populated by thousands of peons who had to toil for four or five years to work off their debts and the fare for the steamer or brig that had carried them to West Kalimantan.[131] Moreover, and this was particularly the case after the Second World War, when output was increased through improved cultivation techniques, copra plantations obtained a competitive advantage over smallholders.[132]

In the Philippines, the extensive smallholder cultivation of copra and abaca in the eastern provinces set them apart from western and central Luzon and the western Visayas, where both rice and sugar production were dominated by the *hacenderos* and marked by sharp social inequalities. In the 1920s, generous profits ended up in the pockets of the absentee *hacenderos* in Manila, while the workers in the cane fields of Negros and Pampanga suffered. Workers in the abaca and copra belts were much better off in those years. Certainly, during the Depression years, the decline of copra prices was more severe than that of Philippine sugar. Wages were about 25 percent lower in the eastern abaca- and copra-growing provinces than in the sugar belts. Yet in terms of living standards, farmers in these provinces were better off than in Negros, for example, because they still had the option to shift from export to food cropping.[133]

Moreover, the profits from indigenous export cultivation, as Jacob van Gelderen (the head of the statistical office in Batavia) argued in the 1920s, were not siphoned off to Europe or to the United States but were either spent on imports or saved in gold or paper currency. During the rubber boom in the 1920s, about 82.4 million guilders in paper money of the Netherlands Indies was extracted from circulation, suggesting that a considerable amount of money had been stashed away to return into the economy over time.[134] Thousands of bicycles (a bicycle cost almost a year's earnings of a coolie at a Deli plantation in those days), hundreds of sewing machines, and dozens of motor cars found their way to smallholder communities in Kalimantan and Sumatra.[135]

In the profoundly Dutch-oriented Minahasa, the profits from copra cultivation were lavishly spent on children's education.[136] Wherever corporate estate enterprise did not rule, the rural economy benefited from its incorporation in the global commodity market. By contrast, a plantation belt such as Deli (East Sumatra) was a typical wealth exporter; it averaged an export surplus double that of the Netherlands Indies.[137] Smallholder commodity production not only entailed a higher retention rate of the profits of cash-crop production for the local economy but also allowed cultivators to spread their risks: the rubber cultivators in Sumatra and Kalimantan, often swidden cultivators, or abaca growers in the eastern provinces of the Philippines continued to grow food crops.[138]

Even in regions where added value was retained rather than siphoned off to the overseas plantation owners or absentee *hacenderos*, the actual cultivators could certainly still be exploited by middlemen. Neither should we cherish illusions about labor conditions, since slaves were frequently employed in indigenous coffee and pepper production well into the nineteenth century, and debt bondage continued for much longer. Every year, thousands of migrants came to the pepper frontiers at the east coast of Aceh as seasonal workers, but many of them had to stay in conditions of debt bondage.[139] They lived in the same debt clutches as the gatherers of forest products in Borneo or the pearl divers in the South Moluccas mentioned in the previous chapter of this book. Many copra and rubber cultivators in West Kalimantan were permanently in debt to the Chinese traders, who controlled the contacts with the outside world and had their own steam liners to Singapore.[140] This debt bondage could easily emerge when farmers no longer grew their own food. Sometimes, favorable prices led cultivators to give up rice cultivation, as was the case with copra growers in South Sulawesi.[141] There were also many farmers who were simply short of hands and time to combine food and cash-crop production.[142] This was a problem that did not disappear after decolonization. In recent times, highland tobacco cultivators in North Sulawesi who were not capable of producing sufficient food for their families ended up debt-chained to coastal traders, who even organized gambling sessions to inflict debts on them.[143] Even if communities of smallholders succeeded in keeping usurers at bay, their prosperity could still have evaporated almost overnight if they had not managed to diversify their activities

Saved from Smallpox but Starving in the Sugar Cane Fields

in a timely fashion. This happened in the Bicol provinces in eastern Luzon, where abaca had brought prosperity but no economic diversification, as most of it was exported as raw material for U.S. and British rope makers.[144]

Nonetheless, the communities of smallholders cultivating abaca, copra, rubber, and coffee usually reaped more of the benefits of their work and enjoyed greater flexibility to respond to the commodity booms and busts than communities that relied on plantation employment. A significant proportion of Java's population was dependent on poorly paid work at the plantations or their extensive supporting infrastructure, without having any other options to become involved in production for the global market. In contrast to the rural populations of the thinly populated parts of Island Southeast Asia, individual farmers in Java—as well as parts of Luzon and the Visayas for that matter—had little chance to engage in commodity production on their own terms, hamstrung as they were by limited resources and population pressure.[145]

Just after 1900, the American labor expert Victor S. Clark remarked in his essay on economic conditions in Java that while the island had made material progress with regard to its public work and plantations, in most other respects it was stationary: "The standard of living and physical well-being of the masses has not risen and wages appear to be falling."[146] Dutch imperialists at that time bluntly stated that Java was exhausted and overpopulated and that the Outer Islands should therefore be opened up to Dutch capital.[147] Although plantation employment in Java boomed during the first twenty-five years of the twentieth century, it brought only temporary relief. By and large, workers in the plantation sectors benefited less from the commodity boom in the 1920s than smallholders and suffered more during the Depression. The Philippines offer a case in point, where the relatively high wages in plantation belts in the 1930s were offset by limited opportunities for workers to grow their own food. This is not to say that conditions were rosy beyond the large European-led plantation economy during the Great Depression. The sharecropping rubber tappers left South Sumatra en masse.[148] In Kalimantan, the glut in rubber prices and the rubber quota also caused hardship, particularly for producers who had neglected their food production and were in the thrall of the middlemen, who just asked for more production at a lower price. Nonetheless, the overall economic performance of the

Outer Islands was better than Java, and in general, there was less hardship during the Depression.[149]

The economic divergence between Java and the Outer Islands is reflected in the fact that in the 1920s the level of imports of consumption goods per capita in Sumatra and Kalimantan was two to 2.5 times higher than in Java, three times higher than in the Moluccas, and seven times higher than in Bali. These differences correlate with the estimates of per capita incomes found by Malines van Ginkel, which were considerably higher in Sumatra and Kalimantan than in Java. Indigenous rubber, pepper, and coffee cultivation did bring some prosperity to many. By contrast, in the former slave-trading regions in the eastern part of the Indonesian archipelago—as well as in Bali and Lombok—per capita income and consumptive imports per capita were slightly under 15 percent of what was earned in Jambi and Bengkulu; the most prosperous residencies in Sumatra.[150] The engagement with the global economy as a supplier of commodities could bring wealth but also further precarity. The additional income brought by plantations to rural societies did mitigate the impoverishment caused by population density, but at the same time, it exposed rural populations to the extractive mechanisms of plantation conglomerates.

CHAPTER FOUR

The Labor-Scarce Commodity Frontiers, 1870s–1942

The audacious pirates who had looted vessels even within sight of major colonial port cities such as Singapore and Surabaya were defeated by naval steam and steel over the course of the nineteenth century. The colonial gunboats eventually brought the slaveholding polities of Island Southeast Asia to heel. The opening of the Suez Canal in 1869 inaugurated the era of modern imperialism, a new stage in the quest for control over resources. Coffee, tea, tobacco, and particularly sugar were shipped to Europe and the United States in increasing quantities, addressing the rising spending capacity of their populations. With tin for canned food, palm oil for soap and margarine, abaca for rope, and last but not least rubber and oil, the region catered to the almost insatiable demand of the industrializing world. Yet even in those decades of what seemed to be unstoppable colonial expansion, plantation estates and corporate capitalism did not bring all of Island Southeast Asia under its sway, as it had done in Java and the northwestern Philippines. Smallholder cash-crop production was resilient. For most of Island Southeast Asia, this peripheralization was a slow process that outlasted colonialism and continued in postcolonial times.

In what follows, the expansion of the plantation economy outside the northern Philippines and Java will be revisited as a process of "incomplete peripheralization." It began in the final years of the nineteenth century, when slave-based commodity production still existed in the peripheries of Island Southeast Asia. In the struggle to increase their control over Chinese-dominated cash-crop cultivation in the outer regions of Island Southeast Asia, colonial administrative centers engineered migration from densely populated provinces toward these areas.[1] Whereas migration to the Philippines and the southern parts of Sumatra occurred more or less spontaneously, Malaysia and North Sumatra had to rely on commercial recruiters. As will be detailed, a free capitalist labor market did not emerge. The North Sumatra plantation belt in particular demonstrates how the combination of plantations' unwillingness to pay market wages and colonial governments' anxiety to control migration engendered a world of trafficking and deceit, which has unfortunately resurfaced in recent decades.

Despite steadfast colonial backing of corporate plantations and mining businesses, only in Java would the European- or American-owned estates control more than half of the cultivation of export crops. At least until the late nineteenth century, colonial support could not make up for the lack of financial stamina and local knowledge, both of which were needed to expand toward the thinly populated territories of Island Southeast Asia. Even in the colonial heartland of Java, they often shared the trade and marketing of products with Chinese entrepreneurs.[2] In the eastern part of the Indonesian archipelago, Bugis merchants assertively engaged in the trade of forest and sea products for the Chinese market, which they bartered for British cloth.[3] Partly as a result of these trading connections, the total value of exports to China from the Outer Islands of Indonesia easily exceeded those to Europe until the 1850s.[4] Only by the end of the nineteenth century had the forests of Island Southeast Asia been turned into frontiers of corporate enterprise. Colonial governments prepared the ground for this by claiming ownership of all the waste land throughout their territories. In the 1870s, the government of the Netherlands Indies, for example, not only enacted its enclosure legislation for Java (see the previous chapter) but also explored how it could be extended all over the Indonesian archipelago.[5] Meanwhile, roads and shipping services were laid out to connect the outer regions to the colonial centers of power, drawing the grid for imperial expansion. The Bugis traders who had once played a central role in the movement of sea and forest products were pushed aside by shipping companies such as the Dutch KPM (Royal Packet Navigation Company). Oil companies entered Sumatra and

Kalimantan, and the first timber companies penetrated the forests of North Borneo, presaging the large-scale corporate destruction of the rain forests later in the twentieth century.[6] However, even in the rubric of extractive commodities, the transnational and highly vertically concentrated oil companies remained an exceptional phenomenon. Coal mines were usually under government control and, most importantly, almost all the tin, gold, and diamond extraction stayed in Chinese hands until the very end of the nineteenth century and in some cases even longer.[7]

RESTIVE SMALLHOLDERS

Island Southeast Asia's sites of mining and cash-crop cultivation showed a varied pattern in terms of ownership and labor relations. Despite the region's reputation as a colonial plantation belt, many crops, for example abaca and copra, were in fact most successfully cultivated as smallholder crops. Some of these smallholder systems proved to be remarkably resilient against the advance of the estate corporations, despite the fact that their crops were in great demand in the West. This was also irrespective of whether these crops were indigenous—such as pepper, abaca, and copra—or had been introduced by the colonial powers. The secret of smallholders' resilience was often the embedding of their production for the market in swidden food-crop cultivation, which enhanced their economic autonomy. Coffee, rubber, and pepper are crops that grow as trees or vines and produce yields for a number of consecutive years. Thus they are highly suitable to be combined with swidden food agriculture.

Most of the corporate mining and plantations would not have survived without the heavy hand of the colonial state, as they were usually economically outperformed by smallholdings and small-scale or artisanal mining. This was even the case in the sugar sector. For Java, it was reckoned in the 1920s that smallholder production was at least 25 percent cheaper than estate cane because it could dispense with the supervision and overhead required by plantations.[8] Not surprisingly, the sugar factories wrested a legal ban on the budding peasant cane sector from the government in the early 1920s.[9] The price of this inefficiency was solely paid by the workers in the field and the cane cutters, as the sugar industry spared their factory workers and overseers in the field (the *mandurs*) who were crucial to ensure smooth operations.[10] Tobacco and tea estates had to compete with smallholder production or operated in symbiosis with smallholders or sharecroppers. In Manado (North Sulawesi), tobacco continued to be grown alongside plantation production, as it was in Java. Actually, more than three-quarters of the tobacco grown in Java was smallholder produce, although it should be noted that most of this was for local consumption.[11] In East Java and Deli (East Sumatra), Dutch pioneers had begun their tobacco estates as putting-out systems, and the Deli plantations kept some of their key features. The so-called field coolies, who carried out the actual planting, tending, and harvesting of the tobacco leaves, were sharecroppers assigned to one *bau* (0.7 hectare) to grow tobacco.[12] In the Priangan, smallholder tea emerged as an offshoot from estates, since the planters encouraged their workers to grow this crop as smallholders. This involved almost a third of the total acreage planted with tea bushes.[13] In addition, tens of thousands of tea smallholdings (varying from 0.2 to fourteen hectares) emerged in West Java, which would expand markedly during the Depression years and yield the capital for further investment, including in textile manufacturing.[14]

The cultivation of pepper resisted all attempts at appropriation by colonial powers. Pepper was the source of Aceh's prowess in the nineteenth century, after it succeeded Banten as the prime pepper grower of the region. It sold its pepper to Chinese traders, to ships from Salem (Massachusetts), or via its Acehnese merchant community in Penang.[15] In Bangka, the Chinese mine owners were extracting more profit from their pepper groves than from tin by the early twentieth century. They turned this island into the world's principal producer of white pepper.[16] Coffee shares many characteristics with pepper, even though it was introduced by the colonizers. From the late eighteenth century onward, it was the most important export crop of colonial Java, the revenues from which were massively siphoned off to the Netherlands. In Sumatra, however, it became predominantly grown by smallholders and received a boost after the revolution in 1791 had decimated coffee supplies from Saint-Domingue. American ships called at the port of Padang every year to fill their holds with coffee grown in Minangkabau.[17] This region was producing so much coffee by the 1840s that it is said that 12,000 porters had to carry the harvested beans from the highlands to the port of Padang.[18] Over the course of the nineteenth century, coffee as a smallholder crop would further expand across Sumatra and Sulawesi, where it gained wide popularity among swidden agriculturalists.[19] In the early twentieth century, a fresh wave of such coffee cultivation followed in West Sumatra, greatly facilitated by newly constructed roads.[20] Coffee cultivation thrived particularly among local communities that were not under the yoke of an economically oppressive local nobility and that felt secure enough to invest in trees that took eight to ten years to bear fruit.[21]

Although intimately linked to the Second Industrial Revolution, rubber was only to a very limited extent vertically integrated with metropolitan corporations. It thrived as a smallholder crop, fitting perfectly with cycles of food production, particularly with swidden cultivation, as the trees could be planted while the land was left fallow to recover from food cropping.[22] Throughout Sumatra and southwestern Kalimantan, smallholder rubber rapidly disseminated after Indonesians had returned from rubber tapping in the Malay Peninsula, where they had acquired the necessary skills and seeds.[23] By about 1940, the total number of smallholder rubber producers in Sumatra and in Kalimantan amounted to an estimated eight hundred thousand, and with the exception of Deli, European-owned plantations were of little consequence.[24] In British Malaya, where large European and American companies held most of the rubber estates, there were still many smaller Chinese and Tamil estates (about 1,500 in 1940) whose owners constituted a thriving middle class and an important factor in the economy of the region.[25] Last but not least, 40 percent of the entire area planted with rubber was owned by smallholders, who would have pushed the rubber estates to the margins in the 1930s if the interwar international rubber restriction schemes had not been so disadvantageous to them.[26]

Rubber smallholders also defied attempts by the Dutch colonial government to encapsulate and sever them from the chain of Chinese traders connecting them with the rubber mills of Singapore. This chain proved to be mutually beneficial because it allowed smallholders to keep their independence and Singapore to emerge as the hub of rubber milling for colonial Indonesia. In the 1920s, the capacity of the city's twenty mills was supplied to the extent of about 80 percent by rubber from Sumatra and Kalimantan. The government in Batavia did not watch with a light heart the loss of potential revenue caused by the raw condition of the exported rubber, and it encouraged investors to build processing factories in Palembang, although without much success.[27] The Royal Packet

Navigation Company (KPM), meanwhile, fruitlessly attempted to force out the Chinese traders from their lucrative intermediary position between the Sumatra smallholders and Singapore rubber mills.[28] In 1934, the Dutch authorities eventually had enough of it and imposed a prohibitive duty on the export of wet rubber. The cultivators in Kalimantan and Sumatra were up to the challenge and ordered thousands of rubber mangles from Singapore, enabling them to diversify the destinations of their exports, as dry rubber was less perishable and hence suitable for transport over the Pacific Ocean to the United States.[29]

REDUCING THE CHINESE IMMIGRANT LABOR FORCE

The resilience of the smallholder sector in the Outer Islands was shored up by labor scarcity and land abundance, a situation diametrically opposed to that of the plantation belts of Java and the northern Philippines. As we have seen, mobility was high in Island Southeast Asia, and plantation estates in Java had been quite successful in attracting labor after the 1860s. They had been doing this by tapping into existing patron-client relationships, and although that violated regulations concerning individual labor contracting, the colonial government did not bother as long as rural order was not disturbed. Indonesia's Outer Islands also had their labor gangs—*kongsis*—but they operated entirely beyond the purview of the colonial state. Rather than being merely labor gangs, the *kongsis* were structures of self-governance that were shaped to survive in a commodity frontier and to take care of the necessary infrastructure such as the construction of dams and water gates.[30]

Domesticating Chinese economic power had always been of key interest to the colonial states in Island Southeast Asia. While the massacres and expulsions of Chinese inhabitants belonged to the past, immigration restrictions, as well as limits on the mobility of Chinese newcomers and ethnic Chinese (that is, Chinese born in the colonies), were still listed in the legal repertoires of the Philippines and the Netherlands Indies. Ethnic Chinese economic acumen was either curtailed or integrated into the colonial economy. As mentioned in the previous chapter, in the Philippines, ethnic Chinese—usually referred to as Mestizos—merged with the Philippine *principales*, becoming a landed class, while the government sought to force them out of trade. Conversely, in Java, the government did not impede Chinese merchant enterprise but was anxious to prevent their ascendancy as a landed class merging with the Indonesian aristocracy. As mentioned in the previous chapter, the forced character of coffee cultivation in the Priangan was inexorably linked to the desire of the VOC to reduce the power of the ethnic Chinese traders and moneylenders in the cash-crop economy. This policy continued progressively in the nineteenth century, when tax farming—which had been outsourced to Chinese collectors—was gradually abolished. These measures were followed a few decades later by cooperative village rice barns and credit, to reduce the role of ethnic Chinese intermediaries.[31]

The colonial governments had set themselves a formidable task to reduce the economic power of ethnic Chinese and Chinese immigrants who were prominently active in almost every sphere of commodity production. Chinese immigrants, for example, had built a substantial sugar belt along the northern coast of Java since the early seventeenth century. On a smaller scale, they would do the same in Penang and in Port Wellesley, just opposite this island on the Malay coast, where they became sugar planters of some consequence over the course of the nineteenth century.[32] British entrepreneurs were incapable of competing with the Chinese sugar millers. In Java, however, the colonial government—backed by metropolitan capital—succeeded in replacing the ethnic Chinese sugar millers by European factories in the 1840s. The emerging sugar conglomerate in Java was a remarkable case of stubborn government intervention pumping millions of guilders into this sector. However, even under Java's Cultivation System, ethnic Chinese capital continued to play a crucial role in the emergence of the plantation sector.

Beyond the northern Philippines and Java, ethnic Chinese and Chinese newcomers were well ahead of the Europeans in the development of plantations and mines. In Johore, the sultanate at the southern tip of the Malay Peninsula, Chinese entrepreneurs had opened up an impressive plantation frontier in the early nineteenth century. They produced pepper and gambier and later on seized on the booming opportunity offered by rubber. In the early twentieth century they employed over two hundred thousand workers who had come from China, almost thirty thousand immigrants from the Indonesian archipelago, and ten thousand from many other parts of the world, together far outnumbering the fifty thousand native Malays.[33] These Chinese entrepreneurs managed to stay independent from European capitalism by limiting their capital needs. First, through their sharecropping system they ably shifted part of the risk to the workers, who were often tied to them by debt. Second, their estates usually combined two crops: first, gambier with pepper and, later on, rubber with pineapples.[34] The crops had complementary cycles, enabling the efficient use of land and labor throughout the year. Moreover, the low profit but steady income of gambier balanced the riskier but more profitable pepper cultivation.

The development of Johore was part of a larger story. Over the course of the nineteenth century, the number of Chinese labor migrants engaged in cultivating cash crops or mining multiplied by ten, reaching the figure of about 1.2 million for British Malaya and over 400,000 for the Netherlands Indies in the 1920s. Further, much of this expansion was accomplished without any outside capital. It was precisely the economic autonomy of the Chinese migrant communities that made them both partners and competitors of the colonial administrations. Control over resources was a key element of colonial expansion, but it appears that colonial administrations were equally, or perhaps even more, guided by their anxiety about the sheer presence of the growing Chinese immigrant populations.[35] The violent clashes between Chinese gold miners and the Dutch authorities in West Kalimantan and with James Brooke in Sarawak in the mid–nineteenth century were not about the ownership of the minerals but about expanding colonialism seeking political control over these immigrant populations.[36]

Tin was an important example of how the desire to control immigration impelled colonial authorities to take control over production. Tin mining was a Chinese business even at times when the VOC had a monopoly of the tin trade in the entire Malay world. The Chinese *kongsis* were actually in charge, and most of the metal was shipped off to Chinese and Indian markets. In the early nineteenth century, Batavia took full control of the export of the Bangka tin but left the *kongsis* structure intact. In the Malay Peninsula, Chinese tin mining was conducted on a relatively modest scale without any interference from the British authorities until well into the nineteenth century. Massive Chinese immigration would, however, change that stance. The emergence of the American food industry as the dominant purchaser of tin triggered a bonanza in the still independent sultanate of Perak, on the western coast of the

Malay Peninsula. It would attract tens of thousands of Chinese miners, which in turn set the stage for colonial intervention.[37] A serious war between different Chinese ethnic groups in 1874 provided the pretext for the British administration of the Straits to extend its rule over Perak and Selangor.[38]

In these years, the colonial powers resorted to mechanization to contain migration. Both the British and Dutch encouraged mechanization in tin mining from the 1880s, without any immediate effect in terms of a declining labor force, however. The number of Chinese miners in Malaya first had to swell to about 150,000 before the introduction of dredges in 1912 began to diminish their numbers, eventually by a third.[39] In Bangka, government-employed engineers and administrators took over the management in 1884, although the ownership was left in the hands of the Chinese headmen. It was, however, because of a lack of outside investment that mechanization progressed much more slowly in Bangka than in the Malay Peninsula, and thus a reduction of the reliance on Chinese labor there was only achieved in the 1930s.[40]

Throughout Southeast Asia, mechanization was promoted to reduce the reliance on increasingly scarce and politically sensitive Chinese labor immigration. Mechanical plows entered the tobacco plantations of Sumatra's east coast in the 1880s, in the same years as the dredges were introduced in the tin mines. Elsewhere in Southeast Asia, at the Siamese rice frontiers, dredges were used for digging canals, and experiments were even undertaken with mechanizing rice cultivation.[41] The path of mechanization was obviously chosen to reduce any reliance on immigrant labor from China without endangering production.

ENGINEERING MIGRATION

Colonial expansion is usually described as a quest for land, oil, and minerals pushed by corporate enterprise that could count on the ministries of the colonies in the metropolitan capitals to protect their interests. For colonial administrations, however, the main concern was not to facilitate this business but to control labor and migratory flows toward the thinly populated but resource-rich territories of British Malaya, Sumatra, and Kalimantan. Colonial governments sought to extend their control in a gradual way, particularly in the nineteenth century, when their hold on the colonial outer regions was still fragile. The leniency shown by the Resident of West Kalimantan toward imports of debt slaves from Sulawesi in the 1870s, for example, strongly resembled the way in which at that time the colonial civil service condoned the atrocities perpetrated against coolies on the opposite shore of Sumatra, in Deli. Civil servants could do little against the power of local planters, whether they were ethnic Arabs, Bugis, Chinese, Dutch, or American. Colonial expansion could not exclusively rely on brute military force and hinged on successful collaboration with local grandees, Chinese businessmen, and Western planters. This also pertained to the realm of labor recruitment.

Of the three colonial powers in Island Southeast Asia, the American administration of the Philippines was the least accommodating to local conditions. It had not compromised on the abolition of slavery in the Philippines, nor had it given in to planters' interests. It had turned a deaf ear to desperate demands by sugar factories in the early 1900s to allow Chinese laborers in. Since the Philippines were part of U.S. territory, the Exclusion Laws of 1882 banning Chinese immigration applied to the Philippines, and the acting governor-general, W. H. Taft, was not prepared to repeal this.[42] The problem of labor shortages would only disappear once the sugar and rice estates of the Philippines began large-scale investments in mechanization.

While mechanization was a perfectly feasible way to reduce the reliance on Chinese labor immigrants on mining and sugar plantations, on the tobacco estates there was only limited room for mechanization, and on rubber plantations it was not an option at all. Planters and the colonial administrations of the Netherlands Indies and British Malaya were therefore searching for other providers of labor. The coastal stretches of Madras, the homeland of the Tamils, were an obvious source of labor supplies, as these were facing a declining land-labor ratio and had little plantation employment to offer.[43] On the eve of the Great Depression, over six hundred thousand Tamil workers were employed on the Malay Peninsula, alongside 1.2 million first-generation Chinese immigrants. In addition, three hundred thousand subjects of the Netherlands Indies, mostly Javanese, lived in British Malaya.[44] Lastly, minor farmers who had lost their means of production through rinderpest or other disasters came from Terengganu and Kelantan to the western and southwestern Residencies of the Malay Peninsula in the 1880s. All in all, Tamil and

Malay migrants—the latter coming both from the peninsula and Indonesia—made up almost half of the required labor force and thus drastically reduced the need for Chinese plantation labor.

The Netherlands Indies were even more successful in stemming the influx of workers from China than was British Malaya. In East Sumatra, Javanese workers were imported from the 1880s onward, but their recruitment was greatly expanded in the early years of the twentieth century.[45] To facilitate the procurement of labor by the plantation estates of Sumatra's east coast, the government of the Netherlands Indies removed the barriers to Javanese emigration from their island in 1906, which it had imposed forty-three years earlier to prevent their enslavement. At the same time, it established a labor inspectorate to monitor recruitment and labor conditions in the plantations and mines on the Outer Islands.[46] At the Deli plantations, the number of Chinese workers declined from 103,768 in 1900 to 50,000 in 1912 and further down to 27,000 in 1920. Over the same twenty years, the number of Javanese labor immigrants rose to over two hundred thousand.[47] By that time, rubber planters were relying almost exclusively on Javanese male and female workers, whereas the tobacco estates kept Chinese workers as sharecroppers—being the most cost-efficient method of cultivation—for the actual planting and tending of the tobacco plants.[48] All in all, by 1930 about 730,000 people had left Java for the Outer Islands, the majority of whom worked in the plantations.[49] By that year, the first-generation Chinese immigrants in the Netherlands Indies numbered a modest 433,842, among a total Chinese population of 1,190,014.[50] Chinese immigration had been successfully contained.

Once the Philippine population had recovered from the ravages of the war, and with agricultural mechanization underway, a labor surplus emerged that was able to supply the commodity frontiers in the south. Filipinos from Luzon and the Visayas fanned out to the thinly inhabited islands of Mindoro, Palawan, and Mindanao, which more than doubled these islands' share of the Philippine population to 20 percent within two generations.[51] Mindoro, located southwest of Luzon, became a producer of copra for the American market, worked by thousands of Ilocanos, who had fled Nueva Ecija after losing their land and being reduced to sharecroppers.[52] Migration to Mindanao was not just an economic project but a political objective. After the American administration had more or less suppressed the Moros resistance on Mindanao, it began to consider colonization by Christian Filipinos as a strategy to tighten its grip on the island, a policy that was intensified once the Philippines were granted self-government in 1934. Rather than handing Mindanao over to American corporate enterprise, the Philippine government was in favor of small-scale settlements from overpopulated areas.[53] It turned out to be a pious wish, as the U.S. Dole Food Company would acquire vast tracts of land in northern Mindanao to grow pineapples with migrant labor from the Visayas and increasingly from Luzon as well.[54] Further, foreign enterprise had already found its way to the southeastern corner of Mindanao well before the 1930s. Pioneered by Americans, the abaca industry in Mindanao was developed by Japanese investors, who hired about ten thousand Japanese workers together with tens of thousands of Filipino laborers to cultivate and harvest their seventy-one plantations in Davao, which was producing 40 percent of all the Philippine abaca by the eve of the Second World War.[55]

FAILED ATTEMPTS TO CONTROL THE LABOR GANGS

The years in which colonial governments and Western enterprise sought to tap alternative supplies of labor for Chinese *kongsi* labor were also a time of intensified efforts to extinguish slavery. Colonial bureaucracies and, in particular, their legal experts were acutely aware of the fact that the commodity frontiers entailed the risk of new forms of slavery emerging, particularly since many of these frontiers were not at all under the effective control of European administrators. Combating slavery and encouraging the flow of labor to resource-rich and thinly populated areas of Island Southeast Asia were potentially conflicting objectives. This was particularly the case because it was widely accepted that labor migrants who had been advanced their fare should not be allowed to walk away from their creditor until they had worked off their debt. The question was how to differentiate between debt bondage as a result of the fare and the abduction of indebted people.

Examples abound in historical records with regard to the difficulties surrounding the drawing up of a legal boundary between labor recruitment and enslavement. British and Dutch authorities more than once discovered that slave traders simply renamed their enslaved cargo as "peons," by which they meant laborers who were kept under bondage because they had to work off their debts.[56] The Dutch colonial government was complicit in such practices in the decades during which it bought slaves in West Africa to enlist them as soldiers and take them to the Netherlands Indies. Of course, these military men were no longer slaves, but neither did they consent to be shipped to the other side of the globe. Only after the British had repeatedly expressed their displeasure with these recruitment practices did the Dutch close their recruitment depot in Ghana in 1842, and even then only temporarily.[57] Meanwhile, in the Netherlands Indies slave markets still existed in European towns, and slaves were still advertised. Slavery and peonage were only banned in 1860, as discussed in chapter 3.[58] Not surprisingly, until that time human traffickers claimed that they stayed within the law with their transport of people under debt bondage. Incidentally, some government officials even agreed with them. The Resident of Sumatra's West Coast saw nothing illegal in the transport of "peons" from Nias to Padang in 1831, and it required the intervention of The Hague to straighten out that there was no legal excuse whatsoever for human trafficking.[59] The purchase of slaves to bring them to plantations was an illegal practice, even if they were set free after a few years. As long as enslaved people were in abundant supply, however, these practices would continue. Much of it escaped the government's gaze, although sometimes government officials reported it, and in rare cases it had international repercussions. This happened in 1846, when a Portuguese navy ship from East Timor intercepted a ship, jointly owned by a European and a Bugis, full of "peons" for a plantation run by a well-known Creole businessman in Makassar.[60]

As soon as the colonial government had cleared one embarrassing gray area, the ever-resourceful traffickers would create a new one. Bugis skippers who provided Bulungan (East Kalimantan) with slaves supplied them with proper passes and letters, and none of these involuntary passengers dared to tell Dutch authorities that they had been abducted against their will.[61] Dutch authorities had a hard time establishing whether people were fugitive slaves or passengers who had run away from paying back their fare—which had to be done by performing work—after being transported to East Kalimantan, for example. Were they slaves, or did they consent to their coerced working conditions as the consequence of their inability to pay their fare from Sulawesi?[62]

The authorities in Singapore faced similar challenges to draw the line between slavery and permissible debt bondage with regard to the influx of Chinese migrants. The debt-bonded workers and their skippers, recruiters, and employers belonged to the same Chinese ethnicity. For centuries and throughout Island Southeast Asia, Chinese *kongsis* worked with seasoned migrants, who were full-fledged shareholders, and with newcomers (*sinkehs*), who still had to repay their passage and subsistence costs.[63] Before the arrival of steamships, most workers traveled on overcrowded Chinese junks to the Malay Peninsula, and their fares were paid either by their foreman or by capitalists in China. Passengers without means became the pawns of the captain of the ship, who handed them over to the recruiters in return for the payment of the fare.[64] Often these skippers were just part of an infrastructure, in which boarding houses at Chinese port cities and in the Straits worked in tandem to drive up their profits to two to four times the amount of the actual fare and lodging costs.[65] They considered the labor migrants as merchandise and spoke about them as "piglets." As early as 1823, Raffles had put in place the first step to protect these Chinese immigrants by setting a limit of two years for debt repayment.[66]

Through this measure, Raffles wanted to reconcile his duty to suppress human trafficking with his willingness to honor the argument of employers that once they took over the debts from the freshly arrived immigrant workers they in fact had advanced part of the wage to these workers. Absconding without redeeming these advances had to be punishable as a criminal offense, the employers argued, and the colonial authorities agreed. As early as in 1832, the Dutch colonial government had prohibited Bangka tin miners from leaving their *kongsis* unless they had paid their debts.[67] Over time, colonial governments sought to regulate this bondage with a labor contract containing a penal sanction against absconding to ensure that the condition was indeed temporary and to protect workers from violence and mistreatment by their employers. The authorities were struggling, however, with limited inspection capacity, and much of the actual recruitment and labor conditions escaped their oversight. European plantation administrators, meanwhile, dealt with their labor force through foremen, such as the Tamil *kangani*, the Chinese *tandil*, the Javanese *mandur*, and the Philippine *kapatas*.[68]

For the Singapore authorities and for the town's prominent Chinese merchants as well, this coolie trade and the involvement of the secret societies caused the additional embarrassment of having a state within a state posing a direct threat to public order in the city.[69] Formal indentureship was an attempt by colonial authorities to regulate an extremely profitable business, which, with all its diplomatic entanglements, began to spiral out of control. These emerged in the late 1860s, when the Chinese imperial court, appeased by the highly welcome migrant remittances, abandoned its age-old disparaging attitude toward its emigrated subjects and began to ask for their protection. The government of the Netherlands Indies heeded this call and issued the so-called Coolie Ordinance in 1868, assigning to its civil servants the task of ascertaining that no coercion was involved in the immigration of Chinese laborers.[70]

In 1877, the government of the Straits established the Chinese Protectorate, which organized the central registration of all labor contracts, to address the concerns of the imperial court of China, rein in the coolie brokers, and act against the criminal and kidnapping practices that surrounded the coolie trade in Singapore.[71] A few years later, the Chinese Immigrants Ordinance was added to ensure that immigrants were not cheated with overcharged recruitment and boarding bills. These measures were not effective, nor did they address the problem of usury at the plantations and mines, where food, tobacco, and opium were frequently sold at 200 to 300 percent above market prices.[72] Regardless of whether it concerned plantations or mines run by either Chinese or European capitalists, most of the workers were trapped in debt and remained in the thrall of the Chinese headman, or captains, who supplied the *kongsis* with working capital.[73] The headmen were the interlocutors between the *kongsis* and the owners of the plantations or mines. In the case of the Bangka tin mines, they were even owners. At any rate, they must be distinguished from foremen, who were also intermediaries but still workers. Throughout Southeast Asia, these headmen reaped huge profits on supplies and credit, while shifting the business risks and losses to the *kongsis*.

Almost simultaneously with the establishment of the Chinese Protectorate, new regulations for Indian immigrant laborers were enacted. A Straits Immigration Agent was put in place to register and grant licenses to workers in the plantations to travel back to India and hire laborers for three years under indentureship, a system that became known as *laukeh* recruitment. While Chinese migrants came under their *kongsi* leaders, Tamil workers were led by their *kanganis*, a system British planters had become acquainted with in Ceylon. The *kangani* was usually the most senior man of a group of relatives or village dwellers. He shared in the profits made by the planters and controlled his laborers by virtue of the social status he already enjoyed back home—and by the fact that most workers were indebted to him.[74] Pressure by the government of India to abolish the penal sanction for Indian workers, combined with diminishing labor supplies in the early years of the rubber boom, convinced the government of British Malaya of the need for a new approach. As a major employer of Tamil laborers for the construction of public works, it had a direct interest in a change to a system of government-assisted migration like those already in place in a number of white settler colonies. Under this new system, implemented in 1910, labor immigration from India was overseen and its funding administered by a government committee, with a junior role allotted to private business.

Although the introduction of government-assisted migration in 1910 did much to mitigate the consequences of the abolition of the penal sanction for Indian workers, it did little to stop the massive desertions. In the middle of the rubber boom, plantations frantically competed for labor, and an equally frantic mobility of the labor gangs headed by their *kanganis* was the result. The sugar plantations did not survive the abolition of the penal sanction and were converted to rubber estates, adding to the further specialization of British Malaya in this crop.[75] All in all, it is a history that plainly contradicts the argument made by Huff and Caggiano that the penal sanction could be abolished in British Malaya thanks to an abundance of labor.[76] It was just the other way around; the penal sanction had become toothless because of labor scarcity and the growing power of the labor gangs.

From the 1880s onward, competition among employers in the Malay Peninsula, Sumatra, and Bangka intensified.[77] The rate of desertion of indentured laborers went up so rapidly in the Malay Peninsula that the indentured system and truck system began to fall apart. The labor gangs saw their bargaining power improving, and at the same time, the workers became less dependent on their creditors. They arrived more and more on their own account with the help of family and relatives already residing in British Malaya, encouraged by letters and remittances. At the time that the formal abolition of the penal sanction was enacted, the majority of workers no longer came to the Malay Peninsula under indentureship. These migrants were, moreover, increasingly worldly-wise and less likely to be cheated by their employers with truck systems.[78] Workers—as well as entire labor gangs—escaped as soon as they saw a chance to free themselves from debts enforced on them.[79] Since only half of these deserters were purportedly caught by the police, thousands of miners found new *kongsis*, and thousands of rubber workers obtained employment at other plantations or may have started their own rubber gardens.[80]

JAVANESE EMIGRATION AND THE PENAL SANCTION

Colonial authorities introduced the penal sanction to regulate recruiting practices, in order to keep them from deteriorating into outright slave trafficking and, in the case of Chinese labor migrants to the Netherlands, to prevent their permanent settlement. It had no role whatsoever in solving labor shortages because that was best done by giving room to the *kongsi* and *kangani* recruitment systems. The Belitung tin mines are a case in point. In sharp contrast to the Bangka mines, these privately owned mines enjoyed the luxury of an oversupply of labor. They could rely on what has been termed *migration systems*: a stable connection between provenance and destination sustained by personal networks. Practically all the new miners arrived under the "patronage" of their relatives in Belitung, as the high-ranking civil servant Hendrik Colijn wrote in 1910. He was sent to the tin island to resolve a conflict between the mine directors and the island's administration, which considered the coolie ordinance indispensable, particularly its clause about obligatory repatriation of the workers at the end of their contract to be paid by the employer. In no way did it want to encourage permanent Chinese immigration.[81] The directors of the company loathed the coolie ordinance and the penal sanction, considering them cumbersome regulations jeopardizing their smooth labor supplies. Even though Colijn concurred with them that the indentured labor regulations were not helpful at all in their case, Batavia sided with the local administrators and ruled that the coolie ordinance was needed to ensure the workers' repatriation to China by the company after the expiry of their contracts.

The entanglement of colonial geopolitics, concerns about human trafficking, and entrepreneurial interests gives the story of the penal sanction its peculiar twists. Its existence cannot be explained in purely economic terms. In some cases, indentured labor contracts were considered but not implemented, in others they were short-lived, and where they survived until the very end of colonial times—namely in Indonesia's Outer Islands—this defied sound economic judgment. Grasping the complexity of this history is of direct relevance to understanding today's problems of coercion and trafficking that accompany the extensive flows of migrants from this part of the world. A case in point is the prolonged existence of the penal sanction in the Outer Islands of the Netherlands Indies until the very end of colonial rule. To understand this story better, it is helpful to discuss it in a wider context and bring in the comparison with the sugar belts of Java and Negros, where in both cases the penal sanction had been lobbied for by the sugar interests. In fact, the penal sanction did exist for a few years in Java. Eventually, the sugar lords reached the same conclusion as their colleagues in British Malaya: that the penal sanction was relatively ineffective. Both in Java and the northern Philippines, employers could rely on patron-client relationships to ensure sufficient labor supplies.

In the Philippines, labor shortages were endemic during the first twenty years of American rule. They were the upshot of high mortality rates during the Philippine Revolution, of a lack of animal power as a result of rinderpest, and last but not least of a ramshackle infrastructure.[82] In 1890, when the Spanish were still ruling, U.S. Secretary of the Interior Dean Worcester noted: "Many a time have I seen rice and sugarcane spoiling in the field, for want of men to harvest them."[83] Workers easily absconded because plantations were vying for their labor, as one observer wrote about Negros in 1910: "Breaches of faith by contractors after receiving advance money are frequent, and numerous instances are cited where out of twenty or thirty men reporting for work and receiving a month's wages in advance, half have escaped within the week."[84] Their attempts, supported by sympathetic officials, to convince Manila to act against desertion were in vain. As early as 1878, the governor of Negros had proposed a penal sanction of fifteen days incarceration for desertion, although this found no favor in the eyes of the Spanish author-ities in Manila.[85] Requests by planters to legalize the practice of advanc-ing their workers' tax obligations in return for which they took their *cedulas personales* (documents that indicated whether their holders had paid their taxes) fell equally on deaf ears with the central government of the Philippines. It declared itself unwilling to mix tax collection with the interests of private parties.[86]

At any rate, the sugar lords did not grumble too loudly about their failure to win over the Spanish authorities in Manila for their cause. They could still rely on the local army and police to control their seasonal laborers, and their tenants and sharecroppers were firmly under their wing as indebted clients.[87] Practices of informal debt bondage were ubiq-uitous in the Philippine sugar sector and were actually defended by the Filipino members in the Philippine Commission, the appointed Senate of the Philippines. Any action against these practices would purportedly have encouraged "abuses on the part of farm laborers working under the share system and the employees of the workshops."[88] The Americans were not impressed, however, and in 1912 legislation was enacted prohibiting "slavery, involuntary servitude, peonage and the sale or purchase of human beings in the Philippine Islands."[89] Yet this ban on bonded labor remained a paper tiger, in particular because of the resilience of the patron-client relationships. This was also what the case of Java shows us.

In contrast to the Philippines, the penal sanction for agricultural workers in Java *was* introduced, in 1872, immediately on the withdrawal of the colonial civil service from conscripting labor for sugar planta-tions.[90] It only survived until 1879, when the Dutch Parliament decided that regulating the labor market for Dutch subjects was not an issue for penal law. By doing so, it defied massive lobbying both from private enter-prise and from colonial civil servants.[91] The option of enacting a penal sanction for Java resurfaced twice on the colonial agenda, once in the 1890s and again in 1913, when labor unrest flared up during the emer-gence of the Sarekat Islam, the first nationalist mass movement in Java.[92] A third attempt to legislate against desertion was made in 1918, when sugar factories in East Java were luring away one another's cane cutters. A regulation was drafted to allow factories to postpone payment of most of the wages until all the work had been carried out.[93] It was never implemented.

As early as the 1890s, most sugar factories in Java were convinced that they did not need a penal sanction because they had a circle of a few miles surrounding them, the so-called *areaal*, allotted to them by the government, within which they could hire land for their cane growing without external competition. Via the village heads and the *mandurs* (foremen), they recruited men and women, which often involved debt contracts. Some factories promoted gambling and opium smoking to keep the workers penniless and indebted.[94] However, that was not the rule, nor was it common in Java's estates to keep workers indebted via a truck system. Most plantation estates were located in densely settled regions where there were enough shops around to keep prices down.[95] Patron-client relationships with nearby villages and, particularly in East Java, seasonal Madurese immigrant labor gangs provided sugar factories and cane fields with sufficient labor.

The apparent lack of a patron-client system for "greasing" recruitment goes a long way toward explaining why the penal sanction was deemed useful in Deli. However, this leaves the question of how this penal sanction was revived for Deli, as it had already been declared illegal for the Javanese—and all Dutch subjects, for that matter—by the Dutch Parliament. The explanation is that the indentured labor system was originally only conceived for Chinese labor, not for Dutch subjects, but that when the first Javanese workers were hired for Deli in 1889, they were tacitly brought under the indentured regime.[96] To end this legal irregularity, a new coolie ordinance was drafted in the early years of the twentieth century that explicitly excluded subjects of the Kingdom of the Netherlands from the penal sanction.[97] This draft was, however, buried after vehement protests by the tobacco planters, who were 75 percent reliant on Javanese workers at the time.

There was nevertheless a general feeling that the days of the penal sanction were numbered. In South Sumatra, it was abolished in 1912, early on during the rubber boom. In these years, entire groups left the plantations of Lampung to find employment in smallholder rubber tapping or to work on the construction of the local railway.[98] They were easily replaced by other workers, who arrived by the hundreds every week across Sunda Strait, either on the ships of the Koninklijke Paketvaart Maatschappij or on a motley fleet of other vessels.[99] Plantations could obtain workers from Java as long as they were allowed to return to their families back in Java during Ramadan. The tobacco belt of Jember in the most eastern corner of Java was served by cheap railway transport that maintained the bonds between the migrant workers and their villages of origin.[100] Likewise, the construction of the South Sumatra railway line just before the First World War would facilitate migration into Lampung and even farther north into Sumatra.[101]

The massive migrations toward the plantations in Java and South Sumatra and the oversupplies of labor for the Belitung mines make one wonder why in the 1920s the plantations in East Sumatra had to pay the astonishing amount of 150 guilders for each coolie (more than a coolie earned in a year), half of which went into the pockets of the recruiters. Actually, the Belitung mines only paid 30 guilders for the fare—which it billed to the Chinese *numpang* (*kongsi*) of which the worker became a member—and 20 guilders as a premium for the *laukeh*.[102] Clearly, it did not appeal to Javanese men and women to leave their homes for a full three years and work in Deli under the shadow of the humiliating and loathed penal sanction for a wage more or less the same as in the Java sugar factories.[103] The only way to hire the tens of thousands of Javanese workers needed by Deli every year was by offering substantial advances and sending expensive crimps to the most remote villages of Java. The high recruitment costs, however, just put a premium on employers' attempts to lure workers from other plantations. The large advances enticed coolies to walk away from the very moment that they had pocketed this money at the recruitment depot in Java.[104] Even by the late 1920s, when conditions had putatively improved, 12 percent of the coolies under penal sanctions deserted in their first year and another 8 percent in the second.[105] The Deli plantations had maneuvered themselves into a vicious circle of depressed wages and awkward labor conditions, on the one hand, and staggering recruitment costs, on the other.

The crimps recruited mostly Javanese who had a good reason to escape from their own communities.[106] Almost 80 percent of the recruited workers for East Sumatra gave false information about their name and the village they came from. Whether this was always done on purpose cannot be determined, but it is certain that quite a few saw Deli as a way to leave debts behind or to elude criminal persecution. Female migrants may have escaped from an unbearable marriage or for want of other options after having been widowed and left with little. Some abandoned their children without notice, hoping that relatives would take care of them. None of these workers wanted to leave traces behind.[107] Above all, it shows that in no way did the migration from Java to East Sumatra resemble the migration of Chinese and Tamil workers, whose labor gangs were embedded in their own villages and constituted migration networks. The fact that Javanese workers for Deli were recruited outside the patron-client relationships made the migration to Deli unique and explains both the longevity of the penal sanction and the widespread trafficking and crimping practices attending it.

LOW-WAGE ENCLAVES, PENAL SANCTIONS, AND TRAFFICKING

The indentured labor regime of the Deli plantations in East Sumatra maintained a low-wage enclave in an environment where commodity booms resulted in a tremendous demand for labor.[108] Smallholder rubber gardens in Sumatra, plantations in the Malay Peninsula, the Belitung mines, and tea plantations in Sumatra offered plenty of opportunities to earn much more than in Deli. The United States Rubber Company did respond to the realities of the labor market by raising wages at its Deli estates, but even for this company it remained to be seen whether that was enough.[109] Labor shortages were huge and left, for example, a third of the rubber trees of the smallholders in Palembang (Sumatra) untapped by the mid-1920s. In those years, a tapper at a small rubber garden in Sumatra could earn up to 75 guilders per month, which was more than the amount a government clerk earned and three times as much as the Deli plantations paid.[110] Indigenous rubber planters even imported labor from the Straits Settlements via their own informal recruitment systems, using Chinese transporters.[111] Chinese traffickers helped deserters from the plantations of East Sumatra by hiding them in lodgings (*kedehs nassi*) and providing fake passes. Javanese workers who deserted not only went to smallholder rubber plots in Sumatra but also crossed the Straits.

To combat these practices, as early as in 1887 the government of the Netherlands Indies had prohibited any recruitment of workers for destinations outside its territory.[112] This ban was far from watertight, and quite a few migrants came illegally via Sumatra to British Malaya.[113] Thousands of them ended up in North Borneo.[114] This cash-strapped tobacco region and later on rubber belt hosted a party of adventurers who put every laborer they could get—according to some, even slaves from nearby Tawi Tawi—on small plots of tobacco land to work as sharecroppers.[115] Illegal recruitment also occurred in the impoverished rural societies of the principalities, where crimps from Singapore conniving with hajis brought people with false passports to their city, where they came under debt contracts and were hired out to plantations. To stem the trafficking of Javanese laborers into the Straits and beyond, the Dutch authorities started a rather fruitless maritime patrol along the east coast of Sumatra.[116] At best, they received some lukewarm assistance from the authorities of British Malaya, who had no interest in stopping this passage and were in fact quite happy with this strengthening of the Malay component of the population and the influx of valuable wet rice-growing skills.[117] By 1931, Javanese were the third-largest immigrant group in British Malaya.

Much of the trafficking of Javanese to the Malay Peninsula and North Borneo was an offshoot of the pilgrimage to Mecca.[118] Between 1860 and 1930, the colonial reports of the Netherlands Indies recorded 628,235 pilgrims departing for Mecca, more than a third of whom traveled during the commodity boom of the roaring twenties.[119] This figure does not encompass all Dutch subjects on pilgrimage, however, since many followed another itinerary via Sumatra, crossing the Straits into Singapore and thereby circumventing the checks and controls of the Dutch colonial authorities. Pilgrims from the eastern part of the archipelago sailed on dhows to Singapore to embark for the port of Jeddah accessing Hejaz.[120] Every year, thousands of Indonesians were stranded in Singapore and signed up to work as indentured laborers. In this huge flow of pilgrimage and labor migration, legalized and illicit practices had become entangled.[121]

Human trafficking, deceit, abuse of power, the confinement of labor migrants, and outright violence are the troublesome continuities that link nineteenth-century commodity production, either under slavery or indenture, with twenty-first-century recruitment for overseas work all over Asia and the Gulf States. Like contemporary governments, colonial authorities tried to reconcile economic interests with their duties to maintain public order and protect their subjects. The colonial government of the Netherlands Indies had set its hopes on regulating the coolie migration through licensed recruitment agencies. In the Javanese port cities from where labor migrants departed, European civil servants were assigned to check whether these workers were leaving voluntarily and knew what job they had been hired to do, a measure that was largely ineffective because these migrants were instructed by their crimps about what to tell the colonial authorities. The crimps meanwhile became increasingly ruthless as the rewards for each coolie they could deliver soared during the rubber boom of the 1910s. Recruiting costs increased from 100 to 160 guilders per worker, of which only about 20 guilders went for the transport from Java to Deli.[122] *Laukeh* recruitment—plantation workers going back home to convince their fellow villagers to sign up—was embraced by the planters as an alternative, but despite the support of the labor inspectors and other authorities of the Netherlands Indies, the commercial recruiters were capable of derailing the *laukeh* recruitment in Java by outbidding the *laukehs* with advances to workers.[123] The effort was compounded by volatile economic conditions during the First World War and its aftermath.[124] Meanwhile, attempts by the colonial government to encourage the settlement of Javanese in East Sumatra, who could provide the plantations with a stable workforce, were fruitless as long as wages were so low in comparison with what was paid everywhere else in Sumatra, particularly by rubber smallholders.

The Deli rubber planters, who clung less stubbornly to low wages and to the penal sanctions than their colleagues in tobacco, suggested following the example of British Malaya by starting government-assisted migration and establishing an insurance fund, which would compensate a plantation for its recruitment expenses when laborers left before the expiration of their contract.[125] Again, however, without a properly functioning *laukeh* system, such a government-assisted scheme still had to rely on the practices of crimps. The same happened in 1916, when the Sumatra plantations received government permission to organize their own recruitment, bypassing the commercial recruitment agencies. This did not put the crimps out of business either.[126] Moreover, always being short of labor, plantations desperately tried to force workers to reengage. For that purpose, gambling sessions and other leisure activities that could rip them off were organized.[127]

Although far from egalitarian, labor gangs—the backbone of migration networks—at least protected workers against the worst exploitation by plantations or mines. Wherever the *kongsi* system was still intact, remittances might have been at an acceptable level, as was the case for the Chinese sharecroppers of the East Sumatra tobacco plantations who returned to China with savings ranging between 50 and 80 guilders. The Chinese miners of Belitung fared even better, as they usually took home over 200 guilders.[128] The Chinese workers' remittances from Bangka were a pittance, however. The colonial civil servant A. D. A. de Kat Angelino concluded in 1919 that a small oligarchy of ethnic Chinese shareholders of these mines, who had replaced the *kongsi* leaders, compensated the losses they incurred through the compulsory sales of tin to the government at fixed low prices by squeezing money from the miners through a truck system and usury. In the six years before De Kat Angelino's report, these shareholders managed to accumulate ten million guilders, which they partly invested in white pepper production. As a result, about 78 percent of the miners returned to China penniless.[129] The Javanese workers in Deli did not fare any better. The colonial civil servant J. W. Meijer Ranneft saw with his own eyes in 1914 that thousands of destitute coolies reengaged immediately on their return to Semarang.[130] The situation had hardly improved by the late 1920s, when various investigations into the matter assessed that migrant workers in Deli could at best save a mere 3 cents per day from their wages.[131] Despite banking facilities created for the purpose, annual remittances amounted to a pitiful 25 cents per average worker in the late 1920s and a mere 65 cents ten years later.[132]

Meanwhile, the planters, particularly the tobacco planters among them, tried to impress on the colonial government that coolies were becoming increasingly insolent and violent and that the prolongation of the penal sanction was thus imperative.[133] It was necessary, they argued, in order to maintain a labor regime that was one and a half times as productive as it would have been with free laborers. With its ten working hours per day, it had contributed to the impressive 30 percent hike in labor productivity that had been achieved in the 1920s, critics wryly observed.[134] It is no coincidence that in the course of the 1920s, the planters no longer defended the penal sanction as a means to stem desertion but as being indispensable to enforce labor discipline on what they would not admit were severely underpaid workers.[135] In the eyes of knowledgeable Social Democrats such as J. E. Stokvis and J. van Gelderen, the penal sanction was the most effective weapon against any form of collective action, a message the latter conveyed to ILO Director-General Albert Thomas, who visited the Netherlands Indies in 1929. There was no doubt among Dutch Social Democrats that indentured labor ought to be outlawed by the ILO Forced Labor Convention, which in fact happened when it was adopted in 1930.[136] This convention gave the American tobacco industry the perfect argument to convince Congress that the Sumatra product should be banned. The tobacco planters of Deli had no choice: in 1931, they declared that the penal sanction no longer had a place in their estates.[137]

They could afford this step, however, because after 1928 the percentage of indentured laborers was already sharply declining in the Outer Islands of the Netherlands Indies. In that year, free migration of Javanese to Deli started after the oil refineries in Balikpapan had shown the way for successful *laukeh* recruitment without a penal sanction.[138] The system was embedded in the social fabric of the village, as not only the family of the worker but also the village head and village scribe had to give their written consent, for which they were paid, respectively, a guilder and 50 cents. Similar to the situation in Java's sugar belts, the local brokers became part of the recruitment system, which would resurface in the context of postcolonial overseas migration. Economic factors worked in favor of free recruitment, as transport had become faster and cheaper over the years, whereas poverty in Java had increased.[139] Technically, the need for a penal sanction diminished, too. The establishment of a dactyloscopic (fingerprint) bureau in Deli's capital Medan in 1926, initially targeted at communist activists, impeded the lively trade in fake passes and discouraged plantations from hiring coolies who had deserted.[140] The desertion problem was further addressed by a government-imposed registration chamber that obliged all employers to register newly arrived overseas workers.[141]

The penal sanction was, however, far from dead: it was still a clause in the contracts of thirty thousand workers throughout Sumatra, Bangka, and Belitung by 1937.[142] Further, their numbers were still growing at the time, with the return of the labor shortages at the plantations of the Outer Islands and smallholders reentering cash-crop production. Moreover, since the village-based recruitment system had been degraded during the Depression years, the government saw no other solution than again to hand out licenses to commercial recruiting agencies, which in turn employed crimps paid per recruited worker.[143] The sad lesson to be learned from this is that trafficking and deceit moved with the economic cycles: they existed before colonialism, alongside the colonial domain, and would outlive colonialism. When labor migration to plantations, for construction and domestic work, mushroomed in Island Southeast Asia from the 1970s, licensed recruiters and their crimps as well as illicit traffickers were doing better business than ever, as we will see in the final chapter.

CHAPTER FIVE

The Periphery Revisited

Commodity Exports, Food, and
Industry, 1870s–1942

The economist and Nobel Prize winner Arthur W. Lewis once lamented plantation economies for their highly regressive taxation regimes, neglect of food production, and low enrollment in education. In his view, gross underspending by colonial governments aggravated the effects of the worsening terms of trade for commodities that marked the interwar years and turned this period into one big depression for the tropics.[1] Taxation in the Netherlands Indies was indeed worrisomely regressive, favoring village elites and, through that, further strengthening patron-client relationships. Meanwhile, corporate enterprise did everything in its power to reduce taxation on its exports.[2] Not much better, and in some respects even worse, was the situation in the Philippines, where the United States had imposed a zero-duty tariff on all trade between itself and its dependency. As a result, the Philippine tax revenue stayed at just 7 percent of the country's GDP in the 1930s, lower than Indonesia at the time.[3] Likewise in British Malaya, export duties on its cash crops were negligible, and opium taxes had to provide half of the Straits' revenue by the mid-1920s.[4]

Meanwhile, the balance of payments gives an indication of the scale of extraction of capital, which was more severe for the Netherlands Indies than for the other two colonies of Island Southeast Asia. Foreign direct investment was a pittance compared with what white settler frontiers in the temperate zones received.[5] For most of the 1920s, the export value was twice as high as the import value for the Netherlands Indies, and capital was massively remitted from its mature plantation sector to Europe and the United States. The Philippines and British Malaya had a much smaller but still considerable trade surplus of about 23 percent in the early 1920s.[6] Moreover, both British Malaya and the Philippines kept substantial reserves in Great Britain and the United States, respectively.[7] Although smallholders dominated the cultivation of marketable crops in most of the extensive space of Island Southeast Asia, exploiting a welcome source of additional income, the majority of the region's population lived huddled together in the plantation and mining belts. The focus of this chapter is on these particular areas. The economies of these relatively small spaces were deeply affected by estate agriculture, and a large proportion of their populations relied on the global commodity market for their subsistence. These conditions were not unlike Lewis's Caribbean background. This was more than anything else the consequence of rapid population growth in Java and in the northern Philippines as well as massive migrations toward plantation and mining provinces all over Island Southeast Asia. Yet rural conditions as well as per capita income in Java compared unfavorably with the relatively densely populated northern Philippines, a fact this chapter will also focus on.

In Java in particular, the combination of fluctuating commodity prices, high demographic growth, low rice prices, and peasants' risk-reducing living strategies all contributed to declining labor productivity in food agriculture and to halting mechanization in the cane fields. The growing population of landless people rarely found full-time employment because work at plantations was usually seasonal, as was much of the nonagricultural labor. Dock work, for example, was at its peak after the milling season, when sugar had to be shipped to overseas markets. The seasonality of the work and the sharp seasonal fluctuations of paddy and milled rice prices brought penury not only to urban and plantation workers but also to marginal peasants who did not produce enough rice to cover their own needs.

While the traditional debate on peripheralization places much emphasis on deindustrialization, the argument proposed in this book is that population densities and modes of labor control—particularly plantations versus smallholder cultivation—should take center stage in our attention. Peripheralization (and the "reversal of fortune" thesis, for that matter) is situated in the countryside, and in order to understand it we need to analyze the workings of the rural economy. While the favorable terms of trade led to intense specialization in cash crops, its potentially detrimental effects made themselves particularly felt in the area of food production, precisely as Lewis has indicated, and less so in the industrial sector. I do not agree with the contention of Bassino and Williamson that the favorable terms of trade for commodities led to the "biggest deindustrialization in the global periphery."[8] The nexus between commodity exports and deindustrialization was a topical issue for Latin America but of less relevance to the on-average poorer, less industrialized, and often more densely populated societies of Island Southeast Asia.

It is also with respect to food production that the American administration in Manila steered a course radically different from Batavia. The former's objective to achieve food self-sufficiency and expand food production while imposing tariffs on rice imports from Mainland Southeast Asia impinged positively on the rural per capita output. Meanwhile, in Java the specialization in exporting plantation products encouraged food imports that distorted the local food market. This in turn was highly detrimental to the capacity of Javanese peasants to generate cash income. Java's rice market was small, only accounting for 15 percent of all the rice available, and half of it was made up of imported rice.[9] Cheap food imports and high prices for export commodities seriously harmed local food production, as the case of British Malaya shows. Here, any attempts to expand food production were simply defeated by the fact that growing export crops paid better than food crops.[10]

Despite the increasing scarcity of irrigated land, rice prices in Java in the 1920s had returned to their low, late-nineteenth-century level, as the combined result of substitution by other crops and cheap rice imports.[11] The low rice prices had a largely unnoticed depressing effect on rural incomes. When the colonial government commissioned an extensive investigation in 1901 into the "Diminishing Welfare" of Java, it recognized that wages had gone down and that for most rural dwellers income was "just sufficient." It also regretted that large quantities of rice had to be imported, but it did not link the precarity of rural subsistence with low food prices and distorted rice markets.[12] On the contrary, since the 1870s the colonial government had encouraged rice imports as a cure for rising rice prices, which moreover peaked sharply in February and March, the rice-scarce months preceding the new harvest. Farmers whose stocks were depleted by that time had to buy on credit and sell just after the harvest to redeem their debts. In fact, fluctuating rice prices engendered speculative practices by rice middlemen all over monsoon and tropical Asia, including the Philippines, where it put a substantial proportion of rural income into the hands of speculators.[13] In Java, this problem was exacerbated because many farmers also sold rice to pay their land rent, and with bad harvests, they had to borrow. Cyclical rice shortages were a key mechanism of perpetual indebtedness, of patron-client relationships, and in Java of tying the countryside to sugar factories. In the late nineteenth century, the experts of the government of the Netherlands Indies identified these problems and addressed them by promoting village rice barns, so-called *desa lumbungs*, as a cooperative measure to save peasants from being in thrall to the moneylenders. These measures were not very successful, however: government investigators discovered in the 1920s that debts amounted to half the annual income of the rural population.[14]

Being genuinely concerned about rice shortages, colonial authorities had turned a blind eye to the discouraging effects of these imports on Java's rice production. Relatively low productivity per hectare and the subsiding role of rice as a source of income were the root causes of the rural poverty of Java. This also strengthened the position of the sugar factories in Java's countryside because with the low paddy prices, cane yielded far more income per hectare than rice.[15] The need for cash made by-employment an absolute necessity, even for peasant families who theoretically might have had enough land to be self-sufficient in food. In addition, in times of bad harvests this by-employment prevented starvation. In the 1930s, the collapse of the sugar industry, combined with bad rice harvests, led to hunger in quite a few sugar districts of Java.[16]

Low food prices and the influx of cheap rice were crucial factors in keeping Java's export crops competitive. Low food prices were far more important in the Netherlands Indies as a cash-crop exporter than in the Philippines, with its privileged access to the U.S. market. Its American administration could afford to allow rice prices to stay above regional market rates, in order to support its policies toward rice self-sufficiency. Together with a redistribution of idle land, this policy augmented the acreage under rice. Furthermore, considerable investments in irrigation resulted in an increase of the yield per acre of over 30 percent. By contrast, in the Netherlands Indies the total budget for irrigation in real terms diminished after 1917. As a result, the acreage under irrigation stagnated, and the yield per hectare in Java declined by a few percent.[17] Meanwhile, in the Netherlands Indies, experimental research on rice improvement was glaringly underfinanced compared with the sums of private money spent on the experimental stations for estate crops. While in the early 1920s the Experimental Station of Pasuruan, with a staff of sixty, succeeded in developing a cane variety with a 30 percent higher yield, nothing comparable was accomplished in the rice fields in those years.[18] It must be acknowledged that the situation was not much better in the Philippines, despite the opening of an experimental agricultural station in Los Baños in 1908. It would take another half-century before this institute earned its fame as the cradle of the Green Revolution.[19] Moreover, it is to the credit of the Dutch colonial governments that, perhaps inspired by the success of Pasuruan, it stepped up its efforts at rice improvement. At the experimental gardens in Bogor, a systematic selection and breeding program commenced in 1926 and reported its first successes on the eve of the Second World War.[20]

Still, the fact that serious research on rice improvement came at such a late stage is indicative of the dominance of plantation interests. As long as cane and paddy competed for the same fields, sugar factories had no interest at all in increasing the yields of rice productivity per acre, and as long as Siam and Burma produced enough rice and the paddy-per-acre yield stagnated in Java, they could make an economically sound case for specialization in sugar exports rather than substituting for food imports. However, this came at a severe cost: low rice prices and stagnating productivity per hectare aggravated the indebtedness of Java's rural population and made it difficult for farmers to pay their land rent.[21]

HANDICRAFTS: REVISITING A DISMAL PICTURE

The starting point of this chapter is the question of why Java fell behind the Philippines economically in the early twentieth century, as well as behind the rest of Island Southeast Asia, for that matter. The gist of the answer is that it should be attributed to population pressure and distortions in Java's rural economy, which was dominated by plantation interests, rather than to putative deindustrialization or to dependence on commodity exports. One could argue against this contention by pointing out that in the 1950s the Philippines were far more industrialized than Indonesia and actually the most industrialized country in Southeast Asia. This may lend some credibility to official figures indicating already relatively high levels of industrialization of the Philippines compared with Java by the early twentieth century.

There are three important caveats to be made here. First, the data is difficult to compare, not least because cottage production was not included in relevant government reporting in the Netherlands Indies, whereas it was listed in the census reports of the Philippines, although underreporting might have taken place.[22] Second, precisely because the manufacturing sector was predominantly in a cottage setting, it was not overly vulnerable to cheap industrial imports. Third, whereas in plantation economies industrialization serving domestic markets might have been impeded, this does not pertain to the export sector. Coal, fuel, and electricity were patently present in the commodity export sector, most notably in sugar production, but since this mechanization increased labor productivity enormously, its overall employment effects were limited and could even have been negative. In fact, the same would be the case for the mechanization of the textile industry in the Philippines and the Netherlands Indies in the 1930s. In sum, the available occupational data needs to be put in context and the way in which and for what purpose they were collected merits proper analysis.[23]

Although the Philippine economy appears to have been slightly more diversified than Java's—it had a well-developed shipbuilding sector, for example—there are also indications that the Dutch authorities may have painted the situation in overly dark colors. As mentioned before, at the turn of the twentieth century, the Dutch Ministry for the Colonies had initiated the Diminishing Welfare investigation, and prominent among the matters of its concern were deindustrialization and lack of industry as causes of growing rural poverty in Java. Working under this assumption, Dutch experts were inclined to underrate the importance of the cottage sector.[24] However, the available data and observations are inconsistent, and the incomplete information precludes any straightforward conclusions about a possible decline in manufacturing. The only rough observation one can make is that over the nineteenth century, nonagricultural employment in Java remained at around 20 percent of the employable population.[25] Some sectors may have declined, although even that is difficult to establish.

Government officials and later on economic historians have been somewhat quick to point out that technological change and cheap imports invariably ruined traditional crafts. For example, it has been suggested that shipbuilding in Java waned, although a paucity of data for the early nineteenth century makes it hard to corroborate this point.[26] It is plausible that railways put part of Java's coastal shipping out of business. It is certain that the introduction of steel ships diminished the demand for timber vessels in Java, a fact that became clear through the recovery of the ship wharfs that crafted wooden vessels during the First World War, when the price of steel rose steeply.[27] Still, it was not a universal trend in the Netherlands Indies. Madura continued to have a flourishing shipbuilding sector, providing its population with an indispensable means of transport.[28] The picture in the Philippines was even more mixed. The arrival of steel ships devastated the vibrant shipbuilding sectors at the Gulf of Lingayen and at Sorsogon.[29] However, in Manila there were still thousands employed in the machine and shipbuilding sector, and Cavite had a large navy wharf. Together, these locations were employing six to seven thousand mechanics.[30]

Even in sectors that had to cope with cheap imports, decline was not the inevitable outcome. In the early twentieth century, Dutch colonial experts claimed that people in Java had given up fishing, noting that fishponds proliferated and that imported dried fish from Siam competed with local fisheries. Their conclusion seems all too plausible because fishing was arduous and ill-paid work.[31] However, in a Residency such as Rembang, the coastal waters were bustling with fishing boats, while at the same time many new fishponds were filled. To all appearances, both sea and pond fisheries in this Residency, as well as elsewhere in South Sulawesi, thrived thanks to increasing demand from the sugar estates of East Java.[32] In other words, we should not take these narratives of decline for granted, particularly not at the time of the booming plantation economy, which exerted a growing demand for food, tobacco, textiles, and other items that could be manufactured locally.

The available data for employment suggests a slightly more diversified labor market in the Philippines than in Java, but in both cases employment in manufacturing workshops and factories was of relatively marginal importance. According to Cavada, about 4 percent of the employable Philippine population was engaged in industrial pursuits in 1876, but his overview is both inconsistent, as it includes transport (shipping), and incomplete, as it probably underestimates female involvement in textiles.[33] For the Netherlands Indies, the *Colonial Report of 1875* lists 2.7 percent of the male employable population as being involved in manufacturing but ignores female work. By 1900, male involvement in manufacturing, construction, and mining was about 11.7 percent of the employable population in the Philippines, compared with a mere 7.5 in Java, according to the available statistics. However, for Java, substantial numbers of workers—in the Madurese salt pans or railway construction, for example—either seem to have been omitted or included in the unspecific category of "coolies and co-workers."[34]

Both in the Philippines and in the Netherlands Indies, manufacturing was predominantly carried out at home by women. The importance of this cottage industry was brought to light by the American census surveyors, who organized a door-to-door survey in the Philippines in 1903. They found out how many farm households combined spinning, weaving, hat making, or fishing and included that in their reporting. From this, we can deduce that 34.5 percent of all employable Filipinas were engaged in manufacturing.[35] By contrast, the *Colonial Report of 1905* gives a figure for Java of a mere 9.0 percent. However, it is far more realistic to assume that cottage handicrafts and peddling were important sources of income for at least a third of all households.[36] The greater the distances from villages to the regional capitals, the more households grew their own cotton, did their own spinning and weaving, made their own pottery, gathered forest produce, collected rattan to plait baskets, and so on.[37] Cottage textiles and pottery were also part of the agricultural rhythm: the sales of these products to local markets helped farming households earn some money and buy food as they ran short of their stocks during the rice-scarce months before the new harvest.

It was moreover the poor regions where the handicrafts were particularly developed, and some were quite successful. The plaited hats exported under the name "Manilas"—they could have equally been made in Tangerang, West Java—caused a craze in Paris. Like weaving and batik, plaiting was hardly rewarding, and it was therefore no coincidence that in Java this industry was located in the poor Residency of Banten, where wages were low and the work usually done in spare hours for additional income. Handicrafts could compete with industrial manufacturing, particularly if mechanization was impossible, as was the case for plaiting but also for embroidery—a well-known export product of the Philippines—and the hand-painted artistic batik cloths of Central Java. Cottage work was moreover competitive because it was carried out in people's spare time, whereas workshops only kept their heads above water by enslaving their workers. At Chinese batik workshops in Rembang, for example, women worked in debt bondage or for the pittance of 2 to 8 cents per day.[38]

The cottage sector was far less vulnerable to external competition than the workshops, which suffered from the imports of cotton textiles by the Dutch Trading Society. It was noted, for example, that by the mid-1840s the textile workshops in the Residency of Banyumas had all but disappeared.[39] Java's textile exports might have gone down since the early nineteenth century, and spinning definitely declined because of the influx of cheap industrial yarn, but cottage weaving was not given up on at all. As Van Nederveen Meerkerk has pointed out, this could not have been the case, because imported cloth only met part of the demand in Java.[40] The gap that needed to be filled was large enough to have engaged a million women (20 to 25 percent of all households) for 20 percent of their time. This continued to be the case until after the First World War, when the combination of imports of cheap Japanese cloth and the attraction of the plantations did lead to a decline in weaving in the Netherlands Indies.[41]

Nonetheless, in certain areas outside Java where smallholders could obtain high prices for pepper, coffee, or rubber, women became involved in cash crops and might have started to buy their cloth even before 1920. In South Sumatra, for example—where cotton was widely grown—local yarn was replaced by the cheaper Manchester product by about 1900, and a few years later weaving was abandoned for rubber tapping. In fact, a similar pattern seems to have developed in Siam and Burma, where cultivating rice for export was much more profitable than weaving.[42]

Likewise, in East Java, where work at plantations was plentiful, there was often not much weaving. Yet we cannot conclude that the presence of plantation employment always kept women away from their looms. In the Priangan, where the thriving tea estates attracted hundreds of thousands of laborers, looms were still present in many households.[43]

Aside from embeddedness in agricultural rhythms, whether local production could resist the onslaught of cheap imports also depended on the quality and productivity of the region's looms, local conditions for cotton cultivation, and local tastes. While looms in Java were quite inefficient, those on the eastern coast of the Malay Peninsula, Central Sumatra, and Nusa Tenggara were fairly advanced and better capable of meeting global challenges. The dryer regions of Indonesia were also better suited to cotton growing. Selayar, an island south of Sulawesi, had been a site of textile production for centuries. Moreover, local textile industries more easily survived the onslaught of British and later on Japanese cheap cloth if they operated in the luxury segment of the market, which was particularly the case for silk cloth, batik, and embroidery.[44]

This evidence of microhistorical character goes against the prevailing broad narrative of British imperialism in the nineteenth century turning manufacturers in the region and elsewhere into commodity producers. By the mid–nineteenth century, Singapore was acting as a clearinghouse from where Southeast Asian markets were flooded with British cotton cloth and yarn, a flow that did destroy local centers of textile exports in this region, as it had done with Indian exports of cotton. The British were opening up agricultural frontiers all over the region, with the aim of creating markets for their industrial manufactures. By the mid–nineteenth century, they had colonized Burma and imposed a free-trade treaty on Siam. Part of this deployment of British economic interests was also the appointment of Nicholas Loney as vice consul in the Philippine harbor town of Iloilo, when the city was opened up to foreign trade in 1855. Yet while he made no secret of his intention to promote sugar production in the western Visayas and to import Manchester cloth, it is not clear to what extent his actions reduced this thriving textile belt to a commodity producer. There is instead ample reason to question the dominant narrative. First of all, many Filipinos and Filipinas wore clothes of abaca or piña (fiber from pineapple leaves), and British attempts to replace these fabrics with cheaper machine-made imitations failed.[45]

Moreover, even the cotton weavers in the Philippines seemed to have maintained themselves against cheap British cloth.[46]

It is undisputed that after the late eighteenth century, a "proto-industrial manufacturing center" for handwoven textiles combining cotton yarn and piña had developed around the port of Iloilo.[47] Here, women even worked in factory-like settings, where many looms had been brought together in large rooms.[48] According to McCoy, the combined effects of cheap cotton imports and the emergence of the sugar frontier of Negros Occidental resulted in the collapse of textile exports from Iloilo to Manila.[49] However, since these exports predominantly concerned piña, why should they have been replaced by cheap cotton cloth? That McCoy signals a decline of the piña cloth arriving from Iloilo in Manila is because he took an extraordinary year as the basis for reconstructing the trend and did not take into account that the liberalization of trade diminished the role of the colonial capital as an entrepôt.[50] Moreover, data from the province of Antique, located on the same island of Panay as Iloilo, indicates that even though the number of weavers declined in the 1870s, the number of looms still increased. This suggests that at a time of growing population pressure, weaving became an even more important source of additional income for women, while the men seasonally migrated to the cane fields and sugar mills of Negros.[51] Since systematically gathered data for the late nineteenth century on the number of looms in operation is scant, we may refer to the census of 1903.[52] This indicates that in Iloilo, 48 percent of the employable women were engaged in manufacturing and that together with Cebu this province accounted for almost 20 percent of Philippine female manufacturing. We may deduce from these figures that the western Visayas were still the Philippine center of textile production, next to Ilocos and Manila.[53] All in all, the available statistical data suggests that at least until the Americans opened up the Philippine market for their textiles and Japanese cloth conquered Southeast Asia, textile manufacturing for the internal market was an important part of the Philippine economy.

Similar to the Netherlands Indies and Malaya, local handicrafts in the Philippines were resilient, which goes against the grain of the grand narrative of British economic imperialism and defies the macroeconomic wisdom of comparative costs. These local handicrafts continued to be pivotal in the living strategies of households that were always short of cash. Nevertheless, one could argue that the British supplies of cheap cloth prevented the thriving Philippine textile sector from moving beyond the cottage sphere and industrializing. This did not happen, but neither did it occur in the sugar industry, even though the latter suffered from serious labor shortages. Apparently, capital was in short supply, although this was just one of the causes. A cotton mill built in Manila in 1897 was doomed to a languishing existence, partly because the cotton grown in the Philippines had a short staple unsuitable for machine spinning. However, even more important might have been the general shortage of labor during the War of Independence and the absence of an urban proletariat large enough to supply this factory with labor on a regular basis.[54] Incidentally, the same labor shortages and high wages at that time inhibited the development of a shipbuilding sector that could conquer foreign markets. Hong Kong, as well as the Surabaya wharf, for that matter, was able to construct and repair ships because they were paying lower wages than their competitors in Manila.[55]

Java's textile sector might have been as resilient as its Philippine counterpart, and even though in other sectors of manufacturing the comparison may look less favorable for Java, this does not necessarily attest to stagnation. A lower proportion of employment does not necessarily translate into a lower proportion of national income, as by definition mechanization means a replacement of human or animal power by machines. This was the case in the sugar industry, a sector in which Java was far ahead of the Philippines for a long time. While, for example, in the 1870s there were still 3,397 sugar mills in the Philippines, sugar production in Java was concentrated in 180 factories.[56] Likewise, although a larger proportion of the employable population in the Philippines was engaged in transport and trade than in Java, this does not point to a more developed sector. On the contrary, while Java at the turn of the twentieth century was endowed with a railway network stretching over thousands of kilometers, and with hundreds of narrow-gauge railways connecting cane fields and factories, the Philippines only had a pitiful 196 kilometers at that time.[57] Furthermore, as they did with respect to manufacturing, the Dutch data gatherers underreported the extensive involvement of women in local trade. There is therefore no reason to believe that Java and the Philippines were that different in terms of the proportion of the population involved in trade. In fact, the economies of

Java and the Philippines differed most significantly with regard to access to land, as will be discussed further on.

RURAL DEPENDENCY ON COMMODITY MARKETS

At the turn of the twentieth century, Island Southeast Asia was no exception to the rule that 80 percent of all households in Asia were engaged in agriculture or fishing and that many members of these households had secondary employment. Moreover, most of the female involvement in agricultural work was invisible in the government statistics, despite the fact that they were the main workforce in the planting and harvesting of the paddy. It would also have been impossible for government monitors not to have seen women planting cane stalks in the fields. However, in the Netherlands Indies only male and female workers who were directly on the plantation's payroll were included in the government statistics. Anyone who carried out seasonal work and was subcontracted by *mandurs* (foremen) remained invisible on paper.

Within the category of agricultural employment, there are major differences in terms of access to land between Java and the Philippines, which are pertinent to the discrepancy between per capita income in the Philippines and in Java in the 1920s. Java had experienced a long-term decline of independent farmers, which is indicated by the fact that the proportion of farmers with their own herd of buffaloes diminished from 50 percent to 26 percent over the nineteenth century.[58] By 1900, about 57 percent of the agricultural workers, or one or more members of Java's 4.4 million rural households, had to work part of their time for wealthier farmers, at plantations, at construction sites, at the docks, or took over corvée requirements from villagers who could afford to have paid replacement.[59] The situation would not change for the better: by 1920, some 60 percent of the agricultural workforce could not subsist from its land. A third of these rural poor worked at plantations and a fifth for other richer farmers.[60] Whereas in Java by-employment had been the answer to population pressure from the mid–nineteenth century, when land became increasingly scarce, in the Philippines peasants could still move from densely populated areas to new frontiers. In the early twentieth century, the American administration rapidly expanded the amount of good agricultural land through its homesteading programs and investment in irrigation. As a result, the number of farms doubled between 1903 and 1918, the percentage of real landless rural workers fell from 34 to 15 percent by 1918, and 65 percent of the rural workers had more than 1 hectare of land.[61] Whereas in Java the planted acreage per capita (including estate land) shrank from 0.21 hectares to 0.2 hectares in the first two decades of the twentieth century, in the Philippines it increased from 0.25 to 0.3 hectares (again, this concerned all arable land).[62] Moreover, in Java an increasing proportion of the arable land was planted with crops less protein rich than rice.

By-employment in estates was crucial for Java's rural population to survive. The majority of Java's rural population lived in precarious conditions and relied heavily on the export sector. However, when the Great Depression set in, the colonial government of the Netherlands Indies seemed to be blatantly unaware of this dependency and hence of the severity of the consequences of the collapse of many sugar factories and plantation estates. This ignorance is almost unbelievable considering that since the days of the massive conscription for cash-crop growing under the Cultivation System, at no point were under 30 percent of Java's rural households involved in growing crops for export.[63] Based on agricultural statistics, we can assume that about 325,000 hectares were planted with estate export crops in 1900, the cultivation of which involved the equivalent of over 565,000 years of work.[64] Since most workers probably spent just a third of their time in the plantations, their total number must have amounted to 1.7 million, a substantial figure compared with just over 4.4 million rural households in Java.

It would become even more impressive. Plantations in Java entered booming years in the early twentieth century and absorbed many precarious laborers who in the 1880s and 1890s were listed in the colonial reports as wood cutters, grass cutters, charcoal burners, and gatherers of firewood.[65] In the first twenty years of the twentieth century, the total number of Javanese who worked part of their time at plantations doubled, while the number of rural households increased by just over a third.[66] This already amounted to a sharp increase in dependency, but that is not all. In addition to the 3.6 million plantation workers in Java, another half a million workers were either permanently or seasonally employed in the colonial infrastructure and government services related to commodity exports. The total number of workers in the state railways doubled between 1912 and 1930 and would have tripled had buses and trucks not made their appearance. Maritime transport grew at the same pace.[67] Further, an extensive labor force of 450,000 to 500,000 Javanese (of whom about 30 percent were female) was employed in plantations, oil extraction, and mines in the Outer Islands. This total of 4.5 million workers made up about 25 percent of the male and 12.5 percent of the female total employable population, most of whom combined plantation labor with working on their own plot or for a richer farmer.[68]

Java's rural economy was highly dependent on export agriculture but, perhaps surprisingly, not as dependent in comparison with the rest of Island Southeast Asia. As for the Philippines, the number of Philippine workers who were partly or fully reliant for their income on the four most important export crops—abaca, sugar, copra, and tobacco—sharply increased from almost four hundred thousand in 1900 to over a million in the early 1930s.[69] At that time, the Philippines might have counted a total employable population of just over seven million people, or almost three million households.[70] In combination with the fact that these million workers were to a greater extent engaged full time in Java, we could conclude that by 1930 the Philippines surpassed Java in terms of dependency on export crops. Moreover, underlying these figures was a shift toward plantation-style production. The important smallholder sector of abaca shifted partly to Davao (Mindanao) in the 1930s, where it became a plantation crop. In the copra sector, although still overwhelmingly in the hands of the smallholder sector, plantations began to emerge too. Moreover, by the mid-1930s half of the Philippines' employment was related to sugar: this was definitely not a smallholder sector. Chapter 3 described how the rural conditions in the western regions of Luzon and the Visayas began to resemble those of Java; the increase of the number of workers employed in the Philippine sugar industry from about 150,000 in 1900 to 450,000 in the 1920s and 1930s marked a major step of the Philippines toward a plantation economy.

The dependency of the Philippines on commodity exports was in turn widely exceeded by British Malaya. According to the census of British Malaya of 1931, an average 43.9 percent of the employed population was dependent on rubber, tin, transport, and commerce, a figure that must have been well over 50 percent in the booming late 1920s.[71] Crucially different from Java was the importance of smallholder production, a feature it shared with Indonesia's Outer Islands and initially also with the Philippines. About 60 percent of the workers in the rubber sector were smallholders and as such less dependent than the Javanese rural population on plantation work. In fact, the workers in the plantation and mining sectors in the western states of the Malay Peninsula, about a third of the total employed population, were overwhelmingly immigrants.[72] What stands out in British Malaya is its service sector, with Singapore as a nodal point of global trade, providing jobs to 17 percent of its employable male population by 1930.[73] Industrial employment in British Malaya was proportionally lower than that of the Philippines or even of Java, if we exclude mining.[74] Yet its bustling trade and its many small rubber estates fostered a wealthy middle class, one much larger than in the Netherlands Indies. This is adequately illustrated by the fact that by 1930 there were 165,000 cars registered in British Malaya and only 85,000 in the Netherlands Indies.[75]

As detailed in chapter 3, the consequences of the Great Depression were particularly severe for the densely populated plantation and mining belts. Money became scarce everywhere, a situation in which people who could fall back on subsistence agriculture were best off. The population of Java and the migrant laborers in British Malaya were most seriously exposed to the volatility of the global commodity markets. The vulnerability of the plantation sector was visibly manifest in the short depression of 1921 to 1922 and less ostensibly at the structural level of a world economy that was becoming less open and more unstable over the course of that decade.[76] Rubber cultivation had gone through its first restriction scheme early on the 1920s, and the Java sugar industry only managed to cope with declining sugar prices through relentlessly saving costs regarding both production and transport. After overproduction of sugar and grain had been impending for some years, in 1929 the market prices of sugar, wheat, and rice went into free fall.[77]

The Philippines escaped the worst of the Depression precisely because it was less integrated in the global economy than the Netherlands Indies and British Malaya. Although Philippine exports lost a third of their value and faced tough restrictions on access to American markets for sugar, their overall volume only slightly diminished.[78] Some loss of employment occurred because of the sugar quota and the decline of the abaca sector, but that was nothing in comparison with the other colonies in Island

Southeast Asia.[79] The export sector of British Malaya lost 60 percent of its value, and half of the over four hundred thousand workers on the rubber plantations and 60 percent of the 120,000 tin miners were laid off.[80] The export sector of the Netherlands Indies shrunk even more, namely by two-thirds: about 80 percent of the sugar factory workers, half of the dockworkers, and a third of the railway workers lost their jobs. Half of the 4.5 million seasonal and permanent jobs in Java's plantation export sector were lost, and on top of an immense loss of income, Javanese society had to feed about two hundred thousand returning Javanese labor migrants who had been laid off in the Outer Islands and an additional fifty thousand laborers from British Malaya.[81]

THE DEPRESSION YEARS AND INDUSTRIALIZATION

By the 1920s, densely populated Java—once the political and economic center of Island Southeast Asia—was lagging far behind in terms of per capita income. Again, it was not because it was more deindustrialized or more dependent on commodity exports than other parts of Island Southeast Asia: Java's poverty was the combined and entangled result of land scarcity, a distorted food market, and dominating plantation interests. The Philippines were still in a better position but were moving toward the same dead end as Java. Demographic growth could no longer be absorbed by the frontiers in Luzon and Negros, which were falling prey to hunger and rural unrest. Meanwhile, the export cash-crop sector went through a fundamental transformation from smallholder to plantation agriculture. In these years, the economic structure of the Philippines and Java were also converging with respect to their industrial sectors.

After 1934, the economy of the Netherlands Indies went through a remarkable transformation, bringing its employment in manufacturing, which stood at a pitiful 4–5 percent of its employable population by 1930, to about 7.1 percent in 1939 (both figures excluding cottage industry).[82] Industrial employment in the Philippines also saw substantial growth. It almost quintupled between 1918 and 1939.[83] However, if we include cottage industry, employment in manufacturing stagnated and female employment in manufacturing declined because of cheap imports from the United States after 1909, from Japan in the 1920s, and the industrialization of textile manufacturing in Manila in the 1930s.[84] The same probably happened in Java in the 1920s, where local weaving declined because of imports.

In addition to being less spectacular under closer scrutiny, Philippine industrialization moved in the opposite direction to that of Java, as it became increasingly supportive of the commodity-producing sector for the U.S. market. Much of the industrial growth came from processing commodities such as abaca, copra, sugar, and tobacco as well as from gold mining. While the cigar industry stagnated after 1920, for example, sugar boomed in the 1920s and early 1930s. So did mining and quarrying, where employment rose from a few thousand in 1918 to 48,000 in the 1930s.[85] The only exception to the modest growth of production for the domestic market was the textile sector.

The Philippine economy, being solidly tied to the American economic orbit, was steered toward commodity production, despite the fact that the Filipino elites were better positioned in national business than their counterparts anywhere else in colonial Asia (with the exception of some entrepreneurial communities in India, such as the Bombay Parsis).[86] Neither could the government of the Philippines change this course, even though it rightfully believed that in the field of commodity exports it was tough to compete with countries such as Indonesia, with its dismally low wages and rough labor conditions.[87] Official government policies toward import-substituting industrialization date from 1934, when the Philippines received commonwealth status in preparation for full independence, scheduled for 1946.[88] However, diversification from export agriculture to manufacturing industry for the home market was sluggish, a fact that some attributed to the conservatism and risk adversity of the *hacendero* class and others to nonexistent duties on American-Philippine trade, from which U.S. industrialists and Philippine sugar planters benefited most. The Agricultural and Industrial Bank, established in 1934 to foster industrialization, brought sugar factories into Philippine hands but did little in terms of industrial diversification.[89]

Again, industrial growth for the domestic market was most visible in the textile sector. While employment in textile and clothing factories amounted to just a few thousand workers in the early decades of the twentieth century, it jumped into the tens of thousands in the 1930s, with dozens of new factories established by Philippine, Japanese, and American entrepreneurs. Moreover, the embroidery sector was fostered by

American companies, which established dozens of firms, mainly in Manila. The boycotts by Chinese traders against Japanese imports in the early 1930s also contributed to the growth of the Philippine textile industry.[90] The total number of people fully employed in this sector, including those who worked in a putting-out system, stood at 183,305 in 1939. By-employment in textiles could have also doubled after the 1918 census was taken, rising to 157,856 for additional employment (both figures include tailors).[91] Much of this growth took place in metropolitan Manila and adjacent Rizal, the center of Philippine artisanship, trade, and services even before American rule.[92]

The first Depression years were not conducive to any investment in industrialization in Island Southeast Asia, particularly because of the sharp currency devaluations implemented by Japan and China. The Philippines were linked to the dollar, British Malaya to the sterling zone, and the Netherlands Indies to the gold standard until as late as 1936. Capital for investment was stashed away in the deflationary early 1930s. Moreover, Java was flooded by cheap Japanese cloth, and its textile sector more or less stagnated.[93] In the second half of the 1930s, conditions improved markedly. The devaluation of the Dutch guilder in 1936 is usually considered to be the turning point for the recovery of the Indonesian economy. This step indubitably impinged positively on exports, but its effect should not be overstated. After all, the sugar industry only partly recovered after it had lost its huge Indian market, while rubber and copra continued to suffer from sharply deteriorating terms of trade.[94] The imposition of tariffs on dyed textile cloth in 1933 and further restrictions on textile imports from outside the Dutch Kingdom constituted other important factors, ones that strongly favored local textile production. But probably the most consequential change was the less apparent reversal of the government policies of low rice prices because this substantially raised rural income.

In 1933, the government of the Netherlands Indies gradually implemented a ban on cheap rice from Mainland Southeast Asia, which had flooded the Java rice market and cut prices by half. This had brought disaster to the Javanese peasants who used to pay their land rent from their paddy sales. They had already been starved of cash after the sugar factories cancelled the lease of their land and opportunities for by-employment at plantation estates had dwindled. The ban introduced in

1933 raised the rice prices and brought much-needed relief. As an additional measure, the government succeeded in convincing The Hague to ship off part of the maize harvests of the Netherlands Indies, which was in abundant supply and threatened to drag down the rice prices as well. Furthermore, Deli plantations and Bangka tin mines were obliged by the government to shift from cheap imports to Java rice. As a result, Java, as well as South Sulawesi and Lombok, became important rice suppliers for the Indonesian archipelago.

Javanese peasants increased their output from 3.5 million tons in 1934 to 4 million in 1939. By that time, they were bringing over 22 percent of their paddy harvest to the market, instead of the 11 percent of five years before. Despite these increased supplies, market prices in Java still went up because about 20 percent of the milled rice was exported to the Outer Islands.[95] As a positive collateral of the expanded market, rice prices became more stable: the seasonal fluctuations decreased from plus or minus 10 to 5–7 percent.[96] The encouragement of a Netherlands Indies rice market through a combination of duties in imports and subventions on interinsular rice exports strengthened purchasing power in Java's countryside, whereas the flattening out of price fluctuations helped reduce rural indebtedness. It is a telling tale of how detrimental the import of cheap rice had been and underlines the importance of the decision by the American administration in the Philippines to pursue rice self-sufficiency early on during its rule.

Obviously, self-sufficiency could only be obtained at low levels of nutrition per capita, and sections of the rural population in Island Southeast Asia still lacked access to sufficient food during the 1930s. This was definitely the case in the plantation belts of the Philippines and Java. Moreover, increasing rural incomes did not automatically generate more nonagricultural business in the countryside. In the case of Java, however, it did. The necessary capital did not come from the so-called cultivation banks, which played such a crucial role in the financing of the plantations and sugar factories of Java. These metropolitan-based banks confined their investments to plantation agriculture after the investments of one of them in the Insulinde coconut oil factories had gone down the drain. It spoiled their appetite to follow the example of the British colonies and develop into fully fledged management agencies engaged in an array of activities. Moreover, in the Netherlands Indies, the European trading houses usually confined themselves to importing goods rather than facilitating their local production. Their ethnic Chinese counterparts were either involved in commodity exports, predominantly sugar, or the import of Japanese goods.[97]

Instead of the large trading houses and the Dutch banks' rural moneylenders, a new source of investment emerged, as in the 1930s indigenous cash-crop production increased relative to foreign-owned plantations in Java.[98] This occurred particularly in West Java's Priangan, where land had become increasingly concentrated in the hands of major landowners and proletarianization had advanced further than elsewhere in the island.[99] The textile industry, for example, emerged near indigenous tea gardens, whose owners had apparently channeled their profits into textiles. An agriculturally prosperous Priangan district such as Sukabumi saw an emergence of artisanal industry of agricultural implements, cutlery, and so on.[100] Moreover, in this part of Java, textile manufacturing had been traditionally an important cottage sector. It is no coincidence that by 1940, 34 percent of Java's textile manufacturing was located in the Priangan.[101] Their workers were overwhelmingly young landless women, of whom 41 percent possessed some basic reading and writing skills, which was far above the average.[102] In fact, this was also the case in the Philippines, where about 73 percent of the 110,000 women employed in the embroidery sector were literate; the national average was just 41 percent.[103]

Between 1936 and 1939, the estimated number of workers in small-scale and secondary industries (not including the cottage industry) increased from 1.66 to 2.8 million in the Netherlands Indies.[104] Impressive as this may sound, most of these jobs were probably not full time. Moreover, the growth of employment in workshops happened at the expense of cottage production, which more or less stagnated in the 1930s.[105] Industrialization reduced the number of hands needed per unit of output. This happened in cigarette manufacturing, where machines partly replaced the handwork of the dominant putting-out system in the 1930s, and it also happened in the textile sector.[106] In the latter, the number of Japanese looms—which were seven times more productive than those of the Javanese—increased from a mere five hundred in 1935 to 49,500 in 1941. Over the same period of time, the number of mechanical looms soared from an underwhelming four hundred to 9,800. The pace of mechanization, and hence of rising labor productivity, was such that in the second half of the 1930s the growth of Java's industrial sector might have eliminated so much of the cottage industry that it could have brought about an overall loss of employment.[107]

All in all, the gains in employment in Java's industry and food agriculture would not have been enough to compensate for the loss of about two million jobs in the export agricultural sector. Meanwhile, Java's population had grown by 20 percent in the 1930s, which meant that these years saw a serious reduction in the proportion of the employed within the total population. The extent of the loss of employment and resulting impoverishment was not clear to most of the government experts at the time. They had, after all, consistently underestimated the level of dependency of Java's rural population on the plantation economy.

TOWARD INTERNATIONAL MIGRATION: EDUCATION AND URBANIZATION

In the early twentieth century, Java and the Philippines were still overwhelmingly rural economies, and the fact that the latter did better in terms of access to land, rice self-sufficiency, and smallholder production of export crops goes a long way in explaining its higher per capita income. What these economies had in common, however, was high rural mobility spurred by increasing rural precarity. The sugar plantation belts, as we saw in chapter 3, became the scenes of an undernourished sharecropping peasantry and rural proletariat. In the 1930s, other convergences in the structure of the respective economies appeared. One was a shift from cottage to industrial textile industry, which encouraged urban migration, particularly of young women in both colonies. Another factor in the convergence was that the plantations lost some of their dominance over Java's economy in the 1930s, while at the same time the Philippines became more reliant on them, and its industrial sector also turned toward commodity exports.

In contrast to these structural economic convergences, urbanization patterns diverged. While the Netherlands Indies—and Java in particular—were still more urbanized than the Philippines by 1900, thirty years later almost 11 percent of the Philippine population was urban (living in cities of more than twenty thousand residents), against 6.7 percent for

Java and 2.8 percent for the Outer Islands.[108] This was a reversal with important implications for later international emigration flows from this part of the world. It pertains directly to the fact that today Malaysia and the Philippines have much higher emigration ratios than Indonesia and that their emigrants are generally better educated. This in turn brings us to the central question of this book: how Island Southeast Asia became a mass exporter of labor. While zooming in on the roles of education and urbanization in this migration, British Malaya will be included in the final section of this chapter. The Straits Settlements, after all, were the most urbanized territories in Southeast Asia, where 59.5 percent of the population consisted of city dwellers as early as in 1911.[109]

Initially, high demographic growth—in the case of British Malaya mainly caused by immigration from southeastern China and Madras—pushed migration toward the plantation frontiers, a mobility facilitated by new means of transport. At the turn of the twentieth century, urban centers started to grow as a concomitant of increasing levels of literacy, a stage of development that conforms to Zelinsky's mobility-transition hypothesis, which was guided by the paradigms of demographic transition and modernization.[110] Although his model has lost much of its appeal because of its determinism, the positive correlation between human development and migration is now increasingly acknowledged. In the late 1980s, Massey had already identified economic development as a driving rather than attenuating factor in migration. The continuous relationship with the colonial and later postcolonial metropolis is another key variable, as Sassen has argued.[111] De Haas recently revived Zelinsky's mobility-transition hypothesis by suggesting, on the basis of extensive empirical research, "that capability- and aspiration-increasing human development is initially associated with generally higher levels of emigration and immigration."[112] This is pertinent to the question of why Philippine and Malaysian migrations in postcolonial times had a stronger cross-cultural character than Indonesian ones, which would stay predominantly within the Malay world.

At the turn of the twentieth century, Island Southeast Asia had entered the phase, as described by Zelinsky, in which a rapidly expanding trek to the cities emerged alongside migration toward the frontiers. In Java, however, this happened at a slower pace than elsewhere in the region, including the Outer Islands of the Netherlands Indies.[113]

Underlying the apparent slowing down of Java's urbanization is a shift from permanent to seasonal urban migration. Surabaya, Semarang, and Batavia offered wages two to three times above Java's average for most of the nineteenth century, and migrants flocked toward their rapidly growing *kampungs*.[114] From the 1870s, these began to grow at the expense of other cities because newly constructed railroads brought sugar and other commodities directly to these cities, bypassing other ports along the northern coast.[115] Over time, however, the same railroads facilitated the travel of seasonal migrants. Permanent urban migration declined both because increasing supplies of labor brought urban wages down and because land scarcity forced marginal peasants to look for by-employment that would enable them to keep their land. Whereas, for example, wages in Batavia were more than twice as high as elsewhere in West Java in 1880, this gap had almost disappeared by 1915.[116] By 1930, Surabaya, Semarang, and Batavia still ranked among the top immigration Residencies of Java, together with the plantation belts of Pasuruan and Besuki, but their growth had become modest in comparison with their economic role.[117] At that time, almost a third of Java's urban work force might have consisted of circular migrants during peak months, many of whom were locked into patron-client relationships with their foremen.[118] The total number of dockworkers in Java alone might have amounted to sixty or seventy thousand in the 1920s, and they were joined by other urban seasonal laborers such as porters, *becak* drivers, and sellers of firewood.

Considering the nineteenth-century European history of urbanization, one would expect that these circular migrations were just a relatively transient phase of preproletarianization. This at least was observed in 1916 by the colonial civil servant Meijer Ranneft, an expert on Java's rural economy.[119] However, after he penned these insights, the means of transportation only further improved and widened thanks to the introduction of buses and trucks, and Java's population density only further increased. Circularity therefore remained a dominant factor in urban migration into postcolonial times.[120] Meanwhile, the reason why the rural population sought by-employment rather than permanent jobs is that most of the work in the urban sector was unskilled and held in lower regard compared with toiling on one's own land.[121] As a rule, farmers clung to their land, and by-employment enabled them to do so. It was part of their sense of belonging to a community and kept their relations with their local patrons intact, which was a crucial source of social security in times of increasing precarity. In early postcolonial times, permanent migration toward the cities increased rapidly. This was only to a limited extent the upshot of higher educational attainment and predominantly because of the endemic violence of the War of Independence (1945–1949) and insurrections in the years that followed. Many people from the countryside sought a safer place in the cities.[122] These were extraordinary years and did not change the basic fact that Java's urban migration continued to exhibit a markedly seasonal character.

In contrast to Manila and Singapore, Batavia had not become the primate city in colonial times (see table 5.1). It was neither the residence of an affluent absentee planters' class like Manila, nor was it the central banking and trading hub of Southeast Asia, a role taken by Singapore.[123] An important reason why 10 percent of the population of British Malaya lived in Singapore (see table 5.1) is that in contrast to Java's coastal cities, immigrants in this city came from much farther away than the rural hinterland: some 75 percent of its population consisted of ethnic Chinese. Finally, in contrast to Manila and Singapore, Batavia had to share its role as the colony's administrative center with the healthier town of Bandung and its role as an export hub with Surabaya and Semarang, which had emerged as the nodal points in the commodity-producing system of Java, providing shipping, insurance, administration, and equipment for the plantations. With just 533,000 citizens, followed by Surabaya with 342,000 inhabitants, Batavia was in no way a primate city by 1930.[124]

TABLE 5.1

The capitals of the Netherlands Indies, British Malaya, and the Philippines in 1830 and 1930

Capital	Size in 1830	% of total population	Size in 1930	% of total population
Batavia	50,000	0.25	533,000	0.88
Manila	97,000	3.88	800,000	6.10
Singapore	26,329	0.55	454,719	10.00

Source: Bosma, "Methodological Paper," 11–12.

The rise of primate cities was a function of permanent migration, and this in turn was correlated to rising educational levels and the emergence of an educated middle class. In Island Southeast Asia, as in many other parts of the world, migrants to cities were significantly better educated than rural populations, which are usually abandoned by young educated people who want to try their luck in the city.[125] In the Philippines, the *hacendero* class had already begun to move toward the cities by the end of the nineteenth century, and their numbers swelled under American rule when political life was budding and the newly established Congress of the Philippines strengthened Manila's role as a center of power. Moreover, the city became the main center of industry, with relatively high wages and the hub of maritime transport, railways, and roads of Luzon.[126] By the late 1930s, the urban industrial centers of Manila and adjacent Rizal offered significantly higher wages for unskilled labor: about 25 percent above the national average.[127] Manila was also considered to be a safe place in the 1930s, when the Huk uprising created a sense of insecurity in Central Luzon.[128] This city had an educated middle class, which made up about 18 percent of the total urban population and included an absentee *hacendero* class with considerable purchasing power.[129] The rural-urban migration became increasingly female and often went via smaller to larger cities. In postcolonial times, families would try to give their daughters a good education and send them to the cities for a skilled job.[130]

Manila emerged as a primate city, surrounded by provinces with relatively high levels of literacy. In the Philippines, the level of literacy was about 10 percent as early as the 1870s, and by 1940, the great majority of the Philippine population could read and write. On the eve of the Second World War, 90 percent of the children aged between seven and ten were at school.[131] Such figures conceal, however, that educational attainment diverged considerably across the Philippine provinces. While the average literacy rate among gainfully employed men and women was 51 and 41 percent, respectively, the figures were as high as 89 percent and 73 percent in Manila and as low as 35 percent and 17 percent in Negros.[132] Farther south in the Muslim territories, the literacy rates were even lower, and these educational arrears would only persist. Meanwhile, in British Malaya, the divergences in educational attainment were almost as large. In the Straits Settlements, literacy among males over fifteen years was over 48 percent and for females 10 to 13 percent, according to the 1931 census, but elsewhere in British Malaya, male literacy ranged between 10 and 15 percent.[133] In the Netherlands Indies, a modest 6.5 percent of all Indonesian males (and less than half a percent of the women) older than fifteen were literate by 1920.[134] These low literacy rates gave little impetus for urban migration. This slightly changed in the 1930s, however, when literacy would increase at a remarkable pace, to 20 percent in 1941, for which the Indonesian nationalist Wild School Movement (*Wilde Scholenbeweging*) of the 1930s deserves much credit and which had also an impact on urbanization and industrialization in Java in the course of that decade.[135]

Colonial Indonesia lagged behind the Philippines and British Malaya not only in terms of education but also in outward-looking orientation. As early as the 1880s, the Philippine *hacenderos* and wealthier tenants tended to send their children to Manila and even to Spain for their education.[136] After 1900, American schoolbooks instilled in the schoolchildren a sense of America as the Promised Land. An outward-looking attitude was also promoted by the circulation of newspapers, which amounted to two hundred thousand households, one in every ten, in the Philippines by 1930. In Indonesia, the total circulation of newspapers was about four hundred thousand in 1948, of which half was in Bahasa, which comprised fewer than one in every thirty households. For British Malaya, the little available data suggests that the total circulation of Malay newspapers was confined to a few thousand. However, a rapidly growing number of bookshops sold newspapers from abroad, including from Egypt, and newspapers were read aloud in coffee shops. Many members of the Chinese and Indian middle classes must have subscribed to British-language newspapers, such as the famous *Straits Times*, because its annual circulation of five thousand copies in the 1930s indicates that its readership was much wider than just the British.[137] Mastery of the English language was a key part of cosmopolitan modernity in the Malay cities, as Hollen has described.[138]

Newspaper circulation and familiarity with English were as unevenly spread as literacy. The western provinces of Luzon and the western states of the Malay Peninsula stood out in this respect, with substantial classes that were familiar with the large Anglophone world. By 1930, over 10 percent of the Chinese and Indian male population of fifteen years and older in Singapore were English literate, and about 4 to 5 percent in the Federated Malay States, where the mines and plantations were concentrated. By 1918, 32.1 percent of the literate Filipinos and 21.5 percent of the literate Filipinas were able to read and write English, and many were living in Manila or at least in an urban environment.[139] In the Netherlands Indies, only a minute section of the population had some knowledge of English, mainly the children of the relatively literate Chinese population, both newcomers and Peranakan, who went to private schools that attached great value to learning the language of international trade.[140]

In addition to these high levels of educational attainment and international exposure, the hiring policies of colonial administrations played a key role in nurturing educational aspirations, particularly because skilled employment was scarce in these commodity-producing economies. In this respect, the Philippines were the most advanced, with only 1 percent of the government posts (mostly teachers) held by American expatriates. In British Malaya, the British held 5.5 percent, mostly in administration and the police, and the metropolitan Dutch in the Netherlands Indies just 3 percent. In the latter colony, however, another 11 percent of all government positions were held by Indies-born Dutch citizens, the majority of whom were culturally oriented to the Netherlands.[141] As a result, few Indonesians were to be found in the middle and higher echelons of government.

Since higher educational levels did not automatically generate higher economic growth or a sectoral change toward industry and services, many higher-educated people might not have been able to find suitable employment.[142] High educational attainment coupled with low wage levels and little skilled employment exerts a strong migration push that was forcefully present in the Philippines, which exhibited extreme social and spatial inequalities. The Ilocos provinces, for example, coupled low income with high educational standards.[143] Such discrepancies drove young people to the cities and tens of thousands to the United States, where they found jobs in the factories, the service sector, and the army. In Malaysia, second-generation Chinese and Tamil emigrants with higher education applied for professions not only in Singapore but all over the world.

The way in which cultural orientation directs mobility can be illustrated by comparing the Ilocanos and the Madurese. Their migration history shared some important features, as both populations migrated extensively in search of new land, both were seafaring, and both sought maritime employment. The crucial difference was the linkage to international migration. As early as the eighteenth century, Ilocanos had moved to Manila to seek maritime employment.[144] Later on, Filipinos could be found on American whaling ships and in increasing numbers on ocean liners as cabin boys.[145] Filipinos sailed under many different flags, while Madurese stayed within the Netherlands Indies or at least on Dutch vessels.[146] Since primary education had reached the tiniest villages of Ilocos at the turn of the twentieth century, educational aspirations ushered in the migration of broad layers of the population. Almost from the very beginning of American rule in the Philippines, the Ilocanos had eagerly learned English. Their *hacenderos* continued to send their children abroad for education, at the risk of their own impoverishment or of having to mortgage their land to their tenants.[147] Ilocanos were also strongly represented among labor migrants heading for the United States. They made up half of the 125,000 Filipinos who enlisted for work in the cane and pineapple fields of Hawaii.[148] Their remittances became an important source of income for the relatively poor Ilocano provinces, which would further encourage migration to the United States.[149] During the First World War, the Ilocanos were well represented among the Filipinos who joined the U.S. Navy. In fact, 5 percent of the American navy crews consisted of Filipinos. Meanwhile, Filipinas could be found in the American hospitals. Between 1934 and 1965, Philippine immigration to the United States was severely restricted, but Philippine immigrants, including Ilocanos, still entered the country via the detour of employment at American bases in Korea and Indochina. Another category consisted of Filipina spouses of American servicemen.[150] Ilocanos have again been well represented among the migrants who came to the United States after the relaxation of the immigration regulations for family reunification and high-skilled workers in 1965. They make up a substantial portion of today's over four million people born in the Philippines or of Filipino descent living in the United States.[151]

CHAPTER SIX

Postcolonial Continuities in Plantations and Migrations

From the 1850s onward, an ongoing specialization in commodity production had linked Mainland and Island Southeast Asia to Japan, Southeast
China, India, the United States, and Europe. Cheap transport had enabled
the emergence of globalized markets for bulk products. Asian interde-
pendence was embodied in labor flows from India and China, rice imports
from mainland Southeast Asia, and plantation belts in Island Southeast
Asia. Commodity chains rather than national policies forged trajectories of economic development, and these in turn shaped migration patterns. This interdependency unraveled during the Depression, a process
that coalesced with the emergence of economic nationalism and nation
building during decolonization but that had already started in the 1930s,
as discussed in the previous chapter.

One of the most visible aspects of disintegration was the return
migration of hundreds of thousands of Chinese and Tamils to their countries of origin. Between 1931 and 1947, the proportion of Indian migrants
in the population of British Malaya shrunk by a third, and in postwar
Malaysia their proportion in the plantation labor force would drop further.[1] While the total proportion of the ethnic Chinese and Chinese newcomers in the population of Malaysia did not diminish, their position
became increasingly insecure. One factor was the role of Chinese workers in the guerrilla uprising of the Communist Party in Malaysia that
started in the late 1940s, in response to bad labor conditions on the

plantations. To quell this uprising, the Chinese population was subjected to massive governmental resettlement schemes.[2] Meanwhile, rising Malay nationalism asserted itself against Chinese and Tamil immigrants. The anti-Chinese attitude of the Malay political elite went so far that they expelled Singapore—where 75 percent of the population was ethnically Chinese—from the federal state of Malaysia in 1965.[3] In this threatening atmosphere, hundreds of thousands of ethnic Chinese left Malaysia.[4] In Indonesia, colonial times had left enough resentment to trigger the departure of about one hundred thousand Sino-Indonesians to China, many of whom were evacuated by the Chinese government in 1959. Ethnic Chinese also became victims of the 1965 massacres and of some anti-Chinese riots in their aftermath.[5]

The anti-Chinese and anti-immigrant sentiments revealed in a grim way the legacies of colonial plural societies and their economic dependence on commodity production by foreign companies. They were the dark side of the nationalist fervor that pushed government policies to nationalize their countries' economies. British Malaya chose in this regard to invest in a strong ethnic Malay farmers' class. Equally strong was the desire to catch up with the level of modernity of the former colonizers. Indonesian and Philippine politicians expected miracles from industrialization, to ward off the looming massive unemployment of a rapidly growing population. However, in their eagerness to follow this path, they sidestepped the immense structural problems in the countryside. This was particularly the case in Indonesia, where land scarcity and dilapidated irrigation works compounded the daunting challenge of feeding a rapidly growing population. The Indonesian government was under great pressure to increase food production, which had stagnated since 1940. The country had to import 7,700,000 tons of rice (12 percent of its needs) in 1952.[6] Prominent Indonesian economists poured scorn on their government for favoring industrialization projects instead of taking serious steps to reduce food imports and alleviate the alarming nutritional deficiencies plaguing the Indonesian population.[7]

This chapter will complete the answer to the question of how Island Southeast Asia became a mass exporter of labor. After decolonization, the governments of Island Southeast Asia were still heavily reliant on commodity exports for their revenue, which went along with a new push toward the frontiers and the continuation and even growth of the plantation sectors. Since the early nineteenth century, an unstinting trek to the frontiers had taken place, which the governments of the Philippines and the Netherlands Indies had further encouraged in order to alleviate population pressures. In the postwar decades, these policies would encounter the limits of the ecological and social absorption capacity of the frontiers. Meanwhile, in all three countries of Island Southeast Asia, mechanization and the ascendency of palm oil and timber production made the new commodity frontiers less labor intensive than the traditional ones, such as tobacco and sugar. Industrialization and urbanization could not fully absorb labor surpluses, either. The widening and growing migration circuits of colonial times would spill over the national boundaries. The patterns of recruitment and client-patron systems of the colonial days, coupled with rising educational standards, facilitated this widening of migration patterns toward East Asia, the United States, and the Arabian Peninsula.

A RENEWED DRIVE TOWARD THE FRONTIERS AND THE RETURN OF THE PLANTATION

In the 1950s, Indonesia's exports almost entirely consisted of tin, rubber, copra, and oil, together contributing over 25 percent of its national income.[8] While acknowledging its dependence on cash-crop exports, the Indonesian government encouraged smallholder production because plantations did not accord with the ideals of national economic development. As a result, the share of estate exports in total export value sank from 54.3 percent in 1938 to 38.6 percent in 1953.[9] The growth of smallholdership was given a boost from American tire manufacturers, who swiftly returned to using natural rubber after the liberation of British Malaya and the Netherlands Indies from Japanese occupation. By the mid-1970s, about three-quarters of the people engaged in rubber cultivation were smallholders, involving six hundred thousand households.[10] The situation was similar in Indonesia, which by about 1990 was the world's second-largest rubber producer: 75 percent of the two million households involved in rubber cultivation and processing were smallholders and predominantly swiddeners.[11]

The plantation as a business model was far from defeated, however, and made a comeback in Island Southeast Asia to become a driving factor in the region's emerging role as a mass exporter of labor. Plantations returned, first because crops such as palm oil, sugar, abaca, and even rubber became increasingly capital intensive.[12] Second, because of their strategic importance for government revenue and balance of payments, state intervention in the production of export crops intensified.[13] The Malaysian government, for example, cast a tightening web of supervision over smallholders in its ambition to enlarge the contribution of rubber cultivation to the national income. In 1956, it established FELDA (Federal Land Development Authority), which was initially conceived as a resettlement scheme to offer farmers viable plots of land, but over time it extended its control over all the agricultural aspects of these settlements, practically turning them into plantations.[14] The government of British Malaya also spent considerable sums on rubber research and on agricultural extension for rubber cultivators.[15] As a result, Malaysian output per hectare rose toward 2.3 times the level of Indonesia, while keeping the price competitive with expanding synthetic rubber production in the industrialized countries. This market share was also maintained at the expense of rubber-cultivating households, many of which fell below the poverty line—while their work became as arduous as that of the plantation estate workers in the old colonial days.[16] The same return to the plantation, but swifter and more radical, occurred in the palm oil sector that would succeed rubber as Malaysia's most important export crop. In this sector, FELDA emerged as the largest enterprise, accounting for nearly 30 percent of the country's palm oil production. Under its regime, resettled landless peasants were more or less working as sharecroppers.

Cronyism and collusion also inflicted much harm on smallholders and reopened the door for plantations. Cooperative structures and commodity boards skimmed off the profits and degraded the farmers to indebted sharecroppers working in plantation-like settings. Struggles about the control over commodity production between central and regional authorities even ignited an armed conflict in eastern Indonesia. In Manado, the struggle between Jakarta and local officials for control over the copra sector sparked a rebellion in the 1950s. This fight between the center and the periphery wreaked havoc on the once crucial copra sector, which declined to a third of its earlier size between 1952 and 1967.[17] Another major onslaught on the smallholder economy occurred when

Sukarno's policies to recast the Java sugar sector from plantation to peasant cultivation were rolled back by his successor, Suharto. Powerful cane-growing peasants, who had merged with the local aristocrats and urban traders, controlled the scene under the guise of cooperative structures. The sugar plantation made an undisguised appearance in the Outer Islands from the 1990s onward, namely as heavily mechanized large-scale enterprises.

In contrast to Malaysia and Indonesia, the government of the Philippines did not even pay lip service to smallholder production and allowed coconut, banana, and pineapple plantations unfettered expansion. Plantation corporations followed the smallholder settlers in Mindanao to engage them in growing bananas and pineapples and force them to quit the production of food crops. On this island, transnational companies controlled the technology and every other aspect of production, and they shifted their business risks onto the shoulders of the growers. This created an impoverished and indebted class of farmers. In the 1990s, the plantation corporations started to replace their tenured work force by casual labor on the extensive banana and pineapple estates.[18] Sugar, the most important export crop, was nominally not produced in plantations, because cultivation and milling had been organizationally separated after the arrival of the large sugar centrals in the 1920s. However, labor was entirely in the thralls of the landlords who controlled the centrals, and these landlords enjoyed tremendous profits, thanks to generous access to the American market after Cuban sugar was banned from the United States in 1962. The Philippine acreage under cane more than doubled in the 1960s, but at the expense of a halving of the yield per hectare. By that time, the Philippine sugar industry had become too inefficient to compete on the global market, where prices were under constant downward pressure.

Sugar was not the only plantation predicament the Philippines had to deal with. At the commodity frontiers of Mindanao, the pineapple and banana plantations of Del Monte and Dole were bulldozing their way over Filipino landholdings, spreading pesticides over the countryside, tricking landowners into leasing out their land on unfavorable terms, and displacing local communities. New sugar factories, such as the Bukidnon factory (Mindanao) established in the 1970, were, despite their outwardly cooperative nature, centrally led capital-intensive enterprises in which a few powerful planters called the shots, to the detriment of many minor farmers, who lost their land. Nutritional conditions in the plantations, local activists reported to concerned consumers in Europe, stood at the outrageously low level of 1,670 kilocalories per day. Fair-trade organizations and human rights groups noted wryly that the Philippines exported pineapples while its population suffered from malnutrition.

While the commodity frontiers were pushed all over Island Southeast Asia, Indonesia and the Philippines resumed the policies of encouraging migration to less-populated islands within their archipelagos in the 1950s and 1960s. FELDA resettled seventy thousand landless households: over four hundred thousand people.[19] From Java, about 2.5 million families, or ten million people, migrated to the Outer Islands between 1950 and 1992, half of whom were spontaneous settlers. While Java's share in Indonesia's population fell back from about 75 to 60 percent over the twentieth century, those of Sumatra and Kalimantan nearly doubled to 20 and 5 percent, respectively.[20] Yet even this substantial migration fell below the ambition of the Indonesian government to unleash a massive chain migration toward the agricultural frontiers. The frontiers were not uninhabited, however, and their local communities suffered from these colonization schemes. Many Javanese rural villagers left under coercion, and the immense operation went against the grain of increasing urban migration fueled by rising educational levels.[21]

Meanwhile, the limited capacity of the frontiers in Indonesia's Outer Islands, which were mostly located in ecologically fragile environments, was poorly understood by the national elites of Indonesia, most notably by President Sukarno.[22] The soil of southern Sumatra, which was less fertile than that of Java, could not sustain the twenty-fold population increase between 1930 and 1990.[23] In the 1980s, the Indonesian government had to take draconian measures to protect the forests and forcibly removed four hundred thousand squatters. Shortage of land compelled these settlers to seek by-employment, which they found at coffee or sugar plantations. Thousands moved farther, toward plantations and construction sites in Malaysia.[24] Once the government realized that "Sumatra could not carry more people," the focus shifted to New Guinea, which was even more politically sensitive. In the 1980s, donor countries and the World Bank stopped sponsoring the transmigration projects but only partly and under pressure from international outrage. By that time, international development consultants had already concluded that transmigration could in no way absorb two million immigrants per year, the equivalent of the 2 percent annual population growth of Java and Bali. Together with a drop in oil prices in 1987, these negative assessments led to the winding down of these colonization schemes.[25]

In the Philippines, the internal migration was even more unsettling than in Indonesia, and this was particularly the case in the predominantly Muslim island of Mindanao. By 1960, the influx of 1.2 million Christian immigrants had turned this once sparsely populated territory into the home of 19 percent of the Philippine population.[26] It was a migration that would only accelerate: almost three million Christians were said to have settled in Mindanao between 1966 and 1976, some as smallholders and others as self-employed artisanal gold miners in the Compostela Valley.[27] Meanwhile, plantation corporations carried out extensive land grabbing, a destruction and violence that attended the colonization of what once was the Islamic south of the Philippines. The Moro rebellion in the 1970s, a new depressing chapter in the islands' four hundred years of conflict, was crushed by the indiscriminate bombing of the cities of Jolo and Zamboanga, which probably left half a million people homeless. It only reached a settlement in 1976, after the involvement of Muammar Gadhafi—the leader of Libya and sponsor of the Moro uprising—as a mediator to negotiate autonomy for the Muslim-populated areas in the southern Philippines.[28]

FALTERING NATIONAL DEVELOPMENT STRATEGIES

Economic nationalism did not fundamentally change the commodity dependency of the Island South. The revival of the plantation did not alleviate the mounting population pressure in the northern Philippines and Java, and neither did government-engineered migrations. The Philippines had already exhausted its potential for agricultural expansion in the 1970s, and Indonesia followed a few years later.[29] The Philippines were in a development deadlock, and their neocolonial status received much of the blame from activists who had participated in the ousting of Ferdinand Marcos. Their victory soon turned sour, and extreme disappointment set in about the direction their country had taken after it had become independent in such high spirits. Shortly after the Second World

War, the Philippines were generally expected to be the first Asian country after Japan to achieve an "industrial take off" thanks to a high literacy rate, faster economic growth than Malaysia and Indonesia, and the beginnings of a diversified economy through the introduction of import-substitution policies in 1949.[30] The proportion of manufacturing in terms of GDP rose to 17.9 percent in 1960, much higher than in Indonesia (10 percent) or Malaysia (13.6 percent, of which only 6.3 was for manufacturing and 7.3 for mining).[31]

In the postwar years, the trend of an increasingly female urban migration continued, and by 1960, this movement had surpassed the migration toward agricultural and mining frontiers in numbers.[32] However, by the 1970s, the Philippine urban economy could no longer absorb the influx to the cities, and the situation worsened after the closing of garment factories. This loss of employment was only partially compensated for by the arrival of electronics assembly lines, which benefited from the oversupply of educated, docile, and single young women. While low-tax export enclaves helped maintain the level of industrialization of the Philippines above that of Indonesia, Malaysia, and Thailand, they brought only temporary relief. In the early 1980s, the industrial output of the Philippines plunged by 19 percent. Although much of this was attributable to the collapse of the sugar industry, which carried great weight as an economic sector, the Philippines also missed the opportunity to attract the parts of the electronics industry that were relocating from the high-income countries of Japan, Hong Kong, and Taiwan to countries with lower wages.[33] Now, a declining industrial basis and a young and relatively well-educated female population became the driving forces behind intense international migration.[34]

The Philippines were also doubly unfortunate in the global commodity markets in the 1970s, in the face of soaring oil prices, on the one hand, and dwindling prices of their own export commodities, such as sugar, copra, and copper, on the other.[35] For bananas and pineapples, the terms of the trade deteriorated by an annual average of 3 percent between the 1960s and 1980s. Protected access of Philippine sugar to the U.S. market, at least until 1974, had bloated an industry that was producing at a cost price 2.5 times above market level.[36] In this constellation, the decision by Coca-Cola and PepsiCo in the early 1980s to switch from Philippine sugar to maize syrup (HFCS) had a devastating effect on the country's sugar exports. It dealt a serious blow to the livelihood of three million workers whose income depended at least partly on sugar. It created havoc particularly in Negros, where the sugar factories ceased grinding cane in 1985.[37] Social discontent fueled armed resistance and military suppression, and peaceful protests were indiscriminately gunned down as well. One such protest, in Escalanda on September 20, 1985, ended in a massacre.[38] The immediate cause of Negros's tragedy was actors in the United States, but it had been in the making from the island's inception as a sugar frontier in the 1850s. Eventually, the collapsing Philippine sugar industry brought President Marcos down along with it.

To the long list of misfortunes needs to be added that the Philippines had turned into a net importer of agricultural products by 1995.[39] This was yet another deep disappointment, considering that the International Rice Institute at Los Baños had been the cradle of the Green Revolution in the 1960s and had facilitated a doubling of rice production in the Philippines in under two decades. By the late 1970s, however, the potential for growth in rice output was exhausted. Moreover, employment opportunities did not grow for the rapidly increasing rural population.[40] Income inequality had already increased in the 1960s to such an extent that an estimated 70 percent of all children between one and four years old were undernourished.[41] This loss of self-sufficiency in food production contrasted sharply with the situation in Malaysia and Indonesia, which had achieved self-reliance in terms of rice production by the late 1970s and 1984, respectively and which contributed substantially to per capita growth.[42]

The predicament of the Philippines has incited a debate that is equally as intense as it is inconclusive. For understandable reasons, cronyism—if not simply large-scale theft—is widely held responsible. After his successful fight with the sugar barons, Ferdinand Marcos had siphoned off huge sums from this sector to his own bank account. While his actions were brazen, the corruption in this country was not unique in the region; it was endemic in Indonesia as well.[43] Neither did Malaysia escape from entrenched interests, for example in rice and tin or timber schemes in Sabah and Sarawak. Yet these did not slow the country's economic growth or impede the government's capability to raise enough revenue for its proper functioning.[44] Moreover, one cannot blame Marcos entirely for the rural destitution, which had held large parts of the Philippine countryside in its ever-worsening grip since the 1930s. Looking for the deeper causes of violence, political instability, and loss of attraction to foreign investors, one cannot ignore the country's high birth rate, amounting to 3.3 percent per annum in the 1960s and early 1970s. Family planning, pursued by Marcos, was resisted in this staunchly Catholic country.[45] Unsurprisingly, the first prime minister of the post-Marcos regime identified the country's demography as its top problem.[46] At present, demographic growth has slowed somewhat to 2 percent, but this is still much higher than the 1.2 percent in Java.[47] In fact, the demographic explosion in the Philippines resembles the 3.1 percent growth figures of Mexico in the 1960s. In Mexico, the existing migration system to the United States expanded with similar rapidity in the 1980s, under pressure from a baby-boom generation that could not be absorbed by the local economy, which was suffering a crisis almost as severe as the one in the Philippines.[48]

In the Philippines, population pressure could no longer be remedied either by the trek to the frontiers or by land reforms. As a result, rural conditions began to resemble those in Java. When *Newsweek* reported in 1987 that an alarming 90 percent of the land in the Philippines was in the hands of 10 percent of the population, it could have described the rural conditions in Java in the same terms.[49] Both in Java and Central Luzon, moreover, the increase of landlessness eroded the old patron-client relationships, at least in the agricultural context, a tendency reinforced by the progressing mechanization of rice cultivation. This engendered a massive expulsion of labor from the countryside.[50] Despite high economic growth in the 1970s and 1980s, the livelihood of the majority of Java's rural population was as precarious as in the late nineteenth century.[51] Circular migrations between the countryside and the cities did not alleviate precarity, let alone bring sustained economic growth to the countryside.[52] Men and women worked as domestic servants, pedicab drivers, food sellers, or collected firewood to sell in the city, just to eke out a subsistence wage.[53]

While the Philippine and Indonesian governments embarked on the export of labor, Malaysia became an immigration country. Its remarkable economic growth hinged on a narrow range of primary commodities, particularly rubber, defying the common wisdom that exports of primary products ushered in peripheralization. Since foreign-owned rubber plantations were of diminishing importance, these revenues directly benefited the Malaysian economy.[54] Moreover, Malaysia's oligopolistic position regarding its prime commodity was in sharp contrast to that of the Philippines, which had no control whatsoever over the global sugar market. Benefiting from the fact that 90 percent of the world's natural rubber production was in the hands of Indonesia, Malaysia, Thailand, and Sri Lanka, their governments succeeded in stabilizing the prices of natural rubber in the context of the UNCTAD negotiations. It was equally as necessary as the fragile agreement concluded under the pressure of a steadily growing share of synthetic rubber.[55] Malaysia managed, however, to untie itself from this dangerously high dependency on its rubber exports. It diversified toward other export crops, such as cocoa, and became the world's largest palm oil exporter. It also successfully upgraded a significant share of its commodity exports toward processed products.[56]

The obvious downside of Malaysia's commodity-based growth was its reliance on reduced wages and cheap immigrant labor, which by the 1980s made up about 50 percent of all plantation estate labor.[57] At the turn of the twenty-first century, the palm oil plantations alone offered work to 470,000 workers, many of whom came from Indonesia and Bangladesh.[58] For example, tens of thousands of Indonesians travel annually to Sabah from the relatively dry and poor East Nusa Tenggara, the region that had suffered so much from piracy and slavery in the previous century.[59] They are attracted by the fact that wages on palm oil plantations are seven to fourteen times as high as the amount they can earn at home.[60] Workers also arrive from other parts of Indonesia, however, and the largest single category of documented Indonesian migrant workers is still in the plantation sector, despite the fact that construction and manufacturing have exerted an increasing demand for labor. If we furthermore take into account the large flow of undocumented Indonesian plantation workers in Sabah—estimates range from 0.6 to 1.7 million—it becomes highly likely that plantation and other agricultural labor still makes up half of all male Indonesian migration toward Malaysia.[61] Many of these Indonesian male migrant workers aspire to blend into the Malay population and hope to obtain a position among its middle class.[62]

Malaysia's postcolonial economy is still chained to its commodity-producing past and does not offer enough skilled employment. Even while massively importing cheap labor, this country has become a country of mass emigration, even more so than Indonesia, relative to the size of its population. The Malaysian economy has been offering too little employment for its educated population, and this is particularly the case for the Indian and Chinese youth who, according to a survey in the 1970s, were overrepresented in secondary education but still less gainfully employed than Malays of the same age.[63] Meanwhile, the educational level of the Malay population, as well as their mobility, increased.[64] Many better-educated Malaysians started to commute to Singapore, and growing numbers are heading abroad. They leave for Taiwan, Japan, the United States (to these countries often as undocumented and circular migrants), and, oddly enough, even toward Indonesia and the Philippines.[65] Meanwhile in Sarawak, governmental settlement schemes following the example of FELDA were thwarted by the availability of cheap Indonesian labor.

In the Philippines, tenant farmers with large families scraped together every peso for the education of their children in the hope that this would lift them out of rural precarity and toward white-collar employment.[66] However, while education and urban life might bring status enhancement, it often did not yield much economic benefit.[67] A generation of highly educated people, for whom investment in education had not brought a release from precarity, provided the recruitment basis for Marcos's policies of promoting labor migration. In the 1970s, the Marcos regime actively encouraged emigration to improve its rapidly deteriorating balance of payments.[68] Moreover, with the banning of all forms of collective action, it had accomplished precisely what the penal sanction on Sumatra's eastern coast had achieved in the past, namely the creation of a servile labor force working for globally competitive wages. Four million labor migrants left the Philippines in the 1980s, turning it into the largest labor exporter after Mexico in those years.[69] Migration in the Philippines is also driven by a mismatch between education and the labor market. In 2007, unemployment among college graduates trained in the service sector reached the figure of 1.1 million, while at the same time, 650,000 vacancies for technical-vocational jobs were recorded.[70] Some of these were filled by Malaysians. About a third of all

Philippine university alumni are abroad, of whom more than half live in the United States, and as a rule they will not return.[71] The same mismatch is looming in Indonesia as well, where many who have obtained university degrees cannot find suitable jobs.[72]

RETURN OF THE DAYS OF INDENTURE

Since the 1980s, emigration from Island Southeast Asia has exploded into a multi-billion-dollar industry exploiting an increasingly female labor force. In Indonesia, domestic work abroad became a second destination alongside plantations. In the Philippines, the once dominant category of sailors among international male migrants became a minority, making up just 15 to 20 percent of the total.[73] The millions of migrant workers are an immense source of revenue. In recent years, their remittances have amounted to over 41 percent of the Philippine export earnings.[74] Emigration has become an industry, in which various official and semiofficial actors skim off migrants' earnings. There are official rates for obtaining the necessary documents in the Philippines and Indonesia, but in general, the fees are excessive and shored up by cartelization of the placement agencies.[75] Particularly in Indonesia under Suharto, a limited number of recruitment agencies obtained a license and had to share their profits with the political and military establishment.[76]

That the authoritarian regimes of Marcos and Suharto were interested in securing remittances and bribes rather than in protecting their citizens should not surprise us. Yet since their removal, any improvement in the conditions of migrant workers has still been disappointingly slow. After the ousting of Ferdinand Marcos in 1986, NGOs that were engaged with migrant workers held high hopes that the Aquino administration would enhance the effectiveness of the protection of overseas workers. However, it still took almost another decade—and the execution in March 1995 of the domestic worker Flor Contemplacion after a dubious conviction by a Singapore court—for the concerns about the safety and well-being of emigrants to be addressed consistently by the government of the Philippines.[77] In Indonesia, the government only became serious about protecting its citizens abroad from 2002 onward. Moreover, whatever government is in charge, it will always depend on the goodwill of the immigrant countries. In that respect, there is little room for optimism. The ILO Domestic Workers Convention (no. 189) of 2011, aimed at protecting domestic workers, has so far only been ratified in twenty-three countries, and none of these receive Philippine or Indonesian guest workers.[78]

However, even if more countries ratified the convention, one could still wonder what difference it would make. The past offers little basis for optimism. Although the 1930 Forced Labor Convention broke the stubborn resistance of the tobacco plantations in Sumatra to the abolition of the penal sanction, it did not eradicate the penal sanction, let alone forced labor. Likewise, since the adoption in 1956 of the Supplementary Convention on the Abolition of Slavery—which stretched the definition of slavery from its confines of legal property to "sufficient similarity"—trafficking and coerced labor conditions have grown rather than diminished in absolute figures.[79] The present mistreatment of migrant workers from Nias, the island that had exported so many slaves in the past, is just one among many examples. In recent times, these workers have been subjected to multiple human rights violations, including extensive child trafficking toward palm oil plantations in East Kalimantan, according to Indonesia's National Commission on Human Rights.[80] Human trafficking has involved debt slaves in the nineteenth century, plantation coolies in the twentieth century, and international labor migrants heading to East Asia and the Gulf States in the twenty-first century. The scale of today's coercion, fraud, deception, and abuse of power cannot leave a shred of doubt about the persistence of human trafficking.[81]

Colonial labor history repeats itself, for example, in the recruiting agencies in Jakarta that confine their clients in compounds, isolate them from their families, and charge them with highly inflated costs. Javanese women heading toward their overseas employment in the twenty-first century are locked up in the same way as Chinese workers were locked up in Singapore in the nineteenth century.[82] Female domestic workers are in high demand today and therefore are lured with advance payments, while their freedom is severely constrained as long as they have not repaid these sums.[83] The recruiters bill the employer for the advance, a mechanism reminiscent of what happened in the old colonial days. The employers in East Asia and the Gulf States deduct these amounts from the wages in monthly installments, resort to holding workers' passports, or even confine workers in their compounds or houses to ensure that they will recover their investment.[84] The insulation of the domestic workers can include prohibiting cellular phones, with the tragic effect that families lose contact with their migrated members.[85] Governments in receiving countries sanction confinement by employers. In Singapore, employers are expected to be the custodians of their workers. Under Saudi law, absconding is a criminal offence for migrant workers. In Malaysia, employers have been allowed to keep their workers' passports, yet going out without a passport entails the risk of being apprehended by the authorities, imprisoned, and deported. Although the governments of Malaysia and Indonesia agreed in 2006 that employers could only keep passports for reasons of safekeeping and with the workers' consent, it was an empty clause considering the leverage the employer had over them.[86] The Malaysian government has been sharply rebuked for this by Amnesty International, among others.[87]

Not only the practices of confinement but also the key elements of the recruitment infrastructure have survived decolonization. Bawean and Riau, which served as corridors for often-illicit migration to the Malay Peninsula in the colonial days, have fulfilled the same role in post-colonial times.[88] The scope of operations for these sponsors widened considerably when new circuits of labor migration emerged alongside the plantation recruitment because of infrastructural improvements in Indonesia and modest industrialization during the 1970s. East Java for example, once an immigrant frontier and today a relatively developed region of plantations and industry, has emerged as a site of prolific labor exports.[89] The actors are familiar as well. In colonial times, pilgrim brokers and recruiters of Arabian descent were channeling Javanese to Mecca via Singapore. Sheikhs worked via local priests to bring pilgrims to Java's port cities.[90] In the 1980s, the relatives of the sheikhs involved in the hajj to Mecca in the colonial era began to train and send female domestic labor to the Gulf States.[91] The recruitment agencies were legitimized by the Indonesian government, with the argument that they protect Muslim women. Many women deeply mistrust these commercial recruiters, however.[92] There are also many negative reports about the mistreatment of domestic and other workers in the Gulf States, and these stories reach the most remote villages in Indonesia. Nonetheless, many women feel attracted to Saudi Arabia, aside from the earnings, by the prospect that their stay there will enable them to make the hajj.[93]

Since migrants can earn ten times as much abroad than at home, they willingly take on the risks of mistreatment, cheating, and extortion by an array of official and semiofficial agencies. Migrants have to cope with these vagaries all the way from the first stages of the recruitment process up to their return home. Terminal 3 at Jakarta Airport, the entry for the returning migrant workers, has become notorious for ripping travelers off.[94] The profitability of the migration industry has also blurred the lines between recruiters and government agencies far more than in colonial times. Indonesian government officials, for example, maintain contacts with FELDA and, via local branches of recruitment agencies, channel migrants to Malaysia. These migrants are contracted via a network of local recruiters (or field agents or sponsors) who are paid per migrant, an exact replica of the recruitment infrastructure in Java for the Deli plantations a century ago.[95] Since the 1970s, the Indonesian workers at the Malaysian plantation estates have been in the thrall of sponsoring contractors and syndicates, who skim off their wages just as they did fifty years ago.[96]

Meanwhile, this brazen exploitation of migrant flows has encouraged alternative migration circuits, particularly between Indonesia and Malaysia. Official recruitment channels are practically unaffordable for migrants, who are driven into the arms of illicit recruitment and migration with forged documents, the latter being almost routine in the Indonesian migration industry.[97] These practices are old, also. In the nineteenth century, thousands of people left Java every year without the necessary written permission, since there were enough vessels around to take them across one of the sea lanes toward the Malay Peninsula. These reemerged in the 1990s, as a combined result of overcharging by licensed recruiters, Malaysian restrictions on Indonesian labor immigration, and attempts to replace Indonesian workers by Bangladeshis.[98] Large numbers of undocumented migrants cross the Malacca Straits from Riau to Johore or travel from the Eastern Archipelago toward Sabah.[99] Unlicensed recruiters with good contacts in Malaysia offer better services—including the procurement of the necessary immigration documents through illegal channels—in return for a payment of half the price charged by the licensed agencies.[100] On an island such as Lombok, which emerged as an important supplier of migrant workers in the 1990s, human traffickers used the old migration and smuggling itineraries of the Bugis, with hiding places in the creeks, to make the dangerous journey to Sabah. This is the same voyage made by the victims of piracy 150 years ago.[101]

The proportion of undocumented passages for Indonesian emigration may amount to almost 40 percent, which is four times as high as in the Philippines. This usually does not involve outright smuggling, and many migrants do hold a visa, but only one that allows them a temporary stay for a family visit or as a tourist. Since the 1990s, the overwhelming majority of undocumented Indonesian male and female migrants in Malaysia have been there thanks to their social networks, because transport has become much cheaper and easier, and because informal recruitment has become increasingly attractive.[102] The family encourages young people to look for employment in Malaysia, and the village head provides a travel document indicating that the person in question is visiting a relative there, which helps circumvent the channel of applying for work permits. It also leads to insufficiently documented labor migration.[103] Older migrants, friends, or relatives resident in Malaysia take care of a visa for a family visit.[104] In a world with erratic migration policies and complicated and corrupt bureaucracies, patron-client relationships have lost nothing in importance. Migrants see them as protection against trafficking recruiters conniving with government officials, a form of cronyism in which the "national economic interest" is used as an excuse to brush aside the rights of laborers. These workers struggle to escape from state-sanctioned bondage, or from employers who literally lock them up, and find their own way as migrants. Migrants have formed their own social networks since time immemorial to survive adverse conditions at the frontiers and resist their exploiters.

The role of patrons in labor recruitment and migration has been firmly established, and the resilience of the mechanisms of patriarchy, clientelism, and debt bondage in postcolonial times should not come as a surprise. Many of the subcontracting mechanisms outlived decolonization while diversifying to other sectors. Although they had predominantly served rural migrations in the nineteenth century, they increasingly linked the rural to the urban spheres in the twentieth, as well as the local to the global.[105] At present-day construction sites, for example, all the labor is delegated to *mandurs* (foremen). They incur all the risks, in return for which they pocket 10 to 20 percent of the total wages.[106] Meanwhile, the long tradition of village heads being instrumental in recruitment for plantations has diversified toward the factories. Their managers call on these functionaries to recruit young people for their workplaces, sometimes sending a bus to pick them up.[107]

With the liberalization of the recruitment industry since the end of the Suharto regime, the number of recruiting agencies has multiplied, and recently, undocumented migration seems to have declined and the role of the *taikong*, the migrant trafficker, to have diminished.[108] Here, we see the parallel with the late 1920s, when the crimps were phased out from the recruitment for Deli through an embedding of migration in the village structure of trust and authority, sponsorship, and subcontracting.[109] Moreover, migrants have become more worldly-wise and capable of comparing different migration options, which has a mitigating effect on the fees charged to them.[110] While urban agencies initially sent their representatives into the villages, today these communities have their own brokers or "sponsors," who are quite often hajis.[111] Village brokers, village heads, and religious authorities supply the potential migrants with funds to go to Jakarta to register with one of the recruitment agencies. These facilitators at the village level are today's patrons, and the migrants their clients.[112] The situation is no different in the Philippines, where most migrants cannot advance the recruitment fee either and where richer villagers or remittances of relatives provide the funding, and through that reproduce patron-client relations.[113] At the village level, where the overlap between formal and informal is as blurred today as it was in the colonial past, the patron is still a regular feature, according to Lindquist, writing about his fieldwork on migration in Lombok. The patron-client relationship is as functional in the recent era of global migration as it was pivotal for labor recruitment in earlier phases of globalizing capitalism.[114]

Today, in the absence of other systems of social security and of banking systems that serve the poor, patron-client relationships will continue to be crucial. Sponsors are indispensable; otherwise, migrants have to borrow for their recruitment fee and airfare on the local informal market, with interest rates that can be as high as 240 percent.[115]

Alternatively, and as happens for example in the Philippines, households sell land in order to obtain a job abroad rather than indebting themselves.[116] However, sponsors also charge high interest rates of up to 100 percent, which devours a substantial portion of the earnings, as recruitment fees are high.[117] Today, the official recruitment costs for a plantation worker in Sabah often amount to a full year's wage, which is no different from the darkest days of coolie recruitment by crimps in Java a century ago.[118] As happened a hundred years ago with Javanese workers in Deli, plantation workers and domestic workers in Malaysia today get caught in cycles of continuous migration, as they can often only save 300 or 400 USD per annum.[119] The amounts arriving back home are also small because many migrants have to pay these high interest rates and are cheated by their middlemen. Yet they continue to deal with the people who rip them off because they mistrust banks, which are also extremely slow.[120] Particularly Indonesian labor migrants who have borrowed money from local sponsors to pay for their recruitment charges will evade the banks, often because the local sponsors demand that workers remit money via them.[121] In Indonesia, just 10 percent of the remittances go through formal banking; most go via Western Union and MoneyGram agents and, particularly, through the hands of the not always reliable local sponsors.

While migrants make considerable sacrifices, their remittances barely generate any prosperity in their home communities. Both in the Philippines and in Indonesia, much of the remittances have to cover day-to-day expenditures. What is left is invested in education for younger siblings or for housing, to be constructed piece by piece as the money comes in over the years.[122] In rural areas of the Philippines, remittances are sometimes used by tenants' families to buy land and Japanese-made water pumps, but in general, only a marginal portion of the remittances is sent for investments.[123] The prestige of consumer goods and the fashionable clothes repatriates are wearing encourage relatives and neighbors to migrate as well. In the end, migration contributes disappointingly little to the diversification of the economy. Island Southeast Asia is far from unique in this respect; the same observation has been made for other high-emigration communities, such as Mexico.[124] With little opportunity to buy land or capital goods, the remittances cause a local "Dutch disease," which is also nothing new: in colonial times, migrants from Ilocos extensively invested their remittances in land, which drove up the prices of already scarce land.[125] The same occurred in the typical emigration island of Bawean (an island north of Java) in colonial times, where many returning after a life abroad bought a plot of overpriced land.[126] In principle, education is a worthwhile investment, but it does not automatically enhance job opportunities, and hence many young people with a college degree from Island Southeast Asia go abroad, where they can earn a lot more even through practically unskilled work.

Parents of domestic workers, who paid for their daughters' educations and held high hopes for their futures, may feel miserable about this, and their agony only deepens given the ongoing negative reporting about labor conditions for domestic workers abroad.[127] Nonetheless, going abroad is alluring to many young women because it gives them increased autonomy, and they convince their families that they can obtain goods that will enhance their family's status. Today, the average remittance for a worker from the Philippines is still much higher than for an Indonesian, which is not just a matter of individual levels of education but also of strong migrant networks that help Filipinos and Filipinas find the best placement.[128] Philippine women, who sometimes serve up to five times abroad, only go through the official channels for their first stay, after which they find their own way.[129] The social composition of the Filipina migrant population, which includes professionals, gives some degree of protection to the most vulnerable domestic servants, a network that also helps migrants find jobs via the irregular circuits. In contrast to Indonesian workers, who mainly come from poor rural villages, Philippine migrants, both males and females, come from urban segments and are better educated, which gives them more social capital.[130]

In the future, these differences between migrants from Indonesia and the Philippines may become less pronounced, as more and more individuals and families become acquainted with the challenges and traps of international labor migration. Exploitative recruiters are increasingly circumvented, and abusive employers are more readily abandoned by workers. Workers are aware of the fact that they are exploited and use their networks to resist it. Their resilience is reminiscent of what happened in the plantation and mining belts of Island Southeast Asia at the turn of the twentieth century. In the colonial days, each year 5 to

10 percent of the indentured workers deserted from the plantations in the Malay Peninsula and East Sumatra.[131] The same desertion rate of 10 percent was reported in 2010, when about thirty thousand maids left their employers in Malaysia, most of them seasoned migrants who absconded, liberating themselves from the debts incurred through inflated recruitment and other costs.[132]

Protest gatherings have been springing up in East Asia, and lines of complaining domestic workers are queuing up at Indonesian and Philippine embassies and consulates throughout Asia and the Middle East.[133] In 2008 and 2009, the Philippine Consulate in Dubai provided legal counseling to over 25,000 of its citizens each year. Thousands complain about extremely long working days, underpayment, and even denial of food.[134] In 2007, frequent mistreatment of female domestic servants by the Indonesian state incited highly visible protests in Hong Kong, which exposed—to anyone not yet aware of it already—the collusion of the Indonesian Consulate General and the labor exporters.[135] With their protests, these activists achieved the ruling that placement agents were no longer allowed to hold workers' passports and that workers were free to change their employment agencies.[136] A silver lining has appeared, thanks to the protest and advocacy groups that foster solidarity among workers, a novelty in the social world of Island Southeast Asia, which for many centuries has been dominated by the vertical solidarity of the patron-client relationships. This labor activism often faces repression, but it can no longer be silenced as easily as it was in colonial times.

Conclusion

Today, more than five million Filipinos, about four million Indonesians, and 1.8 million Malaysians live abroad. Many of these migrants have grandparents who moved from densely populated Central Java to the island's eastern parts, from Ilocos to Manila, to Negros or even further south to Mindanao, and last but not least, from China and Madras to Malaysia.[1] Their journeys were part of migration flows from once wealthy wet rice cultivation societies that lived under the pressure of rapid demographic growth. Growing population pressure was a crucial element in the "reversal of fortune," which contradicts the standard historical explanation that the peripheralization of the region was the outcome of the brutal colonial conquests by the Spanish conquistadores and the Dutch VOC. Likewise, British commercially driven imperialism to open up the Asian markets was only of limited importance. Last but not least, the claim that Island Southeast Asia became a periphery simply because of its role as a commodity supplier in global trade ignores the crucial importance of production systems. Smallholders were capable of engaging with the global economy in ways more beneficial to local communities than plantations, and for centuries, slavery was part of a noncolonial trajectory of engagement with unfolding global capitalism. The upsurge of slave raiding and slavery in the early nineteenth century was not the dire consequence of the disruption of the precolonial maritime economies but attests to the resilience of what Wallerstein has termed the "external arena."

These are all powerful arguments against the perspective of peripheralization as being the result of five hundred years of path dependency. It is this very perspective that has enabled both the world-systems scholars and Acemoglu and his coauthors of *Why Nations Fail* to explain global divergences with a single theory and from a long-term historical perspective. The unavoidable drawback of the unifying power of these theoretical positions is that it produces a homogenization of the peripheries, which is fundamentally ahistorical. This is not a new problem, however, but an inheritance from the days of Raúl Prebisch and the early years of the dependency theory. It suffers from an overemphasis on the deindustrialization of the periphery and a lack of recognition of the importance of demographic factors, labor relations, and mechanisms of migration. This makes it impossible, for example, to explain how even in the halcyon days of colonialism, corporate plantation and mining enterprises did not emerge as the dominant forces all over Island Southeast Asia but still left ample room for smallholders to produce for the global market. Having exposed this tendency toward homogenization, we should not throw out the baby with the bathwater. That would result in a kaleidoscopic perspective in which we discern the varieties but ignore the commonalities of engagement with global markets and the universality of basic mechanisms of survival within agricultural societies. Peripheralization should be studied as a global phenomenon, and it deserves a prominent place within global history and global studies at large; however, it should be approached in an interdisciplinary and comparative fashion. This would entail a more inclusive perspective on the path-dependent character of peripheralization, that it be perceived not as a unilinear, unidimensional phenomenon but as a combination of factors that reinforce one another.

World-systems research and new institutional economic history have both made an important contribution to the study of peripheralization by placing in the foreground the long-term detrimental effects of plantations on economic and social development. It needs to be added, however, that these plantations required specific demographic and social conditions, which in themselves were already key factors in impoverishment. Staggering demographic growth and precolonial patron-client relationships enabled the formation of extensive recruitment systems that served colonial policies of encapsulating local peasantries in plantation economies. The attending processes of enclosure and the extraction of wealth spread out from Java and the northern Philippines over the rest of Island Southeast Asia, with the consolidation of, respectively, Dutch, Spanish, and American colonial rule in this part of the world. After decolonization, the plantations would continue their march into the frontiers, despite the postcolonial preference for smallholder production. Likewise, the migration flows that had their provenance in the early nineteenth century can be seen as a continuous and contiguous movement that only ended in the 1980s for the Philippines and Indonesia, when there were no more frontiers left to move to within their national boundaries.

My aim here was to uncover how the detrimental role of plantations was entangled with demography and labor control. The peripheralization process in Island Southeast Asia was a process of growing rural precarity. This was particularly the case in Java, which changed from the most powerful island of Southeast Asia into one of the poorest and which suffered from land scarcity exacerbated by enclosures as well as a distorted rice market. The latter is a reminder that we should not confine our thinking about the peripheralizing effects of the "terms of trade" to the exchange between industrial manufactures and commodities but that we should also pay due attention to the effects of food imports. That the Philippines escaped the fate of Java, at least until the 1930s, was the combined result of more enabling conditions for smallholder cash-crop cultivation and of a conscious policy of the American administration to promote rice self-sufficiency by imposing tariffs on rice imports and the redistribution of land. Although colonial tariff policies did impede industrialization in the early twentieth century across all of the Global South, at least in Island Southeast Asia, agrarian policies had a much deeper effect on the economic conditions of the still overwhelmingly rural populations. This goes a long way toward explaining the divergent per capita incomes of Java and the Philippines under American administration.

Island Southeast Asia's lengthy engagement with the global economy was attended by labor coercion and coerced migrations in different guises, including kidnapping and debt traps. Oppressive labor regimes in the plantation conglomerates did exist under conditions of labor scarcity—the indentured labor systems attest to that—but these conditions were unstable and ephemeral. Low wages and the repression of labor activism were most effective and enduring where land was scarce and solid patron-client relationships in place. In the colonial heartlands (the northern Philippines and Java), where slavery had more or less disappeared in the eighteenth century, patron-client mechanisms proved indispensable in recruiting people for wage labor. Colonial governments advocated a free labor market with individual labor contracts, only to discover that the plantations and mines ground to a halt without labor intermediaries.

Patron-client relationships greased the wheels of labor supplies. Employers were either at their mercy or had to rely on the expensive and unpalatable practices of crimps. The labor intermediaries, whom we have encountered in this book among Chinese, Philippine, Tamil, and Javanese workers, were not just subcontractors for plantations and mines but also leaders of labor gangs, and they had no qualms about absconding with their workers in search of better treatment. Although exploitative, patron-client relationships offered protection to individual migrants, those under indentured conditions in particular, even to such an extent that they thwarted highly exploitative labor regimes. Many of the tens of thousands of workers who escaped from the mines and plantations of the Malay Peninsula and the Outer Islands of the Netherlands Indies used their contacts to become engaged in commodity production under much better conditions. Many others were cheated and trafficked, like today's international labor migrations from this region, but they resisted with increasing success as the social capital of their migration networks accrued. Conversely, because of the absence of a Javanese migration network connecting local village communities with plantations, and Deli or Chinese villages with the mines of Bangka, the colonial government had to bow to the pressure of planters' associations and legalize commercial recruiting practices and concomitant coerced labor conditions under indenture.

In the final decades of colonial rule, the migration networks that attended these patterns of mobility began to vary in character according to the respective levels of urbanization and education. The Philippine international migration was by and large an extension of earlier urban migrations and systems of maritime labor migration; in the case of Indonesia, the rural seasonal mobility and the old established links with the Malay Peninsula continued to dominate; and in Malaysia, it was the result of a plural society built on commodity exports. The Malaysian and Philippine international migration networks featured relatively high levels of social capital thanks to their urban background, educational attainment, and familiarity with the English language. Indonesian emigrants were clearly disadvantaged in this regard.

Nevertheless, the commonalities are no less important. Island Southeast Asia became a mass exporter of labor as a consequence of its specialization in commodity production in a *plantation* context. As the examples of Indonesia, the Philippines—and, last but not least, postcolonial Malaysia—show, plantation economies can be a powerful source of economic growth but usually only temporarily, as they offer limited opportunities for skilled employment. Likewise, they offer little in terms of local economic diversification. In Malaysia, the "return of the plantation" led to a massive influx of low-skilled labor, while its own growing numbers of higher educated found it increasingly difficult to find suitable employment. In the Philippines, plantation and estate interests compounded the already grave rural problems caused by extreme demographic growth and derailed the agenda of economic nationalism. This crisis had been brewing since the 1930s, and it exploded in the early 1980s. Although Indonesia did not experience such a grave crisis at that time, it did face the limits of transmigration policies as a means to address the problems of population pressure and labor surplus in Java.

At this juncture, new destinations for labor emigration emerged in the Middle East and East Asia. Existing patron-client mechanisms had been subsumed under new commercial recruiting systems, which mushroomed through exponentially increasing margins of profitability. Recruiters, governments, and government officials are never far away to skim off the remittances of the labor migrants. Laborers are still today subjected to debt bondage, and similar to the past, they resist coerced conditions or circumvent them by developing their own migration networks, in which patron-client relationships still play a crucial role. These often illicit channels are more trusted today than are government institutions, although the former can be abusive too. Meanwhile, all the hardship endured by migrants brings disappointingly little in terms of sustained development. As much as by-employment at nearby plantations once was, today's remittances are a crucial source of income for a substantial percentage of households, but the prospects of long-term economic gains are as dim today as they were in the past.

Appendix: Methodological Notes

Data on demography and occupational structures plays a key role in this comparative study on peripheralization. Decent census data is of a relatively recent date. For Indonesia, the first attempt at a census was made under Thomas Stamford Raffles (lieutenant governor-general of Java from 1811 to 1816), and further systematic gathering of data on demography had only begun by the mid–nineteenth century. The first successful and extensive census—including topics such as age distribution, occupations, and migration—had to wait until 1930. In the Philippines, the first census was held in 1876, but this survey did not include items regarding age and occupation. The first comprehensive census was conducted as late as in 1903, by the American colonial administration. Based on the U.S. format, this exercise resulted in a highly informative and thorough survey. In British Malaya, census reports on the Straits appeared from the mid–nineteenth century onward, but the first census containing data on occupations, as well as the first that covered most of the territory of present-day Malaysia, was held in 1911.

Data about demography, farming, plantation employment, and industrialization obtained through three different national systems of statistical surveying had to be brought together in a single format. Moreover, national census records are not only difficult to compare because of diverging definitions and categorizations but are also subject to change over time. I have used a method that was developed by the Global Collaboratory of Labour Relations to make data from highly diverse sources commensurable.[1] The starting point for this systematization was the creation of a comparative framework that began with total population figures.[2] From the available reconstructed total population figures, I first deducted children below ten (about 30 percent of the population). From the remaining 70 percent I deducted another 15 percent to account for the nonemployable either from age or sickness. Knowing that the employable population was about 59.5 percent of the total population in this part of the world in the decades around 1900, the biases with respect to unemployment, informal labor, and gender in the colonial counting methods can be determined and to a certain extent corrected. In line with the methods of the Global Collaboratory, I have included data on mixed employment, a crucial category, considering the importance of the cottage industry. Furthermore, I have drafted employment figures in export agriculture based on total acreage and the figures for the average required labor force per hectare for each specific crop. Finally, since about 80 percent of all people in Island Southeast Asia were agriculturally employed until the end of the colonial period, it is crucial to make a distinction between independent, dependent, sharecropping, landless agricultural workers, and enslaved agricultural workers. This was feasible for the twentieth century by combining agricultural and occupational statistics.

The results of this reworking of the available data can be found in my "Methodological Paper: Island Southeast Asia and the Global Collaboratory Labour Relations." The reworkings of census and other material that forms the basis of the paper are stored at the IISH dataverse and can be found at http://hdl.handle.net/10622/NCJVLW.

Notes

INTRODUCTION

1. The terms "Island Southeast Asia" and "Maritime Southeast Asia" are both used to distinguish the Philippines, Indonesia, and the Malay Peninsula from mainland Southeast Asia. The first term is more often used among prehistorians and biologists, whereas Maritime Southeast Asia is more popular among historians. However, since the term "Maritime" has the specific connotation "of human activity oriented toward the sea," I prefer the word "Island," which denotes the physical geography of this part of the world.

2. These figures are derived from the International Organization for Migration (IOM) for the year 2015. See http://www.iom.int/countries.

3. In absolute figures, the growth was from about 8.6 million in 1600 to 15.3 million in 1800 and 318.3 million in 2000. See: "Clio Infra," https://www.clio-infra.eu/datasets/searchresults.

4. See http://www.iom.int/countries/malaysia.

5. See, for example, the seminal article by Massey, "Economic Development and International Migration in Comparative Perspective."

6. This concerns, for example, Mexico, which was an industrializing country in the early nineteenth century but in the course of that century became a supplier of raw materials to the United States.

7. Acemoglu and Robinson, *Why Nations Fail.*

8. See Sokoloff and Engerman, "History Lessons."

9. Acemoglu, Johnson, and Robinson, "The Colonial Origins of Comparative Development"; Acemoglu, Johnson, and Robinson, "Reversal of Fortune."

10. See, for example, Peer Vries's review article, "Does Wealth Entirely Depend on Inclusive Institutions and Pluralist Politics?"

11. Bosma, *The Sugar Plantation in India and Indonesia*, 35–38; Roy, "Factor Markets and the Narrative of Economic Change in India," 142–43.

12. Acemoglu, Johnson, and Robinson, "Reversal of Fortune," 1235.

13. Acemoglu, Johnson, and Robinson, "Reversal of Fortune," 1258.

14. Bankoff and Boomgaard, "Introduction: Natural Resources and the Shape of Asian History, 1500–2000," 8–10; Van Schendel, *Three Deltas*, 297; Boomgaard, "From Riches to Rags?," 187; Henley, "Forced Labour and Rising Fertility in Colonial Indonesia," 9.

15. Zelinsky, "The Indochinese Peninsula," 137.

16. Hall, *A History of Early Southeast Asia*, 231; Krom, *Hindoe-Javaansche Geschiedenis*, 398.

17. See Dove, "The Agroecological Mythology"; Boomgaard, "From Riches to Rags?," 189. Also see Pigeaud, *Java*, 4:300.

18. In terms of food security, swidden agriculture might have been much less vulnerable than wet rice cultivation. For a discussion on this subject, see Boomgaard, "From Riches to Rags?," 193–195.

19. Dove, "Agroecological Mythology." It should be mentioned in this regard that in many rural areas of fourteenth-century Java, *ladang* (swidden) agriculture was still predominant. See Pigeaud, *Java*, 4:494.

20. Wolters, "Geographical Explanations for the Distribution of Irrigation Institutions," 220, 223; Wisseman Christie, "Water and Rice in Early Java and Bali," 246–47.

21. The notion of a paternalistic attitude of major landowners toward the landless in Java's countryside was, however, present in academic writings of the time. See Van der Kroef, "Social Structure and Economic Development in Indonesia," 397.

22. Geertz, *The Development of the Javanese Economy*, 33–40; Firman, "Population Mobility in Java," 82.

23. Clark, *Labor Conditions in the Philippines*, 895–96.

24. See Alexander and Alexander, "Shared Poverty as Ideology"; Benjamin White, "'Agricultural Involution' and Its Critics."

25. Kaut, "Utang No Loob," 265, 270–72.

26. See in this respect Kratoska, "The Peripatetic Peasant."

27. Pigeaud, *Java*, 4:474; De Graaf, *De Regering van Sultan Agung*, 262–63; Charney, "Crisis and Reformation," 192; Andaya, *Perak, the Abode of Grace*, 42–43;

Boomgaard, "Human Capital," 87–88; Talens, *Een Feodale Samenleving,* 52; Sutherland, "The Sulu Zone Revisited," 146.

28. This was pointed out by Evsey Domar in his famous article "The Causes of Slavery or Serfdom."

29. See Moertono, *State and Statecraft,* 134–51; Rothenbuhler, *Rapport,* 35–49. Tax revenue as a proportion of national income of the Netherlands Indies ranged between 7 and 10 percent, whereas total revenue ranged between 15 and 17 percent between 1920 and 1940. See Booth, "The Burden of Taxation," 94, 96.

30. The policies of sedentarism and peasantization by rulers in Southeast Asia were extensively discussed by James Scott. See, for example, Scott, "Freedom and Freehold," 50–51. For taxation and tribute in the Philippines under early Spanish rule, see, for example, Alonso, "Financing the Empire."

31. Clark, "Labour Conditions in Java," 924.

32. Taxation in precolonial Java was extensive, although often inconsistent. See Moertono, *State and Statecraft,* 134–51; Rothenbuhler, *Rapport,* 35–49. For taxation and tribute in the Philippines under early Spanish rule, see, for example, Alonso, "Financing the Empire."

33. For the 1920s, data is provided on per capita income for Java and the Outer Provinces by Meijer Ranneft Huender and Fievez de Malines van Ginkel, respectively. For Java, we could assume that the income of a poor *sawah* owner represents the average income, which would be about 69 guilders per household member. Meijer Ranneft and Huender, *Onderzoek naar den Belastingdruk,* 10. By contrast, the average income in Sumatra per household member was between 52 and 174 guilders, depending on the Residency in which it was located, but in most Residencies well beyond 100 guilders. Fievez de Malines van Ginkel, *Verslag van den Belastingdruk,* 10–11.

34. Bassino and Williamson, *From Commodity Booms to Economic Miracles,* 8.

35. See Van Nederveen Meerkerk, "Challenging the De-Industrialization Thesis."

36. This period is termed by Barbier as "The Golden Age of Resource-Based Development." See Barbier, *Scarcity and Frontiers,* 368–462.

37. Williamson, "Land, Labour, and Globalization in the Third World," 56, 81.

38. See Sokoloff and Engerman, "History Lessons."

39. Just to mention one example, the privileged position of plantations to the detriment of smallholders and the economy at large was extensively and hotly debated in the West Indies in the 1960s and 1970s. See Beckford, "Aspects of the Present Conflict Between the Plantation and the Peasantry in the West Indies."

40. UNCTAD, *Commodities and Development Report 2015;* Byerlee, Falcon, and Naylor, *The Tropical Oil Crop Revolution,* 190, 191, 201.

41. Van Schendel, *Three Deltas*, 295.

42. Acemoglu, Johnson, and Robinson, "Reversal of Fortune," 1264.

43. Tomich, "Rethinking the Plantation," 17.

44. Barlow, *The Natural Rubber Industry*, 50–51; Kaur, "Indian Ocean Crossings," 164.

45. De Zwart and Van Zanden, "Labor, Wages, and Living Standards in Java, 1680–1914," 229; Williamson, *Real Wages and Relative Factor Prices in the World Economy*, appendix table 3.4.

46. According to data presented by Clark, wages in the Java sugar industry may have declined by 10 to 20 percent between 1883 and 1900. See Clark, "Labor Conditions in Java," 936. According to Van Zanden and Marks, growth of GDP per capita for 1840–1860 was 0.4 percent, 0.2 percent for 1860–1880, 1 percent for 1880–900, and actually 2.5 percent for 1900–1913. Van Zanden and Marks, *An Economic History of Indonesia*, 50.

47. Schneider, *Inleiding tot de Studie*, 49.

48. Booth, *Colonial Legacies*, 147.

49. Van Gelderen, *Voorlezingen*, 103, 105.

50. Findlay and Lundahl, "Resource-Led Growth," 39.

51. In 1915, a Social Democratic member of parliament, H. H. van Kol, made a government-commissioned trip to Japan to study the prospects of an industrialization policy for the Netherlands Indies. See Van Kol, *Japan*. For the sharply competitive wage levels of Japan and coastal cities of China, see Clark, "Labor Conditions in the Philippines," 781, 820.

52. Doeppers, *Manila, 1900–1941*, 141.

53. As Benton and Herzog have argued, establishing colonial control involved a multitude of agents and interests leading to negotiated outcomes and complicating the notion of sovereignty. Benton, *A Search for Sovereignty*, 279–80; Herzog, *Frontiers of Possession*, 243.

1. SMALLPOX VACCINATION AND DEMOGRAPHIC DIVERGENCES IN THE NINETEENTH CENTURY

1. Acemoglu, Johnson, and Robinson, "Reversal of Fortune," 1264n15. For an overview of a critique on this position, see Vries, *Escaping Poverty*, 37–39.

2. Reid, *Southeast Asia in the Age of Commerce*, vol. 2, esp. chap. 5, "The Origins of Southeast Asian Poverty," 267–325.

3. Lieberman, *Strange Parallels*, 1:19, 22.

4. Wallerstein, *The Modern World-System*, 2:273.

5. Maddison, "Dutch Income," 645; Bulbeck et al., *Southeast Asian Exports*, 6.

6. Nagtegaal, *Riding the Dutch Tiger*, 126–28, 136, 148, table 12; De Zwart, "Globalization and the Colonial Origins," 140; Andaya, "Cloth Trade," 39–43; Hall,

"The Textile Industry in Southeast Asia," 119; Glamann, *Dutch-Asiatic Trade*, chap. 7; Kwee Hui Kian, "The End of the 'Age of Commerce,'" 291–92.

7. Pigafetta, sailing with Magellan around the world in the 1520s, counted 25,000 houses in Brunei, which we have to take with a grain of salt. Nicholl ("Notes on Some Controversial Issues," 38) makes it clear that it was probably just 25,000 inhabitants. Reid suggests that Malacca city had a population of 100,000, who could be fed thanks to extensive rice imports (*Southeast Asia in the Age of Commerce*, 2:67, 70–71; "The Structure of Cities," 238). Lockard ("The Sea Common to All," 230) conjectures more cautiously between 50,000 and 100,000, whereas Borschberg (*The Singapore and Melaka Straits*, 157, 185) disavows the figure of 100,000 as derived from Dalboquerque's fantasies. Furthermore, as Talens (*Een Feodale Samenleving*, 46–51) argues, it is highly unlikely that Banten had about 200,000 inhabitants in 1682 (claimed by Guillot, "La politique vivrière," 100). For Makassar, Reid ("Pluralism and Progress," 436) conjectures a size of 100,000 inhabitants between 1640 and 1660, but this is also based on circumstantial evidence of rice imports. Valentijn's figures about large Javanese port cities have been refuted by Nagtegaal (*Riding the Dutch Tiger*, 91–93). For the revisionism, see also Raben, "Cities and the Slave Trade," 121.

8. On a smaller scale and in Southeast Asia itself, Colombijn analyzed the inherent volatility of the different ports at Sumatra's east and west coast, which were vying for the role of an entrepôt for the products of the hinterland, most notably pepper. Colombijn, "The Volatile State," 520.

9. With regard to the dry-rice basis of Palembang, see Hill, *Rice in Malaya*, 21. For the reliance on external food supplies of Aceh, see, for example, Amrith, *Crossing the Bay of Bengal*, 55. Brunei's surrounding slopes were ecologically unsuitable for wet rice agriculture, and here Dayaks conducted swidden agriculture. Wet rice cultivation in lower districts had not developed sufficiently, despite that Javanese immigrants had been attracted to do so. Healey, "Tribes and States," 4, 15. According to Reid, about 6,000 tons of rice were imported into Malacca annually, which was enough to feed 50,000 people, and more food came overland or via small *prahus*. Reid, "The Structure of Cities," 237; Reid, *Southeast Asia in the Age of Commerce*, 2:69. Malacca attracted from Sumatra Minangkabau immigrants, known as competent wet rice growers, who settled in the interior near the city, but this concerned a relatively small population counting fewer than 30,000 members by the early nineteenth century. Hill, "Rice in Malaya," 145.

10. Manguin, "Trading Ships," 266–67, 270; Hall, *A History of Early Southeast Asia*, 216.

11. See also Guillot, "La politique vivrière."

12. For the Tonkin delta, Gourou (*Les paysans du delta Tonkinois*, 154) mentions villages, which were perfectly rural in character but still could have 10,000 or more inhabitants.

13. For an overview of the demographic growth of Batavia and Ommelanden, see Raben, "Cities and the Slave Trade," 128.

14. Villiers, "Manila and Maluku," 147.

15. Newson, *Conquest and Pestilence*, 124–25.

16. Newson, *Conquest and Pestilence*, 256–57; Newson, "Disease and Immunity," 1845.

17. Corpuz, *An Economic History of the Philippines*, 28.

18. De la Costa et al., "Muhammad Alimuddin I," 44. In 1718, the Spanish stationed a garrison in Zamboanga at the most western tip of Mindanao after they had vacated this stronghold in 1663.

19. De la Costa et al., "Muhammad Alimuddin I," 54; Vandermeer, "Population Patterns," 323; Warren, *Iranun and Balangingi*, 82–85.

20. Corpuz (*The Roots of the Filipino Nation*, 1:624) attributes the decline of the population of the Philippines in the early seventeenth century largely to raids by the Moros. See also Vidal, *Historia de la pirateria*, 1:71; Newson, *Conquest and Pestilence*, 85. The estimates for the total number abducted from the Philippines between the 1560s and 1800 range from several hundred thousand to two million. Clarence-Smith, *Islam and the Abolition*, 15.

21. Newson, *Conquest and Pestilence*, 76, 78–79, 107–8; Corpuz, *An Economic History of the Philippines*, 35.

22. Newson, *Conquest and Pestilence*, 259; Corpuz, *The Roots of the Filipino Nation*, 1:627.

23. Wisseman Christie, "Water and Rice," 243; Wisseman Christie, "States Without Cities," 24, 29, 30. For the numismatic history of Java before the arrival of the VOC, see Van Aelst, "Majapahit Picis."

24. Reid, "Introduction: Slavery and Bondage," 31; Jacobs, "Un règlement des comptes," 169; Boomgaard, "Fluctuations in Mortality," 7.

25. Boomgaard, "Fluctuations in Mortality," 8.

26. Boomgaard, "Fluctuations in Mortality," table 10.

27. Knaap, "The Demography of Ambon," 238. For Banda's population before 1623, see Villiers, "Trade and Society," 726–27. According to Van Fraassen (*Ternate*, 1:90), the population fell from 7,000 to 2,000 in the seventeenth century. See also Boomgaard, "Fluctuations in Mortality," 7.

28. The population of the Ambon islands increased from 52,669 in 1673 to 63,780 in 1692. Knaap, "The Demography of Ambon," 234. For the early nineteenth century, a figure of 59,000 has been quoted. De Graaff en Meylan, "De Moluksche eilanden," 241.

29. In contrast to Rickles and Feenstra, I do not believe that an annual population growth of a full percent could have been achieved without smallpox vaccination. I therefore suggest that Java's population must have been around 5.8 million by the mid–eighteenth century. Rickles, "Some Statistical Evidence," 30; Feenstra, "Dutch Coins," 168.

30. Velthoen, "Contested Coastlines," 199, 206. For a contemporary account on the Bajau, see Van Verschuer, "De Badjo's."

31. For a discussion of Warren's claim ("A Tale of Two Centuries," 129) that 68,000 slaves were employed in commodity production in the Sulu sultanate and its dependencies, see Sutherland, "The Sulu Zone Revisited." Velthoen ("Contested Coastlines," 203–4) emphasizes that for the East Sulawesi coastal waters, there is not much evidence of the extensive employment of slaves in the trepang fisheries; slaves were used for food production. For enslaved pearl divers in the Sulu islands, see "Berigten Omtrent den Zeeroof," 20:413. In 1900, when slave raiding had been practically suppressed, there were still between 5,000 and 20,000 slaves reported for the Sulu archipelago. Salman, *The Embarrassment of Slavery*, 71.

32. These under-researched demographic consequences were alluded to in Reid, "Low Population Growth," 43. See also Boomgaard, "Human Capital, Slavery," 91–92, and Warren, *Iranun and Balangingi*, 121.

33. Forrest (*A Voyage*, 354) claimed that the population of the Sulu sultanate had been about 60,000, whereas Hunt ("Some Particulars Relating to Sulo," 41–42) arrives at a figure of 200,000 inhabitants for the Sulu islands around 1810. Whether this discrepancy is the result of different counting methods or a massive influx of slaves, as Warren (*Sulu Zone*, 209) argues, is difficult to tell.

34. Reid, *The Contest for North Sumatra*, 7; Bosma, "Smallpox," 91.

35. Snouck Hurgronje, *De Atjehers*, 1:21, 23, 24–25, 394.

36. Although the population figure of 340,000 cited by Tideman is for 1930, the territory of Bone in the nineteenth century was much larger. Tideman, *Het Landschap Bone*, 5.

37. This estimate is based on Forrest's account of the total militia of Ternate and its dominions of 90,700. See Forrest, *A Voyage to New Guinea*, 36–37. Devastation and population decline was not always caused by piracy. The Sula Islands, off the east coast of Sulawesi, lost most of their population in the early nineteenth century when their revolt against Ternate was brutally repressed. Van der Hart, *Reize Rondom Celebes*, 118. Also see Bosscher and Matthijsen, "Schetsen," 92.

38. Jackson, *The Chinese in the West Borneo Goldfields*, 20.

39. Ritter (*Indische Herinneringen*, 115) even estimated the number of Chinese in West Kalimantan at 60,000. Somers Heidhues (*Golddiggers*, 130) deems these

estimates of over 40,000 "probably exaggerated," in which she follows Veth's assessment that in 1868, the total Chinese population was just 24,230. At that time, the mines had already petered out, however, and miners had left for Sarawak. See the footnote by P. J. Veth on page 33 of Gronovius, "Verslag over de residentie Borneo's Westkust, 1827–1829." See, further, Jackson, *The Chinese in the West Borneo Goldfields*, 24; and Yuan Binling, "Chinese Democracies," 70, 174–76.

40. NA (National Archive, the Hague), MvK (Ministerie van Koloniën) I, 3084, "Rapport over den afloop der zending van de Kommissaris voor de West kust van Borneo M. Francis, 1832"; "Een Inlandsche Nederzetting," 43–44.

41. Somers Heidhues, *Golddiggers*, 146.

42. Schwaner's (*Borneo*, 1:66–67) descriptions of the mines indicate that the number of miners involved ranged from 250 to 1,200, and since we may assume that there were a dozen of these mining sites, the total number of miners could have ranged from 5,000 to 10,000.

43. Dodge, "Population Estimates," 439–40; Mohamad, *The Malay Handloom Weavers*, 21, 33; Hill, *Rice in Malaya*, 34; Talib, "The Port and Polity of Terengganu," 214–15.

44. See Dias-Trechuelo, "Eighteenth-Century Philippine Economy: Mining," 774, 777.

45. Table 1.1 only includes the Chinese coolies working in the Ommelanden of Batavia. See Atsushi, "Toward Cities," 197–99. According to Raffles (*The History of Java*, 1:70), the entire ethnic Chinese population in Java stood at 91,441 in 1815.

46. Smith and Shui-Meng, "The Components of Population Change," 253–55; Doeppers and Xenos, "A Demographic Frame," 4. With regard to the inaccuracy of early-nineteenth-century data, see, for example, "Remarks on the Philippine Islands and Their Capital Manila 1819–1820," in Blair and Robertson, *The Philippine Islands*, 51:78. Tables of the *Guia oficial de las islas filipinas* present widely divergent figures for births minus deaths in 1858 (2.24%), in 1862 (1.03%), in 1864 (2.20%), and in 1879 (1.77%). See IISH Dataverse, Bosma, "Demography," File "Philippines Natural Growth and Migration 1858–1896 (19 March 2017)." As Owen (*Bikol Blend*, 50) observed, the demographic data collected under the Spanish rule is unreliable. However, it remains consistently within the range of high demographic growth. The Philippine census of 1903 provides details about natural population growth for the 1880s and 1890s, and apart from years with cholera and the resumption of smallpox caused by the Philippine Revolution (1896–1898) and the War of Independence (1899–1902), population growth could easily have exceeded 2 percent per annum. *Census Philippines* 1903, 3:17.

47. Boomgaard, *Children of the Colonial State*, 202.

48. For Siam in the first half of the nineteenth century, Skinner, for example, projects a growth rate of about 0.38 percent (from 4.75 million in 1825 to 5.25. million in 1850). See Skinner, *Chinese Society in Thailand*, 70. For Burma, see Resnick, "The Decline of Rural Industry," 56, 58. See, further, Reid, "Southeast Asian Population History," 5; Richell, *Disease and Demography*, 8–17. For the growth of Indonesia's Outer Islands, see Bosma, "Smallpox"; for the Malay Peninsula, see Bosma, "Methodological Paper," 6, table 1.3.

49. National Archive The Hague, MvK I, inv. no. 3089, "Opgaaf der bevolking der Moluksche eilanden 1840"; Bosma, "Smallpox," 91–92, table 2.

50. According to Reid, Sulu and Mindanao may have had a population of 230,000 by 1800. Reid, *Southeast Asia in the Age of Commerce*, 1:14; Reid, "Low Population Growth," 36. An estimated 75 percent of this population was Muslim, which amounted to 10 percent of the total Philippine population at that time. The Philippine census of 1903 counted 350,000 Muslims among an entire population of over seven million. *Census Philippines* 1903, 2:49.

51. For the demographic figures of the Malay Peninsula, see Bosma, "Methodological Paper," 6, table 1.3.

52. Dodge, "Population Estimates," 447; Hill, *Rice in Malaya*, 55, 58. Late-nineteenth-century population growth was also recorded in Kedah (ceded to the British by Siam in 1909). See Mahmud, "The Population of Kedah," 205.

53. Boomgaard, "Smallpox, Vaccination, and the Pax Neerlandica," 599–600; see also Bosma, "Smallpox."

54. Java was visited by severe cholera epidemics every thirty years, which in combination with food shortages led to declining populations in central Java in the late 1840s. In the Philippines, cholera claimed over 100,000 victims within 1.5 years in 1902–1903. Worcester, *A History of Asiatic Cholera*, 21; Breman, "Java," 271; Boomgaard, "Morbidity and Mortality in Java," 50.

55. De Jong Boers, "Mount Tambora in 1815"; Zollinger, *Verslag van eene Reis naar Bima*, 150–51; Reinwardt and de Vriese, *Reinwardt's Reis naar het Oostelijke gedeelte*, 317. The deadliest typhoon that struck the Philippines was the Haiphong of 1881, which resulted in 20,000 casualties in this archipelago alone. http://www.britannica.com/event/Haiphong-cyclone.

56. Junghuhn mentions the curiously precise figure of 232,995 for the number of casualties from the Padri War (1803–1837) in the Minangkabau highlands. Junghuhn, *Die Battaländer*, 1:264, 2:56; Müller, *Reizen en Onderzoekingen in Sumatra*, 91. For the Java War, see Carey, *The Power of Prophecy*, 653. The total death toll at the Indonesian side of the Aceh War (1873–1903) has been estimated at about 60,000 during military campaigns and another 25,000 caused by disease and exhaustion in labor camps, and these figures may well be underestimates. Wesseling, *A Cape of Asia*, 68.

57. For estimates of the number of casualties from the wars of independence of the Philippines, see, for example, Bankoff, "Wants, Wages," 67. Henley ("Population and the Means of Subsistence," 358) does not attribute much weight to volcanic disasters as factors in demographic stagnation or decline. For an example of the ravages of a hurricane, see Kolff, *Reize*, 65–66.

58. De Zwart, "Globalization and the Colonial Origins," 137; Feenstra, "Dutch Coins," 181–82; De Zwart and Van Zanden, "Labor, Wages," 229.

59. Boomgaard, "In the Shadow of Rice," 600. Research into the effects of the Columbian Exchange on Southeast Asia in nutritional terms is still in its infancy. See Boomgaard, "From Riches to Rags," 194–95; and Nunn and Qian, "The Columbian Exchange," 184.

60. Fornier, "Economic Developments in Antique Province: 1800–1850"; Doeppers and Xenos, "A Demographic Frame," 6.

61. See Razzell, "Population Change in Eighteenth-Century England"; and Davenport, Schwartz, and Boulton, "The Decline of Adult Smallpox," 1312.

62. Leung, "Variolation," 8; Leung, "The Business of Vaccination," 30. The crucial role of smallpox vaccination in early-nineteenth-century demographic transition in Europe has been detailed in Mercer, "Smallpox and Epidemiological Change," 306. See also Rutten, *De Vreselijkste Aller Harpijen*, 412; and for Costa Rica, Brignoli, *La población de Costa Rica*, 219–20, 234.

63. Banthia and Dyson, "Smallpox in Nineteenth-Century India," 657–58, 678. Apart from the famine years, the average annual mortality from smallpox in Madras Presidency was less than 0.1 percent by the late nineteenth century. Lardinois, "Famine, Epidemics, and Mortality," 457.

64. For the Philippines, I took the figures published by Xenos and Shui-Meng ("Nagcarlan," 209, 213–18) for Lagcarlan (Laguna). For Java, see Breman, "Java," 276; and Boomgaard, *Children of the Colonial State*, 172.

65. Lucieer, "Het Kindertal," 546–47, 549, 557. See also Andaya, "Women and Economic Change," 174; Reid, "Low Population Growth," 41; and Schadenberg, "Die Bewohner von Süd-Mindanao," 9.

66. Rappard, "Het Eiland Nias," 478, 560.

67. Roth, *The Natives of Sarawak*, 1:106.

68. For the Malthusian factor, see Tammes, "De Biologische Achtergrond," 197; and Henley, *Fertility, Food, and Fever*, 610.

69. Spyer, *The Memory of Trade*, 14–15; Chew, *Chinese Pioneers on the Sarawak Frontier*, 77, 109, 114.

70. Thompson, "Jean Marie Despiau," 44, 60; Thompson, *Vietnamese Traditional Medicine*, 114; Pearson, "Vaccination"; Naono, "Vaccination Propaganda," 34; Highet, "Small Pox," 17.

71. Naono, *State of Vaccination*, 103–15; Bhattacharya, Harrison, and Worboys, *Fractured States*, 63–70; Naono, "Inoculators," 96–97; Naono, "Vaccination Propaganda," 32. See also Brimnes, "Variolation." The rates of variolation for Bihar, Orissa, and the northern part of Madras Presidency were an estimated 50 percent. For Bengal, the estimates range from 60 to 80 percent. Banthia and Dyson, "Smallpox in Nineteenth-Century India," 659; Arnold, *Science, Technology, and Medicine*, 72.

72. Naono, *State of Vaccination*, 175–77; Highet, "Small Pox," 20, 22; Thompson, *Vietnamese Traditional Medicine*; Gourou, *Les paysans*, 188.

73. Lee, "Smallpox and Vaccination, I (1819–1829)," 525–26.

74. The consequences were devastating because the incubation time was ten to fourteen days, but during that period a patient is already contagious via respiration.

75. Lee, "Smallpox and Vaccination, III (1850–1859)," 17–18; Lee, "Smallpox and Vaccination, IV (1860–1872)," 127–30; *Singapore Free Press and Mercantile Advertiser*, August 24, 1849. Whereas the census of 1845 gave a population of 57,421 for Singapore and its dependencies, the census of 1849 gave only 52,801. For the figures for 1845, see "Statement of the Census of the Island of Singapore and Its Dependencies Taken in the Month of July 1845," *Singapore Free Press and Mercantile Advertiser*, August 21, 1845; and for 1949–1850, see "Census of Singapore and Its Dependencies Taken Under the Order of Government in the Months of November and December 1849," *Singapore Free Press and Mercantile Advertiser*, February 1, 1850.

76. Lee, "Smallpox and Vaccination, IV (1860–1872)," 132–34.

77. *Straits Times*, April 11, 1889; "Small Pox in Penang," *Straits Times Overland Journal*, December 26, 1881; "Small-Pox in the Straits and Burma," *Singapore Free Press and Mercantile Advertiser*, March 16, 1899.

78. In 1912, for example, a quarter of the population of the town Terengganu reportedly died from smallpox. Dodge, "Population Estimates," 442; Manderson, *Sickness and the State*, 47.

79. See Razzell, "Population Change"; Davenport, Schwartz, and Boulton, "The Decline of Adult Smallpox," 1312. See also Razzell, "The Decline of Adult Smallpox."

80. See Thompson, "To Save the Children."

81. Martín, "El Legado," 42–43.

82. Martín, "El Legado," 57–60.

83. Franco-Paredes et al., "The Spanish Royal Philanthropic Expedition," 1288; Colvin, "Arms Around the World," 79, 83.

84. *Reglemento de Vacuna*, 7–8, 37–38; Lopez-Yrastorza, *Memoria*, 25; Bantug, "Carlos IV," 98–100. For an extensive and balanced discussion concerning the

effects of smallpox vaccination under Spanish rule, see De Bevoise, "Until God Knows When." For the preservation of the vaccine, see Bantug, *A Short History of Medicine in the Philippines*, 66.

85. Turot, *Emilio Aguinaldo*, 3.

86. De Bevoise, "Until God Knows When," 169–70.

87. Bosma, "Smallpox," 74.

88. HTK 1851–1852, *Koloniaal Verslag* 1851, 262; *Encyclopaedie* 1917, 4:499.

89. Van der Chijs, *Nederlandsch-Indisch Plakaatboek*, 14:48. For the arrival of smallpox vaccine in Bengkulu in 1803, see Bennett, "Passage Through India," 211; Neelakantan, "Eradicating Smallpox in Indonesia," 63.

90. Schoute, *Occidental Therapeutics*, 110–11.

91. For the role of the village priests in vaccination efforts, see, for example, Breman, *Koloniaal Profijt*, 19.

92. Within the first three years after 1820, about 355,000 people, mainly children, had been vaccinated in Java, and to this figure another 200,000 to 250,000 might be added as a result of earlier vaccinations. "Koepok-inenting" (1846), 112; Boomgaard, "Smallpox and Vaccination," 127; Swaving, "Numerieke Verdeeling," 290–91. An incidental outbreak of smallpox in 1868 was immediately answered by an increased effort of 1,284,798 vaccinations and 722,938 revaccinations in 1868. Veth, *Java*, 1:488. Newspapers still reported outbreaks of smallpox around 1870, but these diminished in significance. See, for example, *Bataviaasch Handelsblad*, November 15, 1871.

93. See Boomgaard, "Smallpox and Vaccination on Java." See also Boomgaard, "Morbidity and Mortality," 63; Boomgaard, "Smallpox, Vaccination, and the Pax Neerlandica," 603–4.

94. Schoute, "De Geneeskunde," 950.

95. Tillema, "*Kromoblanda*," 3:29.

96. Bantug, *A Short History of Medicine in the Philippines*, 67.

97. Kai Khiun Liew, "Terribly Severe Though Mercifully Short," 239.

98. The measures were far from watertight, however, as in 1907 the Deli planters decided to establish a quarantine station. Modderman, Volker, and Van der Veen, *Gedenkboek*, 129. Interestingly enough, in the quarantine ordinance of 1911, smallpox had disappeared from the list of epidemic diseases that required quarantine. Van der Kemp, *De Quarantaine- en Epidemie-Voorschriften*, 54, 79; Hekmeijer, *Quarantaine Ordonnantie*.

99. De Bevoise, "Until God Knows When," 157–58, 162, 173.

100. Tillema, "*Kromoblanda*," 3:23, 30; Kolff, *Reize*, 213.

101. À Campo, *Koninklijke Paketvaart Maatschappij*, 687.

102. Roth, *The Natives of Sarawak*, 292. The case of influenza exposed once again how vulnerable the smaller islands must have been to smallpox,

particularly since no proper medical assistance could be offered there. *Bataviaasch Nieuwsblad*, April 16, 1919. *Nieuws van den Dag voor N.I.*, April 9 and 29, 1919.

103. Resistance in Java was confined to Banten and the Priangan. Winkler and Noordhoek Hegt, *Aanteekeningen*, 33.

104. De Bevoise, "Until God Knows When," 159.

105. For an overview of this resistance, see Bosma, "Smallpox," 76–77.

106. For Lombok, see Van der Kraan, *Lombok*, 134.

107. Roth, *The Natives of Sarawak*, 290–93; "Smallpox at Brunei," *Straits Times*, August 3, 1904; "Epidemic in Brunei," *Straits Times*, August 12, 1904.

108. Compulsory vaccination was introduced in Britain in 1853 and in Prussia in 1884. See Hopkins, *The Greatest Killer*, 87–91. According to Bantug (*A Short History of Medicine in the Philippines*, 39), vaccination was compulsory in the Philippines under Spanish rule, although no sanctions were applied in the case of noncompliance.

2. THE EXTERNAL ARENA: LOCAL SLAVERY AND INTERNATIONAL TRADE

1. Austin, "Cash Crops and Freedom," 18; Lovejoy and Hogendorn, *Slow Death for Slavery*, 305n1. See also Salau, "The Role of Slave Labor."

2. Hopper, "Slaves of One Master," 225.

3. Mann, *Sahibs*, 159–60; Warren, *Iranun and Balangingi*, vi. An important contribution to this debate is also Damir-Geilsdorf et al., eds., *Bonded Labour*, in which five out of its eight contributions refer explicitly to the linkage between capitalism and slavery beyond the orbit of European colonial domination.

4. Lieberman, "A Zone of Refuge," 338–39.

5. An example of this historiography is Tarling, *Piracy and Politics*, 7–8.

6. Lapian, "Violence and Armed Robbery," 139.

7. Christians and Muslims enslaved Alfurs and Papuas in the Moluccas, the Spanish enslaved Negritos in the Philippines, aboriginals or *orang asli* were enslaved by the Malay in the Malay Peninsula, the Dayaks in Kalimantan by the Malay or made peons by the Chinese, the Torajas were enslaved by the Bugis, the mountain dwellers of Sumba by the Endehnese, the Butonese from interior by the coastal pirates, the gentile populations by the Christian populations around the scattered VOC forts in the Moluccas, and the inland Dayaks by the Sea Dayaks or Iban.

8. "Berigten Omtrent den Zeeroof," 20 (1873): 316; Hunter and St. John, *Adventures of a Naval Officer*, 68.

9. Hall, Hirsch, and Li, *Powers of Exclusion*, 10.

10. Warren, "Sino-Sulu Trade," 50–51. Some of the figures given by Warren about the required labor to produce sea products have been contested by Sutherland as being exaggerated. See Warren, *Iranun and Balangingi*, 217, 220, 401; Sutherland, "The Sulu Zone Revisited."

11. Forrest, *A Voyage*, 344–45. In the first half of the nineteenth century, an estimated 500 slaves were brought to the northeastern tip of Borneo annually to be put in the forest to work there. Warren, "Slave Markets," 166.

12. Velthoen, "Contested Coastlines," 203.

13. Warren, *Iranun and Balangingi*, 209. Also see, for example, the Batta sailor Jadee in the account of Sherard Osborne in *The Blockade of Kedah*, 40; Müller, *Proeve eener Geschiedenis*, 52.

14. Raffles (*The History of Java*) estimated that the Iranun numbered not less than 10,000. See St. John, "Piracy in the Indian Archipelago," 253. Warren (*Iranun and Balangingi*, 87) estimates the total number of Iranun in the early nineteenth century to be between 10,000 and 15,000. According to Vidal (*Historia de la piratería*, 1:84), the number of warriors was 18,140. Comyn's (*The State of the Philippines*, 248) claim that the sultan of Sulu was maintained by about 50,000 pirates seems to be an exaggeration. For the clients of the Malay states, see Mills, Turnbull, and Bassett, "British Malaya 1824–1867," 261–62.

15. NA, MvK I, inv. no. 1787, Verb. August 6, 1847, no. 353.

16. Warren, *Iranun and Balangingi*, 144; Barrantes, *Guerras piráticas*, 148–64. Local successes in repelling the pirates were reported, for example, in Antique, the western coastal strip of Panay (Fornier, "Economic Developments: 1800–1850," 414) and for eastern Luzon (Owen, *The Bikol Blend*, 6).

17. "The Piracy and Slave Trade," 3:632; Warren, *Iranun and Balangingi*, 108. In the late 1820s and 1830s there seems to have been a setback in the struggle against piracy, but this need not have afflicted the coasts of Luzon and the Visayas. See Warren, "The Port of Jolo and the Sulu," 306. See also Vidal (*Historia de la pirateria*, 1:375), who mentions that 6,000 Filipinos were captured by the Moros in 1836.

18. Hunt, "Sketch of Borneo," 19.

19. Andaya, *Perak*, 333, 335; "The Piracy and Slave Trade," 3:584, 587–88; Warren, *Iranun and Balangingi*, 61, 137–38. Atsushi, *Changes of Regime*, 124–28; Cornets de Groot, *Notices historiques*, 4; Müller, *Proeve eener Geschiedenis*, 49–52; Veth, *Borneo's Wester-afdeeling*, 361; Horsfield, "Verslag Aangaande het Eiland Banka," 211–20; Andaya, *Perak*, 377.

20. Velthoen, "Contested Coastlines," 212–13; Warren, *Iranun and Balangingi*, 70–71; Teitler, Van Dissel, and à Campo, *Zeeroof en Zeeroofbestrijding*, 25; Van Eijbergen, "Geschiedkundige Aanteekingen"; Kruyt, "De Bewoners van den Banggai-archipel," 66.

21. Warren, "A Tale of Two Centuries," 135; "Nouvelles de Java," *Journal de la Haye,* September 12, 1834. Although many abductions, particularly of fishermen, went unnoticed by authorities, there is enough on record to reconstruct the overall pattern and geographical shifts of slave raiding in this part of Island Southeast Asia, as is demonstrated by à Campo, "Patronen, Processen," 95–98.

22. NA, MvK I, inv. no. 1787, Verb. August 6, 1847, no. 353.

23. Cornets de Groot, *Notices Historiques,* 5–6; Warren, *Iranun and Balangingi,* 290; "The Piracy and Slave Trade," 3:582–83, 586, 629. "Atjeh—Beschouwingen van den oud-soldaat Veritas," 333.

24. *Singapore Chronicle and Commercial Register,* May 7, 1836; "The Piracy and Slave Trade," 4:145, 156; "More Atrocious Piracies," *Singapore Chronicle and Commercial Register,* August 25, 1831; "More Piracy," *Singapore Free Press and Mercantile Advertiser,* April 13, 1837; "Atrocious Piracies," *Singapore Chronicle and Commercial Register,* August 11, 1831; *Straits Times,* August 12, 1846.

25. Crawfurd, quoted in "The Piracy and Slave Trade," 4:45.

26. "The Piracy and Slave Trade," 3:634.

27. Tarling, *Piracy and Politics,* 76; "The Piracy and Slave Trade," 4:145.

28. Atsushi, "Pirates or Entrepreneurs," 78–79; Leyden, "Sketch of Borneo," 50–53; Tagliacozzo, "Smuggling," 147; Wong Lin Ken, "The Trade of Singapore," 63.

29. With regard to the lack of collaboration between Dutch and Spanish fleets in combating piracy, see NA, MvK II, inv. no. 1557, Verb. January 6, 1865, no. 15, inv. no. 2102; Verb. July 4, 1868, no. 10 and inv. no. 2111; and Verb. July 27, 1868, no. 6.

30. "Berigten Omtrent den Zeeroof," 20 (1873): 407; Tarling, *Piracy and Politics,* 168. The Dutch newspapers of the Netherlands Indies reported that about 290 people were captured in 1861 and 478 in 1862. In addition, twelve people liberated from pirates were reported in 1861 and 616 in 1862. See IISH, Dataverse, Bosma "Demography," File "19th C. Slavery in the Outer Islands of the Netherlands Indies (March 19, 2017)."

31. Wright, "The Anglo-Spanish-German Treaty," 66; Schult, "Sultans and Adventurers," 404.

32. Bhar, "Sandakan," 121. Schult, "Sultans and Adventurers," 405–6; Wright, "The Anglo-Spanish-German Treaty," 68–69; Warren, "Sino-Sulu Trade," 72–73.

33. Wright, "The Anglo-Spanish-German Treaty," 70–75. Spanish and Dutch sources mention the import of slaves from Sulu, some of whom had been raided from the Tawi Tawi islands located between Jolo and Borneo. Worcester, *The Philippine Islands,* 208; HTK 1892–1893, *Koloniaal Verslag* 1892, 59; NA, MvK II, Mail report 1890, no. 389.

34. See Tregonning, "The Elimination of Slavery." In a petition by Sultan Hashim in 1906, the high commissioner was, among other things, asked to provide assistance to recover runaway slaves. Singh, *Brunei,* 112.

35. IISH, Dataverse, Bosma "Demography," File "19th C. Slavery in the Outer Islands of the Netherlands Indies (March 19, 2017)."

36. Van Hoëvell, "De Zeeroverijen der Soloerezen," 103; *Java-bode*, June 9, 1860; HTK 1871–1872, *Koloniaal Verslag* 1871, 253; HTK 1877–1878, *Koloniaal Verslag* 1877, 36; HTK 1879–1880, *Koloniaal Verslag* 1879, 22; Teitler, Van Dissel, and à Campo, *Zeeroof en Zeeroofbestrijding*, 104.

37. Kniphorst, *Historische Schets*, 22; "Beschrijving van het Eiland Soemba," 297.

38. HTK 1877–1878, *Koloniaal Verslag* 1877, 36; Needham, "Sumba and the Slave Trade," 7; Widjojo, *The Revolt of Prince Nuku*, 127–30. Van Fraassen, *Ternate*, 1:79.

39. Welie, "Slave Trading and Slavery," 72; Bigalke, "Dynamics of the Torajan Slave Trade," 344; "Beschrijving van het Eiland Soemba," 298; NA, MvK I, inv. no. 2798, GB 12 January 1827, no. 9. In 1876, Papua, Bugi, and Toraja slaves were still being traded by merchants in Makassar and Ternate. NA, MvK II, Mail report 1876, no. 654; Mail report 1877, no. 509. As late as 1892, it was reported that 100 to 200 people from Nias were enslaved and possibly the same number killed. NA, MvK II, Mail report 1892, no. 106; Lekkerkerker, "Bali 1800–1814," 317; "[De] Afschaffing van de Slavernij," 31; Bigalke, *Tana Toraja*, 24, 42–43; Sarasin and Sarasin, *Reisen in Celebes* 2:28, 62; Atsushi, "Tropical Products Out," 513–14; Bigalke, "A Social History," 66.

40. Haga, *Nederlandsch Nieuw Guinea*, 2:60, 90, 448–49; Van Fraassen, *Ternate*, 1:82; Riedel, "De Sluik- en Kroesharige," 101, 154, 252, 293, 320.

41. NA, MvK II, Mail report 1888, no. 216.

42. NA, MvK II, Mail report 1870, nos. 633 and 669; Mail report 1871, no. 522.

43. NA, MvK II, Mail report 1894, no. 268.

44. "Beschrijving van het Eiland Soemba of Sandelhout," 297; Needham, "Sumba and the Slave Trade," 26, 33–35; HTK 1890–1891, *Koloniaal Verslag* 1890, 62; NA, MvK II, Mail report 1888, no. 868; Mail reports 1889, nos. 148 and 869; Riedel, "Timor en Onderhoorigheden," 7, 10; Bigalke, "A Social History," 66; Van der Kraan, "Bali: Slavery," 337. Slaves from New Guinea were still being imported in East Seram during the early years of the twentieth century. See KITLV, collectie A. P. van de Siepkamp, Letters of [A. J. Quarles de Quarles], Resident of Amboina.

45. This estimate is based on the assumption that between 300 to 400 pirate vessels were plying the waters of Island Southeast Asia and on reports that on average a vessel could carry 20 or so captives. St. John, "Piracy in the Indian Archipelago," 258; Warren, "The Port of Jolo: International Trade," 193. Warren, "The Port of Jolo and the Sulu," 316. Warren suggests that 65 percent of the 200,000 captives traded at the slave market of Sulu between 1770 and 1848 came from the Philippines and 35 percent from the eastern part of the Indonesian

archipelago. Warren, "Slave Markets," 169. Not all the slaves reached this slave market, of course, and considering the momentous shift in slave raiding toward the Indonesian archipelago in the late eighteenth and early nineteenth centuries, a 50-50 division seems fairly plausible.

46. With regard to the import of slaves from Nias, see Snouck Hurgronje, *De Atjehers*, 1:21, 134; and see Pruys van der Hoeven, *Een Woord over Sumatra*, 2:56.

47. "Het Landschap Donggala," 521.

48. Abeyasekere, "Slaves in Batavia," 292; Van der Kraan, "Bali: Slavery," 331–37; Allen, *European Slave Trading*, 155; Allen, "Satisfying the 'Want for Labouring People,'" 63. In 1827, three French slave ships were discovered at Sumatra's west coast by Dutch authorities, but that must have been an exception because their usual destination was Bali. See MvK I, inv. no. 570, Verbaal August 16, 1827, no. 63. According to Peggs (*Slavery in India*, 81), many slaves from Bali were still being transported to Mauritius by the late 1830s.

49. HTK 1890–1891, *Koloniaal Verslag* 1890, 63. For the year 1877, it was reported that still about 500 slaves were deported from Sumba, and trafficking conducted by Endehnese was still observed by 1886. NA, MvK II, Mail report 1877, no. 224; Mail report 1886, no. 625.

50. "Berigten Omtrent den Zeeroof," 7 (1858): 358.

51. "Berigten Omtrent den Zeeroof," (1852–1853) contains 38 witness accounts. Boyle, *Adventures*, 286.

52. "Slave Trade at Nias," 185–86.

53. Dalton, "Mr. Dalton's Papers on Borneo," 16.

54. Reid ("Inside Out," 77–83) lists five hypotheses to explain why the rice-growing populations in Sumatra moved into the interior, and one of them is that it was thought to be less vulnerable to marauding. Junghuhn and Neubronner von der Tuuk found out during their stays in this part of Sumatra in the 1840s that the Bataks had long ago moved into the interior because of the depredations of the pirates. Sternagel, *Der Humboldt von Java*, 154.

55. Vosmaer, "Korte Beschrijving," 110; Warren, "A Tale of Two Centuries," 135; Kolff, *Reize*, 93–94.

56. Van Welie, "Slave Trading and Slavery," 74.

57. Gooszen, *A Demographic History*, 230; Knapen, *Forests of Fortune?*, 135–36.

58. There is ample evidence of slavery as an institution that also reduced birth rates among the slave masters. Slaveholding also indirectly impinges adversely on demographic growth, as it may negatively affect agricultural output. Snippets of evidence suggest that slaves put on paddy fields produced less than "free" farmers. Lucieer, "Het Kindertal," 557–58; Henley, "Population and Means of Subsistence," 366–68; Adriani and Kruijt, *De Barée-sprekende Toradja's*, 164.

59. As Terray observed: "il n'y a pas de reproduction naturelle ou biologique des captifs, parce que les descendants des captifs ne sont pas eux-mêmes captifs." See Terray, "La captivité," 437. See also Lovejoy, *Transformations in Slavery*, 276. Mortality rates exceeding birth rates is another universally observed phenomenon among slave populations. This has been reported for the Banda Islands. See National Archive, The Hague, MvK I, inv. no. 3089, "Opgaaf der bevolking der Moluksche Eilanden." For Lampung, Cornets de Groot ("Nota over de Slavernij," 477–78) reported that slavery quickly disappeared after the Dutch established control over this residency in the 1850s, and no new slaves arrived.

60. NA, MvK I, inv. no. 1563, Verb. April 8, 1844, no. 9.

61. Bosma, "Methodological Paper," 36.

62. Adriani and Kruijt, *De Barée-sprekende Toradja's*, 159; Vroklage, *Die Sozialen Verhältnisse*, 1:256.

63. Bowie, "Slavery in Nineteenth-Century Northern Thailand," 108.

64. See also Mbeki and Van Rossum, "Private Slave Trade," 96; Van Rossum, *Kleur-rijke Tragiek*, 13.

65. Reid, "'Closed' and 'Open' Slave Systems," 158–59. With regard to the normative character of the distinction between raiding and enslaving through a *bellum iustum*, see Vink, "Freedom and Slavery," 37. Patterson (*Social Death*, 105), Terray ("La captivité," 395), and Lasker (*Human Bondage*, 16–17) also distinguish between raiding and capturing as part of an act of war. However, in Island Southeast Asia—where slave raiding was conducted as part of extensive maritime pursuits—the line between kidnapping and warfare was hard to draw.

66. Quirk signals this mentality among civil servants in Africa, but it holds equally true for Southeast Asia: Quirk, *The Anti-Slavery Project*, 11; Stanziani, *Sailors*, 132.

67. According to Reid, the majority of these slaves were debt slaves. Reid, "Introduction: Slavery and Bondage," 12; Reid, "'Closed' and 'Open' Slave Systems," 159. One of the reasons Boomgaard gives for widespread slavery in weak polities of Southeast Asia pertains to the nexus between the lack of food security—particularly occurring in wet rice agriculture—and indebtedness, which in turn ushers in enslavement. Boomgaard, "Human Capital," 91. However, Reid argues that famines were infrequent and that the most important example of people selling themselves into slavery was survivors of the eruption of Tambora. Reid, "'Closed' and 'Open' Systems," 159.

68. Parliamentary Papers, November 1882, C. 3429, "Further Correspondence Respecting," 3ff.

69. Cornets de Groot, "Nota over de Slavernij," 478.

70. Kooreman, "De Feitelijke Toestand," 1:363; Kolff, *Reize*, 318.

71. Vroklage, *Die Sozialen Verhältnisse Indonesiens*, 1:256, 281; Adriani and Kruijt, *De Barée-sprekende Toradja's*, 158–59.

72. Nieboer, *Slavery as an Industrial System*, 193; Adriani and Kruijt, *De Barée-sprekende Toradja's*, 158; Roos, *Soemba*, 10–11.

73. Debt slavery and peonage should not be conflated with pawnship, which pertains to a mechanism in which human beings were given as collateral for economic transactions. Moreover, pawning was a contractual arrangement that did not necessarily involve labor. Lovejoy and Richardson, "The Business of Slavery," 73–75. Falola and Lovejoy and Austin have pointed out that for West Africa, pawnship was a nexus between kinship systems and modern markets, but precisely because of that, its scale was always limited, usually concerning one or two people, and prone to disappear with further commercialization of the economy. Falola and Lovejoy, "Pawnship in Historical Perspective," 8; Austin, "Human Pawning," 187, 201, 210.

74. See Martínez, "The End of Indenture?"; Spyer, "The Eroticism of Debt," 517.

75. See Znoj, "Politics of Bonded Labour"; Marsden, *History of Sumatra*, 212–13.

76. Warren, *The Sulu Zone*, 90–92, 138–40.

77. Somers Heidhues, *Golddiggers*, 35; Healey, "Tribes and States," 17; Boyle, *Adventures*, 210–11; NA, MvK I, inv. no. 3084, "Rapport over den afloop der zending van de kommissaris voor Westkust van Borneo, M. Francis, 1832." "Bijdragen tot de Kennis van Borneo," 191; Veth, *Borneo's Wester-afdeeling*, 315–16; Chew, *Chinese Pioneers on the Sarawak Frontier*, 56; "Bijdrage tot de Kennis der Binnenlandsche Rijken," 341.

78. Engelhard, "De Afdeeling Doessonlanden," 196; Sutherland, "Slavery and the Slave Trade," 271.

79. *De Oostpost*, May 16, 1855; NA, MvK II, Mail report 1890, no. 530; Mail report 1897, no. 438.

80. Linehan and Sheppard, "A History of Pahang," 128; Horner, "Batoe-Eilanden," 358. Cushner, *Landed Estates*, 8; Vroklage, *Die Sozialen Verhältnisse*, 1:67; Parliamentary Papers, July 1882, C. 3285, "Correspondence Respecting Slavery," 6.

81. *Java-bode*, August 4, 1858.

82. Bowie, "Slavery in Nineteenth-Century Northern Thailand," 129–30; The British civil servant F. A. Swettenham observed in Perak—and this was definitely not confined to this particular sultanate but existed throughout the Malay world—the forcible detention of people said to be indebted: "Very often there was no real debt; the creditors invented one, or inflicted a fine for an offence never committed, and then compelled the reputed debtor, with his wife and family, to enter his service and treated them all as chattels." See Swettenham, *British Malaya*, 195–96; KITLV, Collectie J. van Swieten, H 997, inv. no. 150, Brief

van J. van Swieten aan de minister van Koloniën inzake de slavernij onder Batak-kers 1871.

83. NA, MvK II, inv. no. 1455, Verb. March 31, 1864, no. 26, Letter of A. J. F. Jansen, governor of "Celebes en Onderhoorigheden" to the governor-general, January 14, 1861.

84. Kooreman, "De Feitelijke Toestand," 1:651; Van Braam Morris, "Het Landschap Loehoe," 514–16, not only blames gambling but also the use of opium as a cause of enslaving; Bigalke, *Tana Toraja*, 24, 27–28. Opium addiction is also mentioned as a cause of enslaving in Lampung. "De Lampongsche Distrikten," 320.

85. Bigalke, *Tana Toraja*, 42–43; Bigalke, "A Social History," 62, 66.

86. Velthoen, "Contested Coastlines," 175–176; NA, MvK II, Mail report 1876, no. 654; Mail report 1891, no. 103; Mail report 1877, no. 509.

87. Ruibing, *Ethnologische Studie*, 43. Slaves from Nias were brought to Padang for coffee cultivation in the early nineteenth century. See Dobbin, *Islamic Revivalism*, 98. With regard to the employment of slaves in the pepper groves of Lampung, see Talens, *Een Feodale Samenleving*, 72; Andaya, "Women and Economic Change," 175; Andaya, *To Live as Brothers*, 96–98. For Banten, see Djajadiningrat, *Critische beschouwing van de Sadjarah bantēn*, 48. In the case of the Banten sultanate, these slaves were obtained from pirates, and increasing action against piracy in the eighteenth century diminished labor supplies and the production of pepper. Rovere van Breugel, "Bedenkingen," 150–51; Reid, *Southeast Asia in the Age of Commerce*, 2:35. According to the *Sumatra Courant* of June 10, 1874, Aceh pepper cultivation was entirely reliant on peons from Nias and the Batak lands.

88. Heersink, *The Green Gold*, 35.

89. Zollinger, "Het Eiland Lombok," 309, 312; Amrith, *Crossing the Bay of Bengal*, 55; Bigalke, *Tana Toraja*, 47–48; Junker, *Raiding, Trading, and Feasting*, 232.

90. Boomgaard, "Resources and People of the Sea," 105.

91. *Bataviaasch Handelsblad*, August 1, 1876.

92. Adriani and Kruijt, *De Barée-sprekende Toradja's*, 165.

93. Scott, *The Discovery of the Igorots*, 187.

94. Lovejoy and Hogendorn, *Slow Death for Slavery*, 305, 1; Salau, "The Role of Slave Labor," 155–56.

95. Van der Linden, "Global Labour History," 430.

96. It also pertains to slaves who were brought to Bugis enclaves on Kalimantan's west coast and who were put to work as sharecroppers and soon integrated into the community via marriage. See Müller, *Proeve eener Geschiedenis*, 52.

97. Liefrinck, "Slavernij op Lombok," 514–15.

98. Scott, "Filipino Class," 170–71. In this regard, also see Schwalbenberg, "The Economics of Pre-Hispanic Visayan Slave Raiding." With regard to the number of slaves, see Lannoy, *Iles Philippines*, 4–5.

99. Nieboer, *Slavery as an Industrial System*, 37–39.

100. Gullick, *Malay Society*, 210–13.

101. Roos, *Soemba*, 10.

102. Zollinger, "Het Eiland Lombok," 309, 326.

103. Reid, "Introduction: Slavery, Bondage," 4.

104. Fynn-Paul, "Empire, Monotheism," 15–16.

105. Cruikshank, "Slavery in Nineteenth Century Siam," 322; Hoskins, "Slaves, Brides, and 'Other Gifts,'" 104, 106; Patterson, *Social Death*, 241; Pelras, "Patron-Client Ties," 397–99, 403; Acciaioli, "Kinship and Debt," 603, 614, 617; Eviota, *The Political Economy of Gender*, 55. For a comparison, see Manning, *Slavery and African Life*, 162.

106. Larkin, *The Pampangans*, 37–38.

107. Hoadley, *Towards a Feudal Mode*, 127; Aguilar, *The Clash of Spirits*, 70.

108. Loh Fook Seng, "Slavery in the Straits Settlements," 181; Yang, "Indian Convict Workers," 180, 197, 200–1; Jackson, *Immigrant Labour*, 12–15.

109. *Staatsblad van Nederlandsch Indië*, 1822, no. 10.

110. Salman, *The Embarrassment of Slavery*, 49, 71, 77, 88, 89, 106.

111. Salman, *The Embarrassment of Slavery*, 77–78; Clark, "Labor Conditions in the Philippines," 775.

112. Worcester, *Slavery and Peonage*; Byler, "Pacifying the Moros."

113. Salman, *The Embarrassment of Slavery*, 226, 246; Clark, "Labor Conditions in the Philippines," 775, 837.

114. NA, MvK II, inv. 1375. Verb. September 1, 1863, no. 9.

115. Haga, *Nederlandsch Nieuw Guinea*, 2:448–49.

116. HTK 1896–1897, *Koloniaal Verslag* 1896, 71.

117. NA, MvK II, inv. no. 1330, Verb. April 29, 1863, no. 15.

118. NA, MvK II, Mail report 1876, no. 860; Mail report 1891, no. 696.

119. NA, MvK II, Mail report 1878, no. 78, no. 499.

120. *Nieuws van den Dag voor Nederlandsch-Indië*, March 4, 1903.

121. NA, MvK II, Mail report 1895, no. 164, no. 313.

122. NA, MvK II, Mail report 1890, no. 389; Mail report 1891, no. 474; Mail report 1892, no. 229.

123. HTK 1906–1907, *Koloniaal Verslag* 1906, 122; HTK 1910–1911, *Koloniaal Verslag*, 1910, 100; HTK 1912–1913, *Koloniaal Verslag* 1912, 78; HTK 1914–1915, *Koloniaal Verslag* 1914, 60; HTK 1915–1916, *Koloniaal Verslag* 1915, 78; HTK 1916–1917, *Koloniaal Verslag* 1916, 76; Cornets de Groot, "Nota over de Slavernij," 482.

124. Jackson, *Immigrant Labour*, 2. With regard to the slave raiding among the aboriginal Malays, see Endicott, "Slave Raiding in the Malay Peninsula"; Lim Teck Ghee, "Reconstituting the Peasantry," 194.

125. Swettenham, *British Malaya*, 196.

126. Boon Kheng, "Malay Politics," 96.

127. Linehan and Sheppard, "A History of Pahang," 128; Clarence-Smith, "The British 'Official Mind,'" 126.

128. Sheppard, "A Short History of Trengganu," 57; Gullick, *Malay Society*, 213.

129. Morris, "Slaves, Aristocrats, and Exports," 304; Clarence-Smith, "The British 'Official Mind,'" 127; Singh, *Brunei*, 117. See also Tregonning, "The Elimination of Slavery."

130. *Bataviaasch Handelsblad*, January 6, 1890.

131. NA, MvK II, Mail report 1889, no. 772.

132. Mantra, "Indonesian Labour Mobility," 173–77; E. Benjamin Skinner, "Indonesia's Palm Oil Industry Rife with Human Rights Abuses," *Bloomberg Businessweek*, July 20, 2013; "Forced, Child, and Trafficked Labour in the Palm Oil Industry," *World Vision Action*, April 2013, http://campaign.worldvision.com.au/wp -content/uploads/2013/04/Forced-child-and-trafficked-labour-in-the-palm -oil-industry-fact-sheet.pdf.

3. SAVED FROM SMALLPOX BUT STARVING IN THE SUGAR CANE FIELDS: JAVA AND THE NORTHWESTERN PHILIPPINES

1. Kratoska, "Rice Cultivation and the Ethnic Division," 284.

2. Rouffaer, *De Voornaamste Industrieën*, 12–13; De Zwart, "Globalization and the Colonial Origins," 137; Feenstra, "Dutch Coins," 183; Carey, "Waiting for the 'Just King,'" 93.

3. With the notable exception of the Igorots inhabiting the mountainous Cordilleras, who were forced into compliance by a range of military expeditions in the 1830s. Habana, "Gold Mining in Benguet to 1898," 479–80.

4. Alonso, "Financing the Empire," 86.

5. Boncan, "Colonial Copper Coinage," 521–22.

6. Diaz-Trechuelo, "Eighteenth-Century Philippine Economy: Agriculture," 113–16.

7. McHale and McHale, *Early American-Philippine Trade*, 21–22.

8. De Haan, *Priangan*, 1:87–88, 251.

9. De Haan, *Priangan*, 1:119, 123; Hoadley, *Towards a Feudal Mode*, 103, 105, 107, 121; Purwanto, "Peasant Economy and Institutional Changes," 4.

10. De Klein, *Het Preangerstelsel*, 39–40. Also see Breman, *Koloniaal Profijt*.

11. De Klein, *Het Preangerstelsel*, 43–44.

12. "De Afschaffing van het Passenstelsel," 236.

13. Most of the labor migrants to the sugar mills were free laborers, though some pressganging might have been involved. NA, Collection Schneither, inv. no. 88, Cheribon, 2. Also see Bosma, "Methodological Paper," 25.

14. This is based on the assumptions that 52 percent (3,901,500) of the total population of Java of 7.5 million was employable and older than sixteen and that within this total employable population only the men were hired for the types of work mentioned here. Moreover, since about 40 percent of these men were independent and usually married farmers, it would leave about a population of a million men from whom wage workers could be recruited. Within their social and gender category, 15 percent were working on a wage basis outside the home of their kin. Bosma, "Methodological Paper," 24–25.

15. Bosma, *The Sugar Plantation*, 37.

16. Knight, "From Plantation to Padi-field," 182–92.

17. Carey, "Waiting for the 'Just King,'" 99.

18. Land registration proved to be technically so complicated that it was not before the 1920s that agricultural land in parts of the Netherlands Indies (Java, Bali, and South Sulawesi) was measured and classified. See Booth, "The Burden of Taxation," 102.

19. The proportion of the households involved in the Cultivation System declined over time, but 35 to 40 percent is a reasonable estimate for the 1840s. The amount of time committed to cultivation conscription was nominally sixty-six days, but in reality the burden could be much higher. Fasseur, *The Politics of Colonial Exploitation*, 16, 256–59.

20. Knight, "Capitalism and Commodity Production," 124–25.

21. Carey, "Waiting for the 'Just King,'" 86, 88.

22. Boomgaard, *Children of the Colonial State*, 192–95, 202–3.

23. Knight, "Capitalism and Commodity Production," 139.

24. Bosma, *The Sugar Plantation*, 120.

25. Kano, *Indonesian Exports*, 400.

26. Bosma, "The Discourse on Free Labour," 410.

27. Elson, "Sugar Factory Workers," 148.

28. With regard to the gradual abolition of corvée and tributary labor, see Wahid, "From Revenue Farming," 44–45; and Fokkens, *Afschaffing der Laatste Heerendiensten op Java*, 6–9, 29. The abolition of cultivation conscription in the Principalities—in fact apanage rights that were leased by plantation estates—only took place in 1926, and even then communal conscription labor, as well as corvée for road construction and repair, was maintained for most of this

territory, which was exceptional for Java although common for the Outer Islands. See Van den Haspel, *Overwicht in Overleg*, 208–9. Only in the Mangkunegara, one of Java's four Principalities, was corvée converted into monetized taxes.

29. De Jesus, *The Tobacco Monopoly*, 79, 96.
30. Knight, "Capitalism and Commodity Production," 139.
31. Bosma, "Migration and Colonial Enterprise," 158.
32. HTK 1875–1876, *Koloniaal Verslag* 1875; and HTK 1885–1886, *Koloniaal Verslag* 1885, Bijlage A, IV. "Beroepen en Bedrijven."
33. See Bosma, "Migration and Colonial Enterprise," 160. The *Diminishing Welfare Reports, 1880–1905*, provide patchy data for in and out migrations per Residency, on the basis of which Gooszen produced a quantified overview. Gooszen, *A Demographic History*, app. 3.1, 119–21.
34. Pelzer, *Pioneer Settlement*, 256, table XXV.
35. Lekkerkerker, "Sapoedi en Bawean," 473.
36. De Jonge, *Handelaren en Handlangers*, 22; Lekkerkerker, "Java's Overbevolking," 876; De Jonge, "State and Welfare," 91, 97.
37. Pelzer, *Pioneer Settlement*, 176. Lekkerkerker, "Java's Overbevolking," 879; Bleeker, "Fragmenten eener Reis over Java" (1849), 2:30, 122, 127. See also De Jonge, *Handelaren en Handlangers*, 18; Tennekes, "De Bevolkingsspreiding," 339–40.
38. Nederburgh, *Tjilegon*, 4–8.
39. See Haspel, *Overwicht in Overleg*, 6; Swettenham, *British Malaya*, 195–96; *Nieuws van den Dag voor N.I.*, January 31, 1919.
40. Margana, "Hybridity," 107.
41. Bosma, "Migration and Colonial Enterprise," 159.
42. Widjojo, *Population Trends in Indonesia*, 36; Bleeker, "Nieuwe Bijdragen tot de Kennis," 597.
43. The tea plantations and the additional smallholder tea production in the Priangan Mountains involved 70,000 households in the early twentieth century, or about 300,000 people, based on an average household size of 4.5 people. Bosma, "Migration and Colonial Enterprise," 164.
44. Meijer Ranneft ("Volksverplaatsingen op Java," 70, 78), for example, alludes to considerable migration from Pekalongan into the Pamelang department of Tegal, where various sugar factories were located.
45. Tennekes, "De Bevolkingsspreiding," 342–44, 389; Spaan, *Labour Circulation*, 95–96.
46. Lekkerkerker, "Java's Overbevolking," 879.
47. Legarda, *After the Galleons*, 64–71, 82–83, 98, 105, 116.
48. Corpuz, *An Economic History of the Philippines*, 66.

49. Legarda, *After the Galleons*, 125; Diaz-Trechuelo, "Eighteenth-Century Philippine Economy"; Owen, *Prosperity Without Progress*, 46.

50. McLennan, "Peasant and Hacendero," 147.

51. Cushner, *Landed Estates in the Colonial Philippines*, 7.

52. Corpuz, *An Economic History of the Philippines*, 28.

53. Bankoff, "Wants, Wages," 64.

54. Roth, "Church Lands," 142–43; McLennan, "Land and Tenancy," 653, 654, 657.

55. McLennan, "Land and Tenancy," 655–56; Arcilla, "Slavery, Flogging," 402; McLennan, "Peasant and Hacendero," 63, 143.

56. Clark, "Labor Conditions in the Philippines," 775, 776; Lasker, *Human Bondage*, 131; quoted in McLennan, *Changing Human Ecology*, 74.

57. Larkin, *The Pampangans*, 53–54.

58. Larkin, "Philippine History Reconsidered," 620.

59. See, for example, Lopez-Gonzaga, *Crisis in Sugarlandia*.

60. Doeppers, *Manila*, 56; Larkin, *The Pampangans*, 56–62. According to McLennan, the Mestizo families must have already taken their positions before the British occupation of the Philippines, which implies in his view that the commercialization of agriculture dated from the mid–eighteenth century. McLennan, "Land and Tenancy," 663.

61. Xenos, "The Ilocos Coast," 47.

62. McLennan, "Peasant and Hacendero," 171.

63. *Census of the Philippine Islands 1903*, 4:180.

64. McLennan, "Peasant and Hacendero," 200.

65. *Census of the Philippine Islands 1903*, 2:20–21. According to Larkin ("Philippine History Reconsidered," 614), "By 1900, Negros Occidental, Panay, Capiz, Cebu, Tarlac and much of Nueva Ecija, most primarily jungle in 1820, were well-populated agricultural regions devoted mainly to rice and sugar."

66. Bassino, Dovis, and Komlos, "Biological Well-Being," 12. Also see the map on page 23 of this paper, where recruits from frontier provinces and commodity producing provinces such as Cagayan, Nueva Ecija, Pampanga, Ambos Camarines, and Negros Occidental are all among above the national average height.

67. Lewis, "Migration in the Northern Philippines," 121, 128; McLennan, "Peasant and Hacendero," 189; Gleeck, *Nueva Ecija*, 26, 88. The population of Nueva Ecija, for example, increased by 69.3 percent between 1903 and 1918, whereas the average increase was just 35.1 percent. See *Census of the Philippine Islands 1918*, 2:20; Storer, "The Philippines," 302.

68. *Census of the Philippine Islands 1918*, 4-1:226, 231.

69. *Census of the Philippines 1939*, 1:1–4, table 15, "Persons 10 years old and over classified by usual occupation, sex, and citizenship: 1939." Also, see IISH

Dataverse, Bosma, "Demography," file "Excerpts from 1939 Philippine Census (March 19, 2017)."

70. This high figure was attributable to relatively low labor productivity in the sugar sector of the Philippines compared with Java and Hawaii. Labor input per unit production in the Philippines was twice as high as in Hawaii. Runes, *General Standards of Living*, 6–9.

71. Bosma, *The Sugar Plantation*, 163, 176.

72. McCoy, "A Queen Dies Slowly," 297–98; Lopez-Gonzaga, "The Roots of Agrarian Unrest," 162; See also Loney, *A Britisher in the Philippines*.

73. Legarda, *After the Galleons*, 309.

74. McCoy, "A Queen Dies Slowly," 315.

75. Billig, "Syrup in the Wheels of Progress," 124.

76. Aguilar, "Sugar Planter–State Relations," 53.

77. Lopez-Gonzaga, "The Roots of Agrarian Unrest," 165.

78. Aguilar, *Clash of Spirits*, 111–13, 141–43; McCoy, "Sugar Barons," 114.

79. Bankoff, "Wants, Wages," 68; Aguilar, *Clash of Spirits*, 128.

80. Clark, "Labor Conditions in the Philippines," 747–48.

81. Worcester, *The Philippine Islands*, 259–60; Carter, "Economic Questions," 688–89.

82. Aguilar, *Clash of Spirits*, 218; McCoy, "A Queen Dies Slowly," 326.

83. While the actual land under cane amounted to 168,000 hectares, factories usually forced cultivators to keep their land fallow as early as four months in advance of planting. Moreover, since the total cycle of cane was 15 months, between April and June of every year, twice as much land was taken by cane. With regard to the difficult relationship between rice and cane and the conflicting needs with respect to labor and irrigation in Java's sawah agriculture, see Alexander and Alexander, "Sugar, Rice, and Irrigation," esp. 213. See also Booth, "Irrigation," 41; and Knight, "Did 'Dependency' Really Get It Wrong," 163.

84. Bosma, "Methodological Paper," 30. Also, see chapter 5 of this book.

85. Knight, *Commodities and Colonialism*, 160–62, 197–99; Bosma, *The Sugar Plantation*, 190.

86. Ingleson, *Workers, Unions, and Politics*, 28.

87. Friend, "The Philippine Sugar Industry," 183, 192; Knight, *Commodities and Colonialism*, 69–77; Bosma, *The Sugar Plantation*, 176–77. According to Meijer Ranneft and Huender (*Onderzoek naar den Belastingdruk*, 29) and corroborated by Wellenstein, the land rent was weighing disproportionally on the population, particularly since more and more marginal land had been taken into production. Wellenstein, "Het Rapport Meyer Ranneft-Huender," 263, 269.

88. Van der Eng actually suggests an improvement of both calorie and protein intake per capita. Van der Eng, "Food for Growth," 597–98, 603–4.

89. Brown, "The Influenza Pandemic of 1918," 241; *Bataviaasch Nieuwsblad*, December 12, 1918, April 10, 1919; *Sumatra Post*, February 17, 1919.
90. The most recent figures for India are by Chandra et al., "Mortality." Based on discrepancies in census data, Chandra ("Mortality from the Influenza Pandemic") conjectures that the number of victims were 4.26 to 4.37 million for Java alone. That would amount to 10 percent of the total population. Reading the newspapers of those days, it seems that 10 percent is much too high and that 6 percent is a more realistic figure. By the end of 1918, the death toll already stood at 1.5 million, according to the colonial health authorities (*Sumatra Post*, November 23, 1918). Moreover, there were second and third waves that came almost immediately after the first. *Nieuws van den Dag voor N.I.*, April 12, June 11, 12, 1919. *Bataviaasch Nieuwsblad*, August 13, 16, September 17, 1919; *Bataviaasch Nieuwsblad*, June 29, November 23, 1920. The influenza also lingered on relatively long in the Netherlands Indies, which is apparent from the fact that as late as November 1920 there were reports about coolies arriving from Java in Deli suffering from influenza that caused deaths among them. *Sumatra Post*, December 11, 1920.
91. Kratoska, "The British Empire," 129; Chiba, "The 1919 and 1935 Rice Crises," 534–35; Mansvelt, *Rice Prices*, 45–46. For the Philippines, my estimate of the death toll is 300,000. This is based on the fact that the general death rate rose from 22.89 per thousand in 1917 to 40.79 per thousand in 1918. For a total Philippine population of 10,314,310 recorded in the census of 1918, this constitutes a difference of 184,626 people, which can be almost exclusively ascribed to influenza. Moreover, the mortality rate in 1919 was still high at 37.51 per thousand, which was again about 15 per thousand higher than in 1917 or in 1920. See also Galeago, "The Philippines in the World," 273–78. For British Malaya, the current estimate is 1 percent of the population, but this is highly unlikely as it assumes that the mortality in Singapore was the standard and that the pandemic left the peninsula in early 1919. Kai Khiun Liew, "Terribly Severe," 222, 251. See also Lee et al., "Twentieth-Century Influenza Pandemics in Singapore." Moreover, the 1921 census (Nathan, *The Census of British Malaya*, 20) indicates that it was impossible to determine how many died from influenza because these causes were reported under different names. According to this census, the casualty rate from influenza was about 2.9 percent.
92. Galeago, "The Philippines in the World," 275.
93. In the 1920s, the average available kilocalories did not fall below 2,000 per capita per day thanks to the substitution of rice by other food crops. Protein intake, however—which was already at a marginal 40 grams per day—must nonetheless have fallen slightly in these years. Van der Eng, "Food for Growth," 597–98, 603–4; Booth, "Measuring Living Standards," 1154, 1156.

94. Runes, *General Standards of Living*, 23.

95. Bankoff, "Wants, Wages," 80–81; Koningsberger, "Een Bezoek aan de Philippijnen," 1227.

96. Scott, "Patron-Client Politics," 31–32.

97. Dennison, "Philippine Labor," 280.

98. Chiba, "The 1919 and 1935 Rice Crises," 540.

99. Runes, *General Standards of Living*, 22; Coolie Budget Commission, *Living Conditions*, 109, 130.

100. Runes, *General Standards of Living*, 5, 21–23.

101. C. P., "Philippine Coconut Industry," 247; Dennison, "Philippine Labor," 279. *Census of the Philippines: 1939*, 1:1–4, table 19. See also IISH Dataverse, Bosma, "Demography," file "Excerpts from 1939 Philippine Census (March 19, 2017)."

102. Bosma, "Sugar Dynasty," 90.

103. Hirschman, *National Power*, vi, vii, 13.

104. The Payne-Aldrich Act of 1909 established free trade between the United States and the Philippines.

105. Porter, "Philippines," 192–93. See also Booth, *Colonial Legacies*, 94.

106. O'Brien, "Intercontinental Trade," 97.

107. Friend, "The Philippine Sugar Industry," 190–91.

108. Wernstedt and Simkins, "Migrations," 87; Hayase, "American Colonial Policy," 509–10.

109. Rice, "Philippine Copra," 157–60.

110. For the ownership of the coconut oil factories, see Aguilar, *The Clash of Spirits*, 207.

111. "Uitvoer van Klapperproducten uit Nederlandsch-Indië," 105.

112. Snodgrass, *Copra and Coconut Oil*, 67–69, 94.

113. Barbier, *Scarcity and Frontiers*, 368–462. See also O'Brien, "Intercontinental Trade," 98.

114. Legarda, *After the Galleons*, 139; Broeze, "The Merchant Fleet," 269.

115. Bosma, "Sugar and Dynasty," 87; *Landbouwatlas*, 2:14.

116. Quirino, *A History of the Philippine Sugar Industry*, 51.

117. Purwanto, *From Dusun to the Market*, 65; Lulofs and Van Vuuren, *De Voedselvoorziening van Nederlandsch-Indië*, 70–71.

118. Kratoska, "Rice Cultivation and Ethnic Division," 282.

119. Kratoska, "Rice Cultivation and Ethnic Division," 283, 287, 293–94; Kratoska, "The British Empire," 146. Chew, *Chinese Pioneers on the Sarawak Frontier*, 156. Kaur, "The Impact of Railroads," 709; Bauer, *The Rubber Industry*, 5; Ooi Keat Gin, "For Want of Rice," 19.

120. Hooley, "American Economic Policy," 468.

121. Apart from the First World War and the Depression years, the farmers of mainland Southeast Asia enjoyed favorable terms of trade for their rice, which led to extensive imports of consumer goods. Resnick, "The Decline of Rural Industry"; Adas, "The Ryotwari in Lower Burma," 114–15.

122. Van Schendel, *Three Deltas*, 83.

123. Van Schendel, *Three Deltas*, 87, 121; Van der Eng, *Agricultural Growth*, 166.

124. Stover, "Tropical Exports," 50.

125. Van der Eng, *Agricultural Growth*, 260–65, table A 1.2.

126. Even in East Sumatra, the bulwark of plantation agriculture, the proportion of estate rubber did not exceed 84 percent, a high percentage but not a monopoly. Thee Kian Wie, "Plantation Agriculture," 36. The total share of the value of indigenous crops in the exports of Sumatra's east coast was actually 22 percent in 1926. See Fievez de Malines van Ginkel, *Verslag van den Economischen Toestand*, 6.

127. Snodgrass, *Copra and Coconut Oil*, 48.

128. Heersink, "Selayar and the Green Gold," 47–48.

129. Snodgrass, *Copra and Coconut Oil*, 57.

130. Heersink, "Selayar and the Green Gold," 54, 56, 59.

131. "Een Inlandsche Nederzetting," 45–47.

132. Borja, "The Philippine Coconut Industry," 387–88.

133. See Wolters, "Uneven Impact and Regional Responses"; Doeppers, "The Philippines in the Great Depression," 60, 63, 67. *Census of the Philippines: 1939*, 1:1–4, tables 18–19. According to my weighted data on daily wages in centavos derived from the census data, the figures for "sugar provinces" were 68 for Tarlac, 67 for Pampanga, 62 for Negros Occidental, and 41 for Batangas. The figures for the copra provinces were 46 for Camarines Sur, 54 for Samar, 43 for Leyte, 44 for Albay, and 44 for Sorsogon. See IISH Dataverse, Bosma, "Demography," File "Excerpts from 1939 Philippine Census (March 19, 2017)."

134. Van Gelderen, *Voorlezingen*, 111. The amount of cash stashed away in the copra belt of Selayar alone was an estimated five million guilders in 1920. See Heersink, "Selayar and the Green Gold," 59.

135. Purwanto, *From Dusun to the Market*, 321, 333. In Palembang, for example, a surge in consumption and investments can be surmised from the trade statistics. Zed, "The Dualistic Economy," 255.

136. Leirissa, " 'Copracontracten,' " 271.

137. Thee Kian Wie, "Plantation Agriculture," 117. This condition is described by Cardoso and Faletto in their *Dependency and Development in Latin America*, 71, as a plantation enclave.

138. Purwanto, *From Dusun to the Market*, 259.

139. HTK 1893–1894, *Koloniaal Verslag* 1893, Bijlage B, 2–3; Drewes, *Two Achenese Poems*, 11.

140. Somers Heidhues, *Golddiggers*, 160–61.

141. Heersink, "Selayar and the Green Gold," 59–65.

142. Stubbs, "Malaysia's Rubber," 87.

143. Li, *Land's End*, 52–53.

144. See Owen, *Prosperity Without Progress*.

145. Pelzer, "Swidden Cultivation," 275.

146. Clark, "The Conditions of Labor in Java," 954.

147. Colijn, "Onder het Staatsbestuur," 33; Baker, "Economic Reorganization," 338.

148. Purwanto, *From Dusun to the Market*, 270.

149. Williamson, "Globalization," 38–39; Touwen, "Entrepreneurial Strategies," 153–54, 165–66.

150. De Waard, "Een en ander," 27; Fievez de Malines van Ginkel, *Verslag van den Economischen Toestand*, 15; Fievez de Malines van Ginkel, *Verslag van den Belastingdruk*, 10–14.

4. THE LABOR-SCARCE COMMODITY FRONTIERS, 1870s–1942

1. Kratoska, "Rice Cultivation and the Ethnic Division," 284.

2. Claver, *Dutch Commerce*, 283–348.

3. Atsushi, "Tropical Products Out," 521.

4. This estimate was only based on Dutch port statistics and therefore underrepresents the total exports to China. Atsushi, "Tropical Products Out," 514–15.

5. Kaur, "A History of Forestry," 127; Peluso and Vandergeest, "Genealogies," 775; Maxwell, *Present and Future Land Systems*; Bankoff, "Coming to Terms," 25. Investigations into local customary law regarding land titles on waste land were conducted in a range of Outer Islands in the 1870s. See, for example, Wit, *Resumé van het onderzoek*.

6. Boyle, *Adventures Among the Dyaks*, 147; John, "The Timber Industry," 57.

7. In Benguet, gold mining in Luzon was carried out for centuries by the Igorot until the American administration decided to open up the region to corporate enterprise. Habana, "Gold Mining in Benguet: 1900–1941," 9, 25. Antimony was the single most important export commodity of Sarawak up to the 1870s, mined in the Sarawak river basin by Dayaks under coerced conditions until James Brooke, the first raja of Sarawak, seized this enterprise. Kaur, "The Babbling Brookes," 66; Craufurd [*sic*], "A Sketch of the Geography of Borneo," 75.

8. Bosma, *The Sugar Plantation*, 190.

9. Bosma, *The Sugar Plantation*, 190–91.

10. Dennison, "Philippine Labor," 280–81.

11. For indigenous tobacco cultivation in Manado, see HTK 1893–1894, *Koloniaal Verslag* 1893, Bijlage B, 14; *Landbouwatlas* II, 14.

12. Pelzer, *Die Arbeiterwanderungen*, 94–95; Breman, *Koelies*, 137.

13. Bosma, "Migration and Colonial Enterprise," 164.

14. Purwanto, "Peasant Economy and Institutional Changes," 7.

15. Putnam, *Salem Vessels*; Phillips, *Pepper and Pirates*. According to Newbold (*Political and Statistical Account*, 1:55), there were 347 Acehnese living in Penang in the early 1830s.

16. Sutter, "Indonesianisasi," 20.

17. Dobbin, *Islamic Revivalism*, 96.

18. Dobbin, *Islamic Revivalism*, 108.

19. Kooreman, "De Feitelijke Toestand," 136.

20. Huitema, *De Bevolkingskoffiecultuur*, 63.

21. Purwanto, *From Dusun to the Market*, 28.

22. Bauer, *The Rubber Industry*, 58–59.

23. Purwanto, *From Dusun to the Market*, 208.

24. Sutter, "Indonesianisasi," 19; Zed, "The Dualistic Economy," 254–55.

25. Parmer, *Colonial Labor Policy*, 9.

26. Bauer, *The Rubber Industry*, 200–2; Thee Kian Wie, "Plantation Agriculture," 36. The total share of the value of indigenous crops in the exports of Sumatra's East Coast even reached 22 percent in 1926. Fievez de Malines van Ginkel, *Verslag van den Economischen Toestand*, 6.

27. Purwanto, *From Dusun to Market*, 208.

28. Purwanto, *From Dusun to Market*, 282, 312, 314.

29. Huff, "The Development of the Rubber Market," 300, 302.

30. Chew, *Chinese Pioneers on the Sarawak Frontier*, 27.

31. For the abuses of tax farming, see Vitalis, "Over de Pachten"; and Wahid, "From Revenue Farming," 73.

32. Hill, *Rice in Malaya*, 83, 84; Parmer, *Colonial Labor Policy*, 7; Hollen Lees, "International Management," 45–46. Hollen Lees, *Planting Empire*, 24.

33. Lake, "Johore," 296; Jackson, "Chinese Agricultural Pioneering," 97.

34. Jackson, "Chinese Agricultural Pioneering," 80–82. See also Huff, "Sharecroppers."

35. Hoadley, *Towards a Feudal Mode of Production*, 137–38; Claver, *Dutch Commerce*, 169. For a longue durée overview of the Chinese economic position in Southeast Asia, arguing that this antedated the expansion of colonial mining and plantations, see Kwee Hui Kain, "Chinese Economic Dominance."

36. Kaur, "The Babbling Brookes," 73, 75.

37. Jackson, *Immigrant Labour*, 34–35; Wong Lin Ken, *The Malay Tin Industry*, 27.

38. Jackson, *Immigrant Labour*, 37.

39. Wong Lin Ken, *The Malay Tin Industry*, 56–60, 219; Drabble, *An Economic History of Malaysia*, 71.

40. NA, MvK II, inv. no. 1950, Verb. February 28, 1919, no. 6 "Rapport De Kat Angelino," 13; Ross, "The Tin Frontier," 462; Somers Heidhues, *Bangka Tin*, 129–30. With regard to the mechanization of the Belitung mines in the 1920s, see Billiton Maatschappij N.V., *Gedenkboek Billiton*, 2:78.

41. Johnston, "Opening a Frontier," 32; Wickizer and Bennett, *The Rice Economy*, 264.

42. Aguilar, *Clash of Spirits*, 126–27; Bankoff, "Wants, Wages," 72.

43. With regard to the overpopulation of the Kaveri Delta, see Van Schendel, *Three Deltas*; Guilmoto, "The Tamil Migration Cycle," 112; Kumar, *Land and Caste*, 114, 119.

44. Kessler, *Islam and Politics*, 69; Dodge, "Population Estimates," 447–48; Vlieland, "The Population of the Malay Peninsula," 64, 67. See also Bahrin, "The Growth and Distribution."

45. Modderman, Volker, and Van der Veen, *Gedenkboek*, 147–48.

46. After 1863, any Javanese and Madurese who wanted to travel overseas needed a pass signed by the regent, the highest Indonesian official of a department, before they could leave, a formality that was abolished in 1906. Modderman, Volker, and Van der Veen, *Gedenkboek*, 114. See also *Staatsblad van Nederlandsch-Indië 1863*, no. 83.

47. HTK 1902–1903, Koloniaal Verslag 1902, Bijlage A. "Statistiek betreffende de Bevolking," 6; *Nota over de Invoering van Staatstoezicht*, 57; *Verslag van de Arbeidsinspectie en Koeliewerving* (1914), 94.

48. For the figures, see, for example, Thee Kian Wie, "Plantation Agriculture," 76. Breman, *Koelies*, 140.

49. *Volkstelling* 1930, VIII, 18. In addition to the 300,000 inhabitants of the Netherlands Indies living in British Malaya at that time, another 32,000 Javanese were living in the Dutch colony of Suriname and about 20,000 in New Caledonia. Lockard, "The Javanese as Emigrant," 44. For New Caledonia, see Maurer, "The Thin Red Line," 872.

50. *Volkstelling* 1930, VII, 23.

51. Storer, "The Philippines," 302.

52. Schult, "Deforestation and Mangyan in Mindor," 158–59; McLennan, "Peasant and Hacendero," 359.

53. Pelzer, *Pioneer Settlement*, 129.

54. Pendleton, "Land Utilization," 181; Pelzer, *Pioneer Settlement*, 127–59; Wernstedt and Spencer, *The Philippine Island World*, 550–51. See also Wernstedt and Simkins, "Migrations."

55. Spencer, "Abaca," 101–2; Pelzer, "The Philippine Abaca Industry," 71; Hayase, "American Colonial Policy," 513.

56. "The Piracy and the Slave Trade," 144; Van der Hart, *Reize rondom het Eiland Celebes*, 114.

57. NA. MvK I, inv. no. 1064, Verb. March 12, 1836, no. 14, inv. no. 1292, Verb. April 1, 1840, no. 23, inv. no. 1284, Verb. February 21, 1840, nos. 22 and 28, inv. no. 1303, Verb. May 30, 1840, no. 18, inv. no. 1323, Verb. September 14, 1840, nos. 3, 9, 10, and inv. no. 1418, January 17, 1842, no. 66.

58. Slaves were even advertised in the official colonial journal *Javasche Courant*. See NA, MvK I, inv. no. 1743, Verb. October 29, 1846.

59. NA, MvK I, inv. no. 799. Verb. June 16, 1831, 29; and NA, MvK I, inv. no. 800. Verb. June 30, 1831, 28.

60. NA, MvK I, inv. no. 1728, Verb. August 24, 1846, no. 27.

61. *Java-bode*, October 29, 1873.

62. NA, MvK II, Mail report 1889, no. 149.

63. Jackson, *Chinese in the West Borneo Goldfields*, 61; Jackson, *Immigrant Labour*, 34.

64. Jackson, *Immigrant Labour*, 42–44.

65. Manderson, *Sickness and the State*, 80–81; Hollen Lees, "International Management," 50; Ng Siew Yoong, "The Chinese Protectorate," 83.

66. Yen Ching-hwang, *A Social History*, 5.

67. Jackson, "Mining in 18th-Century Bangka," 51–52; NA, MvK II, inv. no. 1950, Verb. February 28, 1919, no. 6, De Kat Angelino, chap. 2, 4, 7.

68. Baak, "About Enslaved Ex-Slaves," 123.

69. See Ng Siew Yoong, "The Chinese Protectorate."

70. *Staatsblad van Nederlandsch-Indië*, 1868–1888, "Oostersche Vreemdelingen. Voorschriften tegen misleiding en dwang bij het aangaan en ten uitvoerleggen van huurovereenkomsten."

71. Ng Siew Yoong, "The Chinese Protectorate," 79.

72. Wong Lin Ken, *The Malayan Tin Industry*, 70–75; Parmer, *Colonial Labor Policy*, 101.

73. Jackson, "Chinese Agricultural Pioneering," 78, 81, 87.

74. Parmer, *Colonial Labor Policy*, 21–22.

75. Hollen Lees, "International Management," 47–49.

76. See Huff and Caggiano, "Globalization."

77. Trocki, "Singapore," 215; Modderman, Volker, and Van der Veen, *Gedenkboek*, 36; Heidhues Somers, *Bangka Tin*, 57–58, 62–63; NA, MvK II, Mailrapport no. 591, 1903, Resident van Banka, H. van der Wolk, aan de gouverneur-generaal, missive 30-5-1903, no. 1588.

78. According to Wong Lin Ken (*The Malayan Tin Industry*, 67), the percentage of credit-ticket labor migrants (the so-called *sinkehs*) declined from about

40 percent in 1880 to 12.5 percent in 1896. This is, however, according to official figures. Although more and more immigrants came with help of relatives, recruiters still sometimes pressed their recruits to misinform the officials of the Chinese Protectorate that they had *not* come under the credit-ticket system to keep them out of official indentureship and thus keep them in their own power. Parmer, *Colonial Labor Policy*, 30, 101.

79. Wong Lin Ken, *The Malayan Tin Industry*, 97, 185, 203, 223–25; Jackson, *Immigrant Labour*, 113. The power of the labor gangs has also been noted for plantations in South India. Baak, "About Enslaved Ex-Slaves," 139.

80. Hollen Lees, "International Management," 49; Kaur, "Indonesian Migrant Workers in Malaysia," 7.

81. NA, Archive Billiton Maatschappij, inv. no. 255, "Rapport van H. Colijn," 4, 9, 33, 57. See also Billiton Maaschappij N.V., *Gedenkboek Billiton*, II, 60–61. For the oversupplies of labor, see NA, Archive Billiton Maatschappij inv. no. 40, Jaarverslag 1894–1895, 26, inv. no. 42, Jaarverslag 1911/1912, 5.

82. Bankoff, "Wants, Wages," 67.

83. Worcester, *The Philippine Islands*, 75.

84. Walker, *The Sugar Industry*, 20.

85. Aguilar, "Sugar Planter–State Relations," 58–59.

86. Clark, "Labor Conditions in the Philippines," 777; Aguilar, "Sugar Planter–State Relations," 60.

87. Aguilar, "Sugar Planter–State Relations," 67; McCoy, "Sugar Barons," 119.

88. Salman, *The Embarrassment of Slavery*, 172.

89. Worcester, *Slavery and Peonage*, 4.

90. NA, MvK II, Mail report 1872, no. 259.

91. See Bosma, "The Discourse on Free Labour"; Stanziani, *Sailors*.

92. Breman, *Koelies*, 310; Brouwer, *De Houding van Idenburg en Colijn*, 31.

93. The so-called Banyuwangi arrangement was only drafted for the most eastern and most thinly populated Residency of Java. Drafted in 1918, this regulation was never enacted. See Alkema, *Arbeidswetgeving*, 8.

94. Elson, "Sugar Factory Workers," 148n37; Knight, *Commodities and Colonialism*, 79.

95. "Koelie Ordonnantien," 74; Kantoor van de Arbeid, *Verslag van de Arbeidsinspectie*, 1937 and 1938, 87–90.

96. Van Blommestein, *De Nieuwe Koelie-Ordonnantie*, 12, 13, 30.

97. Van Blommestein, *Ontwerp eener Ordonnantie*, 61.

98. Burger, *Landverhuizing*, 116.

99. Heijting, *De Koelie-Wetgeving*, 136.

100. Burger, *Landverhuizing*, 150, 152–53.

101. Purwanto, *From Dusun to the Market*, 264.

102. Meijer Ranneft, "Misstanden bij de Werving," 56; Middendorp, *Twee Achterlijke Arbeidssystemen*, 49; NA, Archive Billiton Maatschappij, inv. no. 25, "Rapport H. Colijn," 4.

103. With regard to the wages of the seasonal and tenured workers in the sugar sector, see Levert, *Inheemsche Arbeid*, 247–48, 330; Huender, *Overzicht van den Economischen Toestand*, 101.

104. *Nota over de Invoering van Staatstoezicht Werving*, 37.

105. Van Blankenstein, *De Poenale Sanctie in de Practijk*, 22. For the entire working population the figure was about 5 percent by the mid-1920s. *Verslag Arbeidsinspectie* 1925, 46.

106. Meijer Ranneft, "Volksverplaatsingen op Java," 70. For a succinct analysis of the recruitment practices under indenture, see Houben, "Colonial Capitalism," 67–70.

107. Van Blankenstein, *De Poenale Sanctie*, 43–45; Lamb, "Time of Normalcy," 549.

108. Even in the Deli plantations, wages for free laborers (who mostly came from West Kalimantan) were much higher than for the indentured laborers. *Verslag Arbeidsinspectie* (1920), 28.

109. Lamb, "Time of Normalcy," 536; Yacob, "Model of Welfare Capitalism," 161; Gould, *Americans in Sumatra*, 602. NA, Archive Billiton Maatschappij, inv. no. 255, "Rapport H. Colijn," 20 and inv. no. 42, Jaarverslag 1916, 42.

110. Purwanto, "Peasant Economy and Institutional Changes," 16–17; Purwanto, *From Dusun to the Market*, 258, 266.

111. Burger, *Landverhuizing*, 116.

112. *Nota Over de Invoering van Staatstoezicht*, 3.

113. *Verslag Arbeidsinspectie* (1925), 14–15.

114. *Nota Over de Invoering van Staatstoezicht*, 8. To maintain control over Javanese labor emigration to British Malaya, the Dutch authorities had ruled that Javanese workers going to the region had to migrate under indenture, a measure that was only abolished in 1932. *Verslag Arbeidsinspectie* (1926), 17–18; Parmer, *Colonial Labor Policy*, 109; Tate, "Planting in Nineteenth-Century Sabah," 59; Lee, "The Population of British North Borneo," 229. Pekelharing, *De Groote Cultures*, 30.

115. Tate, "Planting in Nineteenth-Century Sabah," 51, 54; David and Jackson, "The Tobacco Industry," 97–98, 103; Lee, "The Population of British North Borneo," 230–31, 242; Worcester, *The Philippine Islands*, 208; Van Verschuer mentions the Tawi Tawi islands together with Bulungan and Berou as sites of intensive slave trade. Van Verschuer, "De Badjo's," 5.

116. *Verslag Arbeidsinspectie* (1925), 46.

117. Winstedt, *History of Johore*, 169; *Verslag Arbeidsinspectie* (1926), 17. *Nota Over de Invoering van Staatstoezicht*, 10; Spaan, "Taikongs and Calos," 95; Kratoska, "Rice Cultivation and the Ethnic Division," 301.

118. *Nota Over de Invoering van Staatstoezicht*, 10.

119. Bosma, "Migration and Colonial Enterprise," 172; Vredenbregt, "The Haddj," 140–45, 148–49.

120. Vredenbregt, "The Haddj," 98–99; Vredenbregt, "Bawean Migrations," 117, referring to C. Snouck Hurgronje, *Ambtelijke Adviezen*, 2:1416, 1442; Spaan, "Taikongs and Calos," 95.

121. Vredenbregt, "The Haddj," 127; Husson, "Indonesians in Saudi Arabia," 122; Roff, *The Origins of Malay Nationalism*, 36–39. For the role of the Chinese protectorate in Singapore in registering labor contracts, see Ng Siew Yoong, "The Chinese Protectorate." Since compared with their respective population size, ten times as many Malays from the Malay Peninsula as inhabitants of the Indonesian archipelago went on hajj in the early decades of the twentieth century, it cannot be excluded that Javanese departed as subjects of the British Crown to Mecca. McDonnell, "The Conduct of the Hajj," 631.

122. Modderman, Volker, and Van der Veen, *Gedenkboek*, 148, 153; Meijer Ranneft, "Misstanden bij de Werving," 56; *ADEK Verslag* 1919–1920, 5.

123. According to Modderman, Volker, and Van der Veen, *Gedenkboek*, 111, 153–56; Broersma. "Vrije Volksverplaatsing," 176, 179.

124. ADEK Verslag, 1919–1920, 7.

125. See Schneider, *Inleiding tot de Studie*; Planterscomité, *Overzicht*, 42; Gallagher, *De Afschaffing van het Contract System*, 19–23.

126. Pelzer, *Arbeiterwanderungen*, 101; Modderman, Volker, and Van der Veen, *Gedenkboek*, 166, 187.

127. For the diminishing recruitment costs, see ADEK Verslag 1923, 15; 1926, 12; Pelzer, *Arbeiterwanderungen*, 103.

128. *Verslag Arbeidsinspectie* (1917–1918), 108; Cheong Lee Kam Hing and Leeu Poh Ping, "Chinese Overseas Remittances," 83; NA, Archive Billiton Maatschappij, inv. no. 255, "Rapport H. Colijn," 18–20, inv. no. 166, Jaarverslag 1924, inv. no. 41, Jaarverslag 1908/1909, 6, inv. no. 42, Jaarverslag 1916, 5.

129. For the 78 percent returning penniless and the accumulation of the ten million guilders, see Ezerman's letter to the "Directeur Binnenlandsch Bestuur of 31 October 1919," pp. 2 and 5 in NA, MvK II, inv. no. 1950, Verb. February 28, 1919, no. 76. For the ownership of the mining and their methods of profit making, see in the same Verbaal the report by De Kat Angelino, chap. 1, 10, 11, 22–23.

130. Meijer Ranneft, "Misstanden bij de Koeliewerving," 15.

131. Langeveld, "Arbeidstoestanden," 320. See also "Een Delische Idylle," *De Tribune. Revolutionair Volksblad. Orgaan Communistische Partij Nederland Sectie Communistische Internationale*, June 9, 1927.

132. In 1928, the total remittances amounted to 41,620.20 guilders (Modderman, Volker, and Van der Veen, *Gedenkboek*, Bijlage 5^c), and in 1937, 140,000 guilders. *Verslag der VEDA*, 1937, 17. For the total number of Javanese workers in Sumatra's East Coast, see *Indisch Verslag* 1938, II, 226.

133. Modderman, Volker, and Van der Veen, *Gedenkboek*, 192.

134. E. Kupers, in *International Labour Conference, 12th Session Compte Rendu Provisoire, no. 31, 20 June 1929*, 547, 549. Retrieved from IISH, Collection Stokvis, no. 91.

135. Van Blankenstein, *De Poenale Sanctie*, 61; Middendorp, *Twee Achterlijke Arbeidssystemen*, 45–47.

136. Handelingen Volksraad, February 31, 1931, 2363–2364, accessed in IISG, Coll. Stokvis, no. 91; IISH, Albert Thomas Papers, 982.

137. *Verslag Arbeidsinspectie* (1930, 1931) and (1932), 39; Modderman, Volker, and Van der Veen, Gedenkboek, Bijlage 5^a.

138. *ADEK Verslag*, 9.

139. *Verslag Arbeidsinspectie* (1926), 14–15.

140. NA, Deli Maatschappij, inv. no. 344, "Dactyloscopisch Bureau der D.P.V. en A.V.R.O.S. 1925–1950," 3; Van Blankenstein, *De Poenale Sanctie*, 22–23; Modderman, Volker, and Van der Veen, *Gedenkboek*, 108–9.

141. *Indisch Staatsblad 1931*, no. 95; NA, Deli Maatschappij, inv. no. 344, "Dactyloscopisch Bureau der D.P.V. en A.V.R.O.S. 1925–1950," 12; Langeveld, "Arbeidstoestanden," 304.

142. *Verslag Arbeidsinspectie* 1938–1939, Bijlage 4; In the Bangka tin mines, the penal sanction was only abolished in 1939, after Chinese miners had been replaced by a Javanese labor force. Ross, "The Tin Frontier," 8–13; Somers Heidhues, *Bangka Tin*, 129–30.

143. *Verslag Arbeidsinspectie* 1937–1938, 17–18; *Verslag der VEDA* 1937, 7.

5. THE PERIPHERY REVISITED: COMMODITY EXPORTS, FOOD, AND INDUSTRY, 1870s–1942

1. Lewis, "The Export Stimulus," 34, 36.

2. Alexander and Alexander, "Protecting Peasants," 382; Van Zanden and Marks, *An Economic History*, 126–28; Bosma, *Karel Zaalberg*, 391.

3. Hooley, "American Economic Policy," 472. In the Netherlands Indies, government expenditure as a share of GDP was 7 percent in the 1920s and actually rose to 10 percent in 1936–1939. Booth, "The Burden of Taxation," 94. It should

be pointed out, as Booth has done, that defense expenditure in the Netherlands Indies was higher than in the Philippines and British Malaya and that this absorbed a substantial portion of the government budget. Booth, *Economic Change*, 21.

4. Booth, *Colonial Legacies*, 75; Gerritsen, "Belastingen," 63.

5. In 1913, investment in USD per capita was 10 for the Philippines, 12 for the Netherlands Indies, and 58 for British Malaya, whereas it ranged from 200 to 400 for white settler colonies. Barbier, *Scarcity and Frontiers*, 387.

6. Korthals Altes, *De Betalingsbalans*, 144–47; Van Gelderen, *Voorlezingen*, 103, 105. For British Malaya, see Kratoskayo, "Imperial Unity," 272. See also Booth, *Economic Change*, 22.

7. Booth, *Colonial Legacies*, 110.

8. Bassino and Williamson, "From Commodity Booms," 8.

9. Mansvelt, *Rice Prices*, 19.

10. Kratoska, "Rice Cultivation," 286.

11. See Ulbe Bosma and Bas van Leeuwen's forthcoming data on rice prices. For now, see Mansvelt, *Rice Prices*.

12. For the depressed rural income and wages, see *Overzicht van de Gewestelijke Onderzoekingen*, IXb, 56, 63.

13. Wickizer and Bennett, *The Rice Economy*, 179.

14. Alexander and Alexander, "Protecting Peasants," 382.

15. Gonggrijp, *Over de Invloed van het Westers Grootbedrijf*, 13–14; Bosma, *The Sugar Plantation*, 176.

16. Djojohadikoesoemo, *Het Volkscredietwezen in de Depressie*, 21, 26; *Sumatra Post*, February 21, 1935.

17. In Java, after having grown from 2.24 million hectares in 1910, the area under paddy stagnated at about 3.5 million hectares in the 1920s. The area under rice would increase again in the 1930s after the collapse of export agriculture. In the Philippines, it had increased from 1.04 million hectares in 1910, to 1.48 in 1918, and 1.81 in 1930, but more or less stagnated in the subsequent decade. Wickizer and Bennett, *The Rice Economy*, 314. For the rice yields per hectare, see Wickizer and Bennet, *The Rice Economy*, 318–19; Chiba, "The 1919 and 1935 Rice Crises," 529. In Java, the government budget for irrigation went up from 6.4 million guilders in 1917 to 8.2 million in 1926, while nominal wages rose by 40 percent between 1913 and 1926, most of this after 1918. For the irrigation budget of 1917, see HTK 1916–1917, Bijlage B, "Begrooting van Nederlandsch-Indië voor het dienstjaar 1917," 33; for 1926, see HTK 1925–1926, Bijlage B, "Begrooting van Nederlandsch-Indië voor het dienstjaar 1926," 17. For nominal wages, see Dros and Van Dooren, *Wages 1820–1940*, 30.

18. See Bosma and Curry Machado, "Turning Javanese," 108.

19. Hooley, "American Economic Policy," 467–68.

20. Barker, Herdt, and Rose, *The Rice Economy of Asia*, 58; Van der Eng, "Development of Seed-Fertilizer," 22–23, 28, 31; Van der Eng, "Food for Growth," 601.

21. The bottleneck in the economic development of colonial Indonesia, and to a lesser degree in the Philippines, might have been the result of stagnating productivity in food agriculture rather than the high percentage of the population employed in this sector. In terms of extra-agricultural employment, none of the colonies in Island Southeast Asia compared unfavorably with Korea or Thailand, where respectively 79.6 and 84.2 percent of the population was engaged in agriculture by 1930. Booth, "Indonesian Colonial Economic Performance," 146.

22. *Census of the Philippine Islands 1903*, 4:464–65.

23. *Census of the Philippine Islands 1918*, 4-1:226; Bosma, *The Sugar Plantation*, 159.

24. See in this respect Rouffaer, *De Voornaamste Industrieën*.

25. Bosma, "Methodological Paper," 24–29.

26. HTK 1875–1876, *Koloniaal Verslag* 1875, Bijlage A, No. IV, "Beroepen en Bedrijven"; HTK 1895–1896, *Koloniaal Verslag* 1895, Bijlage A, Bijlage No. V, "Beroepen en Bedrijven."

27. HTK 1918–1919, *Koloniaal Verslag* 1918, Hoofdstuk O, 232.

28. Rouffaer, *De Voornaamste Industrieën*, 50–51.

29. McLennan, "Peasant and Hacendero," 136. Owen (*Prosperity Without Progress*, 171–72) mentions the emergence of shipyards in Sorsogon by the mid–nineteenth century, which disappeared with the emergence of the steamships.

30. Clark, "Labor Conditions in the Philippines," 819–20.

31. Masyhuri, "Fishing Industry and Environment," 253–56; Boomgaard, "Resources and People of the Sea," 97–98. Fish imports increased from 19.5 million kilograms in 1891 to 33.9 kilograms in 1900. See Van Deventer, *Overzicht van den Economischen Toestand*, 251.

32. Van Deventer, *Overzicht van den Economischen Toestand*, 118; Bottemanne, "De Indische Zeevisscherij," 455; Tideman, "De Zeevischerij in Rembang en Bodjonegoro," 13.

33. According to Cavada, *Historia*, 2:410–11, there were 133,384 people engaged in industry, transport, and services. Assuming that 59.5 percent of the total tributary population of 5,504,356 (*Censo de poblacion 1876*, 46) was employable, this would amount to 4 percent. For the late-nineteenth-century Philippines there is a variety of other data available, but it would require a major research effort to mine this material. See Cullinane, "Accounting for Souls"; and Doeppers, "Civil Records."

34. For the number of men involved in manufacturing in 1875, see HTK 1875–1876, *Koloniaal Verslag* 1875, Bijlage A, 12–13. For the male employment in manufacturing in 1900–1905, see Bosma, "Methodological Paper," 15. For the number of nonagricultural workers in Madura, see HTK 1907–1908, *Koloniaal Verslag* 1907, Bijlage A, VI, 36–37. For employment in salt making, see Jonge, "State and Welfare," 92. The number of railway workers in 1905 ranged between 15,000 and 20,000, according to Van Deventer, *Overzicht van den Economischen Toestand*, 217.

35. *Census of the Philippine Islands 1903*, 2:112. According to the *Census of Philippines 1903*, 2:92–93, practically all female manufacturing work was cottage production.

36. Alexander and Alexander, "Protecting Peasants," 378.

37. Sollewijn Gelpke, *Naar Aanleiding van het Staatsblad*, 242–43, 260–61. For Java, we do not have precise data about textile manufacturing but only for Javanese female involvement in crafts, which is 291,998, of whom 51,429 were in by-employment. The latter figures appear to be unrealistically low. HTK 1907–1908, *Koloniaal Verslag* 1907, Bijlage A, 36–37. See also Matsuo, *The Development of the Javanese Cotton Industry*, 13.

38. See extracts from De Kat Angelino's *Batikrapport* in Lasker, *Human Bondage*, 301–6.

39. Bleeker, "Fragmenten eener Reis" (1850), 2:91.

40. Van Nederveen Meerkerk, "Challenging the De-industrialization Thesis," 1232, table 1.

41. Dalenoord, "Textiel-Nijverheid," 169–72.

42. Post, "The Formation," 612; Purwanto, *From Dusun to the Market*, 74–75; HTK 1891–1892, *Koloniaal Verslag* 1891, Bijlage FFF, 12; Watson Andaya, "Women and Economic Change," 174; Hall, "The Textile Industry," 121.

43. Rouffaer, *De Voornaamste Industrieën*, 11–12; Matsuo, *The Development of the Javanese Cotton Industry*, 16–18, 20; Van der Eng, "De-industrialisation," 10.

44. Reid, *Southeast Asia in the Age of Commerce*, 1:95; HTK 1893–1894, *Koloniaal Verslag* 1893, Bijlage B, 3–4. Rouffaer, *De Voornaamste Industrieën*, 13. See Mohamad, *The Malay Handloom Weavers*.

45. Lannoy, *Iles Philippines*, 81.

46. Legarda, *After the Galleons*, 152; Sawyer, *The Inhabitants of the Philippines*, 250.

47. Mallat, *Les Philippines*, 303.

48. Bowring, *A Visit to the Philippine Islands*, 359.

49. McCoy, "A Queen Dies Slowly," 301, 303–7. Declining margins in the textile trade were mentioned by Nicholas Loney as an incentive for Mestizo Chinese entrepreneurs to invest in sugar production in Negros. See Lopez-Gonzaga, "The Roots of Agrarian Unrest," 163.

50. As a rule, Philippine textile exports abroad from Manila were marginal from the 1850s onward. *Census of the Philippine Islands 1903*, 4:467. Moreover, as Wickberg (*The Chinese in Philippine Life*, 55) has indicated, Chinese traders had been replacing Mestizo-Chinese traders after the opening of Iloilo as an international harbor and after having been granted the freedom to trade.

51. Fornier, "Economic Developments in Antique Province: 1850–1900," 156.

52. Cavada (*Historia*, 2:410) lists 47,320 looms for the entire Philippines, which is probably an underestimation since Fornier counted over 7,000 looms for Antique alone. Fornier, "Economic Developments in Antique Province: 1850–1900," 156.

53. This figure is based on the assumption that 59.5 percent of the total female population were employable and that the total female population of Iloilo was 205,939. *Census of the Philippine Islands 1903*, 2:865–66. The same census explicitly mentions relatively extensive female employment in Capiz, Batangas, the Iloco provinces, and la Unión in the weaving sector. *Census of the Philippine Islands* 1903, 2:100.

54. Clark, "Labor Conditions in the Philippines," 809–10.

55. Clark, "Labor Conditions in the Philippines," 819–20.

56. Cavada, *Historia*, 2:410.

57. Hooley, "American Economic Policy," 471; Corpuz, "Railroads," 62.

58. Bosma, "Methodological Paper," 21, 37.

59. Fernando, "Changing Character," 8–9. On the basis of 25 million inhabitants of Java and Madura, a household size of 4.57, and the fact that 80 percent of the population was dependent on agricultural employment, the total number of households reliant on by-employment would be 4.4 million.

60. Meijer Ranneft and Huender, *Onderzoek naar den Belastingdruk*, 10.

61. According to the Philippine census of 1903, of the total of 1,236,327 males engaged in agriculture, 815,453 either owned or rented a "farm," of whom 290,770 cultivated less than 0.35 hectares and 241,457 between 0.35 and 1 hectare. *Census of the Philippine Islands 1903*, 4:196. According to the census of 1918, the number of farms had increased from this 815,453 to 1,955,276, of which 741,437 were smaller than 0.35 hectares and 455,640 between 0.35 and 1 hectare. *Census of the Philippine Islands 1918*, 3:7. The estimation of the total rural landless population is a conservative one. Assuming an employable male population of 2,740,906 (which is 85 percent of all Philippine males older than 10 [instead of all men older than 10 as indicated in the *Census of the Philippine Islands 1918*, 3:7]), and assuming that over 80 percent of employable men in the rubric of "domestic and personal service" were actually agricultural laborers without land (*Census of the Philippine Islands 1918*, 2:77), this would amount to 353,028 or 12.88 percent of the male employable population being agricultural

laborers without land, or 15.0 percent of the total rural workforce (namely 1,995,276 farm owners plus 353,028 landless rural workers).

62. By 1918, the available area of arable land per capita in the Philippines was 0.25 hectares against 0.21 hectares in Java. *Census of the Philippine Islands 1918*, 3:6, 8; *Landbouwatlas*, 2:28, 46. In addition to the 9,654,440 hectares tilled by Javanese smallholders, which amounted to 0.28 *bau* per head, there were another 2,002,636 rented by estates, of which 779,148 was planted. For 1940, see Booth, *Colonial Legacies*, 39.

63. In 1840, 470,673 households were conscripted for coffee cultivation, 148,247 for sugar, and 207,118 for indigo, figures that would go down to, respectively, 466,207, 189,325, and 103,214 in 1860. Fasseur, *Kultuurstelsel*, 256–59. After the expiration of the Cultivation System, only coffee production stagnated, but the production of sugar increased seventeenfold between 1870 and 1929, tobacco fifteenfold, and tea emerged as an entirely new crop between 1840 and 1900. Mansvelt, *Exportcultures van Ned.-Indië*, table 5.

64. Bosma, "Methodological Paper," 30.

65. HTK, *Koloniale Verslagen*, 1892 (Bijlage A, No. IV, 14–15), 1897 (Bijlage A, No. V, 14–15), 1902 (Bijlage A, No. V, 16–17), 1907 (Bijlage A, No. VI, 37), "Beroepen en Bedrijven."

66. From agricultural production data for Java, we can surmise that in the 1920s, about 600,000 hectares of estate land were planted, involving approximately 1.2 million years of work annually. The *Landbouwatlas*, 2:14, provides figures for acreage in 1922: for sugar, 228,000 *bau*; rubber, 231,000 *bau*; coffee, 140,000 *bau*; tea, 114,000 *bau*; tobacco, 40,000 *bau*; quinine, 21,000 *bau*; and cacao, 10,000 *bau*. For the amount of work per *bau*, see Bosma, "Methodological Paper," 42.

67. Van Nus, "De Staatsspoorwegen," 10, 27; *Een halve eeuw paketvaart*, 401–7.

68. See the article by Danielle Teeuwen about the gender division of plantation labor (forthcoming).

69. See Bosma, "Methodological Paper," 42.

70. The figure for the employable population is based on a rough population figure for the Philippines for 1930 of 13 million and the assumption that 59.5 percent of the population was employable.

71. The figures are 36.5 percent for Singapore, 54.5 percent for the Federal Malay States, and 33.1 percent for the less colonized UMS. The calculation is based on Huff, "Entitlements," 294. We moreover have to take into account that by the late 1920s, the percentages must have been higher, as by 1931 possibly 150,000 workers in the rubber sector had already lost their job. The number of tin workers had already dropped from 120,000 to fewer than 78,000.

72. Vlieland, *British Malaya: A Report on the 1931 Census*, 99.

73. Bosma, "Methodological Paper," 16.

74. Drabble, *An Economic History of Malaysia*, 137.

75. Yacob, "Ford's Investment," 802.

76. Chase-Dunn et al., "Trade Globalization," 86.

77. Latham, "From Competition to Constraint," 94–95.

78. Wolters, "Uneven Impact," 85–87.

79. Bosma, "Methodological Paper," 42.

80. Huff, "Entitlements," 290, 309, 310, 315, 319.

81. Cool, "De Bestrijding der Werkloosheidsgevolgen," 218; Bahrin, "The Growth and Distribution," 275–80; *Verslag Arbeidsinspectie*, 1930, 1931, and 1932, Bijlage 4 and 5; Ingleson, "Urban Java," 285, 301, 305.

82. For the percentage in 1930, see Bosma, "Methodological Paper," 16. The percentage of 6.8 is based on an estimated total Indonesian population of 69 million in 1939, of whom I assumed 59.5 percent were employable. The available data does not allow for a division according to gender. In absolute figures, manufacturing employment in colonial Indonesia rose from 1.7 to 1.8 million in 1931 and to 2.8 million in 1939, of which 300,000 was in larger industrial manufacturing. Van Oorschot, *De Ontwikkeling van de Nijverheid*, 85–87. Van der Eng arrives at a higher figure of 15 percent because he takes the gainfully employed population as a starting point and includes the cottage industry. Van der Eng, "Government Promotion of Labor-Intensive Industrialization," 178. Meanwhile, the share in manufacturing of the GDP in the Netherlands Indies rose from 8 percent in 1931 to 12 percent in 1939. Booth, *The Indonesian Economy*, 88.

83. In the Philippines, employment in industry (including rice husking and sugar mills) had already increased from 79,906 to 143,465 between 1903 and 1918. In addition to the 8,354 industrial establishments, there were 124,487 household industries employing 50,571 men and 15,040 women. *Census of the Philippine Islands 1918*, 4-1:200, 600. The number of workers employed in the household industry rose to 391,111 in 1939. *Census of Philippines: 1939*, I, part 1–4 [weaving, plaiting, embroidery, utensils, and furniture], table 21. Industrial employment would further increase to 400,596 males and 271,623 females in 1939. *Census of the Philippines: 1939*, I, 1–4, table 15. See also IISH Dataverse, Bosma, "Demography," File "Excerpts from 1939 Philippine Census (March 19, 2017)"; Hooley, "American Economic Policy," 470.

84. With regard to the detrimental impact of the American imports, see, for example, Cortes, *Pangasinan 1901–1968*, 58.

85. *Census of the Philippine Islands 1918*, 4-1:203–9; Shepherd, *Industry in Southeast Asia*, 88, 90–93; Doeppers, *Manila*, 21–22.

86. For the observation about Filipino ownership of the industrial assets, see Booth, *Colonial Legacies*, 122.

87. Brown, "Some Comments," 209.

88. Shepherd, *Industry in Southeast Asia*, 120.

89. Doeppers, *Manila*, 30–31.

90. Doeppers, *Manila*, 526–30.

91. The census of 1903 gives a total figure of 569,906 for all spinning and weaving. *Census of the Philippine Islands 1903*, 4:498–99, 2:113. The census of 1918 gives a figure of 79,141 for all cottage textiles. *Census of the Philippine Islands 1918*, 4-1:622–25. For 1939, see *Census of the Philippines: 1939*, 1:1–4, tables 15 and 21.

92. While being the residence of just 6.5 percent of the Philippine population, 19 percent of all male and 12.5 percent of all female industrially employed were living in these two provinces by 1939, and these figures would only increase after the war. See IISH Dataverse, Bosma, "Demography," File "Excerpts from 1939 Philippine Census (March 19, 2017)." See also Doeppers, *Manila*, 53; Doronila, "The Transformation," 105.

93. In the 1920s, daily wages for female workers in the cane fields and sugar factories ranged from 30 to 40 cents per day, whereas in textiles 20 or even 10 cents was common. In the 1930s, wages in the plantations went down to 10 to 14 cents. Yet total female employment in Java's commercial textile and garment sector, for example, only modestly increased from 547,898 to 676,000 between 1930 and 1936. *Volkstelling 1930*, 3:94. See also Kagotani, "Japan's Commercial Penetration," 199–205. Levert, *Inheemsche arbeid*, 247–48; White, "Diversification," 50; Djojohadikusumo, *Het Volkskredietwezen*, 24–25.

94. Sitsen, *Industrial Development*, 54.

95. Mansvelt, *Rice Prices*, 19.

96. Van Zanden, "On the Efficiency of Markets," 1038.

97. Sitsen, *Industrial Development*, 28; Claver, *Dutch Commerce*, 279, 355.

98. Sitsen, *Industrial Development*, 2–5, 11.

99. Scheltema, "De Ontwikkeling," 295–99, 301.

100. Sitsen, *Industrial Development*, 15.

101. Burger, *Sociologisch-Economische Geschiedenis*, 121.

102. Warmelo, "Ontstaan en groei," 21; White, "Economic Diversification," 50.

103. *Census of Philippines: 1939*, I, part 1–4, table 16.

104. Djojohadikoesoemo, *Het Volkscredietwezen in de Depressie*, 197; Sitsen, *Industrial Development*, 5.

105. Van der Eng, "Government Promotion of Labour-Intensive Industrialization," 178.

106. Whereas cottage production through putting out (*bakul*) diminished from 46,670 to 32,362 workers between 1929 and 1934, the number of factory workers increased from 18,835 to 47,771. Van der Reijden, *Rapport*, 3:145.

107. *Indisch Verslag* 1939, 1:169; Sitsen, *Industrial Development*, 33; Burger, *Sociologisch-Economische Geschiedenis*, 2:121.
108. Bosma, "Methodological Paper," 11; Volkstelling 1930, 8:5. For the Philippines, see United Nations, *Growth of the World's Urban and Rural Populations*, 99.
109. Vlieland, *British Malaya*, 45.
110. Zelinsky, "The Hypothesis of the Mobility Transition."
111. Massey, "Economic Development"; Sassen, *The Mobility of Labor and Capital*.
112. De Haas, "Migration Transitions," 40.
113. Goantiang, "Growth of Cities in Indonesia," 107.
114. Bosma, "Migration and Colonial Enterprise," 159; Bleeker, "Fragmenten" (1849), 2:30.
115. Meijer Ranneft, "Volksverplaatsingen op Java," 175.
116. Dros and Van Dooren, *Wages 1820–1940*, 75–88, table 5.
117. Bosma, "Migration and Colonial Enterprise," 174.
118. Ingleson, *Workers, Unions, and Politics*, 12; Ingleson, "Life and Work," 457, 459.
119. Meijer Ranneft, "Volksverplaatsingen op Java," 69.
120. Hugo, "Circular Migration," 72–73; Hugo, "Migration to and from Jakarta," 192.
121. Aguilar, *Clash of Spirits*, 71; Meijer Ranneft, "Volksverplaatsingen op Java," 70.
122. See Hugo, "Forced Migration in Indonesia"; McNicoll, "Internal Migration in Indonesia," 43–48.
123. In 1913, the exports from British Malaya (including Sarawak and British North Borneo) amounted to 200 million USD, which was four-fifths of the size of the exports from Indonesia and four times as large as those of the Philippines. Much of these exports were, however, re-exports, which reflects the role of Singapore as a transit port. Stover, "Tropical Exports," 47–48.
124. *Volkstelling 1930*, 8:78, 79.
125. McNicoll, "Internal Migration," 84–85.
126. Nava, "Internal Migration," 19.
127. *Census of the Philippines: 1939*, 1:1–4, table 19. For a proxy of the wages for unskilled labor, see IISH Dataverse, Bosma, "Demography," File "Excerpts from 1939 Philippine Census (March 19, 2017)."
128. Doeppers, *Manila*, 57, 81, 82.
129. Doeppers, "Metropolitan Manila," 516.
130. Trager, "Family Strategies," 1265, 1270, 1275.
131. *Census of the Philippine Islands 1903*, 2:87; Hayden, *The Philippines*, 465, 471; Storer, "The Philippines," 297. Fox, "Primary Education," 218, 223; Foronda, "Education in the Ilocos," 117, 119; Clark, "Labor Conditions in the Philippines," 854. Adult literacy was also rapidly increasing thanks to a considerable spread of adult education in the Philippines in the 1930s. Furnival, *Educational Progress*, 95.

132. *Census of the Philippines: 1939*, 1:1–4, table 16; IISH Dataverse, Bosma, "Demography," File "Excerpts from 1939 Philippine Census (March 19, 2017)."
133. Vlieland, *British Malaya: Report of the 1931 Census*, 94, 328.
134. *Volkstelling 1920*, 2:155.
135. Van Leeuwen, *Human Capital*, 9.
136. Foronda, "Education in the Ilocos," 120.
137. For Indonesia the figure for 1948 has been taken. See Lubis, "The Press in Indonesia," 93. For the Philippines, see Furnivall, *Educational Progress*, 123; for Malaya, see Emmanuel, "Viewspapers," 19; Matheson Hooker, *Writing a New Society*, 76–80.
138. Hollen Lees, *Planting Empire*, chap. 6.
139. Vlieland, *British Malaya: 1931 Census*, 354–55, 358–59; *Census Report of the Philippine Islands 1918*, 2:62.
140. *Volkstelling 1930*, 7:106.
141. In British Malaya, there were 836 Europeans and 140 Eurasians out of a total of 11,964 civil servants (military excluded). Of the total number of 11,964 teachers, 369 were European and 452 Eurasian. See Vlieland, *Report on the 1931 Census*, tables 121–23, 129–31, 137–39. In the Netherlands Indies, out of the total number of 103,619 European Civil Servants, 86,585 were non-European in 1930. Of all the metropolitan civil servants, just over 3 percent were born in the Netherlands or elsewhere in Europe and firmly held the top positions together with metropolitan trained Eurasians. Gerke, "De Personeelsvoorziening," 183.
142. See, for example, Van Leeuwen, *Human Capital*, 229.
143. *Census of the Philippines 1939*, 1:1–4, tables 9 and 16; IISH Dataverse, Bosma, "Demography," File "Excerpts from 1939 Philippine Census (March 19, 2017)." See also Chua et al., "Urban-Rural Income."
144. McLennan, "Peasant and Hacendero," 172.
145. Cordova, *Filipinos*, 9.
146. Madurese might have represented a considerable segment of the approximately 9,000 Javanese and other colonial subjects sailing under the Netherlands Indies flag, as well as being among the approximately 2,000 Javanese and other colonial subjects sailing under the Dutch flag. Van Rossum, *Hand aan Hand*, 31, 38.
147. Sharma, "Towards a Political Economy," 27.
148. Sharma, "Towards a Political Economy," 17. Also, see Posadas and Guyotte, "Unintentional Immigrants."
149. Doeppers, "The Philippines in the Great Depression," 73.
150. Gonzales and Holmes, "Philippine Labour Diaspora," 301.
151. See Liu, Ong, and Rosenstein, "Dual Chain Migration"; Smith, "Social Demography," 323; Pertierra, "Lured Abroad," 59.

6. POSTCOLONIAL CONTINUITIES IN PLANTATIONS AND MIGRATIONS

1. Fernandez, Hawley, and Predaza, *The Population of Malaysia*, 10–11, 13.
2. Pryor, "Malaysia: Patterns of Population Movement," 80, 82, 97; Hirschman, "Demographic Trends in Peninsular Malaysia," 118.
3. Vlieland, *British Malaya: A Report on the 1931 Census*, 48, 52.
4. Hirschman, "Net External Migration."
5. McNicoll, "Internal Migration in Indonesia," 50; Braithwaite et al., *Anomie and Violence*, 294.
6. Van der Kroef, "Indonesia's Rice Economy," 379.
7. *De Locomotief*, March 13, 1952.
8. Van der Kroef, "Indonesia's Economic Difficulties," 18.
9. Van der Kroef, "Indonesia's Economic Difficulties," 21.
10. Stubbs, "Malaysia's Rubber," 84n1; Yahya, "Labor Flexibility," 149.
11. Dove, "Smallholder Rubber," 136.
12. McHale, *Rubber and the Malaysian Economy*, 71.
13. Mehmet, "Rubber," 27.
14. Bahrin and Lee, *FELDA*, 4–5, 37–57; see Sutton and Buang, "A New Role."
15. *Report of the Mission of Enquiry*, 49; McHale, *Rubber and the Malaysian Economy*, 71.
16. Stubbs, "Malaysia's Rubber," 88; Mehmet, "Rubber," 24; Barlow, *The Natural Rubber Industry*, 103.
17. Rice, "Sumitro's Role," 191–92; Van der Kroef, "Social Structure," 411–13.
18. Eviota, *The Political Economy of Gender*, 107; Feranil, *The Philippine Banana Industry*, 17–18, 24–25, 37.
19. Koninck and Déry, "Agricultural Expansion," 22; Oberai, "Land Settlement Policies," 144–45.
20. Koninck and Déry, "Agricultural Expansion," 7, 9. For the population data of 1900–1905, see HTK 1901–1902, *Koloniaal Verslag* 1900, Bijlage A, "Statistiek betreffende de Bevolking," 4–5; and Bosma, "Smallpox," 90.
21. Wijst, "Transmigration in Indonesia," 25; Hardjono, *Transmigration in Indonesia*, 26. See also Komitee Indonesië, "Transmigratie"; and Lagerberg, "Indonesische Transmigratie."
22. Wertheim, "Sociological Aspects," 192.
23. Hugo et al., *The Demographic Dimension*, 42–43.
24. Elmhirst, "Displacement, Resettlement," 134–35, 137, 140, 145, 147–48.
25. IISG, Komitee Indonesië, inv. no. 29, 30; Arndt, "Transmigration," 51.
26. Wernstedt and Spencer, *The Philippine Island World*, 138–39; Feranil, *The Philippine Banana Industry*, 12; Wernstedt and Simkins, "Migrations," 95.

27. In the mining sector, artisanal gold mining grew massively in Mindanao, engaging an estimated 125,000 to 500,000 workers. Verbrugge, "The Economic Logic," 1031, 1034. Ahmad, "Class and Colony," 9; IISG, Collection Social Movements, inv. no. 13.

28. Algado, "The Political Economy," 168.

29. Hill, "Structural Change," 57.

30. Sicat, "Philippine Economic Nationalism," 13; Booth, *Colonial Legacies*, 166.

31. Booth, *The Indonesian Economy in the Nineteenth and Twentieth Centuries*, 88. Doronila, "The Transformation," 103; Drabble, *An Economic History of Malaysia*, 188; Carroll, *The Filipino Manufacturing Entrepreneur*, 37–38.

32. Abad, "Internal Migration," 131, 133.

33. De Dios and Williamson, "Deviant Behavior," 15.

34. Sloane, "The Philippine Censuses," 61.

35. Sicat, "The Philippines in 1983," 250.

36. Ku, "The Political Economy," 106; Billig, "Syrup in the Wheels of Progress."

37. Pineda-Ofreneo, "The Philippine Sugar Crisis," 464. See also Jagan and Cunnington, *Social Volcano*.

38. IISG, Social Movements Philippines, inv. no. 28.

39. Boyce, *The Philippines*, 29; Ofroneo, "Growth and Employment," 115.

40. Boyce, *The Philippines*, 78–79; Balisacan, "Agricultural Growth," 546, 548.

41. Mangahas, "The Philippine Social Indicators," 78.

42. Kratoska, "Rice Cultivation and the Ethnic Division," 312; Timmer, "Building Efficiency," 136.

43. Van der Kroef, "Indonesia's Economic Difficulties," 19.

44. White, "Beginnings of Crony Capitalism," 394, 404–5, 410, 413, 415.

45. Sicat, "The Economic Legacy of Marcos," 19; Maddison, *The World Economy*, 218.

46. Hunt, "Catholicism and Philippine Population Problem," 214.

47. McDonald, "The Demography of Indonesia," 36, 48, 42. The populations of Sumatra and Kalimantan have been growing much faster than of Java since the 1970s. McDonald, "The Demography of Indonesia," 45, 52.

48. See Hanson and McIntosh, "The Demography of Mexican Migration."

49. *Newsweek*, June 15, 1987; IISG, Collection Social Movements, inv. nos. 24 and 25. Various pamphlets of the KMP (Kilusang Magbubukid nq Pilippinos). See also Kerkvliet, "Land Reform"; Fegan, "The Philippines"; Schul, "A Philippine Sugar Cane Plantation," 161, 166, 168; Aguilar, "The Philippine Peasant as Capitalist," 52.

50. Kerkvliet, *The Huk Rebellion*, 253, 255, 267; Van der Kroef, "Social Structure," 395–98; Fegan, "The Philippines," 138–39.

51. Breman and Wiradi, *Good Times*, 60; Booth, *The Indonesian Economy*, 9. For the "involution" in the service sector, see Marks, *Accounting for Services*, 157; Hugo, "International Labor Migration and the Family," 274; White, "Economic Diversification," 57.

52. Hugo, "Circular Migration," 74–75; Hugo, "Indonesia: The Impact of Migration on Villages."

53. Firman, "Labour Allocation," 86–87, 97.

54. Tharian and Sethuraj, "Dynamics of World Natural Rubber," 55; Thoburn, "Exports and Economic Growth in West Malaysia," 109.

55. Stubbs, "Malaysia's Rubber," 95, 104–5; Tharian and Suthuraj, "Dynamics," 1356.

56. Lim Teck Ghee and Muhammad Ikmal Said, "Rice Peasants," 182; Talbot, "Tropical Commodities," 719.

57. Mehmet, "Rubber," 29.

58. Saravanamutti, "The Political Economy," 123, 127; Pye et al., "Precarious Lives," 330.

59. Lindquist, "Labour Recruitment," 122.

60. Hugo, "International Labor Migration," 281; Hugo, "Indonesian Labour Migration to Malaysia," 55. Also see Vatikiotis, "Escape from Poverty," 21.

61. IOM, *International Migration*, 63.

62. Hernández-Coss, *The Malaysia-Indonesia Remittance Corridor*, 1; Vatikiotis, "Worrisome Influx," 21; Vatikiotis, "Swamped Plantations," 26.

63. Hirschman, "A Note on Labor Underutilization," 96; Hirschman, "Educational Patterns," 488.

64. CIRCED, *The Population of Malaysia*, 37–38.

65. Hugo, "International Migration," 401–2; Hugo, "Migration and Development in Malaysia."

66. Fegan, *Folk-Capitalism*, 83–84.

67. Abad, "Internal Migration in the Philippines," 138.

68. Gonzales, "Philippine Labour Migration," 119; Algado, "The Political Economy," 132. See also Acacio, "Managing Labor Migration."

69. Simkin, "Migration as a Response," 262. The National Demographic Survey conducted in the Philippines in 1973 found that 42.6 percent of the women in the sample were migrants and that the majority were settled migrants. Lauby and Stark, "Individual Migration," 476; Algado, "The Political Economy," 138.

70. Maca and Morris, "The Philippines," 476.

71. Hugo, "International Migration," 406.

72. McDonald, "The Demography of Indonesia," 48–49.

73. Gonzales, *Philippine Labour Migration*, 37–39; Algado, "The Political Economy," 75; Battistella, "Philippine Overseas Labour," 259.

74. Hugo, "International Labour Migration," 406.

75. Gonzales, *Philippine Labour Migration*, 87; Sim, "Women Versus the State," 56.

76. Sim, "Women Versus the State," 55.

77. Gonzales, *Philippine Labour Migration*, 125, 127.

78. C189—Domestic Workers Convention, 2011 (no. 189), https://www.ilo.org/dyn /normlex/en/f?p=NORMLEXPUB:12100:0::NO::P12100_ILO_CODE:C189.

79. ILO Convention no. 29, 1930, was followed by ILO Convention no. 105, 1957. See http://www.ilo.org/ilolex/english/index.htm. See also Quirk, "The Anti-Slavery Project," 570.

80. Skinner, "Indonesia's Palm Oil Industry"; "Forced, Child, and Trafficked Labour in the Palm Oil Industry," *World Vision Action*, http://campaign.worldvision .com.au/wp-content/uploads/2013/04/Forced-child-and-trafficked-labour-in -the-palm-oil-industry-fact-sheet.pdf.

81. See in this regard, article 3 of the Palermo Protocol: http://www.ohchr.org /EN/ProfessionalInterest/Pages/ProtocolTraffickingInPersons.aspx. Vlieger, "Domestic Workers," 191–92.

82. Killias, "'Illegal' Migration," 901; Sim, "Women Versus the State," 56. Also see Rudnyiki, "Technologies of Servitude."

83. Semyonov, "Labor Migration," 63–64.

84. Ueno, "Strategies of Resistance," 499; Johnson, "Freelancing in the Kingdom," 461.

85. Lindio-McGovern, "Alienation and Labor Export," 221; IOM, *Labour Migration from Indonesia*, 16.

86. Pye et al., "Precarious Lives," 331; Hernández-Coss, *The Malaysia-Indonesia Remittance Corridor*, 51; Johnson, "Freelancing in the Kingdom," 461; Killias, "'Illegal' Migration," 903, 907.

87. Amnesty International, *Trapped*, 7.

88. Mantra, "Indonesian Labour Mobility," 176; Spaan, "Taikongs and Calos," 97.

89. Spaan, *Labour Circulation*, 147–48.

90. Lockard, "The Javanese Emigrant," 42; Vredenbregt, "Bawean Migration," 115, 117, 119. Vredenbregt refers here to *Ambtelijke Adviezen*, van C. Snouck Hurgronje, II, 1416, 1442.

91. Spaan, "Taikongs and Calo," 106; Rudnyckyj, "Technologies of Servitude," 408, 414.

92. Sim, "Women Versus the State," 58.

93. Tagliacozzo, *The Longest Journey*, 210; Lindquist, "Labour Recruitment," 123.

94. Rudnyckyj, "Technologies of Servitude," 428.

95. Lindquist, "Labour Recruitment," 124.

96. Mehmet, "Rubber," 29.

97. Kaur, "Indonesian Migrant Workers," 24; Rudnyckyj, "Technologies of Servitude," 426.

98. Kaur, "Indonesian Migrant Workers," 26.

99. Hugo, "Migration in Indonesia," 54; Saravanamuttu, "The Political Economy," 145.

100. Martin, "Merchants of Labour," 3; Ford, "Indonesian Women," 6. According to Hernández-Coss et al. (*The Malaysia-Indonesia Remittance Corridor*, 22), the recruitment fee for the undocumented channel was just 170 USD.

101. Mantra, "Indonesian Labour Mobility," 169–70, 173, 176; Hugo, "Indonesian Labour Migration to Malaysia," 47; Mantra, "Illegal Indonesian Labour Movement," 64.

102. Hugo, "Indonesian Labour Migration to Malaysia," 56.

103. Mantra, "Indonesian Labour Mobility," 171, 174.

104. Mantra, "Indonesian Labour Mobility," 168–69.

105. Doeppers, *Manila*, 100, 102; Spaan, *Labour Circulations*, 217.

106. Firman, "Population Mobility," 87, 89.

107. Hugo, "Migration in Indonesia," 54.

108. Lindquist, "The Elementary School," 71–72n3.

109. Lindquist, "Labour Recruitment," 126.

110. Lindquist, "Labour Recruitment," 128.

111. Breman and Wiradi, *Good Times*, 116–17; Spaan, *Labour Circulation*, 289–301.

112. Rudnyckyj, "Technologies of Servitude," 415; Hugo, "International Labor Migration and the Family," 289; IOM, *International Migration*, 42.

113. Algado, "The Political Economy," 245; Pertierra, "Lured Abroad," 67.

114. Lindquist, "The Elementary School," 74, 89.

115. Ranveigg Agunias, *Migration's Middlemen*, 12.

116. Banzon-Bautista, "The Saudi Connection," 153.

117. Lindquist, "Labour Recruitment," 128.

118. Hernández-Coss et al., *The Malaysia-Indonesia Remittance Corridor*, 22, 25.

119. Hernández-Coss et al., *The Malaysia-Indonesia Remittance Corridor*, 23, 25, 49; IOM, *International Migration*, 2, 3, 4, 93.

120. Mantra, "Illegal Indonesian Labour Movement," 67; Mantra, "Indonesian Labour Mobility," 179–80; Algado, "The Political Economy," 253–54.

121. Hernández-Coss et al., *The Malaysia-Indonesia Remittance Corridor*, 22, 50. According to the IOM (*International Migration*, 101), half of the money from Malaysia is remitted through informal channels.

122. Hugo, "International Labor Migration and the Family," 291–93; Semyonov and Gorodzeisky, "Labor Migration," 634.

123. Banzon-Bautista, "The Saudi Connection," 153; Hugo, "International Labour Migration and Migration Policies," 409; Arcinas, Bautista, and David, *The Odyssey*, 78.

124. Pertierra, "Lured Abroad," 56; Massey et al., *Return to Aztlan*, 212, 216–17.

125. Sharma, "Towards a Political Economy," 27; Hugo, "International Labour Migration and Migration Policies," 409.

126. Lekkerkerker, "Sapoedi en Bawean," 475.

127. Hugo, "International Labor Migration and the Family," 286; Lauby and Stark, "Individual Migration," 485–86; Lindquist, "Labour Recruitment," 123; Williams, *Maiden Voyages*, 146–47.

128. Eversole and Shaw, "Remittance Flows and Their Use," 181.

129. Martin, *Merchants of Labour*, 12.

130. Hugo, "International Labour Migration and Migration Policies," 410.

131. Johnson, "Freelancing in the Kingdom," 470.

132. This figure is mentioned by the government-licensed Malaysian Association of Foreign Maid Agencies (Persatuan Agensi Pembanturu Rumah Asing Malaysia). See also Lindquist, "Labour Recruitment," 116. Malaysia is far from the only country confronted with the desertion of domestic workers. See, for example, Loveband, "Position the Product," 345.

133. See, for example, Silvey, "Transnational Domestication," 17; De Regt, "High in the Hierarchy," 601.

134. Rannveig Agunias, *Migration's Middlemen*, 25, 27.

135. Sim, "Women Versus the State," 57–62, 66–67.

136. Sim, "Women Versus the State," 70.

CONCLUSION

1. The IOM report on Indonesian migration of 2010 points to several generations of migratory labor and migration systems. See IOM, *Labour Migration from Indonesia*, 37.

APPENDIX: METHODOLOGICAL NOTES

1. "Global Collaboratory on the History of Labour Relations, 1500–2000," https://collab.iisg.nl/web/labourrelations.

2. In the case of Island Southeast Asia, I had to make a reconstruction for Indonesia's Outer Islands, for which figures were completely absent for the nineteenth century. See Bosma, "Smallpox."

Bibliography

ARCHIVES

International Institute of Social History

Albert Thomas Papers, "Voyage Russie-Chine-Japon-Indies Neerlandaises (novembre-decembre 1928, janvier-février 1929)."

Bosma, Ulbe. "Data on Demography, Migration, Slavery, and Employment for the Netherlands Indies, the Philippines, and British Malaya, 1800–1950." 2017. IISH dataverse, http://hdl.handle.net/10622/NCJVLW.

Collection J. E. Stokvis, inv. no. 91.

League of Nations Collection, inv. nos. 135, 136, and 137.

Social and Political Movements of the Philippines.

National Archive, The Hague (NA)

Archief van de NV Deli Maatschappij, Dochtermaatschappijen en Gefuseerde Bedrijven.

Archive Billiton Maatschappij, inv. nos. 40–42 and 166 (jaarverslagen), inv. no. 255, Rapport van H. Colijn, adjunct-regeringskommisaris, betreffende een conflict tussen het Gouvernement van Nederlands-Indië en de maatschappij over het zogenoemde arbeidsvraagstuk. Met bijlagen. 1910.

Coll. Schneither, 83–100 Statistieke opgaven betreffende de residentiën op Java, 1816–1824.

Ministerie van Koloniën (1814–1849) (MvK I), inv. nos. 0359, 0429, 0498, 2954, 3041, 3065A, 3067, 3075, 3077, 3080, 3081, 3088, and 3089.

Ministerie van Koloniën (1849–1950) (MvK II) Mail reports.

NA, VOC archives, inv. nos. 1315, 1489, and 7784.

Koninklijk Instituut voor Taal-, Land en Volkenkunde, Leiden (KITLV)

Collection A. P. van de Siepkamp.

Collection J. van Swieten.

BIBLIOGRAPHY

Abad, Ricardo G. "Internal Migration in the Philippines: A Review of Research Findings." *Philippine Studies* 29, no. 2 (1981): 129–43.

Abeyasekere, S. "Slaves in Batavia." In *Slavery, Bondage, and Dependency in Southeast Asia*, ed. Anthony Reid, 86–314. New York: St. Martin's, 1983.

À Campo, Joseph N. F. M. *Koninklijke Paketvaart Maatschappij: Stoomvaart en Staatsvorming in de Indonesische Archipel 1888–1914*. Hilversum: Verloren, 1992.

——. "Patronen, Processen en Periodisering van Zeeroof en Zeeroofbestrijding in Nederlands-Indië." *Tijdschrift voor Sociale en Economische Geschiedenis* 3, no. 2 (2006): 78–107.

Acacio, Kristel. "Managing Labor Migration: Philippine State Policy and International Migration Flows, 1969–2000." *Asian and Pacific Migration Journal* 17, no. 2 (2008): 103–32.

Acciaioli, G. "Kinship and Debt: The Social Organization of Bugis Migration and Fish Marketing at Lake Lindu, Central Sulawesi." *Bijdragen tot de Taal-, Land- en Volkenkunde* 156, no. 3 (2000): 588–617.

Acemoglu, Daron, Simon Johnson, and James A. Robinson. "The Colonial Origins of Comparative Development: An Empirical Investigation." *American Economic Review* 91, no. 5 (2001): 1369–401.

——. "Reversal of Fortune: Geography and Institutions in the Making of the Modern World Income Distribution." *Quarterly Journal of Economics* 117, no. 4 (2002): 1231–94.

——. *Why Nations Fail: The Origins of Power, Prosperity, and Poverty*. New York: Random House, 2012.

Adas, Michael. "The Ryotwari in Lower Burma: The Establishment and Decline of a Peasant Proprietor System." In *Land Tenure and Peasant in South Asia*, ed. Robert Eric Frykenberg, 100–19. New Delhi: Orient Longman, 1977.

ADEK Verslag. See *Verslag van het Algemeen Delisch Emigratie Kantoor*.

Adriani, N., and Albert C. Kruyt. *De Barée-sprekende Toradjas van Midden-Celebes*. 3 vols. Batavia: Landsdrukkerij, 1912–1914.

Aguilar, Filomeno V. *Clash of Spirits: The History of Power and Sugar Planter Hegemony on a Visayan Island*. Quezon City: Ateneo de Manila University Press, 1998.

——. "The Philippine Peasant as Capitalist: Beyond the Categories of Ideal-Typical Capitalism." *Journal of Peasant Studies* 17, no. 1 (1989): 41–67.

——. "Sugar Planter–State Relations and Labour Processes in Colonial Philippine Haciendas." *Journal of Peasant Studies* 22, no. 1 (1994): 50–80.

Ahmad, Aijaz. "Class and Colony in Mindanao. Colonization Destroyed the Basis of Moros Society." *Southeast Asia Chronicle* 82 (1982): 4–10.

Alexander, Jennifer, and Paul Alexander. "Protecting Peasants from Capitalism: The Subordination of Javanese Traders by the Colonial State." *Comparative Studies in Society and History* 33, no. 2 (1991): 370–94.

——. "Shared Poverty as Ideology: Agrarian Relationships in Colonial Java." *Man* 17, no. 4 (1982): 697–19.

——. "Sugar, Rice, and Irrigation in Colonial Java." *Ethnohistory* 25, no. 3 (1978): 207–23.

Algado, Dean Tiburcio. "The Political Economy of International Labor Migration from the Philippines." PhD diss., University of Hawai'i, 1992.

Alkema, B. *Arbeidswetgeving in Nederlandsch-Indië inzonderheid met het Oog op de Oostkust van Sumatra*. Haarlem: H. D. Tjeenk Willink, s.a. 1929.

Allen, Richard B. *European Slave Trading in the Indian Ocean, 1500–1850*. Athens: Ohio University Press, 2015.

——. "Satisfying the 'Want for Labouring People': European Slave Trading in the Indian Ocean, 1500–1850." *Journal of World History* 21, no. 1 (2010): 45–73.

Alonso, Luis. "Financing the Empire: The Nature of the Tax System in the Philippines." *Philippine Studies* 51, no. 1 (2003): 63–95.

Amjad, R. "Philippines and Indonesia: On the Way to Migration Transition." *Asian and Pacific Migration Journal* 5, no. 2–3 (1996): 339–66.

Amnesty International, *Trapped: The Exploitation of Migrant Workers in Malaysia*. London: Amnesty International, 2010.

Amrith, Sunil. *Crossing the Bay of Bengal: The Furies of Nature and the Fortunes of Migrants*. Cambridge, MA: Harvard University Press, 2013.

Andaya, Barbara Watson. "The Cloth Trade in Jambi and Palembang Society During the Seventeenth and Eighteenth Centuries." *Indonesia* 48 (1989): 26–46.

——. *Perak, the Abode of Grace: A Study of an Eighteenth-Century Malay State*. Kuala Lumpur: Oxford University Press, 1979.

——. *To Live as Brothers: Southeast Sumatra in the Seventeenth and Eighteenth Centuries*. Honolulu: University of Hawai'i Press, 1993.

——. "Women and Economic Change: The Pepper Trade in Pre-Modern Southeast Asia." *Journal of the Economic and Social History of the Orient* 38, no. 2 (1995): 165–90.

Arcilla, José. "Slavery, Flogging, and Other Moral Cases in 17th-Century Philippines." *Philippine Studies* 20, no. 3 (1972): 399–416.

Arcinas, Fe. R., Cynthia Bautista, and Randolf S. David. *The Odyssey of the Filipino Migrant Workers to the Gulf Region.* Quezon City: University of the Philippines, 1987.

Arndt, H. W. "Transmigration: Achievements, Problems, Prospects." *Bulletin of Indonesian Economic Studies* 19 (1983): 50–73.

Arnold, David. *Science, Technology, and Medicine in Colonial India: The New Cambridge History of India.* Cambridge: Cambridge University Press, 2000.

"Atjeh—Beschouwingen van den Oud-Soldaat Veritas." *Tijdschrift voor Nederlandsch-Indië* 22, no. 1 (1893): 321–61.

Atsushi, Ota. *Changes of Regime and Social Dynamics in West Java: Society, State, and the Outer World of Banten, 1750–1830.* Leiden: Brill, 2006.

——. "'Pirates or Entrepreneurs?' The Migration and Trade of Sea People in Southwest Kalimantan, c. 1770–1820." *Indonesia* 90 (2010): 67–95.

——. "Tropical Products Out, British Cotton In: Trade in the Dutch Outer Islands Ports, 1846–69." *Southeast Asian Studies* 2, no. 3 (2013): 499–526.

Austin, Gareth. "Cash Crops and Freedom: Export Agriculture and the Decline of Slavery in Colonial West Africa." *International Review of Social History* 54, no. 1 (2009): 1–37.

——. "Human Pawning in Asante, 1820–1950: Markets and Coercion, Gender and Cocoa." In *Pawnship in Africa: Debt Bondage in Historical Perspective,* ed. Toynin Falola and Paul E. Lovejoy, 187–224. Boulder, CO: Westview, 1994.

Baak, Paul E. "About Enslaved Ex-Slaves, Uncaptured Contract Coolies, and Unfreed Freedmen: Some Notes About 'Free' and 'Unfree' Labour in the Context of Plantation Development in Southwest India, Early Sixteenth Century–Mid 1990s." *Modern Asian Studies* 33, no. 1 (1999): 121–57.

Bahrin, Tunku Shamsul. "The Growth and Distribution of the Indonesian Population in Malaya." *Bijdragen tot de Taal-, en Land- en Volkenkunde* 123, no. 2 (1967): 267–86.

Bahrin, Tunku Shamsul, and Boon Thong Lee. *FELDA, 3 Decades of Evolution.* Kuala Lumpur: FELDA, 1988.

Baker, Christopher. "Economic Reorganization and the Slump in South and South East Asia." *Comparative Studies in Society and History* 23, no. 3 (1981): 325–49.

Balisacan, Arsenio M. "Agricultural Growth, Landlessness, Off-Farm Employment, and Rural Poverty in the Philippines." *Economic Development and Cultural Change* 41, no. 3 (1993): 533–62.

Bankoff, Greg. "Coming to Terms with Nature: State and Environment in Maritime Southeast Asia." *Environmental History Review* 19, no. 3 (1995): 17–37.

——. "Wants, Wages, and Workers." *Pacific Historical Review* 71, no. 1 (2005): 59–86.

Bankoff, Greg, and Peter Boomgaard. "Introduction: Natural Resources and the Shape of Asian History, 1500–2000." In *A History of Natural Resources in Asia: The Wealth of Nature*, ed. Greg Bankoff and Peter Boomgaard, 1–18. New York: Palgrave Macmillan, 2007.

Banthia, Jayant, and Tim Dyson. "Smallpox in Nineteenth-Century India." *Population and Development Review* 25, no. 4 (1999): 649–80.

Bantug, J. P. "Carlos IV y la introducción de la vacuna en Filipinas." *Anuario de Estudios Americanos* 12 (1955): 75–129.

——. *A Short History of Medicine in the Philippines Under the Spanish Régime, 1565–1898*. Manila: Colegio Médico-Farmacéutico de Filippinas, 1953.

Banzon-Bautista, Cynthia. "The Saudi Connection: Agrarian Change in a Pampangan Village, 1977–1984." In *Agrarian Transformations, Local Processes, and the State in Southeast Asia*, ed. G. Hart et al., 144–58. Berkeley: University of California Press, 1989.

Barbier, Edward B. *Scarcity and Frontiers: How Economies Have Developed Through Natural Resource Exploitation*. Cambridge: Cambridge University Press, 2011.

Barker, Randolph, Robert W. Herdt, and Beth Rose. *The Rice Economy of Asia*. Baltimore, MD: Johns Hopkins University Press, 1985.

Barlow, Colin. *The Natural Rubber Industry: Its Development, Technology, and Economy in Malaysia*. Kuala Lumpur: Oxford University Press, 1978.

Barrantes, V. *Guerras piráticas de filipinas contra mindanaos y joloanos: corr. é ilustradas por don Vicente Barrantes*. Madrid: M. G. Hernandez, 1878.

Bassino, Jean-Pascal, Marion Dovis, and John Komlos. "Biological Well-Being in the Late 19th Century Philippines." NBER Working Paper Series 21410. Cambridge, MA: National Bureau of Economic Research, 2015. http://www.nber.org/papers/w21410.

Bassino, Jean-Pascal, and Jeffrey G Williamson. "From Commodity Booms to Economic Miracles: Why Southeast Asian Industry Lagged Behind." Discussion Paper 10611. London: Centre for Economic Policy Research, 2015.

Battistella, G. "Philippine Overseas Labour: From Export to Management." *Economic Bulletin* 12, no. 2 (1995): 257–73.

Bauer, P. T. *The Rubber Industry: A Study in Competition and Monopoly*. Cambridge, MA: Harvard University Press, 1948.

Beckford, George L. "Aspects of the Present Conflict Between the Plantation and the Peasantry in the West Indies." Part 2. *Caribbean Quarterly* 18, no. 1 (1972): 47–58.

Bennett, Michael. "Passage Through India: Global Vaccination and British India, 1800–05." *Journal of Imperial and Commonwealth History* 35, no. 2 (2007): 201–20.

Benton, Lauren. *A Search for Sovereignty: Law and Geography in European Empires, 1400–1900.* New York: Cambridge University Press, 2010.

"Berigten Omtrent den Zeeroof." *Tijdschrift voor Indische Taal-, Land- en Volkenkunde* 3 (1855): 1–31; 7 (1858): 350–78; 18 (1872): 435–57; 20 (1873): 302–26, 399–433.

"Beschrijving van het Eiland Soemba of Sandelhout." *Tijdschrift voor Nederlandsch-Indië* 17, no. 1 (1855): 278–312.

"Bevolking van Java en Madoera." *Tijdschrift voor Nederlandsch-Indië* 1 (1839): 154–71.

Bhar, Supriya. "Sandakan: Gun Running Village to Timber Centre, 1879–1979." *Journal of the Malaysian Branch of the Royal Asiatic Society* 53, no. 1 (1980): 120–49.

Bigalke, Terance William. "Dynamics of the Torajan Slave Trade in South Sulawesi." In *Slavery, Bondage, and Dependency in Southeast Asia,* ed. Anthony Reid, 341–63. New York: St. Martin's, 1983.

——. "A Social History of 'Tana Toradja.'" PhD diss. University of Wisconsin, 1981.

——. *Tana Toraja: A Social History of an Indonesian People.* Singapore: Singapore University Press, 2005.

Bhattacharya, Sanjoy, Mark Harrison, and Michael Worboys. *Fractured States: Smallpox, Public Health, and Vaccination Policy in British India, 1800–1947.* Hyderabad: Orient Longman, 2005.

"Bijdragen tot de Kennis der Binnenlandsche Rijken van het Westelijk Gedeelte van Borneo." *Tijdschrift voor Nederlandsch Indië* 1 (1849): 338–56.

"Bijdragen tot de Kennis van Borneo." *Tijdschrift voor Nederlandsch-Indië* 1 (1853): 173–200.

Billig, Michael S. "'Syrup in the Wheels of Progress': The Inefficient Organisation of the Philippine Sugar Industry." *Journal of Southeast Asian Studies* 24, no. 1 (1993): 122–47.

Billiton Maatschappij N. V. *Gedenkboek Billiton, 1852–1927.* The Hague: Nijhoff, 1927.

Blair, Emma H., James A. Robertson, and Edward G. Bourne. *The Philippine Islands, 1493–1803: Explorations by Early Navigators, Descriptions of the Islands and Their Peoples, Their History and Records of the Catholic Missions, as Related in Contemporaneous Books and Manuscripts, Showing the Political, Economic, Commercial, and Religious Conditions of Those Islands from Their Earliest Relations with European Nations to the Beginning of the Nineteenth Century.* Cleveland: A. H. Clark, 1903–1909.

Bleeker, P. "Algemeene Staat der Inlandsche Bevolking van Java, over de jaren 1845, 1846, 1847 en 1848." *Tijdschrift voor Nederlandsch-Indië* 2 (1850): 204–5.

——. "De Statistische Opname der Residentie Cheribon." *Tijdschrift voor Nederlandsch-Indië* 1, no. 2 (1863): 1–12.

——. "Fragmenten eener Reis over Java. Reis door Oostelijk Java." *Tijdschrift voor Nederlandsch-Indië* 2 (1849), 17–38, 117–44, 177–90, 266–70; 1 (1850): 1–50, 89–113, 165–91, 245–74, 309–14, 397–415; 2 (1850): 1–22, 81–98, 142–59, 219–38.

——. "Nieuwe Bijdragen tot de Kennis der Bevolkingsstatistiek van Java." *Bijdragen tot de Taal-, Land- en Volkenkunde* 16, no. 1 (1869): 447–637.

Boncan, Celestina P. "Colonial Copper Coinage in the Tobacco Monopoly, 1769–1837." *Philippine Studies* 34, no. 4 (1986): 518–27.

Boomgaard, Peter. *Children of the Colonial State: Population Growth and Economic Development in Java, 1795–1880*. Amsterdam: Free University Press, 1989.

——. "Fluctuations in Mortality in 17th-Century Indonesia." Conference paper, Asian Population History, Taipeh, January 4–8, 1996. Liège: International Union for the Scientific Study of Population, 1996.

——. "From Riches to Rags? Rice Production and Trade in Asia, Particularly Indonesia, 1500–1950." In *A History of Natural Resources in Asia: The Wealth of Nature*, ed. Greg Bankoff and Peter Boomgaard, 185–203. Houndmills: Palgrave Macmillan, 2007.

——. "Human Capital, Slavery, and Low Rates of Economic and Population Growth in Indonesia, 1600–1910." *Slavery and Abolition: A Journal of Slave and Post-Slave Studies* 24, no. 2 (2003): 83–96.

——. "In the Shadow of Rice." *Agricultural History* 77, no. 4 (2003): 582–610.

——. "Morbidity and Mortality in Java, 1820–1880: Changing Patterns of Disease and Death." In *Death and Disease in Southeast Asia: Explorations in Social, Medical, and Demographic History*, ed. Norman Owen, 48–69. Singapore: Oxford University Press, 1987.

——. "Resources and People of the Sea in and Around the Indonesian Archipelago." In *Muddied Waters: Historical and Contemporary Perspectives on Management of Forests and Fisheries in Island Southeast Asia*, ed. Peter Boomgaard, David Henley, and Manon Osseweijer, 211–234. Leiden: KITLV, 2005.

——. "Smallpox and Vaccination on Java, 1780–1860: Medical Data as a Source for Demographic History." In *Dutch Medicine in the Malay Archipelago, 1816–1942: Articles Presented at a Symposium Held in Honor of Prof. Dr. D. de Moulin*, ed. A. M. Luyendijk-Elshout, 119–31. Amsterdam: Rodopi, 1989.

——. "Smallpox, Vaccination, and the Pax Neerlandica, Indonesia, 1550–1930." *Bijdragen tot de Taal-, Land en Volkenkunde* 159, no. 4 (2003): 590–617.

Boon Kheng, C. "Malay Politics and the Murder of J. W.-W. Birch, Resident in Perak, in 1875: The Humiliation and Revenge of the Maharaja Lela." *Journal of the Malaysian Branch of the Royal Asiatic Society* 71, no. 1 (1998): 74–105.

Booth, Anne. "The Burden of Taxation in Colonial Indonesia in the Twentieth Century." *Journal of Southeast Asian Studies* 11, no. 1 (1980): 91–109.

——. *Colonial Legacies: Economic and Social Development in East and Southeast Asia.* Honolulu: University of Hawai'i Press, 2007.

——. *Economic Change in Modern Indonesia: Colonial and Post-Colonial Comparisons.* Cambridge: Cambridge University Press, 2016.

——. "Indonesian Colonial Economic Performance in an East Asian Perspective." In *Indonesian Economic Decolonization in Regional and International Perspective,* ed. J. Thomas Lindblad and Peter Post, 133–56. Leiden: KITLV, 2009.

——. *The Indonesian Economy in the Nineteenth and Twentieth Centuries: A History of Missed Opportunities.* Houndmills: Macmillan, 1998.

——. "Irrigation in Indonesia." *Bulletin of Indonesian Economic Studies* 13, no. 1 (1977): 33–74; 13, no. 2 (1977): 45–77.

——. "Measuring Living Standards in Different Colonial Systems: Some Evidence from South East Asia, 1900–1942." *Modern Asian Studies* 46, no. 5 (2012): 1145–81.

Borja, Luis J. "The Philippine Coconut Industry." *Economic Geography* 3, no. 3 (1927): 382–90.

Borschberg, P. *The Singapore and Melaka Straits: Violence, Security, and Diplomacy in the 17th Century.* Singapore: Singapore University Press, 2010.

Bosscher, C., and P. A. Matthijssen. "Schetsen van de Rijken van Tomboekoe en Banggai." *Tijdschrift voor Indische Taal-, Land- en Volkenkunde* 2 (1854): 65–107.

Bosma, Ulbe. "The Discourse on Free Labour and the Forced Cultivation System: The Contradictory Consequences of the Abolition of Slave Trade for Colonial Java, 1811–1863." In *Humanitarian Intervention and Changing Labor Relations: The Long-Term Consequences of the Abolition of the Slave Trade,* ed. Marcel van der Linden, 387–418. Leiden: Brill, 2011.

——. Karel Zaalberg. *Journalist en Strijder voor de Indo.* Leiden: KITLV, 1997.

——. "Methodological Paper: Island Southeast Asia and the Global Collaboratory Labour Relations (Java, Outer Islands of the Netherlands Indies, the Philippines and British Malaya)." Version 7. March 2017. IISH Dataverse. Data on Demography, Migration, Slavery and Employment for the Netherlands Indies, the Philippines and British Malaya 1800–1950. http://hdl.handle.net/10622/NCJVLW.

——. "Migration and Colonial Enterprise in Nineteenth Century Java." In *Globalising Migration History: The Eurasian Experience (16th–21st centuries),* ed. Jan Lucassen and Leo Lucassen, 151–79. Leiden: Brill, 2014.

——. "Smallpox, Vaccinations, and Demographic Divergences in Nineteenth-Century Colonial Indonesia." *Bijdragen tot de Taal-, Land- en Volkenkunde* 171, no. 1 (2015): 69–96.

——. "Sugar and Dynasty in Yogyakarta." In *Sugarlandia Revisited: Sugar and Colonialism in Asia and the Americas, 1800 to 1940*, ed. Ulbe Bosma, Juan Giusti-Cordero, and G. Roger Knight, 73–94. New York: Berghahn, 2007.

——. *The Sugar Plantation in India and Indonesia: Industrial Production, 1770–2010*. Cambridge: Cambridge University Press, 2013.

Bosma, Ulbe, and Jonathan Curry-Machado. "Turning Javanese: The Domination of Cuba's Sugar Industry by Java Cane Varieties." *Itinerario* 37, no. 2 (2013): 101–20.

Bottemanne, J. "De Indische Zeevisscherij." *Koloniaal Tijdschrift* 24, no. 5 (1935): 444–58.

Bowie, Katherine A. "Slavery in Nineteenth-Century Northern Thailand: Archival Anecdotes and Village Voices." In *State Power and Culture in Thailand*, ed. E. Paul Durrenberger, 100–38. New Haven, CT: Yale University Southeast Asia Studies, 1996.

Bowring, John. *A Visit to the Philippine Islands*. London: Smith, Elder & Co, 1864.

Boyce, James K. *The Philippines: The Political Economy of Growth and Impoverishment in the Marcos Era*. Houndmills: Macmillan, 1993.

Boyle, Frederick. *Adventures Among the Dyaks of Borneo*. London: Hurst and Blackett, 1865.

Braithwaite, John, et al. *Anomie and Violence: Non-truth and Reconciliation in Indonesian Peacebuilding*. Acton, A.C.T.: ANU E Press, 2010. http://press.anu.edu.au?p=19121.

Breman, Jan. "Java: Bevolkingsgroei en Demografische Structuur." *Tijdschrift van het Koninklijk Nederlandsch Aardrijkskundig Genootschap* 80, no. 3 (1963): 252–308.

——. *Koelies, Planters en Koloniale Politiek*. 3rd rev. printing. Leiden: KITLV, 1992. Originally published in 1987.

——. *Koloniaal Profijt van Onvrije Arbeid: het Preanger Stelsel van Gedwongen Koffieteelt op Java, 1720–1870*. Amsterdam: Amsterdam University Press, 2010.

Breman, Jan, and Gunawan Wiradi. *Good Times and Bad Times in Rural Java*. Leiden: KITLV, 2012.

Brignoli, Héctor Pérez. *La población de Costa Rica, 1500–2000. Una Historia Experimental*. San José: Editorial Universidad de Costa Rica, 2010.

Brimnes, Niels. "Variolation, Vaccination, and Popular Resistance in Early Colonial South India." *Medical History* 48, no. 2 (2004): 199–228.

Broersma, R. "Een Vrije Volksverplaatsing Java-Deli." *Koloniale Studiën* 3, no. 2 (1919): 171–201.

Broeze, F. J. A. "The Merchant Fleet of Java, 1820–1850. A Preliminary Survey." *Archipel* 18 (1979): 251–69.

Brouwer, B. J. *De Houding van Idenburg en Colijn tegenover de Indonesische Beweging.* Kampen: J. H. Kok, 1958.

Brown, C. "The Influenza Pandemic of 1918 in Indonesia." In *Death and Disease in Southeast Asia,* ed. Norman G. Owen, 235–56. Singapore: Oxford University Press, 1987.

Brown, Ian. "Some Comments on Industrialisation in the Philippines During the 1930s." In *The Economies of Africa and Asia in the Inter-war Depression,* ed. Ian Brown. London: Routledge, 1989.

Brumund, J. F. G. "De Expedities van de Stoomboten Hekla en Samarang in 1851 tegen Zeeroovers, benevens Eenige Bijzonderheden omtrent de Overwinning door de Nederlandsche Marine in 1848, en nu onlangs in 1851, door de Spanjaarden op de Sultan van Solok behaald." In *Indiana. Verzameling van Stukken van Onderscheiden Aard, over Landen, Volken, Oudheden en Geschiedenis van den Indischen Archipel,* ed. J. F. G. Brumund, 67–156. Amsterdam: P. N. Van Kampen, 1853.

Bulbeck, David, et al. *Southeast Asian Exports Since the 14th Century: Cloves, Pepper, Coffee, and Sugar.* Singapore/Leiden: Institute of Southeast Asian Studies/ KITLV, 1998.

Burger, D. H. *Sociologisch-Economische Geschiedenis van Indonesia.* 2 vols. Amsterdam: Koninklijk Instituut voor de Tropen. 1975.

Burger, E. J. *Landverhuizing bij de Inheemsche bevolking in Nederlandsch-Indië als Koloniaal-Economisch Verschijnsel.* Den Helder: C. de Boer Jr., 1927.

Byerlee, Derek. "The Fall and Rise Again of Plantations in Tropical Asia: History Repeated?" *Land* 3, no. 3 (2014): 574–97.

Byerlee, Derek, Walter P. Falcon, and Rosamond L. Naylor. *The Tropical Oil Crop Revolution: Food, Feed, Fuel, and Forests.* New York: Oxford University Press, 2017.

Byler, C. "Pacifying the Moros: American Military Government in the Southern Philippines, 1899–1913." *Military Review* 85, no. 3 (2005): 41–45.

Cardoso, Fernando Henrique, and Enzo Faletto. *Dependency and Development in Latin America.* Berkeley: University of California Press, 1979.

Carey, Peter. *The Power of Prophecy: Prince Dipanagara and the End of an Old Order in Java, 1785–1855.* Leiden: KITLV, 2008.

——. "Waiting for the 'Just King': The Agrarian World of South-Central Java from Giyanti (1755) to the Java War (1825–1830)." *Modern Asian Studies* 20, no. 1 (1986): 59–137.

Carroll, John J. *The Filipino Manufacturing Entrepreneurs.* Ithaca, NY: Cornell University Press, 1965.

Carter, William H. "Economic Questions Affecting the Visayan Islands." *North American Review* 180, no. 582 (1905): 688–93.

Cavada, Augustin Mendez de Vigo de la. *Historia geográfica, geológica y estadística de Filipinas. Con datos geográficos, geológicos y estadísticos de las islas de Luzon, Visayas, Mindanao y Joló; y los que corresponden a las Islas Batanes, Calamianes, Balabac, Mindoro, Masbate, Ticao y Burias, situadas al n. so. y s. de Luzon.* Manila: Imp. de Ramirez y Giraudier, 1876.

Censo de poblacion de las Islas Filipinas ... 1876. Manila: Establecimento Tipográfico del Real Colegio de Santo Tomas, 1878.

Census of the Philippine Islands, Taken Under the Direction of the Philippine Commission in the Year 1903, in Four Volumes. By Joseph Prentiss Sanger, Henry Gannett, and Victor H. Olmsted. Bureau of the Census United States/Philippine Commission (1900–1916). Washington, DC: Government Printing Office, 1905.

Census of the Philippine Islands Taken Under the Direction of the Philippine Legislature in the Year 1918, in Four Volumes. By Ignacio Villamor and Felipe Buencamino. Manila: Bureau of Printing, 1920.

Census of the Philippines: 1939. See Commission of the Census.

Chandra, Siddharth. "Mortality from the Influenza Pandemic of 1918–19 in Indonesia." *Population Studies* 67, no. 2 (2012): 185–93.

——. "The Role of Female Industrial Labor in the Late Colonial Netherlands Indies." *Indonesia* 74 (2002): 103–35.

Chandra, Siddharth, Goran Kuljanin, and Jennifer Wray. "Mortality from the Influenza Pandemic of 1918–1919: The Case of India." *Demography* 49 (2012): 857–65.

Charney, Michael W. "Crisis and Reformation in a Maritime Kingdom of Southeast Asia: Forces of Instability and Political Disintegration in Western Burma (Arakan), 1603–1701." *Journal of the Economic and Social History of the Orient* 41, no. 2 (1998): 185–219.

Chase-Dunn, Christopher, Yukio Kawano, and Benjamin D. Brewer. "Trade Globalization Since 1795: Waves of Integration in the World-System." *American Sociological Review* 65, no. 1 (2000): 77–95.

Cheong, Kee Cheok, Lee Kam Hing, and Leeu Poh Ping. "Chinese Overseas Remittances to China: The Perspective from Southeast Asia." *Journal of Contemporary Asia* 43, no. 1 (2013): 75–101.

Chew, Daniel. *Chinese Pioneers on the Sarawak Frontier.* Singapore: Oxford University Press, 1990.

Chiba, Yoshihiro. "The 1919 and 1935 Rice Crises in the Philippines: The Rice Market and Starvation in American Colonial Times." *Philippine Studies* 58, no. 4 (2010): 523–56.

Chua, Karl Kendrick, Louie Limkin, John Nye, and Jeffrey G. Williamson. "Urban-Rural Income and Wage Gaps in the Philippines: Measurement Error, Unequal Endowments, or Factor Market Failure?" *Philippine Review of Economics* 52, no. 2 (2015): 1–21.

Clarence-Smith, William Gervase. "The British 'Official Mind' and Nineteenth-Century Islamic Debates Over the Abolition of Slavery." In *Slavery, Diplomacy, and Empire: Britain and the Suppression of the Slave Trade, 1807–1975*, ed. Keith Hamilton and Patrick Salmon, 125–42. Brighton: Sussex Academic Press, 2009.

——. *Islam and the Abolition of Slavery*. London: Hurst & Co., 2006.

Clark, Victor S. *Labor Conditions in Java—Bulletin of the Bureau of Labor*. Washington, DC: Government Printing Office, 1905.

——. *Labor Conditions in the Philippines—Bulletin of the Bureau of Labor*. Washington, DC: Government Printing Office, 1905.

Claver, Alexander. *Dutch Commerce and Chinese Merchants in Java: Colonial Relationships in Trade and Finance, 1800–1942*. Leiden: Brill, 2014.

Colijn, H. "Onder het Staatsbestuur." In *Neerlands Indië, Land en Volk, Geschiedenis en Bestuur, Bedrijf en Samenleving*, ed. H. Colijn, 1–33. Amsterdam: Uitgevers-maatschappij Elsevier, 1912.

Colombijn, Freek. "The Volatile State in Southeast Asia: Evidence from Sumatra, 1600–1800." *Journal of Asian Studies* 62, no. 2 (2003): 497–529.

Colvin, Thomas B. "Arms Around the World: The Introduction of Smallpox Vaccine Into the Philippines and Macao in 1805." *Review of Culture/Revista de Cultura* 18 (2006): 71–88.

——. "The Real Expedición de la Vacuna and the Philippines, 1803–1807." In *Global Movements, Local Concerns: Medicine and Health in Southeast Asia*, ed. Laurence Monnais and Harold J. Cook, 1–23. Singapore: Singapore University Press, 2012.

Commission of the Census. *Census of the Philippines: 1939*. 5 vols. Manila: Bureau of Printing, 1940–1943.

Comyn, Tomas de. *State of the Philippine Islands, Being an Historical Statistical and Descriptive Account of That Interesting Portion of the Indian Archipelago Translated from Spanish with Notes and a Preliminary Discourse by William Walton*. London: T. and J. Allman, 1820.

Cool, F. J. "De Bestrijding der Werkloosheidsgevolgen in Nederlandsch-Indië gedurende 1930–1936." *De Economist* 87 (1938): 135–47, 217–43.

Coolie Budget Commission. *Living Conditions of Plantation Workers and Peasants on Java*. Trans. Robert van Niel. Modern Indonesia Project. Ithaca, NY: Cornell University, 1956.

Cordova, Fred. *Filipinos: Forgotten Asian Americans, a Pictoral Essay, 1763–Circa 1963*. Dubuque, Iowa: Kendall/Hunt, 1983.

Cornets de Groot, H. F. W. "Nota over de Slavernij en het Pandelingschap in de Residentie Lampongsche Districten." *Tijdschrift voor Indische Taal-, Land en Volkenkunde* 17 (1882): 452–87.

Cornets de Groot, J. P. *Notices historiques sur les pirateries, commises dans l'archipel Indien-Oriental, et sur les mesures prises pour les réprimer par le gouvernement néerlandais, dans les trente dernières années.* The Hague: Belinfante Frères, 1847.

Corpuz, A. G. "Railroads and Regional Development in the Philippines: Views from the Colonial Iron Horse, 1875–1935." PhD diss., Cornell University, 1989.

Corpuz, Onofre D. *An Economic History of the Philippines.* Quezon City: University of Philippines Press, 1997.

——. *The Roots of the Filipino Nation.* Quezon City: Aklahi Foundation, 1989.

C. P. "Philippine Coconut Industry to Fight Legislation." *Far Eastern Survey* 7, no. 21 (1938): 246–47.

Craufurd [*sic*], John. "A Sketch of the Geography of Borneo." *Journal of the Royal Geographical Society of London* 23 (1853): 69–86.

Cruikshank, R. B. "Slavery in Nineteenth-Century Siam." *Journal of the Siam Society* 63, no. 2 (1975): 315–33.

Cullinane, Michael. "Accounting for Souls: Ecclesiastical Sources for the Study of Philippine Demographic History." In *Population and History: The Demographic Origins of the Modern Philippines,* ed. Daniel F. Doeppers and Peter Xenos, 281–346. Manila: Ateneo de Manila University Press, 2000.

Cushner, Nicholas P. *Landed Estates in the Colonial Philippines.* Monograph Series 20. New Haven, CT: Yale University Southeast Asia Studies, 1976.

Dalenoord, G. "Textiel-Nijverheid in Nederlandsch-Indië." *Koloniale Studiën* 10, no. 1 (1926): 167–77.

Dalton, J. "Mr. Dalton's Papers on Borneo etc." In *Notices of the Indian Archipelago, and Adjacent Countries; Being a Collection of Papers Relating to Borneo, Celebes, Bali, Java, Sumatra, Nias, the Philippine Islands, Sulus, Siam, Cochin China, Malayan Peninsula, etc.,* ed. J. H. Moor. Singapore: s.n., 1837.

Damir-Geilsdorf, Sabine, Ulrike Lindner, Gesine Müller, et al. *Bonded Labour: Global and Comparative Perspectives (18th–21st Century).* Bielefeld: Transcript, 2016.

Davenport, Romola, Leonard Schwarz, and Jeremy Boulton. "The Decline of Adult Smallpox in Eighteenth-Century London." *Economic History Review* 64, no. 4 (2011): 1289–1314.

David, W. John, and James C. Jackson. "The Tobacco Industry of North Borneo: A Distinctive Form of Plantation Agriculture." *Journal of Southeast Asian Studies* 4, no. 1 (1973): 88–106.

"De Afschaffing der Slavernij in Nederlandsch Indie." *Tijdschrift voor Nederlandsch-Indië* 7, no. 2 (1878): 1–33.

"De Afschaffing van het Passenstelsel." *Tijdschrift voor Nederlandsch-Indië* n.s. 1, no. 2 (1863): 236–39.

De Bevoise, Ken. "Until God Knows When: Smallpox in the Late-Colonial Philippines." *Pacific Historical Review* 59 (1990): 149–85.

De Dios, Emmanuel S., and Jeffrey G. Williamson. "Deviant Behavior: A Century of Philippine Industrialization." Discussion Paper 2013-03. School of Economics, University of the Philippines, 2013.

De Graaf, Hermanus J. *De Regering van Sultan Agung, Vorst van Mataram, 1613–1645: En die van Zijn Voorganger Panembahan Sédaing-Krapjak, 1601–1613*. The Hague: M. Nijhoff, 1958.

De Haan, F. *Priangan. De Preanger-Regentschappen onder het Nederlandsch Bestuur tot 1811*. Batavia and The Hague: Kolff en Martinus Nijhoff, 1912.

De Haas, Hein. "Migration Transitions: A Theoretical and Empirical Inquiry Into the Developmental Drivers of International Migration." Oxford: International Migration Institute Working Paper 24. 2010.

De Jesus, E. C. *The Tobacco Monopoly in the Philippines: Bureaucratic Enterprise and Social Change, 1766–1880*. Quezon City: Ateneo de Manila University Press, 1980.

De Jong Boers, Bernice. "Mount Tambora in 1815: A Volcanic Eruption in Indonesia and Its Aftermath." *Indonesia* 60 (1995): 37–59.

De Jonge, Huub. *Handelaren en Handlangers. Ondernemerschap, Economische Ontwikkeling en Islam op Madura*. Dordrecht: Foris, 1988.

——. "State and Welfare in the Late Colonial Period, the Madura Welfare Fund (1937–1941)." *Asian Journal of Social Science* 32, no. 1 (2004): 91–104.

De Klein, Jacob Wouter. *Het Preangerstelsel (1677–1871) en Zijn Nawerking*. Delft: J. Waltman Jr., 1931.

De la Costa, Francis Jourdan, A. Dalrymple, and Vizentio de Aziviedo. "Muhammad Alimuddin I, Sultan of Sulu 1735–1773." *Journal of the Malaysian Branch of the Royal Asiatic Society*, 38, no. 1 (1965): 43–76.

"De Lampongsche Distrikten op het eiland Sumatra." *Tijdschrift voor Nederlandsch-Indië* 14 (1852): 245–75, 309–33.

Dennison, Eleanor. "Philippine Labor Under the Commonwealth." *Far Eastern Survey* 7, no. 24 (1938): 277–82.

Departement van Landbouw, Nijverheid en Handel. *Landbouwatlas van Java en Madoera*. 3 vols. Weltevreden: Mededeelingen van het Centraal Kantoor van de Statistiek, 1926.

De Regt, Marina. "High in the Hierarchy, Rich in Diversity: Asian Domestic Workers, Their Networks, and Employers' Preferences in Yemen." *Critical Asian Studies* 40, no. 4 (2008): 587–608.

De Rovere van Breugel, J. "Bedenkingen over den Staat van Bantam." *Bijdragen tot de Taal-, Land- en Volkenkunde* 5, no. 1 (1856): 10–170.

De Waard, J. "Een en ander over de Uit- en Invoercijfers van Sumatra's Oostkust." *Koloniale Studiën* 12, no. 5 (1928): 10–32.

De Zwart, Pim. "Globalization and the Colonial Origins of the Great Divergence: Intercontinental Trade and Living Standards in the Dutch East Company's Commercial Empire, c. 1600–1800." PhD diss., Utrecht University, 2015.

De Zwart, Pim, and Jan Luiten van Zanden. "Labor, Wages, and Living Standards in Java, 1680–1914." *European Review of Economic History* 19, no. 3 (2015): 215–34.

Díaz-Trechuelo, Maria Lourdes. "Eighteenth-Century Philippine Economy: Agriculture." *Philippine Studies* 14, no. 1 (1966): 65–126.

——. "Eighteenth-Century Philippine Economy: Mining." *Philippine Studies* 13, no. 4 (1965): 763–800.

Djajadiningrat, H. *Critische Beschouwing van de Sadjarah Bantēn: Bijdrage ter Kenschetsing van de Javaansche Geschiedschrijving*. Haarlem: J. Enschedé en zonen, 1913.

Djojohadikoesoemo, Soemitro. *Het Volkscredietwezen in de Depressie*. Haarlem: De Erven F. Bohn N.V., 1943.

Dobbin, Christine. "Economic Change in Minangkabau as a Factor in the Rise of the Padri Movement, 1784–1830." *Indonesia* 23 (1977): 1–38.

——. *Islamic Revivalism in a Changing Peasant Economy: Central Sumatra, 1784–1847*. London: Curzon, 1983.

Dodge, Nicholas N. "Population Estimates for the Malay Peninsula in the Nineteenth Century, with Special Reference to the East Coast States." *Population Studies* 34, no. 3 (1980): 437–75.

Doeppers, Daniel F. "Civil Records as Sources for Philippine Historical Demography." In *Population and History: The Demographic Origins of the Modern Philippines*, ed. Daniel F. Doeppers and Peter Xenos, 347–63. Manila: Ateneo de Manila University Press, 1998.

——. *Manila, 1900–1941: Social Change in a Late Colonial Metropolis*. New Haven, CT: Yale University Southeast Asia Studies, 1984.

——. "Metropolitan Manila in the Great Depression: Crisis for Whom?" *Journal of Asian Studies* 50, no. 3 (1991): 511–35.

——. "The Philippines in the Great Depression: A Geography of Pain." In *Weathering the Storm: The Economies of Southeast Asia in the 1930s Depression*, ed. Peter Boomgaard and Ian Brown, 53–82. Leiden/Singapore: KITLV/ISEAS, 2000.

Doeppers, Daniel F., and Peter Xenos. "A Demographic Frame for Philippine History." In *Population and History: The Demographic Origins of the Modern Philippines*, ed. Daniel F. Doeppers and Peter Xenos, 1–16. Manila: Ateneo de Manila University Press, 1998.

Domar, Evsey D. "The Causes of Slavery or Serfdom: A Hypothesis." *Journal of Economic History* 30, no. 1 (1970): 18–32.

Doronila, Amando. "The Transformation of Patron-Client Relations and Its Political Consequences in Postwar Philippines." *Journal of Southeast Asian Studies* 16, no. 1 (1985): 99–116.

Dove, Michael R. "The Agroecological Mythology of the Javanese and the Political Economy of Indonesia." *Indonesia* 39 (1985): 1–36.

——. "Smallholder Rubber and Swidden Agriculture in Borneo: A Sustainable Adaptation to the Ecology and Economy of the Tropical Forest." *Economic Botany* 47, no. 2 (1993): 136–47.

Drabble, John H. *An Economic History of Malaysia, 1800–1940.* Houndmills: Macmillan, 2000.

Drewes, G. W. J. *Two Achenese Poems: Hikajat Ranto and Hikajat Teungkeu di Meuké.* The Hague: Martinus Nijhoff, 1980.

Dros, Nico, and Petrus Johannes van Dooren. *Wages 1820–1940.* Changing Economy in Indonesia 13. Amsterdam: Royal Tropical Institute, 1992.

Ee, Joyce. "Chinese Migration to Singapore, 1896–1941." *Journal of Southeast Asian History* 2, no. 1 (1961): 33–51.

"Eene Inlandsche Nederzetting." *Tijdschrift voor Nederlandsch-Indië* 5, no.1 (1871): 41–49.

Elmhirst, Rebecca. "Displacement, Resettlement, and Multi-Local Livelihoods: Positioning Migrant Legitimacy in Lampung, Indonesia." *Critical Asia Studies* 44, no. 1 (2012): 131–52.

Elson, R. E. "Sugar Factory Workers and the Emergence of 'Free Labour' in Nineteenth-Century Java." *Modern Asian Studies* 20, no. 1 (1986): 139–74.

Emmanuel, Mark. "Viewspapers: The Malay Press of the 1930s." *Journal of Southeast Asian Studies* 41, no. 1 (2010): 1–20.

Encyclopaedie van Nederlandsch-Indië. 1896. The Hague: Nijhoff, 1917.

Endicott, K. "The Effects of Slave Raiding on the Aborigines of the Malaya Peninsula." In *Slavery, Bondage, and Dependency in Southeast Asia,* ed. Anthony Reid, 216–45. New York: St. Martin's, 1983.

Engelhard, H. E. D. "De Afdeeling Doessonlanden." *Bijdragen tot de Taal-, Land en Volkenkunde* 52, no. 1 (1901): 179–222.

Engelhard, P. "Overzicht der Bevolking en Plantagiën van de Bataviasche en Preanger-Regentschappen 1795." In *Opkomst van het Nederlandsch gezag over Java: Verzameling van Onuitgegeven Stukken uit het Oud-Koloniaal Archief,* ed. J. K. J. de Jonge and M. L. van Deventer, 12:390. The Hague, 1884.

Eversole, Robyn, and Judith Shaw. "Remittance Flows and Their Use in Households: A Comparative Study of Sri Lanka, Indonesia, and the Philippines." *Asian and Pacific Migration Journal* 29, no. 2 (2010): 175–202.

Eviota, Elizabeth Uy. *The Political Economy of Gender: Women and the Sexual Division of Labour in the Philippines*. London: Zed, 1992.

Falola, Toynin, and Paul E. Lovejoy. "Pawnship in Historical Perspective." In *Pawnship in Africa: Debt Bondage in Historical Perspective*, ed. Toynin Falola and Paul E. Lovejoy, 1–26. Boulder, CO: Westview, 1994.

Fasseur, Cornelis. *The Politics of Colonial Exploitation: Java, the Dutch, and the Cultivation System*. Ithaca, NY: Southeast Asia Program, 1992.

Feenstra, A. "Dutch Coins for Asian Growth: VOC-Duiten to Assess Java's Deep Monetisation and Economic Growth, 1724–1800." *Tijdschrift voor Sociale en Economische Geschiedenis* 11, no. 3 (2014): 153–83.

Fegan, Brian. *Folk-Capitalism: Economic Strategies of Peasants in a Philippines Wet-Rice Village*. Ann Arbor: University Microfilms International, 1986.

——. "The Philippines: Agrarian Stagnation Under a Decaying Regime." In *Agrarian Transformations: Local Processes and the State in Southeast Asia*, ed. Gillian Hart, Andrew Turton, and Benjamin White, 125–43. Berkeley: University of Los Angeles Press, 1989.

Fenner, Frank. "Smallpox in Southeast Asia." *Crossroads: An Interdisciplinary Journal of Southeast Asian Studies* 3, no. 2–3 (1987): 34–48.

Feranil, Salvador. *The Philippine Banana Industry: Confronting the Challenge of Agrarian Reform*. Quezon City: Philippine Peasant Institute, 1998.

Fernandez, Dorothy Z., Amos H. Hawley, and Silvia Predaza. *The Population of Malaysia*. World Population Year 1974. Paris: CICRED Series, 1975.

Fernando, M. R. "Changing Character of Work-Force in Colonial Java 1820–1930." Paper presented at the Conference of the Economic History Society of Australia & New Zealand, 1992.

Fievez de Malines van Ginkel, Henri. *Verslag van den Belastingdruk op de Inlandsche Bevolking in de Buitengewesten*. Weltevreden: Landsdrukkerij, 1929.

——. *Verslag van den Economischen Toestand en den Belastingdruk met Betrekking tot de Inlandsche Bevolking van de Gewesten Oostkust van Sumatra en Lampongsche Districten*. Weltevreden: Landsdrukkerij, 1929.

Findlay, Ronald, and Kevin H. O'Rourke. *Power and Plenty: Trade, War, and the World Economy in the Second Millennium*. Princeton, NJ: Princeton University Press, 2007.

Findlay, Ronald, and Mats Lundahl. "Resource-Led Growth—a Long-Term Perspective: The Relevance of the 1870–1914 Experience for Today's Developing Economies." UN University Institute for Development Economics Research (UNU/WIDER) Working Papers 162.

Firman, Tommy. "Labour Allocation, Mobility, and Remittances in Rural Households: A Case from Central Java, Indonesia." *Sojourn: Journal of Social Issues in Southeast Asia* 9, no. 1 (1994): 81–101.

——. "Population Mobility in Java: In Search of Theoretical Explanations." *Sojourn: Social Issues in Southeast Asia* 6, no. 1 (1991): 71–105.

Fokkens, F. *De Afschaffing der Laatste Heerendiensten op Java*. Baarn: Hollandia Drukkerij, 1914.

——. *Eindresumé van het bij Besluit van den Gouverneur-Generaal van Nederlandsch-Indië van 24 Juli 1888 no. 8 bevolen Onderzoek naar de Verplichte Diensten der Inlandsche bevolking van Java en Madoera*. Deel I. Heerendiensten. Batavia: F. B. Smits, 1901.

Ford, Michelle. "Indonesian Women as Export Commodity: Notes from Tanjung Pinang." *Journal of Labour and Management Development* 2, no. 5 (2001): 3–9.

Fornier, Joselito N. "Economic Developments in Antique Province: 1800–1850." *Philippine Studies* 46, no. 4 (1998): 407–28.

——. "Economic Developments in Antique Province: 1850–1900." *Philippine Studies* 47, no. 2 (1999): 147–80.

Foronda, Marcelino A., Jr. "Education in the Ilocos During the Spanish Colonial Period, 1574–1898." *Philippine Studies* 26, no. 1–2 (1978): 112–24.

Forrest, Thomas. *A Voyage to New Guinea, and the Moluccans, from Balambangan: Including an Account of Magindano, Sooloo, and Other Islands; Illustrated with Copper-plates. Performed in the Tartar Galley, Belonging to the Honourable East India Company, During the Years, 1774, 1775, 1776* [. . .]. Dublin: Price etc., 1779.

Fox, Henry Frederick. "Primary Education in the Philippines, 1565–1863." *Philippine Studies* 13, no. 2 (1965): 207–31.

Francis, E. *Herinneringen uit den Levensloop van een Indisch Ambtenaar van 1815 tot 1851*. Vol. 1. Batavia: H. M. van Dorp, 1856.

Franco-Paredes, Carlos Lorena Lammoglia, and José Ignacio Santos-Preciado. "The Spanish Royal Philanthropic Expedition to Bring Smallpox Vaccination to the New World and Asia in the 19th Century." *Clinical Infectious Diseases* 41, no. 9 (2005): 1285–89.

Friedmann, Harriet. "Distance and Durability: Shaky Foundations of the World Food Economy." *Third World Quarterly* 13, no. 2 (1992): 371–83.

Friend, Theodore. "The Philippine Sugar Industry and the Politics of Independence, 1929–1935." *Journal of Asian Studies* 22, no. 2 (1963): 179–92.

Furnivall, J. S. *Educational Progress in Southeast Asia*. New York: International Institute of Pacific Relations, 1943.

Fynn-Paul, J. "Empire, Monotheism, and Slavery in the Greater Mediterranean Region from Antiquity to the Early Modern Era." *Past & Present* 205, no. 1 (2009): 3–40.

Galeago, Francis A. "The Philippines in the World of the Influenza Pandemic of 1918–1919." *Philippine Studies* 57, no. 2 (2009): 261–92.

Gallagher, W. J. *De Afschaffing van het Contract-Systeem voor Javaansche Arbeiders op Landbouw-Ondernemingen ter Oostkust van Sumatra* [*met oorspronkelijke Engelsche tekst*]. Medan: AVROS, 1918.

Geertz, Clifford. *The Development of the Javanese Economy: A Socio-Cultural Approach*. Cambridge, MA: Centre for International Studies, MIT, 1956.

Gerke, P. J. "De Personeelsvoorziening." In *Balans van Beleid. Terugblik op de Laatste Halve Eeuw in Nederlandsch-Indië*, ed. H. Baudet and I.J. Brugmans, 171–185. Assen: Van Gorcum, 1984.

Gerritsen, J. "Belastingen in eenige Tropische Britsche Koloniën." *Koloniale Studiën* 10, no. 1 (1926): 49–67.

Glamann, K. *Dutch-Asiatic Trade 1620–1740*. Copenhagen: Danish Science Press, 1958.

Gleeck, Lewis E. *Nueva Ecija in American Times: Homesteaders, Hacenderos, and Politicos*. Manila: R. P. Garcia, 1981.

Goantiang, Tan. "Growth of Cities in Indonesia." *Tijdschrift voor Economische en Sociale Geografie* (1965): 103–8.

Gonggrijp, G. F. E. *Over de Invloed van het Westerse Grootbedrijf op de Inheemse Samenleving in Nederlandsch-Indië*. Haarlem: Tjeenk Willink, 1930.

Gonzales III, Joaquin L. *Philippine Labour Migration: Critical Dimensions of Public Policy*. Singapore: Institute of Southeast Asian Studies, 1998.

Gonzalez III, Joaquin L., and Ronald D. Holmes. "The Philippine Labour Diaspora: Trends, Issues, and Policies." *Southeast Asian Affairs* (1996): 300–17.

Gooszen, Hans. *A Demographic History of the Indonesian Archipelago, 1880–1942*. Leiden: KITLV, 1999.

Gould, James W. *Americans in Sumatra*. The Hague: Martinus Nijhoff, 1961.

Gourou, Pierre. *Les paysans du delta Tonkinois. Étude de géograpahie humaine*. 1936. Paris: Mouton, 1965.

Gronovius, D. J. van den Dungen. "Over de Goudgraverijen in de Afdeeling Sambas." *Tijdschrift voor Nederlandsch-Indië* 9, no. 2 (1847): 395–98.

——. "Verslag over de Residentie Borneo's Westkust 1827–1829." *Tijdschrift voor Nederlandsch-Indië* 5 (1871): 8–36.

Guia Oficial de las Islas Filipinas. Microfilm. Manila: Center for Research Libraries, 1975.

Guillot, Claude. "La politique vivrière de Sultan Ageng (1651–1682)." *Archipel. Études Interdisciplinaires sur le Monde Insulindien* 50 (1995): 83–118.

Guilmoto, Christophe Z. "The Tamil Migration Cycle, 1830–1950." *Economic and Political Weekly* 28, no. 3–4 (1993): 111–20.

Gullick, J. M. *Malay Society in the Late Nineteenth Century*. Singapore: Singapore University Press, 1987.

Habana, Olivia M. "Gold Mining in Benguet to 1898." *Philippine Studies* 48, no. 4 (2000): 455–87.

——. "Gold Mining in Benguet: 1900–1941." *Philippine Studies* 49, no. 1 (2001): 3–41.

Haga, A. *Nederlandsch Nieuw Guinea en de Papoesche eilanden. Historische bijdrage, 1500–1883.* 2 vols. Batavia: W. Bruining, 1884.

Hall, Kenneth R. *A History of Early Southeast Asia: Maritime Trade and Social Development, 100–1500.* Lanham, MD: Rowman & Littlefield, 2011.

——. "The Textile Industry in Southeast Asia, 1400–1800." *Journal of the Economic and Social History of the Orient* 39, no. 2 (1996): 87–135.

Hall, Derek, Philip Hirsch, and Tania Murray Li. *Powers of Exclusion: Land Dilemmas in Southeast Asia.* Singapore: NUS, 2011.

Hanson, Gord on H., and Craig McIntosh. "The Demography of Mexican Migration to the United States." *American Economic Review* 99, no. 2 (2009): 22–27.

Hardjono, J. M. *Transmigration in Indonesia.* Kuala Lumpur: Oxford University Press, 1977.

Hayase, Shinzo. "American Colonial Policy and the Japanese Abaca Industry in Davao, 1898–1941." *Philippine Studies* 33, no. 4 (1985): 505–17.

Hayden, Joseph Ralston. *The Philippines: A Study in National Development.* New York: Macmillan, 1942.

Healey, Christopher J. "Tribes and States in 'Pre-Colonial Borneo': Structural Contradictions and the Generation of Piracy." *Social Analysis: The International Journal of Social and Cultural Practice* 18 (1985): 3–39.

Heersink, Christiaan. "The Green Gold of Selayar: A Socio-Economic History of an Indonesian Coconut Island, c. 1600–1950: Perspectives from a Periphery." PhD diss., VU University Amsterdam, 1995.

——. "Selayar and the Green Gold: The Development of the Coconut Trade on an Indonesian Island (1820–1950)." *Journal of Southeast Asian Studies* 25, no. 1 (1994): 47–69.

Heijting, H. G. *De Koelie-Wetgeving voor de Buitengewesten van Nederlandsch-Indië.* The Hague: Van Stockum, 1925.

Hekmeijer, F. C. *De Quarantaine-Ordonnantie en de Voorschriften tot Hare Uitvoering.* Batavia: Kolff, 1914.

Henley, David. *Fertility, Food, and Fever: Population, Economy, and Environment in North and Central Sulawesi, 1600–1930.* Leiden: KITLV, 2005.

——. "Forced Labour and Rising Fertility in Colonial Indonesia." *Asian Population Studies* 7, no. 1 (2011): 3–13.

——. "Population and the Means of Subsistence: Explaining the Historical Demography of Island Southeast Asia with Particular Reference to Sulawesi." *Journal of Southeast Asian Studies* 36, no. 3 (2005): 337–72.

Hernández-Coss, Raúl. *The Malaysia-Indonesia Remittance Corridor: Making Formal Transfers the Best Option for Women and Undocumented Migrants.* Washington, DC: World Bank, 2008.

Herzog, Tamar. *Frontiers of Possession: Spain and Portugal in Europe and the Americas.* Cambridge, MA: Harvard University Press, 2015.

"Het landschap Donggala of Banawa." *Bijdragen tot de Taal-, Land- en Volkenkunde* 58, no. 1 (1905): 514–31.

Highet, H. Campbell. "Small Pox, Vaccination, and the New Vaccination Law in Siam." *Lancet* 184, no. 4757 (1914): 1043–45.

Hill, D. R. *Rice in Malaya: A Study in Historical Geography.* 1977. Singapore: Singapore University Press, 2012.

Hill, Hal. "Structural Change and 'Turning Points': The Southeast Asian Experience." In *Promises and Predicaments: Trade and Entrepreneurship in Colonial and Independent Indonesia in the 19th and 20th Centuries,* ed. Alicia Schrikker and Jeroen Touwen, 36–60. Singapore: NUS, 2015.

Hillen, A. *V.E.D.A: Vrije Emigratie van D.P.V. en A.VR.O.S.: (Deli Planters Vereeniging en Algemeene Vereeniging van Rubberplanters ter Oostkust van Sumatra).* Medan: VEDA, 1929.

Hirschman, Albert O. *National Power and the Structure of Foreign Trade.* 1945. Berkeley: University of California Press, 1979.

Hirschman, Charles. "Demographic Trends in Peninsular Malaysia, 1947–1975." *Population and Development Review* 6, no. 1 (1980): 103–25.

——. "Education Patterns in Colonial Malaya." *Comparative Educational Review* 16 (1972): 486–502.

——. "Net External Migration from Peninsular Malaysia, 1957–1970." *Malayan Economic Review* 20 (1975): 38–54.

——. "A Note on Labor Underutilization in Peninsular Malaysia." *Malayan Economic Review* 24 (1979): 89–104.

——. "Population and Society in Twentieth-Century Southeast Asia." *Journal of Southeast Asian Studies* 25, no. 2 (1994): 381–416.

Hoadley, Mason C. *Towards a Feudal Mode of Production: West Java, 1680–1800.* Singapore: Institute of Southeast Asian Studies, 1994.

Hollen Lees, Lynn. "International Management in a Free-Standing Company: The Penang Sugar Estates, Ltd., and the Malayan Sugar Industry, 1851–1914." *Business History Review* 81, no. 1 (2007): 27–57.

——. *Planting Empire, Cultivating Subjects. British Malaya, 1786–1941.* New York: Cambridge University Press, 2017.

Hooley, Richard. "American Economic Policy in the Philippines, 1902–1940: Exploring a Dark Age in Colonial Statistics." *Journal of Asian Economics* 16 (2005): 464–88.

Hopkins, Donald R. *The Greatest Killer: Smallpox in History*. Chicago: University of Chicago Press, 2002.

Hopper, Matthew S. "Slaves of One Master: Globalization and the African Diaspora in Arabia in the Age of Empire." In *Indian Ocean Slavery in the Age of Abolition*, ed. R. Harms, B. K. Freamon, and D. W. Blight, 223–40. New Haven, CT: Yale University Press, 2013.

Horner, L. "Batoe-Eilanden ten Westen van Sumatra gelegen." *Tijdschrift voor Nederlandsch-Indië* 3 (1840): 314–71.

Horsfield, Thomas. "Verslag Aangaande het Eiland Banka (Vertaald uit *The Journal of the Indian Archipelago and Eastern Asia*, 1848)." *Tijdschrift voor Nederlandsch Indië* 1 (1850): 192–228, 352–82.

Hoskins, Janet. "Slaves, Brides, and 'Other Gifts': Resistance, Marriage, and Rank in Eastern Indonesia." *Slavery and Abolition* 25, no. 2 (2004): 90–107.

Houben, Vincent. "Colonial Capitalism and Javanese Transcolonial Labor Migration in Insular Asia." In *Work Out of Place*, ed. Mahua Sarkar, 55–76. Berlin: De Gruyter, 2018.

House of Commons. *Parliamentary Papers*. London, 1695.

Huender, W. *Overzicht van den Economischen Toestand der Inheemsche Bevolking van Java en Madoera*. The Hague: Martinus Nijhoff, 1919.

Huff, W. G. "Boom-or-Bust Commodities and Industrialization in Pre–World War II Malaya." *Journal of Economic History* 62, no. 4 (2002): 1074–115.

——. "The Development of the Rubber Market in Pre–World War II Singapore." *Journal of Southeast Asian Studies* 24, no. 2 (1993): 285–306.

——. "Entitlements, Destitution, and Emigration in the 1930s Singapore Great Depression." *Economic History Review* 54, no. 2 (2001): 290–323.

——. "Sharecroppers, Risk, Management, and the Chinese Estate Rubber Development in Interwar British Malaya." *Economic Development and Cultural Change* 40, no. 4 (1992): 743–73.

Huff, Gregg, and Giovanni Caggiano. "Globalization, Immigration, and Lewisian Elastic Labor in Pre–World War II Southeast Asia." *Journal of Economic History* 67, no. 1 (2007): 33–68.

Hugo, Graeme J. *Circular Migration in Indonesia*. Honolulu: East-West Population Institute, East-West Center, 1982.

——. "Forced Migration in Indonesia: Historical Perspectives." *Asian and Pacific Migration Journal* 15, no. 1 (2006): 53–92.

——. "Indonesia: The Impact of Migration on Villages in Java." In *Migration and Development in Southeast Asia: A Demographic Perspective*, ed. Robin J. Pryor, 204–11. Kuala Lumpur: Oxford University Press, 1979.

——. "International Labour Migration and Migration Policies in Southeast Asia." *Asian Journal of Social Sciences* 40 (2012): 392–418.

——. "International Labor Migration and the Family: Some Observations from Indonesia." *Asian and Pacific Migration Journal* 4, no. 2–3 (1995): 273–301.

——. "Migration and Development in Malaysia." *Asian Population Studies* 7, no. 3 (2011): 219–41.

——. "Migration in Indonesia: Recent Trends and Implications." In *Horizons of Home: Nation, Gender, and Migrancy in Island Southeast Asia*, ed. P. Graham, 45–70. Clayton: Monash University Press, 2008.

——. "Migration to and from Jakarta." In *Migration and Development in Southeast Asia: A Demographic Perspective*, ed. Robin J. Pryor, 192–203. Kuala Lumpur: Oxford University Press, 1979.

——. "Population Movements in Indonesia During the Colonial Period." In *Indonesia: Australian Perspectives*, vol. 1: *Indonesia, the Making of a Culture*, ed. J. J. Fox, 95–134. Canberra: Australian National University, 1980.

Hugo, Graeme J., Terence W. Hull, Valerie J. Hull, and Gavin W. Jones. *The Demographic Dimension in Indonesian Development*. Singapore: Oxford University Press, 1987.

Huitema, W. K. *De Bevolkingskoffiecultuur op Sumatra, met een Inleiding tot Hare Geschiedenis op Java en Sumatra*. Wageningen: H. Veenman, 1935.

Hunt, Chester. "Catholicism and the Philippine Population Problem." *Sojourn: Journal of Social Issues in Southeast Asia* 7, no. 2 (1992): 208–22.

Hunt, J. "Sketch of Borneo or Pulo Kalimantan, Communicated by J. Hunt Esq. in 1812, to the Honorable Sir T. S. Raffles, Late Lieut. Governor of Java." In *Notices of the Indian Archipelago, and Adjacent Countries: Being a Collection of Papers Relating to Borneo, Celebes, Bali, Java, Sumatra, Nias, the Philippine Islands, Sulus, Siam, Cochin China, Malayan Peninsula, etc.*, ed. J. H. Moor, appendix, 12–30. Singapore: s.n., 1837.

——. "Some Particulars Relating to Sulo, in the Archipelago of Felicia by . . ." In *Notices of the Indian Archipelago, and Adjacent Countries: Being a Collection of Papers Relating to Borneo, Celebes, Bali, Java, Sumatra, Nias, the Philippine Islands, Sulus, Siam, Cochin China, Malayan Peninsula, etc.*, ed. by J. H. Moor, appendix, 30–60. Singapore: s.n., 1837.

Hunter, Charles, and Spenser St. John. *The Adventures of a Naval Officer*. London: Digby, 1905.

Husson, Laurence. "Indonesians in Saudi Arabia: Worship and Work." *Studia Islamika* 4, no. 4 (1997): 109–36.

Ingleson, John. "Life and Work in Colonial Cities: Harbour Workers in Java in the 1910s and 1920s." *Modern Asian Studies* 17, no. 3 (1983): 455–76.

——. "Urban Java During the Depression." *Journal of Southeast Asian Studies* 19, no. 2 (1988): 292–309.

——. *Workers, Unions, and Politics: Indonesia in the 1920s and 1930s*. Leiden: Brill, 2014.

IOM (International Organization for Migration). *International Migration and Migrant Workers' Remittances in Indonesia: Findings of Baseline Surveys of Migrant Remitters and Remittance Beneficiary Households.* Makati City, Philippines: International Organization for Migration, 2010.

———. *Labour Migration from Indonesia: An Overview of Indonesian Migration to Selected Destinations in Asia and the Middle East.* Jakarta: IOM, 2010.

Jackson, J. C. "Chinese Agricultural Pioneering in Singapore and Johore, 1800–1917." *Journal of the Malaysian Branch of the Royal Asiatic Society* 38, no. 1 (1965): 77–105.

———. *The Chinese in the West Borneo Goldfields: A Study in Cultural Geography.* Hull: University of Hull Occasional Papers in Geography, 1970.

———. *Immigrant Labour and the Development of Malaya, 1786–1920.* Government Press Malaya, 1961.

———. "Mining in 18th-Century Bangka: The Pre-European Exploitation of a 'Tin Island.'" *Pacific Viewpoint* 10, no. 2 (1969): 28–54.

Jacobs, Hubert. "Un règlement de comptes entre portugais et javanais dans les mer de l'Indonésie en 1580." *Archipel* 18 (1979): 159–73.

Jagan, Larry, and John Cunnington. *Social Volcano: Sugar Workers in the Philippines.* London: WOW Campaigns, 1987.

Jagor, Fedor. *Travels in the Philippines.* London: Chapman and Hall, 1875.

John, David W. "The Timber Industry and Forest Administration in Sabah Under Chartered Company Rule." *Journal of Southeast Asian Studies* 5, no. 1 (1974): 55–81.

John, David W., and James C. Jackson. "The Tobacco Industry of North Borneo: A Distinctive Form of Plantation Agriculture." *Journal of Southeast Asian Studies* 4, no. 1 (1973): 88–106.

Johnson, Mark. "Freelancing in the Kingdom: Filipino Migrant Domestic Workers Crafting Agency in Saudi Arabia." *Asian and Pacific Migration Journal* 20 (2011): 3–4.

Johnston, David B. "Opening a Frontier: The Expansion of Rice Cultivation in Central Thailand in the 1890s." *Contributions to Asian Studies* 1, no. 9 (1976): 27–44.

Junghuhn, Franz. *Die Battaländer auf Sumatra. Im Auftrage Sr. Excellenz des General-Gouverneurs von Niederländisch-Indien Hrn. P. Merkus in den Jahren 1840 und 1841.* 2 vols. Berlin: G. Reimer, 1847.

Junker, Laura Lee. *Raiding, Trading, and Feasting. The Political Economy of Philippine Chiefdoms.* Honolulu: University of Hawai'i Press, 1999.

Kagotani, Naoto. "Japan's Commercial Penetration of South and Southeast Asia and the Cotton Trade Negotiations in the 1930s: Maintaining Relations Between Japan, British India, and the Dutch East Indies." In *The International Order of Asia in the 1930s and 1950s*, ed. Shigeru Akita and Nicholas J. White, 179–206. Farnham/Burlington: Ashgate, 2010.

Kai Khiun Liew. "Terribly Severe Though Mercifully Short: The Episode of the 1918 Influenza in British Malaya." *Modern Asian Studies* 41, no. 2 (2007): 221–52.

Kamerling, R. N. J. *De N.V. Oliefabrieken Insulinde in Nederlands-Indië. Bedrijfsvoering in het Onbekende*. Franeker: Wever, 1982.

Kano, Hiroyoshi. *Indonesian Exports, Peasant Agriculture, and the World Economy, 1850–2000: Economic Structures in a Southeast Asian State*. Singapore: Singapore University Press, 2008.

Kantoor van Arbeid (Nederlandsch-Indië). *Verslag van den Dienst der Arbeidsinspectie en Koeliewerving in Nederlandsch-Indië. From 1923: Verslag van de Arbeidsinspectie voor de Buitengewesten*. Batavia: Weltevreden, 1919–.

Kaur, Amarjit. "The Babbling Brookes: Economic Change in Sarawak, 1841–1941." *Modern Asian Studies* 29, no. 1 (1995): 65–109.

——. "A History of Forestry in Sarawak." *Modern Asian Studies* 32, no. 1 (1998): 117–47.

——. "The Impact of Railroads on the Malayan Economy, 1874–1941." *Journal of Asian Studies* 39, no. 4 (1980): 693–710.

——. "Indian Ocean Crossings: Indian Labor Migration and Settlement in Southeast Asia, 1870–1914." In *Connecting Seas and Connected Ocean Rims: Indian, Atlantic, and Pacific Oceans and China Seas Migrations from the 1830s to the 1930s*, ed. Donna R. Gabaccia and Dirk Hoerder, 134–66. Leiden: Brill, 2011.

——. "Indonesian Migrant Workers in Malaysia: From Preferred Migrants to 'Last to Be Hired' Workers." *Review of Indonesian and Malaysian Affairs* 39, no. 2 (2005): 3–30.

Kaut, Charles. "Utang Na Loob: A System of Contractual Obligation Among Tagalogs." *Southwestern Journal of Anthropology* 17, no. 3 (1961): 256–72.

Kerkvliet, Benedict J. *The Huk Rebellion: A Study of Peasant Revolt in the Philippines*. Berkeley: University of California Press, 1977.

——. "Land Reform in the Philippines Since the Marcos Coup." *Pacific Affairs* 47, no. 3 (1974): 286–304.

Kessler, Clive S. *Islam and Politics in a Malay State: Kelantan, 1838–1969*. Ithaca, NY: Cornell University Press, 1978.

Killias, Olivia. "'Illegal' Migration as Resistance: Legality, Morality, and Coercion in Indonesian Domestic Worker Migration to Malaysia." *Migration Asian Journal of Social Science* 38 (2010): 897–914.

Knaap, Gerrit. "The Demography of Ambon in the Seventeenth Century: Evidence from Colonial Proto-Censuses." *Journal of Southeast Asian Studies* 26, no. 2 (1995): 227–41.

Knapen, Han. *Forests of Fortune? The Environmental History of Southeast Borneo, 1600–1880*. Leiden: KITLV, 2001.

Knight, G. Roger. "Capitalism and Commodity Production in Java." In *Capitalism and Colonial Production*, ed. Hamza Alavi, 119–58. London: Croom Helm, 1982.

——. *Commodities and Colonialism: The Story of Big Sugar in Indonesia, 1880–1942*. Leiden: Brill, 2013.

——. "Did 'Dependency' Really Get It Wrong? The Indonesian Sugar Industry, 1880–1942." In *Historical Foundations of a National Economy in Indonesia, 1890s–1990s*, ed. J. Th. Lindblad, 155–74. Amsterdam: KNAW Verhandelingen, 1996.

——. "From Plantation to Padi-Field: The Origins of the Nineteenth-Century Transformation of Java's Sugar Industry." *Modern Asian Studies* 2 (1980): 177–204.

Kniphorst, J. H. P. E. *Historische Schets van den Zeeroof in den Oost-Indischen Archipel*. 1875–1879.

"Koelie Ordonnantien." *Tijdschrift voor Nijverheid en Landbouw in Nederlandsch-Indië* 46 (1893): 47–79.

Koepok-inenting. Bijdragen tot de Kennis der Nederlandsche en Vreemde Koloniën, Bijzonder Betrekkelijk de Vrijlating der Slaven. Utrecht: C. van der Post, 1846.

Kolff, D. H. *Reize door den Weinig Bekenden Zuidelijken Molukschen Archipel en langs de Geheel Onbekende Zuidwest Kust van Nieuw-Guinea Gedaan in de Jaren 1825 en 1826: Met Eene Kaart/Door D.H. Kolff, Jr. Luitenant ter Zee, 1e Klasse, en Ridder van de Militaire Willems Orde*. Amsterdam: G. J. A. Beijerinck, 1828.

Koloniaal Verslag (Colonial report). *Bijlagen bij de Handelingen van de Tweede Kamer der Staten Generaal 1849–1929*. The Hague. Continued as *Indisch Verslag*, 1931.

Komitee Indonesië. *Transmigratie: een Oproep tot Aktie!* Amsterdam: Komitee Indonesië, 1986.

Koninck, Rodolphy, and Steve Déry. "Agricultural Expansion as a Tool of Population Redistribution in Southeast Asia." *Journal of Southeast Asian Studies* 28, no. 1 (1997): 1–26.

Koningsberger, V. J. "Een Bezoek aan de Philippijnen (19 Augustus–1 September 1928)." *Archief voor de Suikerindustrie in Nederlandsch-Indië* 36, no. 2 (1928): 1221–33, 1251–60.

Kooreman, P. J. "De Feitelijke Toestand in het Gouvernementsgebied van Celebes en Onderhoorigheeden." *De Indische Gids* 5, no. 1 (1883): 171–204, 358–84, 482–98, 637–55; 5, no. 2: 135–69, 346–58.

Korthals Altes, W. L. *De Betalingsbalans Van Nederlandsch-Indië 1822–1939* [The balance of payments of the Netherlands Indies, 1822–1939]. S.l.: s.n.

Kratoska, Paul. "The British Empire and the Southeast Asian Rice Crisis of 1919–1921." *Modern Asian Studies* 24, no. 1 (1990): 115–46.

——. "Imperial Unity Versus Local Autonomy: British Malaya and the Depression of the 1930s." In *Weathering the Storm: The Economies of Southeast Asia in the 1930s Depression*, ed. P. Boomgaard and Ian Brown, 271–94. Singapore: Institute of Southeast Asian Studies, 2000.

——. "The Peripatetic Peasant and Land Tenure in British Malaya." *Journal of Southeast Asian Studies* 16, no. 1 (1985): 16–45.

——. "Rice Cultivation and Ethnic Division of Labor in British Malaya." *Comparative Studies in Society and History* 24, no. 2 (1982): 280–314.

Krom, N. J. *Hindoe-Javaansche Geschiedenis*. 1929. The Hague: Martinus Nijhoff, 1931.

Kruyt, A. C. "De Bewoners van den Banggai Archipel." *Tijdschrift van het Koninklijk Aardrijkskundig Genootschap* 49 (1932): 66–88.

Ku, Charng-Yeong. "The Political Economy of the Philippine Sugar Industry." PhD diss., Ohio University, 1989.

Kumar, Dharma. *Land and Caste in South India: Agricultural Labour in the Madras Presidency During the Nineteenth Century*. Cambridge: Cambridge University Press, 1965.

Kwee Hui Kian. "Chinese Economic Dominance in Southeast Asia: A Longue Durée Perspective." *Comparative Studies in Society and History* 55, no. 1 (2013): 5–34.

——. "The End of the 'Age of Commerce'?: Javanese Cotton Trade Industry from the Seventeenth to the Eighteenth Centuries." In *Chinese Circulations: Capital, Commodities, and Networks in Southeast Asia*, ed. Eric Tagliacozzo and Wen-Chin Chang, 283–302. Durham, NC: Duke University Press, 2001.

Lagerberg, C. S. I. J. "Indonesische Transmigratie in Diskrediet." *Internationale Spectator* 41, no. 12 (1987): 626–31.

Lake, Harry. "Johore." *Geographical Journal* 3, no. 4 (1894): 281–97.

Lamb, Nicole. "A Time of Normalcy." *Bijdragen tot de Taal-, Land en Volkenkunde* 170, no. 4 (2014): 530–56.

Landbouwatlas van Java en Madoera Mededeelingen van het Centraal Kantoor voor de Statistiek no. 33. 2 vols. Weltevreden: Departement van Landbouw, Nijverheid en Handel, 1926.

Langeveld, H. J. "Arbeidstoestanden op de Ondernemingen ter Oostkust van Sumatra tussen 1920 en 1940 in het Licht van het Verdwijnen van de Poenale Sanctie op de Arbeidscontracten." *Economisch- en Sociaal-Historisch Jaarboek* 41 (1978): 294–368.

Lannoy, M. J. *Iles Philippines. Leur situation ancienne et actuelle*. Brussels: Delevigne et Callewaert, 1849.

Lapian, Adrian B. "Violence and Armed Robbery in Indonesian Seas." In *Pirates, Ports, and Coasts in Asia: Historical and Contemporary Perspectives*, ed. John Kleinen and Manon Osseweijer, 131–46. Singapore: ISEAS, 2010.

Lardinois, Roland. "Famine, Epidemics, and Mortality in South India: A Reappraisal of the Demographic Crisis of 1876–1878." *Economic and Political Weekly* 20, no. 11 (1985): 454–65.

Larkin, John A. *The Pampangans: Colonial Society in a Philippine Province.* Berkeley: University of California Press, 1972.

——. "Philippine History Reconsidered: A Socioeconomic Perspective." *American Historical Review* 87, no. 3 (1982): 595–628.

——. *Sugar and the Origins of Modern Philippine Society.* Berkeley: University of California Press, 1993.

Lasker, Bruno. *Human Bondage in Southeast Asia.* Chapel Hill: University of North Carolina Press, 1950.

——. "Training for Native Self-Rule." Supplement in *Educational Progress in Southeast Asia*, ed. J. S. Furnivall, 133–74. New York: Institute of Pacific Relations, 1943.

Latham, A. J. H. "From Competition to Constraint: The International Rice Trade in the Nineteenth and Twentieth Centuries." *Business and Economic History* 17 (1988): 91–102.

Lauby, Jennifer, and Oded Stark. "Individual Migration as a Family Strategy: Young Women in the Philippines." *Population Studies* 42, no. 3 (1988): 473–86.

Lavely, William, and R. Bin Wong. "Revising the Malthusian Narrative: The Comparative Study of Population Dynamics in Late Imperial China." *Journal of Asian Studies* 57, no. 3 (1998): 714–48.

Lee, Vernon J., et al. "Twentieth-Century Influenza Pandemics in Singapore." *Annals of the Academy of Medicine* 37 (2008): 470–76.

Lee, Y. K. "Smallpox and Vaccination in Early Singapore." *Singapore Medical Journal* 14, no. 4 (1973): 525–31; 17, no. 4 (1976): 202–6; 18, no. 1 (1977): 16–20; 18, no. 2 (1977): 126–34.

Lee, Y. L. "The Population of British Borneo." *Population Studies* 15, no. 3 (1962): 226–43.

Legarda, Benito J. *After the Galleons: Foreign Trade, Economic Change, and Entrepreneurship in the Nineteenth-Century Philippines.* Quezon City: Ateneo de Manila University Press, 1999.

Leirissa, R. Z. "'Copracontracten': An Indication of Economic Development in Minahasa During the Late Colonial Period." In *Historical Foundation of a National Economy in Indonesia, 1890s–1990s*, ed. J. Th. Lindblad, 265–77. Amsterdam: KNAW, 1996.

Lekkerkerker, C. "Bali 1800–1814." *Bijdragen tot de Taal-, Land- en Volkenkunde* 82, no. 1 (1926): 315–38.

——. "Java's Overbevolking." *Tijdschrift van het Koninklijk Nederlandsch Aardrijkskundig Genootschap* 54, no. 6 (1937): 866–85.

——. *Land en Volk van Sumatra*. Leiden: Brill, 1916.

——. "Sapoedi en Bawean, Overbevolking en Ontvolking." *Koloniaal Tijdschrift* 24, no. 5 (1935): 459–76.

Leung, Angela Ki Che. "The Business of Vaccination in Nineteenth-Century Canton." *Late Imperial China* 29, no. 1 (2008): 7–39.

——. "'Variolation' and Vaccination in Late Imperial China, ca. 1570–1911." In *History of Vaccine Development*, ed. S. A. Plotkin, 5–12. New York: Springer, 2011.

Levert, P. *Inheemsche Arbeid in de Java-Suikerindustrie*. Wageningen: H. Veenman & Zonen, 1934.

Lewis, Arthur W. "The Export Stimulus." In *Tropical Development, 1880–1913*, ed. W. Arthur Lewis, 13–45. London: Allen & Unwin, 1970.

Lewis, Henry T. "Migration in the Northern Philippines. The Second Wave." *Oceania* 55, no. 2 (1984): 118–36.

Leyden, John. "Sketch of Borneo." *Verhandelingen van het Bataviaasch Genootschap der Kunsten en Wetenschappen* (Batavia) 7 (1814): 41–53.

Li, Tania. *Land's End: Capitalist Relations on an Indigenous Frontier*. Durham, NC: Duke University Press, 2014.

——. "To Make Live or Let Die? Rural Dispossession and the Protection of Surplus Populations." *Antipode* 41, no. 1 (2009): 66–93.

Lieberman, Victor B. *Strange Parallels: Southeast Asia in Global Context, c. 800–1830*. Vol. 1: *Integration on the Mainland Southeast Asia in Global Context, c. 800–1830*; vol. 2: *Mainland Mirrors: Europe, Japan, China, South Asia, and the Islands*. New York: Cambridge University Press, 2003–2009.

——. "A Zone of Refuge in Southeast Asia? Reconceptualizing Interior Spaces." *Journal of Global History* 5 (2010): 333–46.

Liefrinck, F. A. "Slavernij op Lombok." *Tijdschrift voor Indische Taal-, Land- en Volkenkunde* 42 (1900): 508–38.

Lim Teck Ghee. "Reconstituting the Peasantry: Changes in the Landholding Structure in the Muda Irrigation Scheme." In *Agrarian Transformations: Local Processes and the State in Southeast Asia*, ed. Gillian Hart, Andrew Turton, and Benjamin White, 193–212. Berkeley: University of California Press, 1989.

Lim Teck Ghee and Muhammad Ikmal Said. "Rice Peasants." In *Agrarian Transformations: Local Processes and the State in Southeast Asia*, ed. Gillian Hart, Andrew Turton, and Benjamin White. Berkeley: University of California Press, 1989.

Lindio-McGovern, Ligaya. "Alienation and Labour Export in the Context of Globalization." *Critical Asian Studies* 36, no. 2 (2006): 217–38.

Lindquist, Johan. "The Elementary School Teacher, the Thug, and His Grandmother: Informal Brokers and Transnational Migration from Indonesia." *Pacific Affairs* 85, no. 1 (2012): 69–89.

——. "Labour Recruitment, Circuits of Capital, and Gendered Mobility: Reconceptualizing the Indonesian Migration Industry." *Pacific Affairs* 83, no. 1 (2010): 115–32.

Linehan, William, and Mubin Sheppard. *A History of Pahang*. Kuala Lumpur: Malaysian Branch of the Royal Asiatic Society, 1973.

Liu, John M., Paul M. Ong, and Carolyn Rosenstein. "Dual Chain Migration: Post-1965 Filipino Immigration to the United States." *International Migration Review* 25, no. 3 (1991): 487–513.

Lockard, Craig A. "The Javanese as Emigrant: Observations on the Development of Javanese Settlement Overseas." *Indonesia* 11 (1971): 41–63.

——. "'The Sea Common to All': Maritime Frontiers, Port Cities, and Chinese Traders in the Southeast Asian Age of Commerce, ca. 1400–1750." *Journal of World History* 21, no. 2 (2010): 219–47.

Loh Fook Seng, Philip. "Slavery in the Straits Settlements." In *Slavery: A Comparative Perspective*, ed. Robin W. Winks, 178–87. New York: NYU Press, 1972.

Loney, Nicholas. *A Britisher in the Philippines; or, The Letters of Nicholas Loney*. Manila: National Library, 1964.

Lopez-Gonzaga, Violeta. *Crisis in Sugarlandia: The Planters' Differential Perceptions and Responses and Their Impact on Sugarcane Workers' Households*. Bacolod City: La Salle Social Research Center, 1986.

——. "The Roots of Agrarian Unrest in Negros, 1850–90." *Philippine Studies* 36, no. 2 (1988): 151–65.

Lopez Yrastorza, José. *Memoria sobre las vicisitudes de la salud pública en la provincia de Cagayan Islas Filipinas*. Madrid: Imprenta de José Perales y Martinez, 1879.

Loveband, Anne. "Positioning the Product: Indonesian Migrant Women Workers in Taiwan." *Journal of Contemporary Asia* 34, no. 3 (2004): 336–48.

Lovejoy, Paul E. *Transformations in Slavery: A History of Slavery in Africa*. 1983; Cambridge: Cambridge University Press, 2000.

Lovejoy, Paul E., and David Richardson. "The Business of Slaving: Pawnship in Western Africa, c. 1600–1810." *Journal of African History* 42, no. 1 (2001): 67–89.

Lovejoy, Paul E., and Jan S. Hogendorn. *Slow Death for Slavery: The Course of Abolition in Northern Nigeria, 1897–1936*. Cambridge: Cambridge University Press, 1993.

Lubis, Mochtar. "The Press in Indonesia." *Far Eastern Survey* 21, no. 9 (1952): 90–94.

Lucieer, A. I. "Het Kindertal van Volkeren van Nederlandsch-Indië (buiten Java)." *Tijdschrift van het Koninklijk Nederlandsch Aardrijkskundig Genootschap* 41 (1924): 540–63.

Lulofs C., and L. Vuuren. *De Voedselvoorziening van Nederlandsch-Indië*. Batavia: Vereeniging voor Studie van Koloniaal-Maatschappelijke Vraagstukken, 1918.

Maca, Mark, and Paul Morris. "The Philippines, the East Asian 'Developmental States,' and Education: A Comparative Analysis of Why the Philippines Failed to Develop." *Compare: A Journal of Comparative and International Education* 42, no. 3 (2012): 461–84.

MacHale, T., and M. MacHale. *Early American-Philippine Trade: The Journal of Nathaniel Bowditch in Manila, 1796.* Ed. T. McHale and M. McHale. New Haven, CT: Yale University Southeast Asia Studies, 1962.

Maddison, Angus. "Dutch Income in and from Indonesia 1700–1938." *Modern Asian Studies* 23, no. 4 (1989): 645–70.

——. *The World Economy: A Millennial Perspective: Development Centre Seminars.* New Delhi: Overseas Press, 2003.

Mahmud, Zahara. "The Population of Kedah in the Nineteenth Century." *Journal of Southeast Asian Studies* 3, no. 2 (1972): 193–209.

Mallat, J. *Les Philippines. Histoire, géographie, moeurs, agriculture, industrie et commerce des colonies espagnoles dans l'océanie.* 2 vols. Paris: A. Bertrand, 1864.

Manderson, Leonore. *Sickness and the State: Health and Illness in Colonial Malaya, 1870–1940.* Cambridge: Cambridge University Press, 1996.

Mangahas, M. "The Philippine Social Indicators Project." *Social Indicators Research* 4, no. 1 (1977): 67–96.

Manguin, Pierre-Yves. "Trading Ships of the South China Sea: Shipbuilding Techniques and their Role in the History of the Development of Asian Trade Networks." *Journal of the Economic and Social History of the Orient* 36, no. 3 (1993): 253–80.

Mann, Michael. *Sahibs, Sklaven und Soldaten. Geschichte des Menschenhandels rund um den Indischen Ozean.* Darmstadt: Wiss. Buchges, 2012.

Manning, Patrick. *Slavery and African Life: Occidental, Oriental, and African Slave Trades.* Cambridge: Cambridge University Press, 1990.

Mansvelt, W. M. F. *Exportcultures van Ned.-Indië 1830–1937.* Batavia: Centraal Kantoor voor de Statistiek, 1939.

——. *Rice Prices.* Changing Economy of Indonesia 4. The Hague: Nijhoff, 1978.

Mantra, Ida Bagoes. "Illegal Indonesian Labour Movement from Lombok to Malaysia." *Asian Pacific Viewpoint* 40, no. 1 (1999): 59–68.

——. "Indonesian Labour Mobility to Malaysia (a Case Study: East Flores, West Lombok, and the Island of Bawean)." In *Labour Migration in Indonesia: Policies and Practice,* ed. A. Haris Sukamdi and P. Brownlee, 143–84. Yogyakarta: Population Studies Centre, Gadjah Mada University, 2000.

Margana, Sri. "Hybridity, Colonial Capitalism, and Indigenous Resistance: The Case of the Paku Alam in Central Java." In *Sugarlandia Revisited: Sugar and Colonialism in Asia and the Americas, 1800 to 1940,* ed. Ulbe Bosma, Juan Giusti-Cordero, and G. Roger Knight, 95–112. New York/Oxford: Berghahn, 2007.

Marks, Daan. *Accounting for Services: The Economic Development of the Indonesian Service Sector, ca. 1900–2000*. Amsterdam: Aksant, 2009.

Marsden, William. *History of Sumatra. Containing an Account of the Government, Laws, Customs, and Manners, of the Native Inhabitants, with a Description of the Natural Productions and a Relation of the Ancient Political State of That Island*. London: Thomas Payne and Son, 1784.

Martin, Philip. *Merchants of Labor: Agents of the Evolving Migration Infrastructure*. Geneva: ILO, 2005.

Martín, Susana María Ramírez. "El legado de la real expedición filantrópica de la vacuna (1803–1810): las juntas de vacuna." *Asclepio* 56, no. 1 (2004): 33–61.

Martínez, Julia. "The End of Indenture? Asian Workers in the Australian Pearling Industry, 1901–1972." *International Labor and Working-Class History* 67 (2005): 125–47.

Massey, Douglas S. "Economic Development and International Migration in Comparative Perspective." *Population and Development Review* 14, no. 3 (1988): 383–413.

Massey, Douglas, et al. *Return to Aztlan: The Social Process of International Migration from Western Mexico*. Berkeley: University of California Press, 1987.

Masyhuri. "Fishing Industry and Environment off the North Coast of Java, 1850–1900." In *Paper Landscapes: Explorations in the Environmental History of Indonesia*, ed. Peter Boomgaard, Freek Colombijn, and David Henley, 249–60. Leiden: KITLV, 1997.

Mather, Celia E. "Industrialization in the Tangerang Regency of West Java: Women Workers and Islamic Patriarchy." *Critical Asian Studies* 15 (1983): 2–17.

Matheson Hooker, Virginia. *Writing a New Society: Social Change Through the Novel in Malay*. St. Leonards/Honolulu: Allen & Unwin/University of Hawai'i Press, 2000.

Matsuo, Hiroshi. *The Development of the Javanese Cotton Industry*. Tokyo: Institute of Developing Economies, 1970.

Maurer, Jean-Luc. "The Thin Red Line Between Indentured and Bonded Labour: Javanese Workers in New Caledonia in the Early 20th Century." *Asian Journal of Social Science* 38, no. 6 (2010): 866–79.

Maxwell, W. E. *Present and Future Land Systems*. Rangoon: Government Press, 1883.

Mbeki, Linda, and Matthias van Rossum. "Private Slave Trade in the Dutch Indian Ocean World: A Study into the Networks and Backgrounds of the Slavers and the Enslaved in South Asia and South Africa." *Slavery & Abolition* 38, no. 1 (2017): 95–116.

McCoy, Alfred W. "Introduction: The Social History of an Archipelago." In *Philippine Social History: Global Trade and Local Transformations*, ed. Alfred W. McCoy and Ed. C. de Jesus, 1–18. Honolulu: University of Hawai'i Press, 1982.

——. "A Queen Dies Slowly: The Rise and Decline of Iloilo City." In *Philippine Social History: Global Trade and Local Transformations*, ed. Alfred W. McCoy and Ed. C. de Jesus, 297–358. Honolulu: University of Hawai'i Press. 1982.

——. "Sugar Barons: Formation of a Native Planter Class in the Colonial Philippines." *Journal of Peasant Studies* 19 (1992): 106–41.

McDonald, Peter. "The Demography of Indonesia in Comparative Perspective." *Bulletin of Indonesian Economic Studies* 50, no. 1 (2014): 29–52.

McDonnell, Mary Byrne. "The Conduct of the Hajj from Malaysia and Its Socio-Economic Impact on Malay Society: A Prescriptive Analytical Study, 1860–1891." PhD diss., Columbia University, 1986.

McHale, T. R. *Rubber and the Malaysian Economy*. Singapore: MPH Printers Sendirian Berhad, 1967.

McLennan, Marshall S. "Changing Human Ecology on the Central Luzon Plain: Nueva Ecija, 1705–1939." In *Philippine Social History: Global Trade and Local Transformations*, ed. Alfred W. McCoy and Ed. C. de Jesus, 57–90. Honolulu: University of Hawai'i Press, 1982.

——. "Land and Tenancy in the Central Luzon Plain." *Philippine Studies* 17, no. 4 (1969): 651–82.

——. "Peasant and Hacendero in Nueva Ecija: The Socio-Economic Origins of a Philippine Commercial Rice-Growing Region." PhD diss., Berkeley: University of California, 1973.

McNicoll, Geoffrey. "Internal Migration in Indonesia: Descriptive Notes." *Indonesia* 5 (1968): 29–92.

Mehmet, Ozay. "Rubber, Recession, and Malaysia's Economic Development Strategy." *Asian Affairs* 13, no. 2 (1986): 21–34.

Meijer Ranneft, J. W. "Misstanden bij de Werving op Java." *Tijdschrift voor het Binnenlandsch Bestuur* 46 (1914): 1–17, 54–70.

——. "Volksverplaatsingen op Java." *Tijdschrift voor het Binnenlandsch Bestuur* 49, no. 1 (1916): 59–87, 165–84.

Meijer Ranneft, J. W., and W. Huender. *Onderzoek naar den Belastingdruk op de Inlandsche Bevolking*. Weltevreden: Landsdrukkerij, 1926.

Mercer, A. J. "Smallpox and Epidemiological-Demographic Change in Europe: The Role of Vaccination." *Population Studies* 39, no. 2 (1985): 287–307.

Middendorp, W. *Twee Achterlijke Arbeidssystemen voor Inboorlingen in Nederlandsch Oost-Indië (Heerendienst en Poenale Sanctie)*. Haarlem: H. D. Tjeenk Willink & Zoon, s.a.

Mills, L. A., Constance M. Turnbull, and D. K. Bassett. "British Malaya 1824–67." *Journal of the Malayan Branch of the Royal Asiatic Society* 33, no. 3 (1960): 1–424.

Modderman, Pieter W., T. Volker, and G. van der Veen. *Gedenkboek Uitgegeven ter Gelegenheid van het Vijftig Jarig Bestaan van de Deli Planters Vereeniging*. S.l: s.n., 1929.

Moertono, S. *State and Statecraft in Old Java: A Study of the Later Mataram Period, 16th to 19th Century*. Ithaca, NY: Cornell University, 1968.

Mohamad, Maznah. *The Malay Handloom Weavers: A Study of the Rise and Decline of Traditional Manufacture*. Singapore: Institute of Southeast Asian Studies, 1996.

Moor, J. H. *Notices of the Indian Archipelago, and Adjacent Countries; Being a Collection of Papers Relating to Borneo, Celebes, Bali, Java, Sumatra, Nias, the Philippine Islands, Sulus, Siam, Cochin China, Malayan Peninsula etc.* Singapore: s.n., 1837.

Morris, H. S. "Slaves, Aristocrats, and Export of Sago in Sarawak." In *Asian and African Systems of Slavery*, ed. James L. Watson, 293–308. Berkeley: University of California Press, 1980.

Müller, Georg. *Proeve eener Geschiedenis van een Gedeelte der West-Kust van het Eiland Borneo (Getrokken uit het Tijdschrift De Indische Bij)*. Leiden: H. W. Hazenberg en Comp., 1843.

Müller, S. *Reizen en Onderzoekingen in Sumatra gedaan op Last der Nederlandsche Indische Regeering, tusschen de Jaren 1833 en 1838*. 's-Gravenhage: K. Fuhri, 1855.

Nagtegaal, Luc. *Riding the Dutch Tiger: The Dutch East Indies Company and the Northeast Coast of Java, 1680–1743*. Leiden: KILTV, 1996.

Naono, Atsuko. "Inoculators, the Indigenous Obstacle to Vaccination in Colonial Burma." *Journal of Burma Studies* 14 (2010): 91–114.

——. *State of Vaccination: The Fight Against Smallpox in Colonial Burma*. Hyderabad: Orient Blackswan, 2009.

——. "Vaccination Propaganda: The Politics of Communicating Colonial Medicine in Nineteenth-Century Burma." *Soas Bulletin of Burma Research* 1, no. 4 (2006): 30–44.

Nathan J. E. *The Census of British Malaya (The Straits Settlements, Federated Malay States and Protected States of Johore, Kedah, Perlis, Kelantan, Terengganu and Brunei)*. London: Waterlow & Sons, 1922.

Nava, E. L. *Internal Migration in the Philippines, 1939–1948*. Bombay: Demographic Training & Research Centre, 1959.

Nederburgh, S. C. H. *Tjilegon. – Banten. – Java. Iets over des Javaans Lasten en Zijne Draagkracht*. 's-Gravenhage: Martinus Nijhoff, 1888.

Needham, Rodney. *Sumba and the Slave Trade*. Working Paper 31. Oxford: Oxford University, 1983.

Neelakantan, Vivek. "Eradicating Smallpox in Indonesia: The Archipelagic Challenge." *Health and History* 12, no. 1 (2010): 61–87.

Newbold, T. J. *Political and Statistical Account of the British Settlements in the Straits of Malacca viz. Pinang, Malacca and Singapore; on the Peninsula of Malacca.* 2 vols. London: John Murray, 1839.

Newson, Linda A. *Conquest and Pestilence in the Early Spanish Philippines.* Quezon City: Ateneo de Manila University Press, 2011.

——. "Disease and Immunity in the Pre-Spanish Philippines." *Social Science & Medicine* 48, no. 12 (1999): 1833–50.

Ng Siew Yoong. "The Chinese Protectorate in Singapore, 1877–1900." *Journal of Southeast Asian History* 2, no. 1 (1961): 76–99.

Nicholl, Robert. "Notes on Some Controversial Issues in Brunei History." *Archipel* 19 (1980): 25–42.

Nieboer, H. J. *Slavery as an Industrial System: Ethnological Researches.* The Hague: M. Nijhoff, 1910.

Nota Over de Invoering van Staatstoezicht op de Werving van Inlanders op Java en Madoera Bestemd voor de Buitenbezittingen of voor Plaatsen Buiten Nederlandsch Indië met Uitzondering van de Kolonie Suriname. Batavia: Landsdrukkerij, 1907.

Nunn, Nathan, and Nancy Qian. "The Columbian Exchange: A History of Disease, Food, and Ideas." *Journal of Economic Perspectives* 24, no. 2 (2010): 163–88.

Oberai, A. S. "Land Settlement Policies and Population Redistribution in Developing Countries: Performance, Problems, and Prospects." *International Labour Review* 125, no. 2 (1986): 141–61.

O'Brien, Patrick Karl. "Intercontinental Trade and the Development of the Third World Since the Industrial Revolution." *Journal of World History* 8, no. 1 (1997): 75–133.

Ofroneo, Rene E. "Growth and Employment in De-industrializing Philippines." *Journal of the Asia Pacific Economy* 20, no. 1 (2015): 111–29.

Ooi Keat Gin. "For Want of Rice: Sarawak's Attempts at Rice Self-Sufficiency During the Period of Brooke Rule, 1841–1941." *Journal of Southeast Asian Studies* 29, no. 1 (1998): 8–23.

Osborn, Sherard. *The Blockade of Kedah in 1838: A Midshipman's Exploits in Malayan Waters.* Intro. J. M. Gullick. Singapore: Oxford University Press, 1987.

Overzicht van de Uitkomsten der Gewestelijke Onderzoekingen naar de Economie van de Desa en daaruit Gemaakte Gevolgtrekkingen. [Voorw. Van Steinmetz]: Onderzoek naar de Mindere Welvaart der Inlandsche Bevolking op Java en Madoera, IXb 1 En IXb 2. Batavia: Kolff & Co., 1912–1914.

Owen, Norman G. *The Bikol Blend: Bikolanos and Their History.* Quezon City: New Day, 1999.

——. *The Emergence of Modern Southeast Asia: A New History.* Honolulu: University of Hawai'i Press, 2005.

——. *Prosperity Without Progress: Manila Hemp and Material Life in the Colonial Philippines.* Berkeley: University of California Press, 1984.

Parmer, Norman. J. *Colonial Labor Policy and Administration: A History of Labor in the Rubber Plantation Industry in Malaya, c. 1910–1940.* Locust Valley, NY: Published for the Association for Asian Studies by J. J. Augustin, 1960.

Patterson, Orlando. *Slavery and Social Death: A Comparative Study.* Cambridge, MA: Harvard University Press, 1982.

Pearson, Alexander. "Vaccination." *Chinese Repository* 2 (1833–1834): 35–41.

Peggs, James. *Slavery in India. The Present State of East India Slavery, Chiefly Extracted from the Parliamentary Papers on the Subject. Printed March 1828, Aug. 1832, Aug. 1838.* 3rd ed., enlarged. London: G. Wightman, 1840.

Pekelharing, N. R. *De Groote Cultures in Nederlandsch-Indië en eenige Naburige Koloniën [. . .]: Departement Van Landbouw, Nijverheid en Handel.* Weltevreden: Landsdrukkerij, 1924.

Pelras, C. "Patron-Client Ties Among the Bugis and Makassarese of South Sulawesi." *Bijdragen tot de Taal-, Land- en Volkenkunde* 156, no. 3 (2000): 393–432.

Peluso, Nancy Lee, and Peter Vandergeest. "Genealogies of the Political Forest and Customary Rights in Indonesia, Malaysia, and Thailand." *Journal of Asian Studies* 60, no. 3 (2001): 761–812.

Pelzer, Karl J. "The Agrarian Conflict in East Sumatra." *Pacific Affairs* 30, no. 2 (1957): 151–59.

——. *Die Arbeiterwanderungen in Sudostasien.* Hamburg: Friederichsen/De Gruyter, 1935.

——. "The Philippine Abaca Industry." *Far Eastern Survey* 17, no. 6 (1948): 71–74.

——. *Pioneer Settlement in the Asiatic Tropics: Studies in Land Utilization and Agricultural Colonization in Southeastern Asia.* New York: American Geographical Society, 1948.

——. "The Spanish Tobacco Monopoly in the Philippines, 1782–1883, and the Dutch Forced Cultivation System in Indonesia, 1834–1870." *Archipel* 8 (1974): 147–53.

——. "Swidden Cultivation in Southeast Asia: Historical, Ecological, and Economic Perspectives." In *Farmers in the Forest: Economic Development and Marginal Agriculture in Northern Thailand,* ed. P. Kunstadter et al., 271–86. Honolulu: East-West Center, 1978.

Pendleton, L. "Land Utilization and Agriculture of Mindanao, Philippine Islands." *Geographical Review* 32, no. 2 (1942): 180–210.

Pertierra, R. "Lured Abroad: The Case of Ilocano Overseas Workers." *Sojourn: Journal of Social Issues in Southeast Asia* 9, no. 1 (1994): 54–80.

Phillips, James Duncan. *Pepper and Pirates: Adventures in the Sumatra Pepper Trade of Salem*. Boston: Houghton Mifflin, 1949.

Pigeaud, Theodore G. Th. *Java in the Fourteenth Century: A Study in Cultural History: The Nagara- Kertagama by Rakawi Prapanca of Majapahit, 1365 A.D.* 3rd ed., rev. and enlarged by some contemporaneous text, with notes, translations, commentaries and a glossary. The Hague: Nijhoff, 1962.

Pineda-Ofreneo, Rosalinada. "The Philippine Sugar Crisis in an International Setting." *Journal of Contemporary Asia* 15, no. 4 (1985): 455–73.

"The Piracy and Slave Trade of the Indian Archipelago." *Journal of the Indian Archipelago and Eastern Asia* 3 (1849–1850): 581–88, 629–36; 4 (1849–1850): 45–52, 144–62, 400–10, 617–28, 734–46.

Planters Comité. *Overzicht van de Verschillende Adviezen in Zake de Afschaffing van de Poenale Sanctie*. Medan: De Deli Courant, 1920.

Porter, Catherine. "Belated Steps to Aid Philippine Hemp Industry." *Far Eastern Survey* 9, no. 1 (1940): 6–8.

——. "Philippines Has Few Ties with Southeast Asia Colonies." *Far Eastern Survey* 9, no. 16 (1940): 192–93.

Posadas, Barbara M., and Roland L. Guyotte. "Unintentional Immigrants: Chicago's Filipino Foreign Students Become Settlers, 1900–1941." *Journal of American Ethnic History* 9, no. 2 (1990): 26–48.

Post, Peter. "The Formation of the Pribumi Business Élite in Indonesia, 1930s–1940s." *Bijdragen tot de Taal-, Land- en Volkenkunde* 152, no. 4 (1996): 609–32.

Pruys van der Hoeven, A. *Een Woord over Sumatra in Brieven. Verzameld en Uitgegeven door* [. . .]. 2 vols. Rotterdam: H. Nijgh, 1864.

Pryor, Robin J. "Malaysia: Patterns of Population Movement to 1970." In *Migration and Development in Southeast-Asia: A Demographic Perspective*, ed. Robin J. Pryor, 79–97. Kuala Lumpur: Oxford University Press, 1979.

Purwanto, Bambang. *From Dusun to the Market: Native Rubber Cultivation in Southern Sumatra, 1890–1940*. London: University of London, 1992.

——. "Peasant Economy and Institutional Changes in Late Colonial Indonesia." https://socialhistory.org/sites/default/files/docs/ecgrowthpurwanto.pdf.

Putnam, George Granville. *Salem Vessels and Their Voyages: A History of the Pepper Trade with the Island of Sumatra*. Salem: Essex Institute, 1922.

Pye, Oliver, Ramlah Daud, Yuyun Harmono, and Tatat. "Precarious Lives: Transnational Biographies of Migrant Oil Palm Wokers." *Asian Pacific Viewpoint* 53, no. 3 (2012): 330–42.

Quirino, Carlos. *History of the Philippine Sugar Industry*. Manila: Kalayaan, 1974.

Quirk, Joel. *The Anti-Slavery Project: From the Slave Trade to Human Trafficking*. Philadelphia: University of Pennsylvania Press, 2011.

———. "The Anti-Slavery Project: Linking the Historical and Contemporary." *Human Rights Quarterly* 28, no. 3 (2006): 565–98.

Raben, Remco. "Cities and the Slave Trade in Early-Modern Southeast Asia." In *Linking Destinies: Trade, Towns, and Kin in Asian History*, ed. P. Boomgaard, D. Kooiman, and H. Schulte Nordholt, 119–40. Leiden: KITLV, 2008.

Raffles, Thomas Stamford. *The History of Java*. Repr. ed., with an introduction by John Bastin. 2 vols. Kuala Lumpur: Oxford University Press, 1978.

Rannveig Agunias, Dovelyn. *Migration's Middlemen: Regulating Recruitment Agencies in the Philippines–United Arab Emirates Corridor*. Washington, DC: Migration Policy Institute, 2010.

Rappard, Th. C. "Het Eiland Nias en Zijne Bewoners." *Bijdragen tot de Taal-, Land- en Volkenkunde* 61, no. 1 (1909): 477–664.

Razzell, Peter. "The Decline of Adult Smallpox in Eighteenth-Century London: A Commentary." *Economic History Review* 64, no. 4 (2011): 1315–35.

———. "Population Change in Eighteenth-Century England: A Reinterpretation." *Economic History Review* n.s. 18, no. 2 (1965): 312–32.

Reglemento de vacuna de las islas filipinas anotado y adicionado con la legislation del ramo y con formularios. Manila: Emprenta Militar, 1873.

Reid, Anthony. "'Closed' and 'Open' Slave Systems in Pre-Colonial Southeast Asia." In *Slavery, Bondage, and Dependency in Southeast Asia*, ed. Anthony Reid, 156–81. New York: St. Martin's, 1983.

———. "Inside Out: The Colonial Displacement of Sumatra's Population." In *Paper Landscapes: Explorations in the Environmental History of Indonesia*, ed. Peter Boomgaard, Freek Colombijn, and David Henley, 61–89. Leiden: KITLV, 1997.

———. "Introduction." In *Slavery, Bondage, and Dependency in Southeast Asia*, ed. Anthony Reid, 1–43. New York: St. Martin's, 1983.

———. "Low Population Growth and Its Causes in Pre-Colonial Southeast Asia." In *Death and Disease in Southeast Asia: Explorations in Social, Medical, and Demographic History*, ed. Norman G. Owen, 33–47. Singapore: Oxford University Press, 1987.

———. *Southeast Asia in the Age of Commerce, 1450–1680*. 2 vols. New Haven, CT: Yale University Press, 1988.

———. *Southeast Asian Population History and the Colonial Impact*. Liege: IUSSP, 1996.

———. "The Structure of Cities in Southeast Asia, Fifteenth to Seventeenth Centuries." *Journal of Southeast Asian Studies* 11, no. 2 (1980): 235–50.

Reinwardt, C. G. G., and W. H. de Vriese. *Reinwardt's reis naar het Oostelijke Gedeelte van den Indischen archipel, in het Jaar 1821, uit Zijne Nagelaten Aanteeekeningen*

Opgesteld, met een Levensberigt en Bijlagen Vermeerderd. Amsterdam: Frederik Muller, 1858.

Report of the Mission of Enquiry Into the Rubber Industry of Malaya. Kuala Lumpur: Government Press, 1954.

Resnick, Stephen A. "The Decline of Rural Industry Under Export Expansion: A Comparison Among Burma, Philippines, and Thailand, 1870–1938." *Journal of Economic History* 30, no. 1 (1970): 51–73.

Ricklefs, Merle. "Some Statistical Evidence on Javanese Social, Economic, and Demographic History in the Later Seventeenth and Eighteenth Centuries." *Modern Asian Studies* 20, no. 1 (1986): 1–32.

Riedel, J. G. F. *De Sluik-en Kroesharige Rassen tusschen Selebes en Papua*. Gravenhage: M. Nijhoff, 1886.

——. "Timor en Onderhoorigheden in 1878 en later." *Indische Gids* 7, no. 1 (1885): 1–13.

Rice, Lloyd P. "Philippine Copra and Coconut Oil in the American Market." *Far Eastern Survey* 4, no. 20 (1935): 156–61.

Rice, Robert. "Sumitro's Role in Foreign Trade Policy." *Indonesia* 8 (1969): 183–211.

Richell, Judith L. *Disease and Demography in Colonial Burma*. Singapore/ Copenhagen: NUS/NIAS, 2006.

Ritter, W. L. *Indische Herinneringen, Aanteekeningen en Tafereelen uit Vroegeren en Lateren Tijd*. Amsterdam: Van Kesteren, 1843.

Roff, William R. *The Origins of Malay Nationalism*. New Haven, CT: Yale University, 1967.

Roos, Samuel. "Bijdrage tot de Kennis van Taal, Land en Volk op het Eiland Soemba." *Verhandelingen van het Bataviaasch Genootschap* 36 (1872): 1–169.

Ross, Corey. "The Tin Frontier: Mining, Empire, and Environment in Southeast Asia, 1870s–1930s." *Environmental History*, 19, no. 3 (2014): 454–79.

Roth, Dennis Morrow. "Church Lands in the Agrarian History of the Tagalog Region." In *Philippine Social History: Global Trade and Local Transformations*, ed. Alfred W. McCoy and Ed. C. de Jesus, 131–55. Honolulu: University of Hawai'i Press, 1982.

Roth, Henry Ling. *The Natives of Sarawak and British North Borneo. Based Chiefly on the MSS. of the late Hugh Brooke Low Sarawak Government Service*. 2 vols. New York: Truslove & Comba, 1896.

Rothenbuhler, F. J. "Rapport van den Staat en Gesteldheid van het Landschap Sourabaija; met de daarin Gevonden Wordende Negorijen en Dorpen, Item Velden, Bevolking enz., Zoodanig als het een en ander Bevonden is bij de Daarvan Gedanen Opneem door . . ." *Verhandelingen van het Bataviaasch Genootschap van Kunsten en Wetenschappen* 41, no. 3 (1880).

Rouffaer, G. P. *De Voornaamste Industrieën der Inlandsche Bevolking van Java en Madoera.* Aanhangsel tot het Overzicht van den Economischen Toestand der Inlandsche Bevolking van Java en Madoera, door Mr. C.Th. van Deventer. The Hague: Martinus Nijhoff, 1904.

Roy, Tirthankar. "Factor Markets and the Narrative of Economic Change in India, 1750–1950." *Continuity and Change* 24, no. 1 (2009): 137–67.

Rudnyckyj, Daromir. "Technologies of Servitude: Governmentality and Indonesian Transnational Labor Migration." *Anthropological Quarterly* 77, no. 3 (2004): 407–34.

Ruibing, A. H. *Ethnologische Studie Betreffende de Indonesische Slavernij als Maatschappelijk Verschijnsel.* Zutphen: W. J. Thieme & Cie, 1937.

Runes, I. T. *General Standards of Living and Wages of Workers in the Philippine Sugar Industry.* Philippine Council Institute of Pacific Relations, 1939.

Rutten, W. *"De Vreselijkste aller Harpijen": Pokkenepidemieën en Pokkenbestrijding in Nederland in de Achttiende en Negentiende eeuw: een Sociaal-Historische en Historisch-Demografische Studie.* Wageningen: Afdeling Agrarische Geschiedenis, Landbouwuniversiteit Wageningen, 1997.

Salau, Mohammed Bashir. "The Role of Slave Labor in Groundnut Production in Early Colonial Kano." *Journal of African History* 51, no. 2 (2010): 147–65.

Salman, Michael. *The Embarassment of Slavery: Controversies Over Bondage and Nationalism in the American Colonial Philippines.* Berkeley: University of California Press, 2001.

Sarasin, Paul, and Fritz Sarasin. *Reisen in Celebes: Ausgeführt in den Jahren 1893–1896 und 1902–1903.* 2 vols. Wiesbaden: C. W. Kreidel, 1905.

Saravanamuttu, Johan. "The Political Economy of Migration and Flexible Labour Regimes: The Case of the Oil Palm Industry in Malaysia." In *The Palm Oil Controversy in Southeast Asia: A Transnational Perspective,* ed. Oliver Pye and Jayatif Bhattacharya. Singapore: ISEAS, 2013.

Sassen, Saskia. *The Mobility of Labor and Capital: A Study in International Investment and Labor Flow.* Cambridge: Cambridge University Press, 1988.

Sawyer, Frederic H. *The Inhabitants of the Philippines.* New York: Scribner, 1900.

Schadenberg, A. "Die Bewohner von Süd-Mindanao und der Insel Samal. Nach Eignen Erfahrungen." *Zeitschrift für Ethnologie* 17 (1885): 8–37, 45–57.

Scheltema, A. M. P. A. "De Ontwikkeling van de Agrarische Toestanden in Priangan." *Landbouw. Tijdschrift der Vereeniging voor Landbouwconsulenten in Nederlandsch Indië* 3 (1927–1928): 271–305, 317–68.

Schul, Norman W. "A Philippine Sugar Cane Plantation: Land Tenure and Sugar Cane Production." *Economic Geography* 43, no. 2 (1967): 157–69.

Schult, Volker. "Deforestation and Mangyan in Mindoro." *Philippine Studies* 29, no. 2 (2001): 151–75.

———. "Sultans and Adventurers: German Blockade Runners in the Sulu Archipelago." *Philippine Studies* 50, no. 3 (2002): 395–415.

Schneider, P. H. *Inleiding tot de Studie van Vraagstukken in Verband met de Voorgenomen Afschaffing der Poenale Sanctie in de Werkovereenkomsten ter Oostkust van Sumatra, met eene Proeve van een Ontwerp Ordonnantie . . . : in Opdracht van het Bestuur der A.V.R.O.S.* Medan: Algemeene Vereeniging van Rubberplanters ter Oostkust van Sumatra, 1919.

Schoute, D. "De Geneeskunde in Nederlandsch-Indië gedurende de Negentiende Eeuw." *Geneeskundig Tijdschrift voor Nederlandsch Indië* 74 (1934): 938–50.

———. *Occidental Therapeutics in the Netherlands East Indies During Three Centuries of Netherlands Settlement: 1600–1900.* Batavia: Publications of the Netherlands Indies Public Health Service, 1937.

Schwalbenberg, Henry M. "The Economics of Pre-Hispanic Visayan Slave Raiding." *Philippine Studies* 42, no. 3 (1994): 376–84.

Schwaner, C. A. L. M. *Borneo. Beschrijving van het Stroomgebied van den Barito en Reizen langs Eenige Voorname Rivieren van het Zuid-Oostelijk Gedeelte van dat Eiland.* 2 vols. Amsterdam: P. N. van Kampen, 1853–1854.

Scott, James C. "The Erosion of Patron-Client Bonds and Social Change in Rural Southeast Asia." *Journal of Asian Studies* 32, no. 1 (1972): 5–37.

———. "Freedom and Freehold: Space, People, and State Simplification in Southeast Asia." In *Asian Freedoms: The Idea of Freedom in East and Southeast Asia*, ed. David Kelly and Anthony Reid, 37–64. Cambridge: Cambridge University Press, 1998.

———. "Patron-Client Politics and the Political Change in Southeast Asia." *American Political Science Review* 66 (1972): 91–113.

Scott, William Henry. "Class Structure in the Unhispanized Philippines." *Philippine Studies* 27, no. 2 (1979): 37–159.

———. *The Discovery of the Igorots: Spanish Contacts with the Pagans of Northern Luzon.* Rev. ed. Quezon City: New Day, 1982.

———. "Filipino Class Structure in the Sixteenth Century." *Philippine Studies* 28, no. 2 (1980): 142–75.

Semyonov, Moshe. "Labor Migration, Remittances, and Household Income: A Comparison Between Filipino and Filipina Overseas Workers." *International Migration Review* 39, no. 1 (2005): 45–68.

Semyonov, Moshe, and Anastasia Gorodzeisky. "Labor Migration, Remittances, and Economic Well-Being of Households in the Philippines." *Population Research and Policy Review* 27, no. 5 (2008): 619–37.

Sharma, Miriam. "Towards a Political Economy of Emigration from the Philippines: The 1906 to 1946 Ilocano Movement to Hawaii in Historical Perspective." *Philippine Sociological Review* 35, no. 3–4 (1987): 15–33.

Shepherd, Jack. *Industry in Southeast Asia*. New York: Institute of Pacific Relations, 1941.

Sheppard, M. C. "A Short History of Trengganu." *Journal of the Malayan Branch of the Royal Asiatic Society* 22, no. 3 (1949): 1–74.

Sicat, Gerardo P. "The Economic Legacy of Marcos." Discussion paper, School of Economics, University of the Philippines, Quezon, 2011–11. http://hdl.handle.net /10419/93568.

——. "Philippine Economic Nationalism." *Philippine Review of Economics* 62, no. 2 (2008): 1–44.

——. "The Philippines in 1983: Economic Crisis in Perspective." *Southeast Asian Affairs* 11 (1984): 249–65.

Silvey, Rachel. "Transnational Domestication: State Power and Indonesian Migrant Women in Saudi Arabia." CLARA working paper 17. 2004.

Sim, Amy. "Women Versus the State: Organizing Resistance and Contesting Exploitation in Indonesian Labor Migration to Hong Kong." *Asian and Pacific Migration Journal* 18, no. 1 (2009): 47–75.

Singh, D. S. Ranjit. *Brunei, 1839–1983: The Problems of Political Survival*. Singapore: Oxford University Press, 1991.

Sitsen, Peter H. W. *Industrial Development of the Netherlands Indies*. Bulletin 2 of the Netherlands and Netherlands Indies Council of the Institute of Pacific Relations.

Skinner, E. Benjamin. "Indonesia's Palm Oil Industry Rife with Human-Rights Abuses." *Bloomberg Businessweek*, July 20, 2013.

Skinner, G. William. *Chinese Society in Thailand: An Analytical History, with Bibliography, Graphs, Index, Maps and Tabs*. Ithaca, NY: Cornell University Press, 1962.

"Slave Trade at Nias." From the *Singapore Chronicle*, April 24, 1828. In *Notices of the Indian Archipelago, and Adjacent Countries; being a Collection of Papers relating to Borneo, Celebes, Bali, Java, Sumatra, Nias, The Philippine Islands, Sulus, Siam, Cochin China, Malayan Peninsula etc.*, ed. J. H. Moor, 185–88. Singapore, 1837.

Smith, P. "The Social Demography of Filipino Migrations Abroad." *International Migration Review* 10, no. 3 (1976): 307–55.

Smith, P. C., and Shui-Meng Ng. "The Components of Population Change in Nineteenth-Century South-East Asia: Village Data from the Philippines." *Population Studies* 36, no. 2 (1982): 237–55.

Snouck, Hurgronje C. *Ambtelijke Adviezen Van C. Snouck Hurgronje*. 3 vols. The Hague: Martinus Nijhoff, 1957–1965.

——. *De Atjèhers*. Batavia: Landsdrukkerij etc., 1893.

Sokoloff, Kenneth L., and Stanley L. Engerman. "History Lessons: Institutions, Factor Endowments, and Paths of Development in the New World." *Journal of Economic Perspectives* 14, no. 3 (2000): 217–32.

Sollewijn Gelpke, J. H. F. *Naar Aanleiding Van Staatsblad, 1878, No. 110*. Batavia, 1901.

Somers Heidhues, Mary F. *Bangka Tin and Mentok Pepper: Chinese Settlement on an Indonesian Island*. Singapore: Institute of Southeast Asian Studies, 1992.

——. *Golddiggers, Farmers, and Traders in the "Chinese Districts" of West Kalimantan, Indonesia*. Ithaca, NY: Southeast Asia Program Publications, Southeast Asia Program, Cornell University, 2003.

Snodgrass, Katharine. *Copra and Coconut Oil*. Stanford, CA: Food Research Institute, 1928.

Spaan, Ernst. *Labour Circulation and Socioeconomic Transformation: The Case of East Java, Indonesia*. The Hague: Netherlands Interdisciplinary Demographic Institute, 1999.

——. "Taikongs and Calos: The Role of Middlemen and Brokers in Javanese International Migration." *International Migration Review* 28, no. 1 (1994): 93–113.

Spencer, J. E. "Abaca and the Philippines." *Economic Geography*, 27, no. 2 (1951): 95–106.

——. *Land and People in the Philippines: Geographic Problems in Rural Economy*. Berkeley: University of California Press, 1952.

Spyer, Patricia. "The Eroticism of Debt: Pearl Divers, Traders, and Sea Wives in the Aru Islands, Eastern Indonesia." *American Ethnologist* 24, no. 3 (1997): 515–38.

——. *The Memory of Trade: Modernity's Entanglements on an Eastern Indonesian Island*. Durham, NC: Duke University Press, 2000.

St. John, Spenser. "Piracy in the Indian Archipelago." *Journal of the Indian Archipelago* 3 (1849): 251–60.

Stanziani, Alessandro. *Sailors, Slaves, and Immigrants: Bondage in the Indian Ocean World, 1750–1914*. New York: Palgrave MacMillan, 2014.

Sternagel, Renate, and Franz W. Junghuhn. *Der Humboldt von Java: Leben und Werk des Naturforschers Franz Wilhelm Junghuhn 1809–1864*. Halle (Saale): Mitteldt. Verl, 2011.

Storer, Thomas Perry. "The Philippines." In *Tropical Development, 1880–1913: Studies in Economic Progress*, ed. Arthur W. Lewis, 283–308. London: Allen & Unwin, 1970.

Stover, Charles C. "Tropical Exports." In *Tropical Development, 1880–1913: Studies in Economic Progress*, ed. Arthur W. Lewis, 46–63. London: Allen & Unwin, 1970.

Stubbs, Richard. "Malaysia's Rubber Smallholding Industry: Crisis and the Search for Stability." *Pacific Affairs* 56, no. 1 (1983): 84–105.

Sutherland, Heather. "Slavery and the Slave Trade in South Sulawesi, 1660s–1800s." In *Slavery, Bondage, and Dependency in Southeast Asia*, ed. Anthony Reid, 263–85. New York: St. Martin's, 1983.

——. "The Sulu Zone Revisited: Iranun and Balangingi: Globalization, Maritime Raiding, and the Birth of Ethnicity by James Francis Warren." *Journal of Southeast Asian Studies* 35, no. 1 (2004): 133–57.

Sutter, J. O. Indonesianisasi. "A Historical Survey of the Role of Politics in the Institutions of Changing Economy from the Second World War to the Eve of the General Election, 1940–1955." PhD diss., Cornell University, 1959.

Sutton, Keith, and Amriah Buang. "A New Role for Malaysia's FELDA: From Land Settlement Agency to Plantation Company." *Geography* 80, no. 2 (1995): 125–37.

Swaving, C. "Numerieke Verdeeling en Omschrijving der Ziekten, die gedurende 1846–1847 in en buiten het Hospitaal te Buitenzorg op Java Waargenomen zijn door C. Swaving." *Tijdschrift voor Geneeskunde* 3 (1852): 289–356.

Swettenham, F. A. *British Malaya: An Account of the Origin and Progress of British Influence in Malaya*. London: G. Allen and Unwin, 1948.

Tagliacozzo, Eric. *The Longest Journey: Southeast Asians and the Pilgrimage to Mecca*. Oxford: Oxford University Press, 2013.

——. "Smuggling in the South China Sea: Alternate Histories of a Nonstate Space in the Late Nineteenth and Late Twentieth Centuries." In *Elusive Pirates, Pervasive Smugglers: Violence and Clandestine Trade in the Greater China Seas*, ed. Robert J. Antony. Hong Kong: Hong Kong University Press, 2010.

Talbot, John. M. "Tropical Commodity Chains, Forward Integration Strategies, and International Inequality: Coffee, Cocoa, and Tea." *Review of International Political Economy* 9, no. 4 (2002): 701–34.

Talens, Johan. *Een Feodale Samenleving in Koloniaal Vaarwater. Staatsvorming, Koloniale Expansie en Economische Onderontwikkeling in Banten, West Java (1600–1750)*. Hilversum: Verloren, 1999.

Talib, Shaharil. "The Port and Polity of Trengganu During the Eighteenth and Nineteenth Centuries: Realizing Its Potential." In *The Southeast Asian Port and Polity: Rise and Demise*, ed. J. Kathirithamby-Wells and John Villiers, 213–30. Singapore: Singapore University Press.

Tammes, P. M. L. "De Biologische Achtergrond van het Bevolkingsvraagstuk op Noord-Celebes en de Sangihe- en Talaud-Archipel." *Tijdschrift voor Economische Geographie* 31, no. 7 (1940): 177–98.

Tarling, Nicholas. *Piracy and Politics in the Malay World: A Study of British Imperialism in Nineteenth-Century South-East Asia*. Lichtenstein: Kraus, 1978.

Tate, D. J. M. "Planting in Nineteenth-Century Sabah and Sarawak." *Journal of the Straits–Malaysian Branch of the Royal Asiatic Society* 69, no. 1 (1996): 37–63.

Teitler, G., A. M. C. van Dissel, and J. F. N. M. à Campo. *Zeeroof en Zeeroofbestrijding in de Indische Archipel (19e eeuw)*. Amsterdam: De Bataafsche Leeuw, 2005.

Tennekes, J. "De Bevolkingsspreiding der Residentie Besoeki in 1930." *Tijdschrift van het Koninklijk Nederlandsch Aardrijkskundig Genootschap* 80 (1963): 309–423.

Terray, Emmanuel. "La captivité dans le royaume abron du Gyaman." In *L'esclavage en Afrique précoloniale*, ed. Claude Meillassoux, 389–453. Paris: Maspero, 1975.

Tharian, George K., and M. R. Sethuraj. "Dynamics of World Natural Rubber Economy: Its Relevance to India." *Economic and Political Weekly* 31, no. 33 (1996): 1355–58.

Thee Kian Wie. "Plantation Agriculture and Export Growth: An Economic History of East Sumatra, 1863–1942." PhD diss., University of Wisconsin, 1969.

Thoburn, J. T. "Exports and Economic Growth in West Malaysia." *Oxford Economic Papers* n.s. 25, no. 1 (1973): 88–111.

Thompson, Angela T. "To Save the Children: Smallpox Inocculation, Vaccination, and Public Health in Guanajuato, Mexico, 1797–1840." *The Americas* 49, no. 4 (1993): 431–55.

Thompson, C. Michele. "Jean Marie Despiau: Unjustly Maligned Physician in the Medical Service of the Nguyen." In *Vietnam and the West: New Approaches*, ed. Wynn Wilcox, 41–72. Ithaca, NY: Cornell University Press, 2010.

——. *Vietnamese Traditional Medicine: A Social History*. Singapore: NUS, 2015.

Tideman, J. "De Koelieordonnantie en Hare Toepassing." *Koloniale Studiën* 2, no. 2 (1918): 31–74.

——. *De Zeevisscherij in Rembang en Bodjonegoro*. Amsterdam: Koloniaal Instituut [Mededeeling 2], 1932.

——. *Het Landschap Bone*. Amsterdam: Koloniaal Instituut [Mededeeling 8], 1935.

Tillema, H. F. *"Kromoblanda." Over 't Vraagstuk van "het Wonen" in Kromo's Groote Land*. 5 vols. Groningen: s.n. [the author], 1921.

Timmer, C. P. "Building Efficiency in Agricultural Marketing: The Long-Run Role of Bulog in the Indonesian Food Economy." *Journal of International Development* 9, no. 1 (1997): 133–45.

Tomich, Dale. "Rethinking the Plantation: Concepts and Histories." *Review (Fernand Braudel Center)* 34, no. 1/2 (2011): 15–39.

Touwen, J. "Entrepreneurial Strategies in Indigenous Export Agriculture in the Outer Islands of Colonial Indonesia, 1925–38." In *Weathering the Storm: The Economies of Southeast Asia in the 1930s Depression*, ed. P. Boomgaard and Ian Brown, 143–70. Singapore: Institute of Southeast Asian Studies, 2000.

Trager, Lilian. "Family Strategies and the Migration of Women: Migrants to Dagupan City, Philippines." *International Migration Review* 18, no. 4 (1984): 1264–77.

Tregonning, K. G. P. "The Elimination of Slavery in North Borneo." *Journal of the Malayan Branch of the Royal Asiatic Society* 26, no. 1 (1953): 24–36.

Trocki, Carl A. "Singapore as a Nineteenth-Century Migration Node." In *Connecting Seas and Connected Ocean Rims: Indian, Atlantic, and Pacific Oceans and China Seas Migrations from the 1830s to the 1930s*, ed. Donna Gabaccia and Dirk Hoerder, 198–224. Leiden: Brill, 2011.

Turot, Henri. *Emilio Aguinaldo: First Filipino President, 1898–1901.* Trans. Pacifico A. Castro. Manila: Solar, 1986.

Ueno, Kayoko. "Strategies of Resistance Among Filipina and Indonesian Domestic Workers in Singapore." *Asian and Pacific Migration Journal* 18, no. 4 (2009): 497–517.

Uitkomsten der in de Maand november 1920 gehouden Volkstelling. 2 vols. Tabellen. Batavia: Ruygrok & Co., 1922.

"Uitvoer van Klapperproducten uit Nederlandsch-Indië." *Economisch-Statistische Berichten* 22, 1102 (1937): 104–5.

UNCTAD. *Commodities and Development Report 2015: Smallholder Farmers and Sustainable Commodity Development.* New York: United Nations, 2015.

United Nations. *Growth of the World's Urban and Rural Population, 1920–2000.* New York: United Nations, 1969.

Van Aelst, A. "Majapahit Picis: The Currency of a 'Moneyless' Society, 1300–1700." *Bijdragen tot de Taal-, Land- en Volkenkunde* 151, no. 3 (1995): 357–93.

Van Blankenstein, M. *De Poenale Sanctie in de Practijk.* Rotterdam: Van Nijgh & Van Ditmar, 1929.

Van Blommestein, A. F. *De Nieuwe Koelie-ordonnantie Voor De Oostkust Van Sumatra: (Ind. Stbl. 1915 No. 421).* Amsterdam: Scheltema & Holkema, 1917.

——. *Ontwerp eener Ordonnantie tot Regeling van den Arbeid van elders afkomstige Personen in Bedrijven, welke in het Gewest Oostkust van Sumatra geheel of gedeeltelijk buiten de Bevolkingscentra Worden Uitgeoefend, en Memorie van Toelichting, in Voldoening aan eene Opdracht van den Minister van Koloniën Samengesteld.* S.l.: s.n., s.a.

Van Braam Morris, D. F. "Het Landschap Loehoe Getrokken uit het Rapport van den Gouverneur van Celebes." *Tijdschrift voor Indische Taal-, Land- en Volkenkunde* 32, no. 5 (1889): 498–555.

Van Deventer, C. Th., and G. P Rouffaer. *Overzicht van den Economischen toestand der Inlandsche Bevolking van Java en Madoera. Samengest. onder Leiding van en door C.Th. Van Deventer. Met Aanhangsel: De Voornaamste Industrieën der Inlandsche Bevolking van Java en Madoera, door G. P. Rouffaer: Met Reg.* The Hague: Nijhoff, 1904.

Van de Graaff, H. J., and G. J. Meylan. "De Moluksche Eilanden (Rapport 1820)." *Tijd-schrift voor Nederlandsch Indië* 18, no. 1 (1856): 74–137, 167–90, 232–63.

Van den Haspel, C. Ch. *Overwicht in Overleg. Hervormingen van Justitie, Grondge-bruik en Bestuur in de Vorstenlanden op Java 1880–1930.* Dordrecht/Cinnaminson: Foris, 1985.

Van der Chijs, J. A. *Nederlandsch-Indisch Plakaatboek 1602–1811.* Batavia: Lands-drukkerij, 1885–1900.

Van der Crab, P. *De Moluksche Eilanden. Reis van Z.E. den Gouverneur-Generaal Charles Ferdinand Pahud door den Molukschen Archipel.* Batavia: Lange & Co., 1862.

Van der Eng, Pierre. *Agricultural Growth in Indonesia Since 1880: Productivity Change and the Impact of Government Policy.* Groningen: Rijksuniversiteit Gron-ingen, 1993.

——. "'De-industrialisation' and Colonial Rule: The Cotton Textile Industry in Indonesia, 1820–1941." Working Papers in Trade and Development 4. Division of Economics, Research School of Pacific and Asian Studies, Australian National University, Canberra, 2007.

——. "Development of Seed-Fertilizer Technology in Indonesian Rice Agriculture." *Agricultural History* 68, no. 1 (1994): 20–53.

——. "Food for Growth: Trends in Indonesia's Food Supply, 1880–1905." *Journal of Interdisciplinary History* 30, no. 4 (2000): 591–616.

——. "Government Promotion of Labour-Intensive Industrialization in Indonesia, 1930–1975." In *Labour-Intensive Industrialisation in Global History*, ed. Gareth Austin and Kaoru Sugihara, 176–200. New York: Routledge, 2013.

——. "Indonesia's Growth Performance in the Twentieth Century." In *The Asian Economies in the Twentieth Century*, ed. Angus Maddison, D. S. Prasada Rao, and William F. Shepherd, 143–79. Northampton, MA: Edward Elgar, 2002.

——. "Why Didn't Colonial Indonesia Have a Competitive Cotton Textile Indus-try?" *Modern Asian Studies* 47, no. 3 (2013): 1019–54.

Van der Hart, C. *Reize rondom het Eiland Celebes en naar Eenige Moluksche Eilanden gedaan in den Jare 1850 door Z.M. Oorlogsschip Argo en Bromo.* The Hague: K. Ruhri, 1853.

Van der Kemp, P. H. *De Quarantaine- en Epidemie-Voorschriften in Nederlandsch-Indië (Staatsblad 1892 Nos 44 en 45).* Batavia: Landsdrukkerij, 1892.

Van der Kraan, Alfons. "Bali: Slavery and Slave Trade." In *Slavery, Bondage, and Dependency in Southeast Asia*, ed. Anthony Reid, 315–40. New York: St. Martin's, 1983.

——. *Lombok: Conquest, Colonisation, and Underdevelopment, 1870–1940.* Singa-pore: Heineman, 1980.

Van der Kroef, Justus M. "Indonesia's Economic Difficulties." *Far Eastern Survey* 24, no. 2 (1955): 17–24.

——. "Indonesia's Rice Economy: Problems and Prospects." *American Journal of Economics and Sociology* 22, no. 3 (1963): 379–92.

——. "Review of Sociologisch-Economische Geschiedenis van Indonesië." *Pacific Affairs* 50, no. 2 (1977): 163–65.

——. "Social Structure and Economic Development in Indonesia." *Social Research* 23, no. 4 (1956): 394–418.

Van der Linden, Marcel. "Global Labor History and the 'Modern World-System': Thoughts at the Twenty-Fifth Anniversary of the Fernand Braudel Center." *International Review of Social History* 46, no. 3 (2001): 423–59.

Van der Reijden, B. *Rapport Betreffende eene Gehouden Enquête naar de Arbeidstoestanden in de Industrie van Strootjes en Inheemsche Sigaretten op Java: I. West-Java. II. Midden Java. III. Oost-Java. Publ. Van Het Kantoor Van Arbeid, 9 en 10, 12.* Bandoeng, 1934–1936.

Van der Wijst, Ton. "Transmigration in Indonesia: An Evaluation of a Population Redistribution Policy." *Population Research and Policy Review* 4 (1985): 1–30.

Van Eijbergen, H. C. "Geschiedkundige Aantekeeningen omtrent de Noordkust van Ceram vanaf het jaar 1816 tot 1832." *Tijdschrift voor Indische Taal-, Land- en Volkenkunde* 17 (1869): 489–504.

Van Fraassen, Ch. F. "Ternate, de Molukken en de Indonesische Archipel. Van Soa-Organisatie en Vierdeling: een Studie naar de Traditionele Samenleving en Cultuur in Indonesië." 2 vols. PhD diss., Leiden, 1987.

Van Gelderen, J. *Voorlezingen over Tropisch-Koloniale Staathuishoudkunde.* Haarlem: Tjeenk Willink, 1927.

Van Hoëvell, W. R. "De Zeeroverijen der Soloerezen." *Tijdschrift voor Nederlandsch-Indië* 2 (1850): 99–105.

Van Kol, H. H. *Japan.* Rotterdam: s.n., 2016.

Van Leeuwen, Bas. "Human Capital and Economic Growth in India, Indonesia, and Japan: A Quantitative Analysis, 1890–2000." PhD diss., Utrecht University, 2007.

Van Nederveen Meerkerk, Elise. "Challenging the De-Industrialization Thesis: Gender and Indigenous Textile Production in Java Under Dutch Colonial Rule, c. 1830–1920." *Economic History Review* 7, no. 4 (2017): 1219–1243.

Van Nus, J. "De Staatsspoorwegen in Nederlandsch-Indië gedurende de Crisisjaren 1930 t/m 1934." *Koloniale Studiën* 19, no. 1 (1935): 1–29.

Van Oorschot, H. J. *De Ontwikkeling van de Nijverheid in Indonesië.* The Hague/Bandung: Van Hoeve, 1956.

Van Rossum, Matthias. *Hand aan Hand (Blank en Bruin): Solidariteit en de Werking van Globalisering, Etniciteit en Klasse onder Zeelieden op de Nederlandse Koopvaardij, 1900–1945.* Amsterdam: Amsterdam University Press, 2009.

——. *Kleurrijke tragiek. De geschiedenis van slavernij in Azië onder de VOC.* Verloren, De Zeven Provinciën reeks: Hilversum 2015.

Van Schendel, Willem. *Three Deltas: Accumulation and Poverty in Rural Burma, Bengal, and South India.* Indo-Dutch Studies on Development Alternatives. New Delhi: Sage, 1991.

Van Verschuer, F. H. "De Badjo's." *Tijdschrift van het Nederlandsch Aardrijkskundig Genootschap* 7, no. 1 (1883): 1–7.

Van Welie, Rik van. "Slave Trading and Slavery in the Dutch Colonial Empire: A Global Comparison." *NWIG: New West Indian Guide* 82, no. 1–2 (2008): 47–96.

Van Zanden, Jan Luiten. "Linking Two Debates: Money Supply, Wage Labor, and Economic Development in Java in the 19th Century." In *Wages and Currency: Global Comparisons from Antiquity to the Twentieth Century,* ed. Jan Lucassen, 169–92. Bern: Peter Lang, 2008.

Van Zanden, Jan Luiten, and Daan Marks. *An Economic History of Indonesia: 1800–2010.* London: Routledge, 2014.

Vandermeer, Canute. "Population Patterns on the Island of Cebu, the Philippines: 1500–1800." *Annals of the Association of American Geographers* 57, no. 2 (1967): 315–37.

Vatikiotis, Michael. "Escape from Poverty." *Far Eastern Economic Review,* January 11, 1990.

——. "Swamped Plantations." *Far Eastern Review,* April 2, 1992.

——. "Worrisome Influx." *Far Eastern Economic Review,* August 6, 1992.

VEDA-Verslag. See *Verslag der Vrije Emigratie van D.P.V. and A.V.R.O.S.*

Velthoen, Esther Joy. "Contested Coastlines: Diasporas, Trade, and Colonial Expansion in Eastern Sulawesi." PhD diss., Murdoch University, 2002.

Verbrugge, Boris. "The Economic Logic of Persistent Informality: Artisanal and Small-Scale Mining in the Southern Philippines." *Development and Change* 46, no. 5 (2015): 1023–46.

Verslag der Vrije Emigratie van D.P.V. and A.V.R.O.S. Medan, 1928.

Verslag van den Dienst der Arbeidsinspectie en Koeliewerving in Nederlandsch-Indië. See Kantoor van Arbeid.

Verslag van het Algemeen Delisch Emigratie Kantoor. Bandoeng: N.V. Drukkeris, 1920.

Veth, P. J. *Borneo's Wester-Afdeeling, Geographisch, Statistisch, Historisch Voorafgegaan door eene Algemeene Schets des Ganschen Eilands.* Zaltbommel: Joh. Noman en Zoon, 1854.

——. *Java, Geographisch, Ethnologisch, Historisch.* 3 vols. Haarlem: Erven F. Bohn, 1875–1884.

Vidal, José Montero y. *Historia de la pirateria malayo mohametana en Mindanao, Jolo y Borneo.* 2 vols. Madrid: Tello, 1888.

Villiers, John. "Manila and Maluku: Trade and Warfare in the Eastern Archipelago, 1580–1640." *Philippine Studies* 34, no. 2 (1986): 146–61.

——. "Trade and Society in the Banda Islands in the Sixteenth Century." *Modern Asian Studies* 15, no. 4 (1981): 723–50.

Vink, Markus P. M. "Freedom and Slavery: The Dutch Republic, the VOC World, and the Debate Over the 'World's Oldest Trade.'" *South African Historical Journal* 59 (2007): 19–46.

Vitalis, L. "Over de Pachten in het Algemeen, de Onzedelijkheid van Sommige, en de Verdrukking waaraan de Overmatige Misbruiken van andere de Javaansche Bevolking Blootstellen." *Tijdschrift voor Nederlandsch-Indië* 13, no. 2 (1851): 365–86.

Vlieger, Antoinette. "Domestic Workers in Saudi Arabia and the Emirates: Trafficking Victims?" *International Migration* 50, no. 6 (2012): 180–94.

Vlieland, C. A. *British Malaya: A Report on the 1931 Census and on Certain Problems of Vital Statistics.* Malayan Information Agency.

——. "The Population of the Malay Peninsula: A Study in Human Migration." *Geographical Review* 24, no. 1 (1934): 61–78.

Volkstelling 1930 = Census of 1930 in Netherlands India. 8 vols. Batavia: Departement van Landbouw, Nijverheid en Handel, 1933.

Vosmaer, J. Nicholas. "Korte Beschrijving van het Zuid-Oostelijk-Schiereiland van Celebes." *Verhandelingen van het Bataviaasch Genootschap van Kunsten en Wetenschappen* 17 (1839): 63–184.

Vredenbregt, J. "Bawean Migrations: Some Preliminary Notes." *Bijdragen tot de Taal-, Land- en Volkenkunde* 120 (1964): 109–39.

——. "The Haddj: Some of Its Features and Functions in Indonesia." *Bijdragen tot de Taal-, Land- en Volkenkunde* 118 (1962): 91–155.

Vries, Peer. *Escaping Poverty: The Origins of Modern Economic Growth.* Goettingen: V&R Unipress, 2013.

——. "Does Wealth Entirely Depend on Inclusive Institutions and Pluralist Politics?" *Tijdschrift voor Sociale en Economische Geschiedenis* 9, no. 3 (2012): 74–92.

Vroklage, B. A. G. *Die Sozialen Verhältnisse Indonesiens. Eine Kulturgeschichtliche Untersuchung / 1 Borneo, Celebes und Molukken.* Münster: Verlag der aschendorffschen Verlagsbuchhandlung, 1936.

Wahid, Abdul. "From Revenue Farming to State Monopoly: The Political Economy of Taxation in Colonial Indonesia, Java c. 1816–1942." PhD diss., Utrecht, 2013.

Walker, Herbert. S. *The Sugar Industry in the Island of Negros.* Manila: Philippines Bureau of Printing, 1910.

Wallerstein, Immanuel. *The Modern World-System.* Vol 1.: *Capitalist Agriculture and the Origins of the European World Economy in the Sixteenth Century.* Vol. 2:

Mercantilism and the Consolidation of the European World Economy, 1600–1750. New York: Academic Press, 1974–1980.

Warmelo, W. "Ontstaan en Groei van de Handweefnijverheid in Madjalaja." *Koloniale Studiën* 1 (1939): 5–25.

Warren, James Francis. *Iranun and Balangingi: Globalization, Maritime Raiding, and the Birth of Ethnicity.* Quezon City: New Day, 2002.

——. "The Port of Jolo and the Sulu Zone Slave Trade: An 1845 Report." 上智アジア学 25 (2007): 303–22.

——. "The Port of Jolo: International Trade and Slave Raiding." In *Pirates, Ports, and Coasts in Asia: Historical and Contemporary Perspectives,* ed. John Kleinen and Manon Osseweijer, 178–99. Singapore: ISEAS, 2010.

——. "Sino-Sulu Trade in the Late Eighteenth and Nineteenth Century." *Philippine Studies* 25, no. 1 (1977): 50–79.

——. "Slave Markets and Exchange in the Malay World: The Sulu Sultanate, 1770–1878." *Journal of Southeast Asian Studies* 8, no. 2 (1977): 162–75.

——. *The Sulu Zone, 1768–1898: The Dynamics of External Trade, Slavery, and Ethnicity in the Transformation of a Southeast Asian Maritime State.* Singapore: Singapore University Press, 1981.

——. "A Tale of Two Centuries: The Globalization of Maritime Raiding and Piracy in Southeast Asia at the End of the Eighteenth and Twentieth centuries." In *A World of Water: Rain, Rivers, and Seas in Southeast Asian Histories,* ed. Peter Boomgaard, 125–52. Leiden: KITLV, 2007.

Wellenstein, E. P. "Het Rapport Meyer Ranneft-Huender nopens den Belastingdruk op de Inheemsche Bevolking van Java en Madoera." *De Economist* 25, no. 1 (1926): 251–88.

Wernstedt, Frederick L., and Paul D. Simkins. "Migrations and the Settlement of Mindanao." *Journal of Asian Studies* 25, no. 1 (1965): 83–103.

Wernstedt, Frederick L., and J. E. Spencer. *The Philippine Island World: A Physical, Cultural, and Regional Geography.* Berkeley: University of California Press, 1967.

Wertheim, W. F. "Sociological Aspects of Inter-Island Migration in Indonesia." *Population Studies* 12, no. 3 (1959): 184–201.

Wesseling, H. L. *A Cape of Asia: Essays on European History.* Leiden: Leiden University Press, 2011.

White, Benjamin. "'Agricultural Involution' and Its Critics: Twenty Years After." *Bulletin of Concerned Asian Scholars* 15, no. 2 (1983): 18–31.

——. "Economic Diversification and Agrarian Change in Rural Java, 1900–1990." In *In the Shadow of Agriculture,* ed. Paul Alexander, Peter Boomgaard, and Ben White, 41–69. Amsterdam: Royal Tropical Institute, 1991.

White, Nicholas J. "The Beginnings of Crony Capitalism: Business, Politics, and Economic Development in Malaysia, c. 1955–1970." *Modern Asian Studies* 38, no. 2 (2004): 398–417.

Wickberg, Edgar. *The Chinese in Philippine Life, 1850–1898*. New Haven, CT: Yale University Press, 1965.

Wickizer, Vernon Dale, and Merrill Kelley Bennett. *The Rice Economy of Monsoon Asia*. Stanford University, CA: Food Research Institute, 1941.

Widjojo, Muridan. *The Revolt of Prince Nuku: Cross-Cultural Alliance Making in Maluku, c. 1780–1810*. Leiden: Brill, 2009.

Widjojo, Nitisastro. *Population Trends in Indonesia*. Ithaca, NY: Cornell University, 1970.

Williams, Catharina Purwani. *Maiden Voyages: Eastern Indonesian Women on the Move*. Leiden/Singapore: KITLV/ISEAS, 2007.

Williamson, Jeffrey G. "Globalization, Factor Prices, and Living Standards in Asia Before 1940." In *Asia Pacific Dynamism, 1550–2000*, ed. A. J. H. Latham and Heita Kawakatou. London: Routledge, 2000.

——. "Land, Labour, and Globalization in the Third World, 1870–1914." *Journal of Economic History* 62, no. 1 (2002): 55–85.

——. *Real Wages and Relative Factor Prices in the World Economy, 1820–1940: Asia*. HIER discussion paper 1844. Harvard Institute of Economic Research, Department of Economics, Harvard University, 1998.

——. "Relative Factor Prices in the Periphery During the First Global Century: Any Lessons for Today." *Australian Economic History Review* 47, no. 2 (2007): 200–6.

Winkler, C., and J. Noordhoek Hegt. *Aanteekeningen naar Aanleiding van Dr. J. H. F. Kohlbrugge's Opstel over de Vaccinatie-Toestand in Nederlandsch-Indië*. Batavia: Javasche Boekhandel & Drukkerij, 1906.

Winstedt, Richard Olaf. *A History of Johore (1365–1895)*. Kuala Lumpur: Malaysian Branch of the Royal Asiatic Society, 1979.

——. *A History of Malaya*. Kuala Lumpur: Marican & Sons, 1988.

Wisseman Christie, Jan. "States Without Cities: Demographic Trends in Early Java." *Indonesia* 52 (1991): 23–40.

——. "Water and Rice in Early Java and Bali." In *A World of Water: Rain, Rivers, and Seas in Southeast Asian Histories*, ed. Peter Boomgaard, 235–58. Leiden: KITLV, 2007.

Wit, J. K. *Resume van het Onderzoek naar de Regten welke in de Residentie Timor door de Inlandsche Bevolking op de Onbebouwde Gronden Worden Uitgeoefend*. Batavia: Landsdrukkerij, 1877.

Wolf, Diane L. "Female Autonomy, the Family, and Industrialisation in Java." *Journal of Family Issues* 9, no. 1 (1988): 85–107.

Wolters, O. W. *Early Indonesian Commerce: A Study of the Origins of Śrīvijaya.* Ithaca, NY: Cornell University Press, 1967.

Wolters, Willem G. "Geographical Explanations for the Distribution of Irrigation Institutions: Cases from Southeast Asia." In *A World of Water: Rain, Rivers, and Seas in Southeast Asian Histories,* ed. Peter Boomgaard, 209–34. Leiden: KITLV, 2007.

——. "Uneven Impact and Regional Responses: The Philippines in the 1930s Depression." In *Weathering the Storm: The Economies of Southeast Asia in the 1930s Depression,* ed. P. Boomgaard and Ian Brown, 83–108. Singapore: Institute of Southeast Asian Studies, 2000.

Wong Lin Ken. *The Malayan Tin Industry to 1914.* Tucson: University of Arizona Press, 1965.

——. "The Trade of Singapore, 1819–69." *Journal of the Malayan Branch of the Royal Asiatic Society* 33, no. 4 (1960): 4–315.

Worcester, Dean. *A History of Asiatic Cholera in the Philippine Islands. With an Appendix.* Manila: Bureau of Printing, 1909.

——. *The Philippine Islands and Their People: A Record of Personal Observation and Experience, with a Short Summary of the More Important Facts in the History of the Archipelago.* New York: MacMillan, 1901.

——. *Slavery and Peonage in the Philippine Islands.* Manila: Bureau of Printing, 1913.

Wright, L. R. "The Anglo-Spanish-German Treaty of 1885: A Step in the Development of British Hegemony in North Borneo." *Australian Journal of Politics and History* 18, no. 1 (1972): 62–75.

Xenos, Peter. "The Ilocos Coast Since 1800: Population Pressure, the Ilocana Diaspora, and Multiphasic Response." In *Population and History: The Demographic Origins of the Modern Philippines,* ed. Daniel F. Doeppers and Peter Xenos, 39–70. Quezon City: Ateneo de Manile University Press, 1998.

Yacob, Shakila. "Ford's Investment in Colonial Malaya, 1926–1957." *Business History Review* 83, no. 4 (2009): 789–812.

——. "Model of Welfare Capitalism? The United States Rubber Company in Southeast Asia, 1910–1942." *Enterprise and Society* 8, no. 1 (2007): 136–74.

Yahya, Siti Rohani. "Labor Flexibility in Malaysian Rubber Estates." *Pakistan Economic and Social Review* 31, no. 2 (1993): 148–76.

Yang, Anand. "Indian Convict Workers in Southeast Asia in the Late Eighteenth and Early Nineteenth Centuries." *Journal of World History* 14, no. 2 (2003): 179–208.

Yen Ching-hwang. *A Social History of the Chinese in Singapore and Malaya, 1800–1911.* Singapore: Oxford University Press, 1986.

Yuan Bingling. *Chinese Democracies: A Study of the Kongsis of West Borneo (1776–1884)*. Leiden: CNWS, 2000.

Zed, Mestika. "The Dualistic Economy of Palembang in the Late Colonial Period." In *Historical Foundations of a National Economy in Indonesia, 1890s–1990s*, ed. J. Th. Lindblad, 249–64. Amsterdam: KNAW Verhandelingen, 1996.

Zelinsky, Wilbur. "The Hypothesis of the Mobility Transition." *Geographical Review* 61, no. 2 (1971): 219–49.

——. "The Indochinese Peninsula: A Demographic Anomaly." *Far Eastern Quarterly* 9, no. 2 (1950): 114–15.

Znoj, Heinzpeter. "The Politics of Bonded Labour Among Rattan Collectors in South-Western Sumatra, Late 1980s." *Asian Journal of Social Sciences* 38 (2010): 853–65.

Zollinger, H. "Het Eiland Lombok." *Tijdschrift voor Nederlandsch-Indië* 9, no. 2 (1847): 177–205, 301–41.

——. *Verslag van eene Reis naar Bima en Soembawa, en naar eenige Plaatsen op Celebes, Saleijer en Floris, gedurende de Maanden Mei tot December 1847*. Batavia: Verhandelingen van het Bataviaasch Genootschap van Kunsten en Wetenschappen, 1850.

Index

Britain, 38, 131; agricultural frontiers of, 139; compulsory vaccination in, 201n108; Philippine sugar bought by, 89; piracy combating by, 49–50

British Malaya, 160, 220n49; capital of, *154*; demographic growth of, 152; economic growth of, 18–19; educational attainment, 155–56; export sector of, 146; food production inhibited in, 97; immigrant society of, 3; indentured labor in, 118, 223n114; industrial employment in, 145; influenza pandemic, 91; labor migration in, 21–22, 110, 112, 118, 124–25, 154, 159; rubber boom in, 21, 107; slavery in, 54–55, 67; trade surplus of, 131

Brooke, James, 49, 110, 218n7

Brunei, 193n9

Brussels Convention (1902), 90

Bugis merchants, 104, 115, 175

Bukidnon factory, 163

Burma, 37, 91, 97, 138

Burmese, 61, 77, 97

by-employment, 142–43, 153–54, 229n59

cane cutters, 89–90, 105, 121

cane-growing peasants, 162–63

cane-sugar exporters, 71–72

Canlubang sugar central, 88, 96

capitalism, 176; colonial, 93; corporate, 103; global, 3, 180; patron-client relationship and, 68–70; rural, 74, 78; slavery and, 68, 201n3

Carey, Peter, 29

Carlos IV (king of Spain), 39

cash crops, 132; under Cultivation System, 143; monopolies, 84, 89, 98; production, 150; smallholder production, 103

casualty rates, 91

Cavada, Augustin Mendez de Vigo de la, 137

Central Java, 9

Central Luzon, 168

children, 41, 170–72

China, 229n50; exports to, 104, 218n4; migrants from, *31*, 31–32, 108–11, 120, 127, 152, 159–60, 180, 195n39

China bone, 29–30, 37

Chinese Immigrants Ordinance, 117

cholera, 34, 81, 196n46, 197n54

cigarette manufacturing, 150–51

citizen protection, 171–72

citizenship, legal, 63

Clark, Victor, 10, 101

clove cultivation, 24, 29

Coca-Cola, 166

coconut oil, 95, 98–99, 149

coffee cultivation, 73, 80, 97, 98, 101, 102, 106–7, 109, 208n87, 230n63

Colijn, Hendrik, 119

collusion, 162, 179

colonial authorities: coolie migration regulation by, 116, 119, 125–26; hiring policies of, 157; penal sanctions introduced by, 119–24; pilgrimage to Mecca and, 125; rice imports encouraged by, 132–33; slavery suppressed by, 45–46, 51, 65

colonial government: conscripted peasantry working for, 75, 83; extractive powers of, 10; migration control by, 109, 111–16; suppression of slavery and, 64–66

colonialism, 4–5, 9, 10, 22, 24, 44, 93–94, 103, 110, 129, 181

colonial society, 22, 85

colonial wars, 35

commodity frontiers, 18, 61, 71, 114, 161, 163, 164

commodity production: bonded labor for, 77–78; bulk, 9; coconut oil's boom as, 98–99; global trade of, 69; in Kalimantan, 60; of Malaysia, 170; migration patterns and, 159; migration toward, 20–21; patron-client relationships facilitating, 78–79, 83–84; rural populations for, 4; slave labor for, 44, 61, 103–4, 195n31; smallholder, 100–101

commonwealth status, for the Philippines, 147

Communist Party: uprising in Malaysia, 159–60

Contemplacion, Flor, 171

coolie labor: migration of, 19, 21; regulation of, 125–26; trade in Singapore, 117; village elites trafficking in, 78

Coolie Ordinance (1868), 117

copra, 98–101, 162, 217n134

Corpuz, A. G., 194n20

corvée labor, 63, 77, 84, 211n28

migration (*continued*)
development correlated to, 152; of Island Southeast Asia, 19, 152–53; labor recruitment from, 22, 175–76; Madura's and Java's annual average, *82*; maritime labor, 184; mass, 2; mechanization and, 111; networks, 126–27; northern Philippines, *87*; peasants settler's, 19; penal sanction and labor, 128–29; Philippines and global, 183–84; Philippines permanent, 86; Philippines's internal, 165; plantation labor, 79–80; railways facilitating, 153; rice cultivation societies, 180; for sugar factories, 212n44; systems, 119; textile industry and urban, 151; toward commodity-producing frontiers, 20–21; urban, 151, 156, 166

Minahasa, 100

Mindanao, 27, 55, 114, 163, 165, 197n50, 236n27

mines, 196n42; Bangka tin, 110–11, 116–19; Belitung tin, 91, 119, 123; diamond, 31; gold, 31, 61, 218n7, 236n27

Moluccan islands, 29; waters, 46–47

MoneyGram, 177

moneylenders, 73–75, 85, 109, 133

monocropping, 89, 96–97

Moro Province, 65

Moro rebellion, 165

mortality rates, 29, 33; among slaves, 51, 206n59; from influenza, 91, 214n91; in Singapore, 38; from smallpox, 198n63

Munro, Thomas, 74

Napoleonic wars, 40

natural disasters, 34–35, 81

Negros, Philippines: malnutrition in, 92, 146, 167; penal sanctions proposed in, 120–21; sugar factories in, 167; sugar plantation belt of, 88, 89, 90, 91

Netherlands: abolitionism in, 65–66; colonial government of, 115–16; debt bondage prohibited by, 66; labor market regulation by, 121, 137; piracy combated by, 49–50

Netherlands Indies, 41–42; capital of, *154*; coconut oil exports of, 95; economy of,

146; export sector of, 95, 146; government expenditures in, 225n3; irrigation budget of, 134; labor force recruitment in, 124–25; manufacturing in, 231n82; Mecca pilgrims from, 125; penal sanction in, 120; pirates capturing people of, 50–51, 203n30; rice ban of, 148–49; slave market of, 115; slavery in, 55, *56*, 66–67; tax revenue of, 191n29; weaving decline in, 138–39

New Caledonia, 220n49

New Guinea, 42, 164

Newson, Linda A., 26

newspapers, 156–57

Nias, 36, 52–54, 66–67, 115, 172, 204n39

Nicholl, Robert, 193n7

nobility, local, 75

northern Philippines, 6; demographics of, 26–27; economic recovery of, 29; migration between provinces in, *87*; plantation model not suited for, 83–88, 91; population growth of, 20–21

North Sumatra, 104

Nueva Ecija, 86, 113, 213n67

nutritional conditions, 35–36, 86, 91–92, 164, 215n93

O'Brien, Patrick, 94, 96

oil companies, 104–5

Ommelanden. *See* Batavia

opium, 45, 49; debts and, 122, 208

Opium War, 38

Outer Islands, 20; demographic growth in, 32–33; fragile environment of, 164; rubber boom in, 21; slavery in, 54–55; smallholder crops in, 98; sugar industry in, 163; wages low in, 15

Padang, port of, 106–7

palm-oil plantations, 44

Pampanga, 28, 63, 85, 92, 99

patron-client relationships, 7–8; capitalism and, 68–70; commodity production facilitated by, 78–79, 83–84; Cultivation System and, 76; demographic growth and, 181–82; erosion of, 92; global migration and, 176, 183–84; labor and, 10–11, 15, 108, 120, 122; labor recruitment and, 11, 153, 176, 183–84 pawnship, 69, 77, 207n73

Pax Britannica, 67

peasants: cane-growing, 162–63; conscripted, 75; indebted, 75; Java's output by, 149; landholding, 74; rural societies and mobility of, 9–10; sedentary, 64; settler's migration, 19

penal sanctions: in Bangka tin mines, 225n142; in Deli, 122, 124–26, 128; human traffickers and, 120; in Java, 121–22; Javanese labor emigration and, 119–24; labor contracts with, 15, 128–29; labor migration and, 128–29; Negros proposing, 120–21; in Netherlands Indies, 120; South Sumatra abolition, 122

Penang, 38, 64, 106

peons, slaves as, 114–15, 201n7, 207n73

pepper: cultivation, 30, 31, 81, 106, 110; slavery and, 60, 64, 208n87; trade, 24, 25; white, 106, 127

PepsiCo, 166

Perak, 67, 110–11

peripheralization, 4, 16, 20–23, 46, 68, 103, 181; plantations, 20, 103–4; reversal of fortune and, 131–32, 180; rural economy and, 131–32, 182

Philippine Revolution, 120, 196n46

Philippines, 2; abaca and copra production in, 99; agriculture in, 167, 229n61; arable land in, 230n62; birth rate in, 168; Britain buying sugar from, 89; as cane-sugar exporters, 71–72; Canlubang sugar central connected to, 88; capital of, 154; census in, 187, 196n46, 197n50; children's education in, 170–71; coconut oil exports of, 95; commodity exports of, 144–45; commonwealth status of, 147; debt bondage in, 121; demographic growth in, 28, 146; economic growth of, 17–18; employable population in, 230nn70–71, 231n83; export crops reliance of, 144; exports and malnutrition in, 163–64; in global commodities market, 166; global economy integration of, 145–46; global migrations and, 183–84; hacendero class in, 155; handicrafts in, 140–41; HFCS and, 166–67; industrial employment in, 146–47, 227n33, 232n92; industrial take off of, 166; influenza death rate in,

215n91; internal migration of, 165; labor market in, 137; labor productivity in, 214n70; labor recruitment in, 176–77; labor surplus of, 113–14; literacy in, 155–56; manufacturing in, 137; migrant social composition in, 178; national landowning class developing in, 85; neocolonial status of, 165; patron-client relationship in, 8; people abducted from, 194n20; permanent migration to, 86; plantations not suitable in, 91; population of, 27–28, 151–52, 168; railways in, 141; rice frontiers in, 35; rice production in, 226n17; slave raiding in, 27; slavery in, 54–55, 62; smallholder production on, 163; smallpox epidemic in, 42–43; smallpox vaccinations in, 200n92, 201n108; Spanish encomienda system in, 84; sugar industry in, 88–89, 141, 163; sugarlandias in, 91–93; tax revenues of, 130; textile industry in, 148, 229n50; tobacco monopoly in, 72; trade surplus of, 131; typhoon striking, 197n55; U.S. administration of, 112; U.S. import tariffs and, 94; U.S. Navy joined by men from, 158; U.S. pressure against slavery in, 65; vaccination program in, 39; women in, 237n69. *See also* northern Philippines

piña (fiber from pineapple leaves), 139–40

piracy, 27, 28, 45; Britain and Netherlands combatting, 49–50; European navy ships battling, 48–49; health conditions and, 53; Indonesian people captured by, 50–51, 203n30; in Island Southeast Asia, 52; shifted to Indonesian archipelago, 46–47, 51; slavery and, 208n87; Spanish squadrons inflicting damage on, 47; Sulu sultanate and, 46; upsurge of, 44–47

pirate ships, 46, 52–53, 204n45

population: of Batavia, 154; for commodity production, 4; employable, 230nn70–71, 231n82, 231n83; of Java, 29, 211n14; Java's geographic divisions in, 79; Malay Peninsula shift in, 33; of Manila, 154; of Philippines, 27–28, 151–52, 168; of Singapore, 154; from smallpox vaccination, 27; Sula Islands decline in, 195n37

Netherlands Indies, 55, *56*, 66–67; pawnship and, 69; pepper trade and, 208n87; in Philippines, 54–55, 62; in Philippines, British Malaya and Outer Islands, 54–55; piracy and, 208n87; for rice production, 60–61; serfdom transformation of, 62–63; sharecroppers and, 61–62; state formation's role of, 9; Straits Settlements abolishing, 64; transient phase of, 61–62; U.S. pressure against, 65; in West Africa, 61

slaves: birthrates among, 57; from Nias, 204n39; as peons, 114–15, 207n73; Sulu sultanate importing, 30, 203n33; Sumba deporting, 205n49

slaves-for-arms trade, 60

slave trade, 53; ban on, 44; demographic consequences from, *54*; in global economy, 102; in Indonesian archipelago, *54*; in Island Southeast Asia, *57*, *58*; of Netherlands Indies, 115; slaves as peons in, 114–15, 207n73

smallholder production, 11, 13, 17, 68, 73, 128, 131, 138, 144, 146, 151, 165, 180–82, 212n43; cane-growing peasants and, 162–63; cash crop, 103; of crops, 100; in Island Southeast Asia, 105, 181; in Java, 105–6; Outer Islands crop, 98; in Philippines, 163; plantations detrimental to, 191n39; rubber gardens, 122, 124, 126, 145; in rubber sector, 107, 145; sharecroppers and, 106; sugar factories and, 105–6

smallpox epidemic, 26, 42–43

smallpox vaccinations: Carlos IV adopting, 39; demographic growth from, 1–2, 20, 33–36, 86; in Java, 40–41, 43; in Philippines, 39–40, 200n92, 201n108; population decline and, 27; population growth from, 195n29; in Southeast Asia, 37–38, 43

Sokoloff, Kenneth, 5, 13

Southeast Asia in the Age of Commerce (Reid), 20, 23, 44

Spain: Carlos IV king of, 39; conquest by, 26, 27; piracy and, 47, 50–51, 64; Zamboanga garrison of, 194n18

Spanish conquistadores, 23, 84, 180

Spanish-Moro Conflict, 27

Stokvis, J. E., 127

Straits Immigration Agent, 117

Straits Settlements, 32, 152; slavery, 64; smallpox vaccination, 37–38

Straits Times, 156

Suez Canal, 12, 103

sugar industry: cane-growing peasants in, 162–63; in Java, 81–82, 88–91, 94, 96, 109, 122, 133, 141, 145; labor at, 76–77; migration for, 212n44; in Negros, 88–92, 140, 146, 147, 167; in Outer Islands, 163; in Philippines, 99, 145, 166, 167; planting cycles for, 214n83; rice productivity and, 134; smallholder production and, 105–6; women's wages in, 232n93; workers' health conditions in, 92–93

sugarlandias, 85, 90–91, 93

Suharto, 163, 171

Sukarno, 164

Sula Islands, 195n37

Sulu sultanate, 27, 46, 48, 195n33, 197n50, 202n14; slavery in, 195n31; slaves imported by, 30, 203n33; Spanish-Moro Conflict and, 27

Sumatra, 101–2; indigenous crops in, 219n26; North, 104; oil companies entering, 104–5; penal sanctions abolished in, 122; ports of, 193n8; rice crops of, 97, 205n54; West, 107. *See also* Deli

Sumba, 62, 205n49

Supplementary Convention on the Abolition of Slavery (1956), 172

Surabaya, 40, 48, 103, 141, 153, 154

Surakarta, 81

Suriname, 220n49

sweet potatoes, 35

swidden agriculture, 9, 73, 80, 105, 107, 190nn18–19, 193n9

Talens, Johan, 193n7

Tambora volcano, 34, 58

Tamil, 20, 107, 112–13, 116, 118

tariffs, import, 21, 49, 92, 94, 130, 132, 148, 182

Tawi Tawi island, 125, 203n33, 223n115

taxation, 4, 7, 10, 13, 74, 81, 91, 191n32, 191nn29–30; coconut oil, 95; regressive, 130

COLUMBIA STUDIES IN INTERNATIONAL AND GLOBAL HISTORY

Cemil Aydin, Timothy Nunan, and Dominic Sachsenmaier, Series Editors